# 1929

## THE YEAR OF THE GREAT CRASH

*other books by William K. Klingaman*

1919: The Year Our World Began
1941: Our Lives in a World on the Edge

# 1929

## THE YEAR OF
## THE GREAT CRASH

*William K. Klingaman*

HARPER & ROW, PUBLISHERS, New York
*Grand Rapids, Philadelphia, St. Louis, San Francisco*
1817 *London, Singapore, Sydney, Tokyo*

Photos 1, 2, 3, 5, 6, 8, 12, 14 UPI/Bettmann Newsphotos
4, 7, 9, 10, 11, 13 AP/Wide World Photos

1929: THE YEAR OF THE GREAT CRASH. Copyright © 1989 by William K. Klingaman. All rights reserved. Printed in the United States of America. No part of this book may be used or reproduced in any manner whatsoever without written permission except in the case of brief quotations embodied in critical articles and reviews. For information address Harper & Row, Publishers, Inc. 10 E. 53rd Street, New York, N.Y. 10022.

FIRST EDITION

Library of Congress Cataloging-in-Publication Data

Klingaman, William K.
   1929: the year of the great crash.

   Includes index.
   1. Depressions—1929—United States.   2. United States
—Economic conditions—1918–1945.   3. Economic history—
1918–1945.   I. Title.   II. Title: Year of the great
crash.
HB3717 1929.K59   1989        338.5'4'0973        88-45895
ISBN 0-06-016081-0

89 90 91 92 93 CC/RRD 10 9 8 7 6 5 4 3 2 1

*For Nick and Marianne*

# Contents

*Illustrations follow page 270*

# Acknowledgments

I would like to thank my editor and friend, Daniel Bial, who did his usual superb job in streamlining my manuscript and guiding it through the publication process. I also owe a deep debt of gratitude to Donald Cutler for making this project possible in the first place and for encouraging and supporting my efforts all along the way. As usual, my research task was aided immeasurably by Bill Zagar, Francesca Savini, and the always helpful staff at the Morris Library of the University of Delaware, and Dr. Billy Wilkinson and Sally Hearn at the Albin O. Kuhn Library and Gallery at the University of Maryland, Baltimore County. Dr. Ken Ledford, too, deserves many thanks for his invaluable suggestions on my treatment of German affairs in the 1920s.

"The snow of twenty-nine wasn't real snow. If you didn't want it to be snow, you just paid some money."
—*F. Scott Fitzgerald*

"This is a great country, but my advice to you is to forget that fact once in a while."
—*Veteran stockbroker to a young man on Wall Street, 1929*

# Prologue: *A Glimpse of Hell*

Early on the morning of Tuesday, October 29, 1929, the canyons of Wall Street were thronged with thousands of excited thrill-seekers who had come to witness the anticipated carnage. Policemen on horseback and detectives in uniform attempted to keep the mob clear of the entrance to the New York Stock Exchange, but it was no use; every time they succeeded in opening a pathway, the jostling crowd immediately closed ranks again.

Inside, on the floor of the exchange, one could actually feel the tension and fear in the air as the hands of the clock crawled toward ten o'clock and the opening gong. Less than a week earlier, on Black Thursday, the stock market had suffered the most disastrous decline in its history, and the staggering plunge of prices on the following Monday afternoon had only increased the prevailing sense of panic. In brokers' rooms across the country, investors fidgeted nervously and coughed and shifted their feet as they stood and stared in hypnotic fascination at the silent stock ticker, the mechanical courier that would soon deliver, with cold indifference, a verdict of survival or—more likely—utter ruin.

The cataclysm struck in full fury as soon as trading began. In the first thirty minutes of business, immense blocks of stock—50,000 shares at a time of Chrysler, General Electric, International Telephone & Telegraph, and Standard Oil—were dumped on the market by wealthy individuals and institutions at prices that stunned onlookers. AT&T, which had reached a peak of 310 dollars per share in the heady summer days of the bull market, smashed all the way down to 204 in a sickening slide; U.S. Steel skidded past 190 . . . 180 . . . 170 . . . and kept going down; RCA, a former favorite at 110, went begging at 26. Some brokers lost their nerve and sold out their customers needlessly, lending further momentum to the downward spiral. Others lost their minds; spectators watched in mute

*Klingaman*

horror as one trader ran screaming like a lunatic from the floor of the exchange. Those who remained among the shouting, frantic mob took on the furtive, frightened look of hunted things.

By noon, more than 8,000,000 shares of stock had been sold, a furious pace that shattered all previous trading records. Shortly thereafter, the members of the governing committee of the exchange held a secret meeting in a cramped, smoke-filled room beneath the floor of the market and anxiously debated whether to suspend trading completely until the panic subsided.

Across the news tickers that morning came a sequence of terse urgent messages: "Federal Reserve Board is in session in Washington with Secretary Mellon . . . Cabinet is meeting . . . President Hoover conferring with Secretary of Commerce Lamont . . . Leading bankers gathering at the office of J. P. Morgan, Jr. to discuss the deteriorating situation." As the extent of the financial debacle became clear—$15 billion worth of stock values had vanished into thin air, wiping out the life savings of investors across the nation—the human toll began to mount. Businessmen whose companies went bankrupt suffered heart attacks; ruined speculators leaped from hotel windows, or shut all the windows and turned on the gas, or swallowed poison, or simply shot themselves. Behind them, in the wreckage of lifetimes of hard work and dreams and fatal illusions, they left notes that read, "EVERYTHING LOST. TELL THE BOYS I CAN'T PAY WHAT I OWE THEM."

This was the time of the Great Crash, when securities on the nation's stock exchanges lost more than a third of their value in a heartbreaking avalanche that haunted the memories of an entire generation, when the dreams of hundreds of thousands of American investors—mostly members of the middle class, including secretaries, clerks, elderly spinsters, and small businessmen—vanished in the smashup along with their hard-earned savings, when the country was battered by a severe psychological trauma whose effects were still plainly visible more than a decade later. This book is an attempt to recreate the turbulent year of 1929 (or, more precisely, the twenty months from November 1928 through June 1930) by following the fortunes of two dozen characters—some famous and some entirely unknown—against the backdrop of the boom, the crash, and the ensuing depression.

Anyone who writes about the Crash of 1929 should expect three questions to be hurled at him with conspicuous regularity. First, what caused the crash? Second, to what extent was the crash responsible for the Great Depression of the 1930s? And third, can it happen again?

The first question may be easily answered, at least on a superficial level. The crash occurred simply because too many stocks had reached absurdly high levels that were impossible to justify by any rational standard, and because too many people suddenly decided to sell their stocks at the same time, when there were too few buyers, and those who were buying were willing to do so only at greatly reduced prices. As prices tumbled, speculators who had purchased their stocks with borrowed money—using the paper worth of the stocks themselves as collateral—were forced to come up with additional cash to replace the vanished collateral value; if they failed to provide the funds within the specified time, their brokers sold the stocks outright, lending fresh impetus to the flood of liquidation and driving prices further downward. Panic ensued, and the dictates of mob psychology, which had borne the market to unprecedented heights during the boom, subsequently carried it far lower than it need have gone.

In a very real sense, however, this answer only begs the more complicated question of *why* so many investors chose to unload their stocks at the same time. A comprehensive response may be found, I trust, in the following narrative and cannot be fairly summarized here, for it requires a detailed reconstruction of the events that transpired on Wall Street along with an examination of the social, psychological, and cultural milieus in which they occurred.

A similarly comprehensive answer to the second question is virtually impossible. Economics is still a most imprecise science, even with the added advantage of hindsight, and as John Kenneth Galbraith aptly points out, when economists seek to be profound they often succeed only in being wrong.

Nevertheless, there are certain facts that may not be disputed. Basic weaknesses plagued the American economy well before the crash, though some of them were hidden by the glittering apparition conjured up by the promoters of the so-called New Era of perpetual prosperity. By destroying nearly $50 billion worth of security values and drastically reducing the buying power of those American consumers whose discretionary purchases had helped fuel the boom during the 1920s, the crash aggravated these weaknesses and accelerated the decline already in progress. And the lingering memories of the disaster on Wall Street created an unprecedented mood of despair and doubt about the hitherto sacrosanct capitalist system in the United States, a development that helped keep both purchasing and capital investment (and hence industrial employment) distressingly low throughout the decade of the 1930s.

The third question must be answered in two parts. Could the nation suffer another paralyzing stock market crash? Of course; in fact, the inspiration for this book arose from the crash of October 1987, which was nearly as devastating though not as long-lived as its 1929 counterpart.

Although the precise sequence of events is not likely to be repeated, there remains the possibility, indeed the likelihood of further smashups in the future so long as psychological and emotional factors rule the market, as indeed they must.

More important, perhaps, is the question of whether a future crash might result in another depression as severe as the one that plagued America and western Europe during the 1930s. Unfortunately, this, too, is a question with no definite answer. Government spokesmen and financial analysts assure us that there are too many safeguards built into the system to permit a repetition of the Great Depression. And perhaps they are correct. Yet those safeguards were installed to meet known dangers; there is no way to guard adequately against a disaster that strikes from a wholly unexpected quarter. Nor should we always accept reassurances from the economic experts at face value, for one of the most disconcerting revelations visited upon anyone studying the events of 1929 is that all the soothing reasons now given for why it cannot happen here were voiced before, with equal certainty and perhaps a similar measure of self-delusion—in the year of the Great Crash.

In recounting the events of 1929, I have not limited the scope of my study to financial history alone. To understand the critical importance of the crash as the end of an era in the United States—and the dawn of a new and exceptionally violent phase of the twentieth century—one must look beyond Wall Street to the streets of Germany, where the events of 1929 opened the door for the Nazis' sudden rise to power; to the Soviet Union, where Stalin ruthlessly eliminated his opponents and launched his long-suffering nation on the brutal experiment of the first Five-Year Plan; to Palestine, where tensions between Jews and Arabs erupted into open warfare; and to Paris, where the celebrated movable feast of a generation of writers and artists finally terminated in acrimonious bickering and madness.

Standing precisely at the center of the interwar period, 1929 also marked the decisive turning point of two decades of uneasy peace. For ten years after the end of the Great War in November 1918, the world remained obsessed by the searing memories of that unprecedented and entirely unnecessary catastrophe. As the fragile postwar order began to crumble in the late 1920s, the forces of radical change and revolution, which had been forced underground by the triumph of international reaction in 1919, emerged to challenge the establishment with varying degrees of success in the United States, India, Germany, Britain, and Latin America. As the most dramatic event in a worldwide economic crisis, the Great Crash accelerated the process of disintegration, discrediting the status quo and sending the Western democracies spinning into a decade of numbing misery and self-doubt, forcing them to concentrate their energies on domestic affairs and weakening their will and ability to resist totalitarian aggression abroad.

Since I have chosen to present the events of this critical year as they unfolded, to allow the reader to experience 1929 as if he were actually living through it, one word of caution may be in order. Beginning in March of that year, the stock markets in the United States entered upon a period of wild price swings both up and downward. Contemporary observers were badly shaken by these sudden, recurring plunges, and even though the declines would later pale in comparison with the dramatic losses suffered during the crash itself, they should not be dismissed as irrelevant; in fact, the increasingly nervous condition of the market provided (to perceptive observers) one valuable clue to the debacle that lay ahead. Readers therefore should not be misled into expecting the crash to occur after the first, second, or even third shock wave that shook Wall Street in 1929. Tragedy proceeds at its own pace.

I should also point out that most histories of the crash—and there are distressingly few good ones—assert that the disaster took nearly everyone in the world by surprise. As we shall see, this is simply not true. The evidence clearly indicates that a substantial number of professional investors saw the catastrophe approaching (though, of course, no one knew precisely when it would arrive) and sharply reduced their holdings before it arrived. And although most of the nation's business press obdurately refused to acknowledge the possibility of a shattering reverse in stock prices, there were numerous contemporary political and economic analysts who warned that the United States was headed for a major financial disaster in the very near future. Those who chose to ignore the increasingly visible red flags did so at their peril.

# PART ONE:　VANITY

# I

# November 6, 1928: Election Day

In a darkened hospital room at the edge of Hell's Kitchen, on the West Side of Manhattan, the king of easy money lay dying. Through the shadows that drifted slowly across his mind he could hear a weary voice repeating the same question again and again. "Who did it, Mr. Rothstein?" the voice asked in a disinterested, mechanical way. "Who shot you?" But Rothstein would not tell. His only response was to slowly turn his face to the wall and whisper, "If I live, I'll tend to it." Then he closed his eyes and faded deep into unconsciousness once more.

Over the past decade, in the years that had followed the conclusion of that agonizing episode of bloody and senseless slaughter known as the Great War, underworld financier Arnold Rothstein had become the most famous and, arguably, the most powerful man on Broadway. The son of a prosperous wholesale clothing merchant, Rothstein had discovered early in his business career that his unique professional talents were better suited to the risks and rewards of illicit gambling than the world of conventional commerce. In the years before the war, a succession of celebrated triumphs as a gambler and a bookie had earned Rothstein a reputation as a man who bet only on sure things; his most sensational coup came when he provided part of the funds—and most of the muscle—to fix the World Series of 1919. Wholly unscrupulous, moving with deceptive quickness in the smooth and shrewd style that soon became his trademark, Rothstein wisely took the winnings from his wagers and invested them in legitimate enterprises. As the owner of vast real estate holdings (including numerous nightclubs, hotels, and apartment houses) and a small fortune in stocks and bonds, and as the backer of a series of successful Broadway productions and the open-handed host of high-class social and political entertainments, Rothstein established an empire whose foundations rested upon such respectable and unquestionably sound financial assets that banks readily loaned him hundreds of thousands of dollars.

The gambler thus became an indispensable link of respectability in the chain of money and influence that bound New York's powerful Tammany political machine to the constantly changing coterie of gangland chieftains who dominated organized crime activities in the city. Fortified with an abundance of liquid assets, he was able to serve as a source of ready cash for anyone who was in a position to perform a favor for Arnold Rothstein in the not too distant future. John McGraw, the longtime manager of the New York Giants, reportedly owed money to Rothstein; William Randolph Hearst's mistress, actress Marion Davies, gratefully accepted gifts from him; and more than one New York City judge borrowed money from Rothstein at one time or another to survive an unexpected financial crisis.

Rothstein's immense influence throughout the city earned him the nicknames of "the Big Shot," "the Man at the Top," or simply "the Man." With politicians, businessmen, and judges in his pocket, he could fix traffic tickets or prohibition violations, rig elections, or guarantee the dismissal of criminal charges—all for a fee, of course. He protected local gambling clubs and provided capital for bootleggers; he furnished bail for dozens of criminals and allegedly sent goon squads to help break strikes in the garment industry; he routinely received hundreds of thousands of dollars worth of stolen bonds and merchandise and held them until the heat was off before fencing the goods for a sizable profit. As the stock market boom of the twenties got into full swing, Rothstein financed a string of "bucket shops," fraudulent stockbrokers' offices with high-powered salesmen who purported to sell securities but merely took the gullible customers' money and cleared out before the police tumbled onto the scam. Lately Rothstein had made major inroads into the rapidly expanding international drug business, specializing in heroin and cocaine. And because he preferred to avoid unnecessary risks, Rothstein held life insurance policies on many of his clients; if any foolhardy borrower failed to repay a debt and subsequently met with an unfortunate accident, the Man still received what was owed him. Each part of the complex, corrupt structure supported the rest; seen from a distance, the whole tangled web of shady deals and informal arrangements appeared nearly impenetrable. "His fortune was of the sort that it took an Arnold Rothstein himself to manage," noted one contemporary observer. "He was the only person on earth who ever had run that sort of big business; and he was the only person who knew all of its ramifications." By the autumn of 1928, Arnold Rothstein had come to believe that his money and his connections had made him untouchable. He was wrong.

On an unusually warm September weekend, in an all-night session of stud poker and high spade in an apartment at 161 West Fifty-fourth Street, Rothstein lost nearly $350,000. His behavior during and after the game was not calculated to win him any friends. When he won a hand, he pocketed the money; but when he lost, he gave IOU's to his creditors. Caught in the midst of a temporary shortage of cash, Rothstein needed all his available liquid funds for impending narcotics deals and for his massive wagers on the upcoming national elections. (A perceptive student of American political affairs, Rothstein had placed bets worth $1.6 million on the Republican presidential candidate, Herbert Hoover, and on Franklin D. Roosevelt, the Democratic nominee for governor of New York.) So, as he walked out of the apartment on Fifty-fourth Street, he waved to the other players—George McManus, "Nigger" Nate Raymond, Sam and Myer Boston, Alvin C. "Titanic" Thomas, and several out-of-town plungers—and said, "See you later." When someone asked him several days afterward when he planned to pay off his markers, he replied testily that he would do so at a time of his own choosing. "Tell them," he snapped, "they can go bite themselves to death."

On the evening of Sunday, November 4, Rothstein entered Lindy's, his favorite uptown restaurant, where the owners kept a special table for him—in the open, for Rothstein had nothing to fear. A message awaited him: George McManus wanted to see Rothstein in room 349 in the Park Central Hotel. McManus, a gambler and self-proclaimed "commission broker"—an elegant euphemism for a bookie—who had the nasty habit of carrying a loaded pistol in a shoulder holster, had lost $51,000 in cash in the card game six weeks earlier.

Rothstein walked the six blocks to the Park Central and went up to room 349. He found another card game in progress. As Rothstein sat down at the table, someone who had been drinking too much started to berate him for welching on his gambling debts. "You're drunk," Rothstein growled. "When you sober up we'll see how big you can talk to me." The man took out a gun, a Colt .38 Special, pointed it downward, and fired one shot, apparently intending to frighten Rothstein.

But the bullet struck Rothstein in the groin. He rose and snarled, "Is that all, you ———," and staggered out of the room. Clutching at his wound with both hands to stem the flow of blood, his face twisted with anger and anguish, he stumbled down a corridor nearly as long as a football field and then made his way down three flights of stairs. He emerged at the service exit, where a bellboy and the night watchman were on duty. "I'm shot," Rothstein gasped, as he crumpled to the ground. "Get me a taxi." The watchman brought a policeman from a nearby street corner. "Who shot you?" he asked the dying man, who had managed to prop himself up against a wall. "I won't tell you," Rothstein said. An ambulance was summoned, and Rothstein was rushed to the Polyclinic Hospital. A team of detectives searched the area for clues, but not very diligently.

Meanwhile, one of the players in the game in room 349 snatched the gun out of the killer's hands and threw it out of the window. It skidded along the pavement, the barrel twisted by the impact of the fall; a passing taxi driver spotted it and turned it over to the police. Babbling incoherently and distraught to the point of hysteria, the killer reportedly ran to a telephone booth to try to confess to the shooting, but before he could blurt out his story to the operator, three men grabbed the receiver and hustled him away from the booth. The shades were hurriedly drawn in room 349, though the half-filled glasses of whiskey and ginger ale remained on the table, and in a closet there hung a coat with the name George McManus sewn into the label.

Within hours of the shooting, Rothstein's private files were rifled and a great deal of incriminating evidence removed. But enough dynamite remained to destroy dozens of prominent careers. "If the Rothstein papers are ever made public," warned one attorney for the family's estate, "there is going to be a lot of suicides." After a brief perusal of the contents of the files, the district attorney decided that the material was better left uninvestigated; he turned the entire collection over to three lawyers and asked them to send him photostatic copies of any documents that appeared to have a bearing on the shooting. However, federal agents who had less fear of gangland retribution unlocked several of Rothstein's safe deposit boxes, discovering leads that guided them step by step along an international trail of drug smuggling and eventually led to the seizure of millions of dollars' worth of narcotics.

New York's wisecracking mayor, James J. (Gentleman Jimmy) Walker, heard the news of the Rothstein incident at the end of an entertaining evening at the Woodmansten Inn in Westchester, a popular suburban hangout for bored Broadway habitués, gangsters, and restless businessmen with a craving for booze, broads, and a sense of danger. Shortly after midnight, someone walked over to Walker and whispered something in his ear. Jimmy immediately sobered up and told his girlfriend, actress Betty Compton, that they had to leave at once. Bandleader Vincent Lopez asked Walker if he was all right. "Not exactly," the mayor replied.

Lopez, who doubled as Walker's numerologist, stepped down off the bandstand. "Something's happened, Jim. I noticed the 'boys' were acting funny."

"Rothstein has just been shot, Vince," Walker replied. "And that means trouble from hereon in."

From the window of his private railroad car, President Calvin Coolidge could see the crowds of people waiting expectantly in the cold November morning mist on the platform of the old familiar station at Northampton, Massachusetts, where he had begun his political career as a city councilman several decades earlier. To his narrow, squinting eyes, it was not a welcome sight. Uncomfortable among strangers in any circumstances, Coolidge was particularly ill at ease when he was the primary target of attention. So when he stepped crisply off the train precisely at eight o'clock on Election Day, the President rewarded his admirers with a weak wave of his hat and the graceless grimace that passed for a Coolidge smile, and then climbed directly into the car that took him to Memorial Hall, where he pushed his way impatiently through the throngs of waiting voters to receive his own ballot. Three minutes later, he was on his way to the modest nine-room rented house ($32.50 a month) at 21 Massasoit Avenue that he and Mrs. Coolidge shared with the town's high school principal and his family.

Almost as if he could barely wait until time released him from the cares of public office, Coolidge already had packed forty boxes and barrels with personal bric-a-brac—souvenirs, furniture, trophies—accumulated during his five years as Chief Executive, and brought them along on his train. Now, appearing more than a little ludicrous in a frock coat and a top hat (which, as always, looked just a shade too small and sat just a little too high on his head, as if he were a farmer unused to dressing up in fancy clothes), Coolidge stood in front of the house and oversaw the delivery and storage of each carton of goods in the parlor or the appropriate bedroom. Then, while his wife went to visit her invalid mother, who lay gravely ill in the local hospital, the President doffed his hat and closely inspected the scraggly grapevines and shrubs that made up his garden. An hour later, the Coolidges were back on the train, heading south toward Washington.

With his Yankee twang, his taciturn nature, and his dour appearance (Alice Roosevelt Longworth once said he looked like he had been weaned on a pickle), Coolidge seemed almost a caricature of the tight-lipped, phlegmatic New England farmer. He took pride in his provincial heritage—"No Coolidge has ever gone west," he boasted—and made no attempt to cover up his lack of sophistication. Shortly after Coolidge moved into the White House, a Secret Service man was aghast to find him sitting in a rocking chair on the front porch, in full view of the passing traffic on Pennsylvania Avenue. "Mr. President," coaxed the agent, "the other Presidents always use the back portico." Coolidge just shook his head and kept on rocking. "I want to be out here where I can see the streetcars go by," he said.

Congenitally suspicious and almost painfully shy, Coolidge usually sat silently by himself at formal social gatherings. When he invited congressmen and senators to the White House for breakfast, he fed them a traditional Vermont breakfast of sausage and buckwheat cakes, and all the guests munched silently throughout the meal, waiting respectfully for Coolidge to open the conversation—but he never did. His speeches were usually dry recitations of truisms or trifling anecdotes he seized upon to avoid grappling with difficult political problems. His hobbies were sleeping (he frequently kept foreign dignitaries waiting for hours while he took his customary afternoon nap) and fishing, although he appalled purists by using worms to catch trout. And although he had the presidential yacht, the *Mayflower,* at his command, Coolidge almost never went anywhere near the ocean or even the Chesapeake Bay; in fact, he seldom ventured farther than Mount Vernon, just a few safe miles down the Potomac.

Yet Coolidge was no simple-minded, naive country bumpkin. Beneath his protective shell of silence lurked an astute political mind accompanied by an intuitively distrustful nature and a sadistic sense of humor that appeared most frequently in the company of pretentious fools or self-seeking visitors, two categories of human beings who seemed (then as now) to make up at least half the population of official Washington. As governor of Massachusetts, he had deftly seized the once-in-a-political-lifetime opportunity presented by the vastly unpopular Boston policemen's strike in 1919 to vault himself overnight from obscurity into national prominence with the ringing declaration that "there is no right to strike against the public safety by anyone, at any time."

"Silent Cal" became a national character; everyone had his or her favorite Coolidge story. *New York Times* reporter Arthur Krock, for instance, recalled a cruise down the Potomac on the *Mayflower* near the end of Coolidge's tenure in the White House. As the President stood alone by the rail, one of the more obsequious guests gushed in fatuous admiration, "Look at that slight and slender figure! Look at that head, bowed over the rail! What thoughts are in the mind of this man, burdened by the problems of the nation?" After a long pause, Coolidge finally turned around; walking toward the group, he jerked his head back toward the water. "See that sea gull over there?" he said. "Been watching it for twenty minutes. Hasn't moved. I think he's dead."

He was a president made for his times. After the emotional trauma of the Great War and the impassioned crusades for progressive reform and the League of Nations during Woodrow Wilson's administration, and the vulgar, tawdry scandals of Warren Harding's brief reign, the nation welcomed a Chief Executive whose fondest wish was to be left alone. Shortly after he was sworn in following Harding's death in August 1923, Coolidge reportedly confided to former Amherst College classmate Dwight Morrow, who had become a leading partner in J.P. Morgan and Company, "Dwight, I am not going to try and be a great President." Indeed, Americans might have been forgiven for forgetting that they even *had* a president. Coolidge explained his inactivity by citing the advice given him by James Lucey, an elderly shoemaker in Northampton, when Coolidge departed for Washington: "Do not work too hard. Heed what came to others in your place and save your health."

Dedicating his administration to the proposition that "the business of America is business," Coolidge placed the moral and material resources of the federal government at the disposal of the private sector, a policy that appeared to pay immediate dividends as the nation entered a period of unprecedented material abundance shortly after he entered the White House. To Coolidge, as to most Americans in the Roaring Twenties, financial titans such as Morgan and Morrow and industrial giants like Henry Ford and John D. Rockefeller were objects of almost religious veneration. "The man who builds a factory builds a temple," Coolidge once said. "The man who works there worships there." He retained millionaire industrialist Andrew Mellon of Pennsylvania (whose family owned a controlling interest in Gulf Oil, the Aluminum Company of America, Koppers, and Union Trust) as his secretary of the Treasury, and Mellon set to work at once to cut government spending and reduce federal income tax rates on businesses and wealthy individuals (including the Mellon family).

Beneath all the sanctimonious probusiness rhetoric, the Coolidge boom was based upon the tremendous expansion in productive capacity of American factories in the 1920s, particularly in such basic industries as iron, steel, petroleum, chemicals, and light metals. Because America's fundamental transportation and manufacturing systems had been completed before 1914, and because the war had suddenly thrust the United States into an entirely unfamiliar role as a creditor nation possessing a record-breaking stock of European gold, businessmen were free to turn their attention toward refinements in the production and distribution processes. Spurred by military demands during the war, and sustained by the adoption of scientific management techniques in the years immediately afterward, U.S. industrial production nearly doubled between 1919 and 1929. Automobile production skyrocketed; by 1929, Detroit was turning out nearly five million new cars a year. Highway construction (funded primarily by state and local expenditures) provided thousands of new jobs; and as Americans enjoyed the benefits of increased mobility, sprawling networks of suburban development grew up virtually overnight, further fueling the building boom that also provided most of the nation's cities with brand-new skylines, symbolized by the graceful, unadorned, and ultra-modern brick, cement, and stone skyscrapers that kept soaring higher and higher each year. Utility companies expanded their grids throughout the countryside, bringing the blessings of inexpensive electric light and power to most of rural America for the first time; power consumption in the United States increased at the rate of 15 percent a year during the decade. In a never-ending quest for efficiency and greater control over every aspect of their operations, businessmen in the 1920s became obsessed with bigness. Local utility companies merged into mammoth regional empires; nationwide chain stores such as A & P, Piggly-Wiggly, and Woolworth's squeezed out thousands of small, independent retail shops; big-city banks gobbled up defenseless competitors and turned them into branches of multitiered holding companies.

Unfortunately, there was no corresponding expansion of employment or wages to accompany this boom in industrial output—which was, after all, achieved largely by the substitution of machinery for manpower. Without some powerful outside stimulus, production soon would have outpaced consumer capacity. So, to encourage a wider distribution of the mushrooming supply of goods and services, advertising became a major industry in itself. Saving was condemned as hopelessly out of fashion and almost unpatriotic; it was every American's duty to provide himself with as many wristwatches, electric floor scrubbers, Frigidaires, Kriss-Kross razor blades, ultraviolet sun lamps, exercise machines, and canned peas as humanly possible. Advertising "makes new thoughts, new desires and new actions," declared Coolidge approvingly in 1926. "It is the most potent influence in adopting and changing the habits and modes of life, affecting what we eat, what we wear, and the work and play of the whole nation." In preaching their gospel of material abundance, advertisers received an incalculable boost from the invention and popularization of the radio; although the medium had been wholly unknown to most Americans before the war (only one American family in ten thousand owned a radio in 1920), the seemingly unlimited potential of radio captured everyone's imagination during the twenties and revolutionized the nation's communications and entertainment industries. The advent of installment purchasing plans provided additional impetus to consumption; all one needed to buy a new washing machine or diamond necklace was a minimal down payment. As the decade progressed, credit terms became even easier, with payment extended over longer and longer periods.

High-powered sales strategies only camouflaged the basic weaknesses in the American economy, however. At one end of the scale there was too much idle capital; at the other end were too many idle workers. Income and purchasing power were dangerously concentrated in the hands of a favored few: government statistics showed that 90 percent of the nation's wealth was owned by 13 percent of the people. While the number of truly rich Americans kept rising—a study by the Federal Reserve Bank of New York revealed that there were forty thousand millionaires in the United States at the end of 1928, where there had been only seven thousand in 1914—millions of American families remained locked outside the charmed circle of prosperity. Farm income declined steadily throughout the twenties, and unemployment kept climbing until it neared the four million mark by the end of 1928. The coal and textile industries remained depressed for most of the decade, producing pockets of appalling poverty in the South and especially in Appalachia. Federal surveys revealed that two-thirds of American families were struggling to survive on incomes below $2,500, the official minimum standard for a decent living. Lured into exorbitant installment purchases, workers watched as a growing percentage of their wages was sacrificed every week to meet mounting interest payments.

In the second half of the decade, as the struggle among producers for customers grew ever more vicious, it became clear that "prosperity" was the exclusive province of big corporations, as the mortality rate among smaller businesses increased inexorably. "The business structure of the United States is undergoing a rigorous process of 'rationalization,' " explained the managing director of the National Industrial Conference Board in early 1928, "in which many of the smaller companies find it increasingly difficult to compete with the high efficiency standards set by well-managed, large-scale enterprises." The New York *World* was less enthusiastic about the trend: "In the intensive competition which is now under way, and which shows no sign of immediate abatement, only the large organizations able to apply the best that science and skill have to offer are showing satisfactory earnings. This goes far to explain what is sometimes called the 'miracle' of prosperity and falling prices. When the nature of this prosperity is understood its miraculous features become less evident."

Even many large corporations continued to prosper only because they were earning extravagant profits in the stock market. Twenty million Americans had gained their first experience in the world of capital investment by purchasing Liberty Bonds or subscribing to Victory Loans during the war, and once the immediate postwar depression ended, a substantial number of individual investors forsook their traditional suspicion of Wall Street and readily transferred their savings into corporate securities. They were rewarded with a stunning bonanza that surpassed even the most wildly optimistic expectations.

Beginning in the summer of 1921, the stock market entered upon a prolonged upswing broken only by minor setbacks in 1924 and 1926. Like all financial booms, it fed on its own success and a pervasive if illogical spirit of boundless optimism that cheerfully ignored the cracks in the nation's economic foundation. (The Coolidge administration did what it could to hide those cracks altogether; for instance, the federal government consistently—and perhaps deliberately—underestimated the number of unemployed workers in America.) As paper profits pyramided, more investors were drawn into the market, forcing prices even higher and providing corporations with a ready market for the issue of new securities, and the profits earned through speculation were promptly plowed back to purchase greater quantities of stock, pushing the cycle up to the next level. "It was a great game," joked Will Rogers. "All you had to do was to buy and wait till the next morning and just pick up the paper and see how much you made, in print."

Trading volume on the New York Stock Exchange began setting records in 1925; by 1928, 920 million shares were being traded annually, compared with only 173 million in 1921. Speculators favored those giant corporations that had presumably demonstrated their fitness by squeezing out their less efficient competitors; among these favorites were General Motors, Radio Corporation of America, Chrysler, General Electric Company, Montgomery Ward and Company, International Harvester, and Sears, Roebuck and Company. In the midst of such unrestrained enthusiasm, control of Wall Street passed from traditionally conservative bankers to freewheeling financial wizards who promised quick returns and built spectacular empires with other people's money.

The Coolidge bull market was also fueled by Secretary Mellon's ill-advised income tax cuts on corporations and wealthy individuals, which released more capital for speculative purposes, and by the Wall Street equivalent of installment purchasing, known as "buying on margin." Most stockbrokers permitted their clients to buy stocks by putting down only 10 to 20 percent of the total purchase price, often using the inflated value of other stocks as collateral; the difference was advanced by the brokers themselves, who in turn borrowed the funds from banks or corporations on the call-money market. The percentage of brokers' loans made by giant corporations (such as Standard Oil of New Jersey), who were looking for a profitable outlet for surplus cash generated through economies in production, represented an especially unpredictable ingredient in this explosive mix, because these lenders were wholly outside the control of the Federal Reserve Board. Bankers derisively referred to the loans as "bootleg money," and economists pointed out that the funds would benefit the national economy far more if they were invested in productive enterprises that increased employment; but the practice spread rapidly nonetheless. "This is still a free country," huffed one executive whose company was active in the call-loan market. "We have a right to employ our money as we see fit. If we see a chance to get 6, 7 or 8 per cent for our liquid funds through loans on stock market collateral, why shouldn't we take it?" The nation was thus treated to the spectacle of corporations paying their own stockholders returns of only 4 percent, while the company earned rates of 9 percent by investing "surplus" cash in the call-loan market. As the boom began to spiral out of control in 1927 and 1928, corporations came to supply nearly half the funds loaned to brokers. And as these brokers' loans—totaling nearly $5 billion by the autumn of 1928—became the main underpinning of the extended rise in stock prices, the market developed a dangerous and decidedly unhealthy reliance on the maintenance of low interest rates and a federal policy of easy money.

Coolidge was only too happy to comply. After all, he had readily proclaimed the dawn of a New Era of perpetual prosperity in the United States (although he harbored personal doubts about the wisdom and morality of stock market speculation). Whenever the industrial index sputtered or the stock market coughed, Coolidge and Secretary Mellon breathed new life into the faltering boom with encouraging words and a generous relaxation of credit. Given the absence of real and substantive expansion in the American economy, this was a policy that could only end in spectacular disaster. At several critical moments between 1924 and 1928, the Federal Reserve System—of which Mellon was the chairman ex officio—obligingly reduced its interest rates and pumped more money into the economy, creating what Republican journalist William Allen White described as

> a flood of credit that swiftly flowed in a mill race [which] headed through Wall Street to the ends of the earth. Riding on that racing flood, Uncle Sam became the world's creditor. We Americans were proud—even vain—of our position as creditor, and Calvin Coolidge, typifying by some mystic coincidence or curious prescience the spirit of American democracy, as its leader and master gave his blessing to the new order.

Even some enthusiastic boosters thought matters had gotten out of hand when the Federal Reserve Bank of New York led a successful drive to lower the discount rate to 3.5 percent in August of 1927. Although Ben Strong, governor of the New York bank, had taken this remarkable action primarily to assist the Bank of England in stemming the flow of gold from Britain to the United States, the immediate effect was to give further impetus to an already overheated speculative situation.

For his part, Coolidge appears to have realized that the day of reckoning was close at hand ("Papa says there's a depression coming," his wife said one day in an offhand comment), though he obdurately continued to issue public statements encouraging the market to set dizzying new heights. During his summer vacation in the Black Hills of South Dakota in that same fateful month of August 1927, exactly four years after he had succeeded Warren Harding, the President called reporters to his temporary office in Rapid City and, without comment, handed out twenty-five slips of paper that read simply, "I do not choose to run for President in 1928." When they asked for some explanation, Coolidge barked, "There will be nothing more from this office today!" Some political analysts suggested that Silent Cal's cryptic wording meant that he was just being coy, and that he really hoped that the Republican party would draft him by popular acclaim for a third term without any effort on his part. But he never lifted a finger to encourage such speculation, and the American business community made preparations to get along without the best friend it had ever had in the White House. "However much or little Mr. Coolidge may have had to do with the prosperity of the past four years," observed the *Commercial and Financial Chronicle* of New York, "he is credited with having been the backbone of that prosperity."

And so, with a worried glance toward the future, Will Rogers bade President Calvin Coolidge a fond farewell as the nation prepared to elect his successor: "You know, Cal, you been President at a mighty fortunate time in our lives. The Lord has sure been good to us. . . . Now just how long is that going to last?"

Before West Coast promoters turned Las Vegas into the gambling capital of the United States, Americans looked to Wall Street to set the odds on national sporting and political contests. Although the odds makers had suffered an embarrassing defeat in mid-October 1928, making the St. Louis Cardinals a 3–1 choice to defeat the New York Yankees in a World Series the Yankees swept in four lopsided games, they remained virtually unanimous in establishing Herbert Hoover as a solid favorite to succeed Calvin Coolidge in the White House.

By the morning of November 6, the odds had lengthened to 5 to 1 in Hoover's favor. Despite strict rules that forbade members of the New York Stock Exchange from acting as "betting commissioners" (another polite euphemism for bookmakers), many brokerage firms accommodated their regular customers by quietly arranging bets for them; one busy clerk reportedly handled more than $1 million worth of wagers in the last two weeks of the campaign. Betting had been unusually light for a presidential contest—the lightest in twenty years, in fact—largely because the stock market itself seemed to present an even more attractive path to easy money. But as election day approached, the big money started to flow in. Aside from Rothstein's $1.6 million wager on Hoover, the largest bet was the Republican pool of $1 million headed by stock market speculator and automobile entrepreneur William Crapo Durant, president of the Durant Motor Company and one of the founders of General Motors. Durant's challenge was accepted by a group of Democratic businessmen, led by John Jacob Raskob and prominent stock manipulator Michael Meehan, who put up $200,000 of their own money to cover the bet. The diminutive Raskob, who had given up his position as vice-president and director of General Motors several months earlier to serve as Democratic National Committee chairman, had seen reports of the record-breaking crowds who had thronged to his party's rallies all along the East Coast in the final week of the campaign, and, like all political novices who saw rainbows easily, he believed that if anyone could parlay that enthusiastic popular support into a shattering upset at the polls, it was the Democratic presidential nominee: New York governor Alfred Emanuel Smith.

Al Smith was unquestionably the most electrifying national political figure in America during the 1920s, and the most controversial presidential candidate since Theodore Roosevelt. An Irish-American Catholic who had grown up among the rabbit-warren tenements, warehouses, and wharves of New York's Lower East Side, Smith had only an eighth grade education; he preferred to say that he had graduated from the Fulton Fish Market, where he had worked as an assistant bookkeeper for $12 a week and all the flounder he could eat. At the age of twenty-two, Smith entered the service of the Tammany machine; for the next eight years, he dutifully delivered subpoenas and performed other prosaic political tasks, until the sachems of Tammany Hall rewarded his dogged loyalty by sending him to the state legislature in Albany. There he became one of the best-informed and most effective assemblymen New York ever had. He understood and sympathized with the plight of the overworked and underpaid women in the notorious sweatshops of the garment district; he championed the cause of the immigrant who was struggling against the entrenched interests to obtain a precarious foothold in the land of opportunity. He learned the intricacies of the machinery of state government from the bottom up until he knew the system better than anyone else, and in 1918 he was elected governor of New York. Although he was buried in the same Harding landslide that wiped out practically every other Democratic candidate outside the South in 1920, Smith triumphantly returned to the executive mansion in 1922, 1924, and 1926, earning a reputation as the ablest state administrator in the nation.

His foremost political protégé, former assistant secretary of the navy Franklin D. Roosevelt, had placed Smith's name in nomination with an electrifying speech at the Democratic presidential convention in Madison Square Garden in the sweltering summer of 1924—Roosevelt christened

Smith "the Happy Warrior," a nickname that stayed with the governor for the rest of his life—but the Southern and Western wings of the party steadfastly refused to swallow any beer-drinking son of Tammany. Their recalcitrance proved a stroke of good fortune for Smith. While he finally had to settle for reelection as governor, the eventual (after 102 ballots) Democratic presidential nominee, former Wall Street counsel John W. Davis, received one of the worst drubbings in the history of American politics. When the fractious and chastened Democratic delegates reassembled four years later to select a candidate, the Smith forces could no longer be denied their chance for the prize, and the governor won the nomination on the first ballot at a relatively subdued (for the Democrats) convention in Houston. "We offer one who has the will to win—who not only deserves success but commands it," proclaimed Roosevelt as he once again performed the honor of nominating his mentor: "Victory is his habit—the happy warrior, Alfred Smith." And as the bands played "East Side, West Side," Governor Smith set out upon the twenty-first and most difficult electoral campaign of his life.

Because Al Smith—an Irish-Catholic machine politician from the sin-ridden saloons and pool parlors of New York—personally represented the worst nightmares of Protestant rural America, the 1928 Democratic platform deliberately avoided any controversial progressive positions that might further alienate moderate or conservative voters. And to manage his campaign, Smith chose the eminently respectable John Jacob Raskob, a Horatio Alger success story who had risen from the slums of Hell's Kitchen to become a businessman so thoroughly orthodox that he felt comfortable describing himself in *Who's Who* as a "capitalist." Raskob, in turn, promptly established his political headquarters in the indisputably creditable General Motors Building in New York.

This unabashed quest for respectability was not just a cynical political maneuver. For all the outward characteristics that marked him as a product of the tenements—the glass of beer in his hand, the ever-present cigar between his teeth, the husky voice and the vulgar East Side accent that made "radio" sound like "raddio" and "first" like "foist," and of course the trademark brown derby that he waved like a talisman over the crowds of admirers—Smith had a deep yearning for social acceptance and a pronounced distaste for radicalism. "He was not the defiant rebel," observed veteran journalist Thomas L. Stokes. "He catered as well to the man who had it and expected to get more of it. He was not out to do any uprooting—except of prohibition. He discussed fundamental issues, but he never went too far."

Nothing irked Smith more than the suggestion that his candidacy posed a danger to the capitalist system in America. Such charges, Smith snapped angrily, were "a foolish attempt to get the American workingman to believe that the Democratic Party under my leadership is going to prostrate him, drive his children out of his house and leave him helpless and homeless. What a stupid performance—of all the men in the world to urge that against a man who came up from the ranks of labor himself, and if elected President I am going to drive them all out of their home?"

It was Alfred Smith's great misfortune that his Republican opponent in 1928 was Herbert Clark Hoover, a man who would not allow himself to be out-respectabled by anyone. Born in August 1874 in the sober and somnolent Quaker community of West Branch, Iowa (population 365), in a two-room house where he shared a trundle bed with his brother and sister, Hoover enjoyed a typically tranquil Midwestern childhood, picking potato bugs and tilling the rich black soil, until he was suddenly orphaned at the age of nine. After spending a year on his uncle's farm just outside of town, Herbert was sent to the West Coast to live with relatives in Newberg, Oregon (which was even smaller and sleepier than West Branch). Despite the endless hours of hard work, clearing stumps and chopping wood to pay for his board and keep, Hoover always remembered his years in Oregon with affection: there, he said, he had been "so happy and so poor," among the "gleaming wheat fields, abundant fruit, the luxuriant vegetation, and the fish in the mountain streams." One could hardly imagine a childhood environment more wholly dissimilar to the East Side of New York City.

In the fall of 1891, Hoover entered Leland Stanford University as a member of that fledgling institution's first freshman class. In typically industrious fashion, he showed up so bright and early that he was the first student to register, moving into the men's dormitory even before the university was formally opened. Although he did not enjoy a particularly distinguished college career, Hoover did earn a bachelor's degree in geology, and subsequently embarked upon a career as a mining engineer that took the Iowa farm boy around the globe five times over the next two decades, visiting such exotic locations as the diamond mines of South Africa, the vast outback of West Australia (where he traveled by camel and lived among aborigines on a diet of bread, cocoa, and tinned sardines), the silver mines of Burma, Russian copper mines deep in the Ural Mountains, and the imperial mineral projects of northern China, where he and his wife—whom he had courted during one of his infrequent sojourns in America—were among the garrison of foreigners besieged at Tientsin during the Boxer Rebellion. In 1907, Hoover established his own consulting firm with offices (and changes of clothes for him) around the world, and began to specialize in taking over unprofitable engineering operations and turning them, often quite literally, into gold mines. As he learned more about the business aspects of mining operations, Hoover spent less time in the field and more in the company of financiers, promoters, and speculators. He learned his lessons well; by 1914 Herbert Clark Hoover was the most famous, and reportedly the wealthiest engineer in the world.

But the Great Engineer longed for new worlds to conquer, and the outbreak of war in Europe provided the opportunity. As the carnage on the western front bogged down into a hopeless stalemate, the Commission for Relief in Belgium selected Hoover to head its efforts to feed the starving civilians in German-occupied territory; over the following three years, Hoover supervised a massive private philanthropic drive that dispensed $25 million per month and provided food for ten million people, an accomplishment that was all the more remarkable considering Britain's manifest reluctance to allow any supplies at all to pass through its naval blockade of the Continent. (A bitter First Lord of the Admiralty Winston Spencer Churchill called Hoover a son of a bitch for his callous disregard of British military interests.) When the United States entered the Great War in February 1917, President Wilson decided that the nation needed a food dictator to increase American agricultural production and curb domestic consumption. Hoover, of course, realized at once that he was the most qualified man in the country for the job and campaigned shamelessly for the appointment, until Wilson finally gave in and made him United States food commissioner and a member of the administration's unofficial war cabinet.

By the time Kaiser Wilhelm II abdicated and the newborn German republican government requested an armistice in November 1918, Hoover had become the second most famous man in Washington (behind only Wilson) and probably one of the most respected men in the world. Thus he seemed the logical choice to serve as chairman of the postwar Inter-Allied Food Council, coordinating the relief efforts that tried to stem the disastrous tide of starvation, plague, and Bolshevik revolution that swept over central and eastern Europe in 1919; as far as British economist John Maynard Keynes was concerned, Hoover was the only man to emerge from the debacle of the Paris Peace Conference with an enhanced reputation. By this time, however, Hoover's autocratic methods were beginning to grate on the nerves of his European colleagues, who doubtless were not sorry to see him return to the United States later that year.

Not surprisingly, some excitable political managers boosted Hoover for the White House in 1920, though their efforts were complicated by the fact that no one knew whether the Great Engineer was a Democrat or Republican. By the time he cast his lot publicly with the GOP (despite the fact that he had held such a highly visible position in Woodrow Wilson's Democratic administration), Hoover had lost whatever chance he may have had to organize a viable run for the nomination. Besides, the professional politicians treated his candidacy as a joke; he had established no record of faithful party service, he had never even voted in an American election until he was forty years old, and the Republican Old Guard resented his independence and individual celebrity. Nevertheless, President Harding selected Hoover as his secretary of commerce in 1921, and Coolidge, after fruitlessly trying to shuttle him off into the less influential Departments of Interior or Agriculture, reluctantly permitted him to remain in office for several years following Harding's death.

Silent Cal never had much use for Hoover. He referred to him sarcastically as "the boy wonder" and "the smart boy," and despised Hoover's busybody attitude and his persistent intrusion into the affairs of cabinet departments other than his own. (Around the White House, Hoover was known derisively as "Secretary of Commerce and Undersecretary of All Other Departments.") "That man," the President once complained to the secretary of agriculture in a fit of exasperation, "has offered me unsolicited advice for six years, all of it bad!" This, of course, was an exaggeration, because Hoover was one of the few members of the Coolidge administration bold enough to suggest that the Treasury conceivably might wish to dampen the speculative boom on Wall Street instead of encouraging it with an irresponsible policy of easy money.

Otherwise, Big Business had no reason to cavil during Secretary Hoover's tenure at the Commerce Department. Hoover had accepted the post on the condition that he would enjoy a free hand to reorganize the department, and he wasted no time in putting his imprint upon every aspect of its activities. He expanded the foreign trade section and increased American exports by 58 percent, promoted the formation of trade associations (which helped eliminate whatever competitive forces remained in American industry), called for conferences to deal with transportation and unemployment problems, represented the government in major industrial disputes, collected all sorts of obscure statistical data (William Allen White once likened Hoover to an adding machine), organized campaigns to eliminate waste in the private sector, and even butted into the issue of the conservation of fisheries. Actually, Hoover turned out to be a better team player than the Old Guard had expected; he never publicly condemned the tawdry political scandals of Harding's administration, nor did he challenge Coolidge's leadership by supporting costly federal measures for farm relief.

Behind the scenes, however, the doggedly ambitious Hoover was laying his plans to succeed Coolidge, using the organization and influence he had built at Commerce to fashion a personal political machine that quietly began gathering support from moderate and liberal Republicans across the country. When Coolidge issued his terse "I do not choose to run" statement in August 1927, Hoover hurried out to the Black Hills to ask his boss exactly what he meant. Coolidge refused to elaborate (partly because he enjoyed seeing the boy wonder squirm), but Hoover went ahead anyway and allowed his name to be placed on the ballot for the 1928 presidential primary elections. The results proved conclusively that he was the overwhelming choice of the Republican rank and file. He also received valuable endorsements from such influential publications as the *Chicago Tribune* and the Scripps-Howard chain of newspapers. Hoover was praised as "the greatest humanitarian since Jesus Christ" and "the man who"—the man who fed Belgium, the man who won the war with his food conservation drives, the man who saved Europe from Communist revolution. Although the party's Old Guard still viewed him with marked distrust, Hoover received the long-coveted nomination on the first ballot in Kansas City in June 1928, at a convention memorable primarily for its unusually listless atmosphere and the oppressive heat. "One of the oldest and perhaps the noblest of human aspirations has been abolition of poverty," declared the candidate in his lackluster acceptance speech. "We in America today are nearer to the final triumph over poverty than ever before in the history of any land. The poorhouse is vanishing from among us."

The two major party platforms in 1928 were as nearly identical as they could be without a mimeograph. Neither advanced any controversial positions or grappled with the serious social and economic problems facing the nation; both waffled on the issues of prohibition and farm relief; and both boldly declared that they were in favor of high tariffs and continued prosperity. According to Walter Lippmann, the only difference between the two platforms on foreign affairs was that "while both were voluble and vague the Republican took longer to read." In their haste to reassure voters that they, too, were safe for American business, the Democrats forsook the progressive tradition articulated so eloquently by Woodrow Wilson only sixteen years earlier. Indeed, the *Magazine of Wall Street* readily acknowledged that it could find no flaw in either party's statements, nor did either candidate appear to pose a threat to the unhindered control of the economy by private industry: "Hoover will be a little better for big business (which, by the way, dislikes him because it has no wonders or mysteries for him and he looks at it level-eyed), and Smith will be a little more inclined to help the business atoms." "What is happening is that both candidates for the Presidency are kowtowing to the business powers that control," lamented the liberal journal *Nation*. "When Governor Smith's backers portray him as safe and sane for all business they picture him as faithless to the soundest tenets of the Democracy. He ought not to be safe and sane for all business. He ought to be as dreaded by lawless business and that portion of the business world which is seeking to acquire certain birthrights of the American people as was Woodrow Wilson."

In the absence of any clear-cut conflict on the issues, the campaign focused on the personalities of the two candidates. And here the differences could not have been more profound. "This was the battle of the high stiff collar and the brown derby, of 'Onward Christian Soldiers' . . . against that lively air 'The Sidewalks of New York,' " remarked Tom Stokes. H. L. Mencken agreed. "The two men differ as a soldier differs from a book-keeper," wrote the sage of the Baltimore *Sun.* "They are as far apart as Pilsner and Coca-cola."

Smith was the flamboyant actor who cherished his moment in the spotlight, an unpretentious man of the people who inspired genuine love and devotion in the hearts of his admirers, a lifelong politician who never felt more at ease than when he was in the midst of a crowd of ordinary Americans. Mencken was admittedly captivated by the Smith perform-ance. "Cocky, vulgar, even maybe low, [Smith] is never cheap," decided the normally cynical columnist. "He says what he thinks in plain English. . . . Compared to him, Lord Hoover is no more than a pious old woman, a fat Coolidge." Another political commentator described Smith's raucous campaign as "a circus with bands and clowns—of which he was the chief, with animals and sideshows and a cold bottle of beer as you left the tent."

Hoover, on the other hand, was dour, blunt, reserved, and downright podgy. "God made Dr. Hoover virtuous," Mencken liked to say, "but He also made him dull." This was the Great Engineer's first campaign for public office, and he found the experience entirely distasteful. One jour-nalist who accompanied the Hoover campaign remarked upon "the al-most physical horror, the evident recoil, when Herbert Hoover made a public speech. He was a timid person before a crowd. He would hide his face in his manuscript and go to the task as if it were something that must be borne. He would plod through it without relish or enthusiasm." Audi-ences marveled at Hoover's ability to remain completely immobile while delivering a speech; in fact, he made only seven set speeches during the entire campaign. He clung for dear life to platitudes and generalities, extolling "the march of progress," pledging "great constructive mea-sures," and wrapping the whole package in his shopworn vision of "an America healthy in body, healthy in spirit, unfettered youth, eager—with a vision searching beyond the farthest horizons with an open mind, sympa-thetic and generous." Decisive and commanding as a businessman and administrator, Hoover the candidate grew more and more tentative as election day neared.

Smith did everything he could to draw Hoover out of his shell—"What does Mr. Hoover think of this?" he would ask his listeners. "He must have *some* ideas about this?"—but Hoover stolidly refused to budge. Instead, Smith himself became the main issue as American voters wondered whether they wanted a Catholic and an avowed opponent of prohibition as their next president. Abetted by prominent Republican spokesmen (including Assistant Attorney General Mabel Walker Wildebrandt, who openly urged a convention of Methodist ministers to mobilize their congregations for Hoover), a sordid whispering campaign against Smith swept like wildfire across the Midwest and the traditionally solid Democratic South. Otherwise rational people were perfectly prepared to believe that if Smith was elected, he would deliver the nation to Rome and build a tunnel to the Vatican so the Pope, who allegedly was financing the Democratic campaign, could visit the White House at will. There were crosses burning in fields as the Democratic campaign train rolled through the countryside; pamphlets spread lurid tales of "Traffic in Nuns"; in Birmingham, Alabama, the Ku Klux Klan publicly burned Smith in effigy; young boys taunted Smith with the chant "Alcohol Al! Alcohol Al!" Fundamentalist Protestant journals had a field day: the *Baptist and Commoner,* for instance, charged that "the devil's crowd—Catholics, political demagogues, brewers, bootleggers, prostitutes—the whole motley bellygang are for Smith!" One Texas newspaper predicted that if the Democrats captured the White House, "the Romish system will institute persecutions again, and put the cruel, blood-stained heel upon all who refuse her authority." In an article entitled "Unclean Spirits Like Frogs," another Texas paper likened the sons of Tammany to the despicable creatures mentioned in the Book of Revelation; and the *Baptist Courier* denounced Democratic campaign manager John J. Raskob (who was also a staunch Roman Catholic) as "a private chaplain of the papal household. . . . Without doubt he has been on his knees before the Pope."

Such inflammatory allegations led New York columnist Heywood Broun to describe the 1928 presidential campaign as "the dirtiest political fight waged in this country in fifty years." "It will take two generations to sweep up the dirt," confirmed Will Rogers in disgust.

Although responsible Republican newspapers such as the Boston *Transcript* condemned "this diabolical campaign of undercover innuendo," Hoover himself remained silent, save for one mild statement of regret. His managers pretended he knew nothing about the whispering campaign, that he was too busy dealing with important issues to notice such petty goings-on. Certainly the Republican candidate never publicly repudiated the support of hate groups such as the Klan. Outraged, Mencken accused Hoover of sleeping with every species of "degraded pimps and harlots of politics across the table." The *Nation's* Broun was even less charitable: "Naturally Mr. Hoover has been obliged to dispose of his own soul as well during the exigencies of the campaign, and in this respect he has proved himself a superb business man. According to tradition, the deal can be made just once. Mr. Hoover has bettered the technique of Faust. His soul, and not a very big one either, has been bartered off a score of times. In fact, whenever he saw a group of voters."

Energized by Smith's aggressive enthusiasm, the increasingly vituperative campaign rhetoric, and the opportunity—for the first time in history—to listen to most of the candidates' major speeches via radio, Americans awakened from their decade-long political torpor and cheerfully took up sides. Those who supported Hoover cited his "dignified bearing," his business expertise, his humanitarian work, and, above all, his intellectual capabilities as a Thoroughly Modern Expert whose trained, logical mind could solve almost any earthly problem. His support of a constitutional amendment to prohibit child labor attracted liberal voters, including Margaret Sanger, the nation's foremost advocate of birth control: "Most politicians go in for externals but Mr. Hoover has his interest embedded in fundamentals," announced Ms. Sanger approvingly. "It was Mr. Hoover's regard for child life that won me." The president of the World Congress of Jewish Women declared her support for Hoover in recognition of his relief work in Europe. Charles Lindbergh, the sober and supremely self-controlled aviator whose solo flight to Paris in 1927 had made him the most widely admired young man in America, promised via a public telegram to fly home to St. Louis from a Mexican hunting trip to vote for the Great Engineer. Many voters chose Hoover primarily because he was not Smith, which meant that the Hoover camp sheltered some very strange bedfellows: while the Women's Christian Temperance Union urged its members to "Get Down on Your Knees and Pray" for a Hoover victory against the "wet" Al Smith, an informal survey of bootleggers in the Northeast and the Midwest revealed that they, too, backed the Republican candidate almost unanimously. Fearful that Smith might repeal prohibition and put them out of business, some prominent bootleggers reportedly organized some very profitable campaign fund drives for Hoover.

As the "safe" Republican candidate, Hoover appealed to Americans who were satisfied with the status quo in late 1928. The *Wall Street Journal,* of course, endorsed Hoover as "the soundest business proposition for those with a financial stake in the country." Four days before the election, the *Journal* also carried a lengthy statement by Henry Ford commending Hoover as the candidate more likely to maintain both prosperity and prohibition. "No prosperity is possible unless the country is sober," explained Ford, who then proceeded to outline his optimistic vision of America's future under the guidance of the Great Engineer:

We are abolishing panics in this country. It is a long time since we had a panic. We are destroying their sources just as health engineers destroyed the sources of yellow fever. . . .

The reason we must have a new kind of President is that we are on the threshold of a new kind of world. Many people think that this is the industrial age we are living in. They think that the big job is to keep things running just as they are. No. We have scarcely begun. We have yet to enter the industrial and comfortable age. And before we can enter it we must have national leadership, a man who sees the main problem in all its wide reaches . . . a social engineer who can direct and oversee and referee between all parties, and keep them all busy at the main task of creating a prosperity which shall be continued and equally distributed throughout the country.

Always eager to irritate Hoover as much as possible, Coolidge refused to publicly endorse the Republican candidate until November 1, when he finally dispatched a terse telegram: ". . . You are able, experienced, trustworthy and safe. Your success in the campaign seems assured, and I shall turn over the great office of President of the United States of America to your keeping. . . ."

Al Smith, on the other hand, gathered most of his support from voters who wanted a change in the markedly moribund atmosphere of Washington, a President who was willing to open the windows of the White House to allow a breath of fresh air into the stuffy corridors of power. "The country needs a leader with soul and vision," declared one liberal journal, "one less interested in increasing the average income of the American and in the efficiency of business than in putting back into our national life some of that social and national and international idealism which has departed from it since Mr. Wilson put the country into war." Forty Harvard professors, including Felix Frankfurter, endorsed Smith as "the best hope for a return to the liberalism of Roosevelt and Wilson," while chiding Hoover for continued association with the reactionary and corrupt elements of the Republican party.

New York Yankee slugger Babe Ruth, who had surmounted a rough-and-tumble childhood of his own on the streets of Baltimore, said that he admired Governor Smith for his ability to rise above his humble East Side origins; after personally demolishing the Cardinals in the 1928 World Series by scoring nine runs and rapping out ten hits (including three home runs) for a record-setting batting average of .625, Ruth presented Smith with a souvenir baseball from the last game of the series and donned a symbolic brown derby for a series of campaign appearances through the South. (When Republican officials asked him to pose for a photograph with

Hoover, the Babe refused. "Tell him I'll be glad to talk to him if he wants to meet me under the stands," was the most he would allow.) Philosopher and educator John Dewey, too, favored the Happy Warrior; Dewey predicted that the election of Smith would have "a humanizing social effect" on the nation, and would reduce "the hypocrisies and humbugs which occupy so much space in our American social life today." While he admitted that Hoover had been an efficient administrator in times of crisis, Dewey denied that the Great Engineer was a great humanitarian: "If he has any human insight, dictated by consciousness of social needs, into the policies called for by the day-to-day life of his fellow human beings, either in domestic or international affairs, I have never seen the signs of it. His whole creed of complacent capitalistic individualism and of the right and duty of economic success commits him to the continuation of that hypocritical religion of 'prosperity' which is, in my judgment, the greatest force that exists at present in maintaining the unrealities of our social tone and temper."

In the final week of the campaign, as Hoover's private train chugged doggedly westward through blizzards and bitterly cold temperatures toward his adopted home state of California, Smith made one last East Coast swing that culminated in massive rallies that drew a total of more than one million people in New England and New York. The candidate exulted in the popular acclaim. "It is in the air," he told reporters. "It means victory. That is what it means. It is the same all over."

When at last his campaign reached its climax in New York City on November 3, Smith greeted the hundreds of thousands of onlookers who braved a chilling drizzle to cheer his procession from the Battery to Central Park. That evening, Smith told a Madison Square Garden audience of more than twenty-five thousand Democratic loyalists that the Republican party held no patent on prosperity, no magic formula that automatically produced good times whenever the GOP controlled the federal government. "The fact of the matter," he croaked in a voice hoarse from six weeks of nonstop campaigning, "is that in the last fifty years we have had more business depressions and more money panics under Republican administrations than we have had under Democratic administrations."

Unlike the debacles of 1920 and 1924, the Democratic National Committee under Raskob's able fund-raising leadership enjoyed a war chest nearly as substantial as the perennially swollen Republican coffers. (In 1928, for instance, the list of GOP contributors included John D. Rockefeller, movie director Cecil B. De Mille, steel executive Charles Schwab, automobile tire manufacturers Harvey S. Firestone and R. H. Goodrich, several members of the Mellon clan, retail mogul S. S. Kresge, the six Fisher Brothers of General Motors, and film producer Adolph Zukor. On the Democratic side, Raskob himself was the second-largest donor, having contributed more than $100,000 by the end of October.) Nevertheless, Smith's campaign began to run out of funds in the final days just as popular momentum appeared to be swinging to the Happy Warrior. In a desperate attempt to bring the Eastern industrial states into the Democratic column, Raskob convinced a New York banker named Jim Riordan, head of the County Trust Company and an old friend of Governor Smith, to loan the National Committee $1.5 million on the understanding that he would be amply repaid after Smith entered the White House. Because legal restrictions prohibited corporate campaign contributions, Raskob then had to persuade an inner circle of Smith's admirers—including New York *World* editor Herbert Bayard Swope and sports promoter (and reputed rumrunner) Tim Mara, the future owner of the New York Giants football team—to sign a note for the amount of the loan after Raskob assured them that their signatures were simply part of a clever legal fiction, and they would never be called on to pay off the note. Conceived in the euphoria of the final hectic days of the election campaign, the County Trust affair would end in tragedy twelve months later.

Raskob's blind optimism notwithstanding, the New York Stock Exchange advanced broadly on November 5, the day before the election, in expectation of a Hoover victory. Wall Street did not fear Smith; indeed, it seemed that nothing could frighten the great bull market in its present condition, as trading volume records were shattered every month and brokers' loans mounted to an unprecedented total of nearly $5 billion. But Hoover was the choice of most of the financiers because he was a known commodity, a candidate whose campaign rhetoric marked him as a man of undeniable "soundness." Besides, Wall Street looked forward with keen anticipation to the prospect of another four years of the invaluable Mellon at the Treasury.

Around the country, it was one of the more eventful election days in American history, though not all the excitement was caused by the political process. In Chicago's financial district, gunmen poured several rounds of slugs into the body of a rival gangster as he sat in his car across the street from the Continental and Commercial Bank. In Philadelphia, where a special grand jury was investigating the recent plague of underworld slayings and police corruption, three automobiles full of hoodlums armed with machine guns pulled alongside the car of another gang member and riddled it with bullets, killing their victim and miraculously missing a three-year-old girl sitting in the back seat. In Cynthiana, Kentucky, a Hoover supporter shot and killed a Smith voter. At least four people in New England dropped dead from heart attacks induced by the excitement (or stress) of voting for Smith or Hoover. In New York, a despondent

Smith volunteer worker sensed the handwriting on the wall and committed suicide.

To provide passersby with the latest election results, the *New York Times* mounted two circles of lights around the flagpole atop the Times Tower: if the white lights were lit, it meant Smith was ahead; the lights for Hoover were red. Save for a brief flash of white shortly after the polls closed in the East, there was nothing but crimson against the overcast sky for the rest of the evening. To put together a majority of electoral votes, Smith needed to hold the traditionally Democratic South (which was Protestant and dry), detach several states from the normally Republican industrial East, and carry the progressive Northwest. In other words, he needed a political miracle. Will Rogers, for one, knew he would not get one. "This is going to be the greatest lesson in geography that New York City ever had," Rogers predicted on election day. "They never knew how many people live west of the Hudson river."

News of the stunning Republican landslide turned a planned victory rally of Smith loyalists at Yankee Stadium into a wake. As a tribute to their fallen chieftain, actor Harpo Marx played a requiem to the tune of "The Streets of New York" on his harp for the hushed multitude. "It was the only time my own playing ever brought tears to my eyes," he admitted thirty years later.

Coolidge refused to stay up late to listen to the election returns. He told reporters that if the contest had not been decided before his usual 10:30 bedtime, he would go to sleep anyway.

Senator Charles ("Call Me Charlie") Curtis of Kansas, the Republican vice-presidential nominee, also hit the sack early (8:30) that evening. Curtis, who had been raised by his grandmother, a full-blooded Kaw Indian princess, on a reservation outside of Topeka until he was eight years old, was the first American of Indian ancestry to obtain such an exalted political office. He had made one hundred speeches and one thousand appearances from the platform of his campaign train—including one whistle stop where Curtis told a heckler that he was "too damn dumb" to understand what he (Curtis) was talking about—and by November 6, the weary candidate was badly in need of a long rest. "I hope I can get it in Washington," Curtis told reporters, "but if I find I can't, then I'll go somewhere else."

Hoover spent the evening sheltered in his study, receiving telegraph reports as they arrived and marking the latest returns on two big blackboards neatly divided into forty-eight columns marked with each state's electoral votes. The candidate displayed no visible emotion when he received Governor Smith's message of concession and congratulation, nor did he deign to appear when John Philip Sousa's band stopped by to serenade him with his favorite march, "Stars and Stripes Forever." Only when a delegation of Stanford students marched up the hill to his house and sang "The Star-Spangled Banner" and "Auld Lang Syne" did the victorious candidate allow his feelings to break through the barrier of icy reserve; as the President-elect and his wife stood stiffly on their terraced roof to acknowledge the honor, several reporters who were standing near Hoover swore they saw tears in his eyes.

In the cold light of the morning after, the final results looked very much like an unmitigated disaster for the Democratic party. Hoover had captured 444 electoral votes to Smith's 87—the greatest majority since Ulysses S. Grant smothered Horace Greeley in 1872. "The stupendous victory of Herbert Hoover stands above party or section," chortled the Republican New York *Herald Tribune.* "It marks an epoch in American political history. . . . America stands at the threshold of a new era." The solid South had crumbled for the first time since 1876; alienated primarily by Smith's Catholicism, Virginia, North Carolina, Kentucky, Maryland, Florida, Texas, and Tennessee all marched into the Republican column. Hoover received 58 percent of the popular vote, 21 million ballots to Smith's 15 million. The most crushing blow to Smith's personal political future was his failure to carry New York State. "Smith is not only defeated," crowed the *Wall Street Journal,* "he is extinct." Feeling as if he had heaved a particularly disreputable stray cat out of the parlor, Bishop James Cannon, Jr., the self-appointed guardian of Protestant virtue in America, exulted over the repudiation of "the wet sidewalks of our cities, aided and abetted by a selfish, so-called liberal element of high society life." The *New York Times* was kinder to the defeated candidate. Governor Smith had displayed admirable qualities of bold leadership, acknowledged the *Times* respectfully; the nation had benefited from his "vigor, his frankness, his instinctive attitude of regarding nothing alien to him which is human . . . [and] his extraordinary personality." But on election day, "a legend went against a personality, and the legend won."

Beneath the undeniably disheartening statistics, however, the future of the Democratic party was not as bleak as it appeared. Because of the unprecedentedly high turnout in 1928, Smith had garnered more popular votes than any other presidential candidate in history (besides Hoover), more even than Coolidge had won in 1924. His vigorous campaign had brought millions of voters to the polls for the first time, particularly in the industrial cities of the East. The twelve largest metropolitan areas in America had voted for Coolidge in 1924 by a margin of 1.3 million votes; in 1928, they went for Smith. Until that moment, as historian William Leuchtenberg explained, the Democrats had not been particularly an urban party. But in losing the struggle against Hoover, Smith "won the battle for the allegiance of the city and laid the foundation for the urban-based party of the 1930's."

It appeared extremely unlikely, however, that Americans would have Al Smith to kick around anymore. His failure to carry his own home state seemed to eliminate the Happy Warrior from serious contention for national office in 1932. But the party would not have far to search for his replacement. Many commentators had predicted before election day that a victory in the New York gubernatorial race would vault Franklin Delano Roosevelt into national prominence once again, resurrecting a political career that appeared to have died when Roosevelt suffered a crippling attack of infantile paralysis in 1921. "One cannot challenge his integrity, his unselfishness, or his desire to do what is right in accordance with old-fashioned American principles," declared the *Nation* in endorsing his candidacy. "It goes almost without saying that, if his health is completely restored, he will probably be nominated some day for a still higher office than that of Governor." For a while, though, it appeared as if Roosevelt, too, would be buried in the Hoover landslide. Through the early hours of the morning of November 7, the contest between Roosevelt and state attorney general Albert Ottinger seesawed back and forth. "The election has been an elegant horse race," Roosevelt grinned as the final tallies trickled in. "I am having the time of my life. I have never done so much figuring since I left school." In the end, he squeaked past Ottinger by a plurality of only 25,564 votes.

After suffering through five years of the reactionary provincialism of President Coolidge, the European press generally welcomed the election of a man as sophisticated and well traveled as Herbert Hoover. "He will bring to the White House a first-hand acquaintance with Europe and its problems such as no previous President has equalled," predicted Britain's *Daily Express.* "That will not make him any less an American, but it is some guarantee that world politics will be approached with at least a semi-international mind." In Berlin, where headlines described Hoover as "the man who supplied starving Germany with food after the war," all but the ultranationalist and extreme radical newspapers approved the triumph of the Great Engineer. "His brain power makes Mr. Hoover a great statesman," noted the *Deutsche Allgemeine Zeitung,* the journal of German heavy industry. "Let us hope that his heart will impart human warmth to this greatness, for without it nothing truly great was ever accomplished in this world."

Official journals in Moscow optimistically predicted that a far-seeing businessman like Hoover would further expand the rapidly developing economic connections between the Soviet Union and the United States.

While the Vatican naturally was disappointed that Smith had lost, it maintained its customary scrupulous impartiality toward other nations' political affairs; besides, Hoover was an old personal acquaintance of Pope Pius XI, whom he had known in the postwar years as Monsignor Achille Ambrogio Domiano Ratti, apostolic delegate to Poland. And insofar as they shed their usual haughty reserve toward American affairs and deigned to comment at all on the election, most French papers echoed *L'Intransigeant's* praise of Hoover as "a man of action, immediate decisions, [and] the biggest of the world's businessmen"; the only dissent came from those Paris journals that had dared to hope that the more sociable Smith would have restored the American market for French wines.

Wall Street wasted no time in celebrating the Republican victory. The stock exchange had taken a holiday on election day, of course, but many shrewd players had left instructions with their brokers on Monday to purchase stocks as soon as trading opened on Wednesday, on the assumption that Hoover's election would send prices soaring at once. As usual, the exhilarating spectacle of broad-based buying by prominent market operators resulted in an avalanche of purchase orders from the "outside public"—smaller players infected with speculative fever who took their lead from knowledgeable insiders such as Raskob, Durant, and legendary stock manipulator Mike Meehan, but who always remained at least one fateful step behind the professionals.

Even a wave of profit taking by speculators late in the morning could not dampen the market's enthusiasm this day, however; tickers lagged more than forty-five minutes behind the action on the floor as the volume of trading reached the second highest level in the history of the New York Stock Exchange. Virtually the entire market surged forward under the pressure of widespread buying. The usual glamour stocks, including American Telephone and Telegraph, Standard Oil of New Jersey, Anaconda Copper, Montgomery Ward, Kennecott Copper, and Wright Aero, led the advance. "Wall Street now feels that business will continue along the same placid, prosperous lines it has held to for the past four years," explained the *Wall Street Journal.* "The job of the Coolidge administration has been to clear the track of obstacles and obstructions which threatened to block the progress of the business engine. The Hoover administration is likely to be one which will show the engineer the way to attain greater speed with safety. . . . There has never been a President with a fundamental understanding of economics better than Mr. Hoover. There has never been a President who had his capacity of large scale organization to get things accomplished. . . . There is no rift in the lute in sight."

Such optimistic predictions aroused the primordial instinct of greed in tens of thousands of otherwise rational American citizens. Hoover had been elected . . . prosperity was guaranteed . . . stocks could not fail to reach dizzying heights heretofore unknown. Critic Gilbert Seldes was convinced that America at the end of 1928 had become "a mob, a little maddened by the sight of sudden wealth, its hysteria concealed because it was making money, which is the normal thing to do in America." There was an almost indiscriminate wave of stock buying among smaller investors; Will Rogers suggested only half jokingly that the Democratic party should have "had the party incorporated and listed on the Exchange as 'Democratic Hopes and Aspirations, Inc.,' then let somebody buy ten shares to get it started, [and] millions would have bought it on the Exchange that wouldn't think of taking it at the polls. They buy anything there worse than Democrats."

Rogers' comment was not far off the mark. At the end of October, oil executive Harry F. Sinclair, who had been convicted for bribery in the Teapot Dome scandal, decided to float a new issue of stock to raise capital for his latest corporate venture, Sinclair Consolidated Oil. To arouse public interest, Sinclair persuaded well-known stock market operator Arthur W. Cutten to ostentatiously "purchase" (actually, Cutten and his associates only pretended to buy the stock) over a million new shares at $30 per share. Although this price was considerably higher than Sinclair Oil's balance sheet justified, eager investors bid up the price to $36 by the end of the first day of public trading. And the price kept rising. Within weeks, Sinclair, Cutten, and their partners had made an estimated $4 million in profits from the obsessive and wholly unwarranted public demand for the new stock.

Brokers' boardrooms were crowded with men and women entranced by the chattering stock ticker, the marvelous machine that seemed to promise everyone a fortune in easy money. "Good feeling was contagious and pervasive," wrote Robert T. Patterson, "and the little five- or ten-share traders were close kin emotionally to those who dealt in thousand-share blocks. To the former, a few hundred dollars profit was more than most of them could save from hard-earned wages in two or three years. Many, from small trader to large, were quickly becoming richer than they had ever seriously expected to be." Patterson found one scene particularly symbolic of the euphoria that swept the nation in November 1928:

> Off in a corner of one boardroom during the post-election advance, three of these followers—well-dressed gentlemen and respected members of the community—would lounge in the leather-upholstered chairs, hats on back of head, cigars tilted upward. They were long in Wright Aeronautical [i.e., they were gambling that the price of the stock would rise] and enjoying the experience tremendously. When a string of quotations at

successively higher prices followed the ticker symbol WAC as it moved across the Translux, or when a single quotation for WAC at a point or so higher appeared, they would break into a joyous chorus of quacking sounds—"Wac, wac, wac, wac, wac!" Others in the boardroom would laugh happily and sometimes join in, for most of them also were making money in one stock or another.

They buried Arnold Rothstein with a coin in his hand and a white skullcap on his head, in a bronze coffin worth $25,000. Fewer than two hundred people attended his funeral. His murderer remained at large.

The Man had died before sundown on election day, too weak to lift his hand to sign his will before he passed away. He would have won $500,000 on his wagers had he lived through the night; now it did not matter. But Rothstein's restive spirit would linger for twelve more months in Hell's Kitchen, along Broadway, and on Wall Street, until someone finally had to pay for killing the king of easy money.

## II

# Bitter Days of Winter

---

"It is quiet here as in a tomb. Nothing stirs. The silence
is so deep one could almost reach out and take hold of it."
—RICHARD E. BYRD, *Midnight, December 30, 1928*

The *City of New York* drifted silently through the fog and the swirling
light snow, threading a narrow path between the crumbling cliffs of ice
that loomed suddenly out of the mists and white shadows. There was no
sound in the Bay of Whales save for the occasional creaking of a wooden
mast or the waves lapping softly against the sides of the ship. Encrusted
in thick shards of icicles, its decks covered with snow and slush, the square-
rigged icebreaker resembled a ghost ship out of a sailor's nightmares as it
wandered through the eerie Antarctic desolation. There was no color save
for the dark, dry red flecks of whale blood that dotted an ice floe off the
starboard side. From time to time, a member of the crew, his eyes sore
from snow blindness, the skin of his face cracked and broken, glanced
hopefully at the overcast sky for any sign of a break in the cheerless
weather that had plagued the expedition for the past two days. But there
was nothing; only more gray clouds above, and more deadly, monotonous
whiteness below the horizon that stretched out behind them to the edge
of the Ross Sea.

At such times Commander Richard Evelyn Byrd may have blessed
the foresight that led him to bring an ample supply of straitjackets and
handcuffs as security against an outburst of madness on his voyage to the
South Pole. Byrd's expedition, which had reached Antarctica in the closing
days of 1928, was the most handsomely equipped and well-financed mission of scientific exploration in polar history. Fund-raising drives and donations by American corporations and private individuals (including John D.
Rockefeller, Jr., heir to the Standard Oil fortune, Edsel Ford, son of automobile magnate Henry Ford, and aviatrix Amelia Earhart, who had graciously contributed her fee from a cigarette commercial endorsement)
had provided Byrd and his crew of eighty men with nearly $1 million and

a thousand tons' worth of equipment, including two ships (the *City of New York* and the smaller *Eleanor Bolling,* named for Byrd's mother), one hundred dogs, fur parkas supplied by an association of Manhattan furriers, $40,000 worth of scientific equipment that would permit Byrd to carry out a series of complex geological and meteorological studies over a two-year period, more than $2,000 worth of office supplies to record the results of those experiments, the most up-to-date radio and electrical equipment manned by a staff of expert radio operators (who also kept stock speculator Byrd abreast of the latest news from Wall Street), and the item that symbolized the hopes of the entire expedition—an all-metal blue Ford trimotor airplane called the *Stars and Stripes,* designed to carry Byrd over the jagged Antarctic ice cliffs that had proved impassable to Scott, Shackleton, and Amundsen.

On New Year's Day 1929, Byrd and his men disembarked from their ships and camped on the ice of the bay to enjoy a splendid holiday dinner of pork and beans, bread and butter, canned applesauce, peanut butter, biscuits, and hot tea. "Few meals ever tasted better," Byrd wrote in his diary that evening. Fifteen hundred miles away, on the South American side of the Antarctic ice pack, Captain Sir George Hubert Wilkins—Byrd's Australian rival in the race to fly over the Pole—welcomed the new year with a slightly more raucous celebration at his main base on Deception Island. After singing their national anthems and drinking toasts to the success of their mission and their friends, Wilkins and his tiny band of international volunteers amused themselves by detonating live grenades and firing their rifles and revolvers into the air; the cacophony of shrieking steam whistles, clanging bells, and the booming harpoon guns sent hundreds of startled birds scattering in panic and confusion. Since the weather on their side of the Pole that day resembled southern California more than the South Pole, Wilkins' men spent the rest of the afternoon playing a spirited game of soccer.

Byrd represented the quintessential modern explorer who sought to provide for every contingency before he embarked on his mission; Wilkins was a throwback to an earlier age when men depended largely upon their wits to survive in the uncharted wilderness. A survivor of numerous Arctic and Antarctic campaigns led by Vilhjalmur Stefansson and Sir Ernest Shackleford, Wilkins brought with him only a skeletal ground organization and a bare minimum of supplies. He and one colleague planned to fly in a Lockheed seaplane across totally unknown territory toward the Pole. Neither man was particularly adept at operating a radio in an emergency; in case of a forced landing, they would have to walk to safety, relying on Wilkins' self-confidence and experience to guide them across one of the windiest, coldest, and most lifeless regions on earth. Even if they managed to reach their goal by air, their plane would not have sufficient gasoline to return all the way to Deception Island. They could fly back only as far as the Ross Sea, and hope that a passing whaling ship would pick them up.

While Wilkins waited for colder weather to begin his flight, Byrd and his men pushed on toward their main base, "Little America," a natural basin scooped out of a high snow rim on the edge of the Ross Barrier. One bitter night, an edge of the barrier suddenly cracked, throwing tons of snow toward Byrd's ships; the ice pack to which the *City of New York* had been anchored gave way without warning, and the ship lurched violently, throwing overboard one of the aviation mechanics, a man named Benny Roth. He could not swim. His crew mates on deck watched in horror as Roth drifted away, clinging for dear life to a slippery cake of ice that kept spinning in his hands. They launched a lifeboat to rescue him, but Byrd feared they would be too late: "Roth by then was near the end of his strength. He had meanwhile grabbed a second cake of ice, and had one under each arm. But his head would go under every now and then, as his numbed hands slipped and his heavy clothes, which had frozen hard, dragged him down. He called out that he could not hold on much longer, but he remained very calm." Through the sea, still boiling from the impact of the huge blocks of barrier ice that had fallen in the avalanche, and the rivulets of ice that fell with a hissing noise into the swirling water, the rescuers rowed furiously until finally one man could reach out and grab the drowning Roth. "The whole incident took no more than twenty minutes, but it seemed hours," the commander noted in his journal. Encrusted with ice, Roth was taken to the fire room to be thawed.

A few days later, the company set sail to explore King Edward Land. "Never had the Antarctic looked so desolate and utterly useless to the needs of mankind," wrote one member of the crew in despair. "That ever-present barrier stretching eastward, dark and foreboding when the sun was lost to us, and now impeding our progress, had become a living nightmare." In his own journal, Commander Byrd noted, "Bitter days followed."

On the first day of 1929, troubled astrologers in the capitals of Europe hinted darkly that the new year would inflict a spectacular procession of natural tragedies on mankind in the form of violent earthquakes, shipwrecks, floods, and tornadoes. As Pisces and Libra appeared bound for head-on collisions with Capricorn and Leo in the night skies, mystics agreed that no previous period had ever held such dark forebodings. England's venerable *Old Moore's Alamanac* warned that unparalleled political and economic disasters lay ahead over the next twelve months:

governments would topple, society would be shaken by extraordinary crimes and scandals, and the capitalist order would crumble.

Nature did its best to fulfill its share of the prophecies. The pattern of destruction had been established at the end of 1928 when the ancient volcano Mt. Etna erupted in savage fury, hurling huge fiery waves of molten lava across the plains of eastern Sicily, totally obliterating one town, burning several others, and leaving nearly four thousand people homeless. And as Etna finally stopped trembling, the smoke over Mt. Vesuvius ominously began to grow thicker and darker.

As January arrived, the entire European continent descended into the deadliest winter in living memory. Blizzards swept down across central and eastern Europe on the wings of bitter arctic winds, leaving an uncanny silence behind as Germany, Austria, Poland, and the Balkan states lay buried under snowdrifts between three and six feet deep. The Danube froze over completely as temperatures plunged far below zero. Prague suffered the most severe cold wave in 157 years; to the east, tornadoes and nine-foot snow drifts left Constantinople isolated and on the edge of famine. The Black Sea was littered with the wrecks of steamers that had either sunk or run aground in the high winds and crashing waves. Passengers on the luxurious Simplon-Orient Express train were stranded by an avalanche in Thrace for ten agonizing days. Half the locomotives in Czechoslovakia were out of service from cracked or frozen cylinders. Influenza ravaged Hungary, as hospitals in Budapest reported three hundred thousand victims, including a disproportionate number of children; the city's gas supply was cut off as pipes burst underground.

The toll of fatalities claimed by the cold kept climbing into the hundreds as homeless people perished in the streets of nearly every major city. Women and children begged to be arrested so they would have a warm place to sleep. In Budapest, one peasant froze to death as he sat on a horse-drawn wagon, the reins still tight between his fingers. In the countryside of southern Europe, scores of peasants in thatched huts and Gypsies in their flimsy tents and caravans went to sleep and never awoke. Wild animals starved despite the courageous efforts of gamekeepers to provide them with food; piles of frozen carcasses and bones were scattered through the forests. Hunger-maddened wolves abandoned their mountain habitats and invaded villages in the plains, desperate for meat.

Huge icicles hung from the public fountains in the cities of southern Italy, and the sunny Riviera was covered with snow. Shipping shut down completely at the Mediterranean port of Marseilles. Paris had not suffered such severe weather since 1870; after five people perished from the cold, municipal officials erected blazing braziers in the city's squares to warm the homeless, and pawnbrokers released overcoats and bedding to their former owners for free. Britain suffered its worst snowstorms since 1895. Denmark was almost completely ice-locked. In the mountains of Silesia, where grave diggers employed dynamite to break up the ground, the temperature dropped to forty degrees below zero; in the outskirts of Berlin, it sank to twenty below.

Along the streets of Berlin, documentary filmmakers carried movie cameras in boxes disguised as suitcases, patiently recording the kaleidoscopic pattern of daily life in the frozen city, capturing a cross-section of ordinary citizens amid the debris and indifference of modern urban existence in the devastating winter of 1929. "I wanted to show everything," explained cameraman Karl Freund, whose *Berlin, the Symphony of a Great City* became a classic of cinematic realism. "Men getting up to go to work, eating breakfast, boarding trams or walking. My characters were drawn from all the walks of life. From the lowest laborer to the bank president." At night, Berliners warmed themselves in subterranean cabarets or coffee houses such as the famous Romanische Café, where they might encounter a grotesque death's head covering the tormented visage of satiric artist George Grosz (who had recently been convicted of blasphemy for his bitterly iconoclastic drawings of German soldiers crucified by the stupidity of their officers); playwright Bertolt Brecht, appearing strikingly degenerate with his closely cropped black hair, stubbled beard, and perpetually suspicious expression, resembling a twisted habitual criminal more than the author of the season's most celebrated theatrical production, *Die Dreigroschenoper (The Threepenny Opera)*; or nude dancer Anita Berber, already well along the path toward a premature death induced by tuberculosis and an overpowering addiction to cocaine and morphine. Cocktails were all the rage among German high society, as books on mixology dominated the best-seller list; on this New Year's celebration, the most popular drink was a dubious concoction called a Jackie Coogan. In one of the more bizarre fads to sweep across the city in recent years, Berliners in early 1929 had begun to collect baby alligators, which sold for 25 marks (about $6), and meat-eating snakes, particularly coral snakes from the southern United States.

Perched high above the rhythms of everyday life in the city, Albert Einstein sat alone behind the iron door of his fifth-floor attic study in an apartment house on the broad Haberlandstrasse, near the municipal zoological gardens. It was a congenial, upper-middle-class neighborhood, with polished brass nameplates above the doorbells, and a slightly chipped statue of a smug St. George slaying his dragon in the public square across from the modest flat occupied by Professor and Mrs. Einstein. In one corner of Einstein's study, under a high, sloping ceiling, stood a four-foot brass telescope and a large terrestrial globe; across the room was a grand piano upon which the professor called up the spirit of his beloved Mozart. The walls were lined with inexpensive paper-bound books. Einstein guarded his privacy zealously, rarely permitting any intrusions upon his work, and a recent illness had left him nervous and more irritable than usual. But at the start of the new year, he found himself besieged by more than a hundred reporters asking him to explain his latest publication, on which he had labored for the past ten years. This six-page pamphlet (costing 1 mark), entitled *Zur einheitlichen Feldtheorie* (On a Uniform Field Theory), was an attempt to reconcile classic mechanics and modern electrodynamics, to bridge the gap between the laws that control gravitation and those that control the phenomena of electricity and magnetism by studying the properties of space in which both gravity and electricity exist. "I cannot understand why all this noise is being made over my little manuscript," Einstein muttered. "I do not look for publicity. On the contrary, I do not want it."

Visitors fortunate enough to penetrate the defenses of his vigilant wife and obtain an interview with the world's most famous scientist found a man of average height and build, still haggard from poor health, with soft, sad eyes and a bashful, childlike air. His eyebrows seemed to be posed in a perpetually quizzical expression beneath the halo of unruly gray hair that encircled his face. Not particularly robust at the best of times, he appeared almost fragile as he rose to greet each new caller. There was a smell of tobacco in the air from the long-stemmed briar pipe he smoked constantly. Although he spent most of his waking hours alone in his sanctuary, his wife denied that her husband's behavior presented any untoward difficulties. "Professor Einstein is not eccentric," she insisted. "He wears stiff collars when the occasion demands it without protest. He hardly ever mislays things. At least, not more than most men. He knows when it's time for lunch and dinner." For relaxation, he preferred to play the violin, or loll about the beach or sail his boat on the placid waters around the harbor of Lübeck, on the Baltic Sea.

Although Einstein did his best to explain in laymen's terms the details and implications of his unified field theory (it was, he said, "a satisfactory way of bringing the gravitational and electromagnetic fields, so to say, under one hat"), the forest of nearly three dozen abstruse mathematical equations defied the best efforts of all but a handful of experts to decipher Einstein's meaning. "This Einstein has proven a great comfort to us that always knew we didn't know much," chortled Will Rogers. "He has shown us that the fellows that we thought was smart is just as dumb as we are." Most reporters quickly found themselves out of their depth, and concentrated instead upon the human interest aspects of Einstein's support of the troubled Zionist movement in Palestine, or the wise man's general philosophy of life, which he obligingly summarized in pithy quotations such as "If A is success in life, I should say the formula is $A = X + Y + Z$, X being work and Y being play." "And what is Z?" asked a reporter. "That," replied Einstein, "is keeping your mouth shut."

This was not a formula that appealed to President Paul von Hindenburg, the iron-willed field marshal and revered hero of the Great War, whose New Year's address to the German people eloquently expressed his galling disappointment that their brothers and sisters in the Rhineland, the Saar Valley, and the Palatinate remained under foreign (i.e., British and especially French) military domination. Ten years after the guns fell silent, Allied occupation troops were still firmly entrenched on German territory, ostensibly to safeguard the uneasy peace settlement signed at Versailles in June 1919. On the first day of 1929, Hindenburg's nationalist rage and despair were echoed by Chancellor Hermann Mueller—the uninspiring leader of the Social Democratic party who had forged a narrow majority in the Reichstag following the national elections of June 1928—and Foreign Minister Gustav Stresemann, the recipient of the 1927 Nobel Peace Prize and arguably the most impressive international figure produced by the Weimar Republic.

But Stresemann, who had nimbly survived eight cabinet changes over the past decade, faced an even more pressing problem in January 1929 than Allied military occupation. The same treaty that had removed substantial chunks of territory from Weimar's control had saddled the fledgling German republic with an extraordinarily heavy burden of financial reparations (although the final figure was deliberately left unsettled, the first few years' payments were bad enough) to be paid to the Allies over an indefinite period of years. Following the disastrous inflationary spiral that had nearly plunged Germany into total anarchy in the early 1920s, an international conference of bankers had adopted a more realistic and less onerous schedule of reparation payments in 1924. According to the Dawes Plan, named for the habitually profane American financier Charles G. "Hell and Maria" Dawes (who later served as Coolidge's vice-president), Germany was required to make scaled-down annual payments between 1924 and 1928. On the assumption that the German economy would have recovered its equilibrium by 1929, reparations payments were scheduled to rise precipitously in that year to a total of 2.5 billion marks. In other words, Germany's debts were tied to a prosperity index, which kept the future perpetually black from Weimar's point of view; every time the nation struggled to its feet, it was dragged down by an ever heavier burden of tribute exacted by its erstwhile enemies.

At the end of 1928, the Allies' agent general for reparations, a precocious thirty-six-year-old American financier named Seymour Parker Gilbert ("Geeb" to his friends), conducted a thorough examination of the latest German economic statistics to determine whether Berlin could, in fact, meet its forthcoming obligations. Gilbert's report was startlingly unequivocal. In light of the continuing modernization of Germany's heavy industry, the stability of the mark against other international currencies, the rising stores of gold in the Reichsbank, the expansion of German exports, and the apparent return of real wages to their prewar levels of 1913, the agent general firmly concluded that Germany could pay. "No question can fairly rise, in the light of practical experience thus far, as to the ability of the German budget to provide the full amount of its standard contributions under the Dawes Plan," Gilbert reported. "Fundamentally, confidence has been restored and Germany has been re-established as a going concern on a relatively high level of economic activity."

Stresemann was appalled. "Germany's capacity to pay is overestimated abroad," he frantically informed Gilbert in a tense private meeting in Berlin. "Germany gives a false impression of prosperity. The economic position is only flourishing on the surface. Germany is in fact dancing on a volcano." British economist John Maynard Keynes agreed. The Dawes committee, Keynes argued, never had expected Germany to bear the full burden of the 1929 annuity; rather, they had hoped that by postponing the problem for several years, a more equitable settlement could be devised in a less emotional atmosphere.

Unfortunately for the peace of the world, Keynes and the German foreign minister were entirely correct. Although the volume of German exports had shown signs of improvement lately (as Gilbert properly pointed out), Germany still suffered from a trade deficit of nearly 400 million marks per month. Weimar's government expenditures kept rising inexorably, and Mueller's proposed budget for 1929 showed a deficit of 500 million marks even after the imposition of new taxes. Statistics on joblessness were still more disturbing: more than two million Germans were unemployed in January 1929, a sharp increase over the previous two years.

As Stresemann and a host of impartial observers pointed out, German "prosperity" rested precariously upon a ramshackle tower of foreign capital. Between 1924 and 1928, Germany had borrowed the staggering sum of $2,380,000,000—slightly more than the total of her reparations payments during that period. Not surprisingly, considering the impoverished condition of the rest of western Europe, most of the money (nearly $300 million in 1928 alone) had come from American bankers and corporations looking for profitable outlets for their surplus capital. Without this massive infusion of short-term American credits, Germany undoubtedly would have been hard pressed either to fulfill its reparations obligations or rebuild its war-ravaged economic structure. Understandably, though perhaps unwisely, German industrialists had used a substantial portion of these foreign credits to indulge in ambitious expansion of their plants; in other words, they treated the loans as if they were long-term, uncallable credits. Any sudden drop in the volume of foreign loans, therefore, would force German banks to call in the credits extended to industry, and the whole tenuous structure would collapse.

For all practical purposes, Germany was becoming an economic colony of the Allies; foreign investors owned nearly one-fourth of the nation's resources. "We in Germany have for the last few years lived on money pumped into the country," Stresemann acknowledged at the end of 1928. "If a crisis should come upon us, and the Americans should call in their short term credits, we are faced with bankruptcy. . . . I do not know where new taxes are to come from. Statistics show how much has been absorbed by the Municipalities, how much by Industry, and how much foreign money we have accepted to keep us going at all. We are not only militarily disarmed, we are also financially disarmed. We have no kind of resources left."

Perhaps. Certainly American bankers were loath to impose additional reparations burdens upon Germany, since the value of their loans would depreciate alarmingly if the German economy went into another tailspin. From their offices at the Quai d'Orsay overlooking the Seine, however, French authorities in Paris viewed the German dilemma from an entirely different perspective. The late war had devastated France's transportation system and ravaged its industrial base, and the terrible toll of human casualties had left the nation with a falling birth rate (particularly in relation to Germany) and a dearth of able-bodied manpower. The psychological scars still had not healed, nor had the physical wounds. Late in 1928, the urbane German author and statesman Count Harry Kessler visited the battlefields of Verdun and the Marne and recorded his impressions in his diary:

> The burned-out villages on the hills near Verdun herald a truly shattering landscape, a landscape that first inspires horror and gradually a feeling of desolate tragedy. Mile after mile of military cemeteries, charred trees still stretching their limbs to the sky, ruined farms, and constantly in the distance the bare, grey and white shimmer of the chalk downs. Horror and anguish alternate at the sight of this picture. The densely packed little white crosses in the graveyards, thousands upon thousands of them, seem in the broad landscape insignificant, for it is the landscape which harbours the souls of the dead crying for vengeance on those responsible for this crime and which constitutes a perpetual admonition to peace. . . .

Those who come here now should do so in the spirit of the Greeks when they viewed the awe-inspiring mythical figures in their tragedies— to be purged with pity and terror.

Presumably Kessler did not know that the French Parliament already was preparing to authorize construction of a formidable line of underground bunkers and concrete fortifications along precisely this route. The project eventually would be dedicated to the memory of the man who strove tirelessly to bring it to fruition: a crippled war veteran named André Maginot.

France, then, had no intention of permitting Germany to shrug off its treaty obligations. The British government, too, professed itself perfectly satisfied with the status quo. If any changes were made, London insisted that Germany's reparations obligations to Britain be directly and irrevocably bound to Britain's own war debt payments to the United States; it would not permit the former to be scaled down without a corresponding reduction in the latter. In the past, the British Treasury had been whiplashed between Washington's cold and unequivocal refusal to forgive Allied war loans (Coolidge's famous comment was "They hired the money, didn't they?") and France's unscrupulous machinations to grab the lion's share of the reparations pie. "We have given everything, and submitted to everything, and paid everything, and we cannot make any new sacrifice," insisted British chancellor of the Exchequer Winston Spencer Churchill in September 1928. "If it is even thought that we are open-minded and favourable to a review of the position everyone will be benefited as usual at our expense. The French would be quite ready to take full advantage of us." Instead, Churchill testily suggested that his government place "the onus of the situation where it truly lies—upon the United States—for European difficulties."

But the United States had no intention of unilaterally sacrificing its own selfish economic interests in Europe; certainly Hoover had given no indication during the presidential election campaign that he would even consider granting war debt relief to America's erstwhile allies. Nor was he likely to make any significant concessions in the near future, because it was becoming increasingly clear that the flaws embedded in the Dawes Plan would require the convocation of another international conference of experts to settle the whole muddled reparations–war debts question once and for all, and Hoover had no intention of surrendering any bargaining chips in advance.

For the Weimar Republic, the outcome of the impending conference could spell the difference between stability and anarchy. And this generation of Germans already had stared into the maelstrom of chaos. The turmoil of the Spartacist revolt and the radical labor agitation that swept over Germany in 1919, and the uncontrolled inflationary spiral of the early 1920s (exacerbated by the vengeful French occupation of the Ruhr), had left many conservative middle-class Germans with a deep-seated terror of disorder and Communist revolution. The impending reparations crisis—combined with a significant shift of the electorate toward the Left as reflected in the national elections of May 1928—brought these fears to the surface.

Thus by the beginning of 1929, a number of leading German industrialists already had begun to finance certain right-wing political parties as a hedge against any future drift toward bolshevism. One such prudent businessman was Fritz Thyssen, chairman of the board of United Steel Works, the largest steel manufacturer in Germany. Although Thyssen had long been a member of the Nationalist party, a respectable (all things considered) if slightly outspoken group dedicated to the restoration of the Hohenzollern monarchy and the elimination of Jewish influence in German political and economic life, the Nationalists' unexpectedly heavy losses in the 1928 Reichstag elections had disillusioned Thyssen and convinced him to search for an alternative political vehicle. He settled upon an extremist fringe group known as the Nationalist Socialist German Workers' party—the Nazis.

Founded in January 1919 by a second-rate journalist and an unemployed toolmaker amid the swirling atmosphere of intrigue and chaos in postwar Bavaria, the Nationalsozialistische Deutsche Arbeiterpartei had been led out of the fetid back rooms of Munich's beer halls by an ex-German army corporal named Adolf Hitler. Hitler's ludicrous attempt to seize power via a violent putsch in 1923 had earned him nothing but ridicule and a brief stay in prison. For several years, he and his party had been banned from holding public rallies in Berlin and Prussia; but by 1928, Hitler had rebuilt the shattered party structure. Although there were fewer than a hundred thousand active party members nationwide, the Nazis had gathered 810,000 votes—2.6 percent of the total ballots cast—in the May 1928 elections and won 12 seats in the Reichstag, making them the ninth largest party in Germany. (By comparison, the ruling Social Democrats received 9 million votes and 153 seats.) Among the Nazi deputies who took their place in the assembly for the first time were Hermann Göring, an air force hero during the war, and Paul Joseph Goebbels, a clubfooted ex-novelist and student of modern literature.

Two years earlier, Hitler personally had given Goebbels full authority to resuscitate the Nazis' flagging fortunes in Berlin, and the lame little propagandist had accepted the challenge with zeal. Following the dictum that "Berlin needs a sensation like a fish needs water," Goebbels had flooded the city with huge crimson posters that proclaimed the Nazi message: "The bourgeois state is tottering toward its end! And rightly so! Since it is no longer capable of liberating Germany. We must create a new Germany, no longer a class society, a Germany of work and discipline! For this task history has chosen you, worker of the brain and of the fist! In your hands lies the fate of the German people. Remember that and act!" Goebbels and his lieutenants enthusiastically encouraged rampages of brutal violence at Nazi rallies; either they would intimidate the opposition into submission, or the movement would receive new martyrs at the hands of Communist thugs.

Gradually, however, Nazi propaganda was evolving from its brutish origins as a strident manifestation of crude anti-Semitism, directed primarily toward working-class bigots, into a more sophisticated campaign based on economic arguments designed to appeal to clerks, small businessmen, and farmers. Hitler himself unveiled the new message on November 16, 1928, in a historic speech at the Berlin Sportspalast. It was the first time he had ever addressed an open meeting in the city, and more than fifteen thousand curious onlookers crowded into the auditorium that evening to hear the man who called himself Der Fuehrer rage against the threat of Marxist subversion and the humiliating domination of the Fatherland by foreign financial interests. He explained, patiently at first and then with growing fury, that Germany had been enslaved by the schemes of Jewish bankers based in London, Paris, and Wall Street. The German economy was drowning under the crushing burden of reparations and interest payments to foreign investors; by supinely acceding to the Allies' oppressive demands, the Weimar Republic had betrayed the nation's trust and mortgaged the heritage of future generations. As he whipped the crowd into a hysterical frenzy, Hitler exhorted them to join him in a glorious crusade to restore Germany to its rightful place of world domination, to risk everything in "the fight that will one day break the chains!"

By the first week of January 1929, Herr Goebbels had scheduled two more mass meetings in the Sportspalast to bring the Nazi message of bitterness, hatred, and national revival to another twenty-five thousand enthusiastic converts. Events abroad over the next few months would provide him and his beloved Fuehrer with all the ammunition they needed.

# III

# Dawn of a New Year

"This, we believe, is 1929—a morning as bright
and cheerful as the funeral of a hanged man."
—BALTIMORE SUN, *January 1, 1929*

Late on the morning of New Year's Day 1929, Franklin Delano Roosevelt awoke to the sound of thin sheets of sleet slapping against his bedroom window in the executive mansion in Albany. Once he finally got out of bed and looked outside, the governor could see streets covered with a disagreeable layer of leaden slush from the wet snow that had fallen during the night. Roosevelt turned away from the window.

January 1 was inauguration day in Albany, although Roosevelt actually had taken the oath of office in a private ceremony the night before, so the state would not be left without a governor after Al Smith's term expired at midnight. Smith had greeted his successor cordially for the cameras when Roosevelt arrived to take possession of the mansion on the last day of the old year. "God bless and keep you, Frank," he said in his usual ebullient tone as he shook Roosevelt's hand. "A thousand welcomes! We've got the home fires burning."

But if Smith betrayed no outward sign of regret at his departure from the spotlight into the political wilderness, he must indeed have been a consummate actor. It was Smith who had personally chosen a reluctant Roosevelt as the Democratic nominee for governor in 1928, primarily because he believed Roosevelt's popularity outside New York City could help him in his own battle to add the state's crucial forty-five electoral votes to the Democratic column. Even normally cynical political commentators had chided Al for ruthlessly pressuring the crippled Roosevelt into the service of Smith's presidential ambitions, yet this sort of cold calculation expressed perfectly the arms-length relationship the two men had maintained throughout the past decade. Although Roosevelt had served as Smith's floor manager at the convention in Houston in the summer of 1928, they had never been particularly close friends; Roosevelt detested the gluttonous Tammany organization, and Smith apparently believed Roosevelt was something of an intellectual lightweight. Thus the pain of Smith's humiliating loss of New York to Hoover was only compounded by Roosevelt's victory, albeit a narrow one, in the gubernatorial race, and through the black melancholy of defeat Smith could hear political columnists—than whom no two-legged species had a shorter memory—enthrone his successor as the new "chief U.S. Democrat."

In December, Smith had met with Roosevelt to offer his unsolicited advice on state affairs and personnel matters for the incoming administration; he suggested, for instance, that Roosevelt appoint Belle Moskowitz, one of Smith's most trusted advisers, to the position of governor's secretary, where she could keep the administration running smoothly from behind the scenes. Smith seemed genuinely hurt and surprised when Roosevelt rejected that recommendation along with Smith's well-intentioned but egregiously heavy-handed offer to have Mrs. Moskowitz draft Roosevelt's inaugural address to the state legislature.

If Smith had expected his successor to suffer his guidance gladly, he had badly misjudged the man. Few mortals had more confidence in their own intuitive judgment than Franklin Delano Roosevelt. Heir to a family tradition that tempered the pursuit of temporal success with notions of Christian stewardship and social responsibility, Roosevelt acquired early in life a sense of his own destiny as an earthly instrument of the omniscient and omnipotent Deity. The spectacular rise, fall, and resurrection of Roosevelt's political career up to his inauguration as governor appeared to lend credence to this conceit. After graduating from Groton Academy and Harvard University (alas, he failed his finals at Columbia Law School, though he later passed the bar exam), the scion of the Hyde Park branch of the Roosevelt clan had defied convention on his first foray into the political arena in 1910 by winning election to the New York state senate from a traditionally stalwart Republican district. His wholehearted support of Woodrow Wilson's presidential ambitions two years later earned him an appointment as assistant secretary of the navy at the age of thirty, and in 1920 the Democratic National Convention chose Roosevelt—a strong advocate of Wilson's beloved League of Nations—as presidential nominee James M. Cox's running mate.

After Harding and Coolidge buried the doomed Democratic ticket under a popular tide of anti-Wilson sentiment, Roosevelt cheerfully dusted himself off and embarked upon a brief career as a Wall Street corporation counsel. Then the fateful attack of infantile paralysis struck him down at Campobello, nearly killing him before leaving him paralyzed from the waist down for the rest of his life. For the next seven years, as the Democratic party stumbled through the twenties, splintered and bereft of statesmanship, Roosevelt endured a painstaking process of physical rehabilitation. In 1926, he began taking treatments at Warm Springs, Georgia, gradually transforming (mostly with his own funds) that sadly dilapidated resort into a first-rate therapeutic center for victims of crippling illness.

Roosevelt clearly did not want to run for governor in 1928. Although he had earned renewed respect and admiration among the Democratic faithful (and independent liberals) by his graceful performances on behalf of Governor Smith at the 1924 and 1928 national conventions, Roosevelt stoutly resisted the desperate entreaties of Smith and Raskob to enter the gubernatorial race. Publicly, he insisted that he needed several more years of uninterrupted therapy to regain the use of his legs; privately, Roosevelt and his closest adviser, an irreverent gnome of a journalist named Louis Howe, foresaw another Republican landslide in 1928, and they wanted to stay as far away from the scene of the disaster as they decently could.

Not until his wife, Eleanor, joined her voice to Smith and Raskob's chorus did Roosevelt reluctantly consent to run. Even then he fully expected to lose, but he decided that a strenuous crusade on behalf of a righteous cause would still leave him well placed to make his own run for the presidency, perhaps in 1936. So he turned his gubernatorial campaign into a showcase for his considerable easygoing personal charm. On hearing rumors that he would not live past January 1, or that he planned to resign immediately after his inauguration in favor of the Democratic nominee for lieutenant governor, Herbert Lehman, Roosevelt just threw back his large, handsome head and laughed. "Most people who are nominated for the Governorship have to run," he told reporters, "but obviously I am not in a condition to run, and therefore I am counting on my friends all over the state to make it possible for me to walk in." Then he set out to crisscross the state on an arduous tour that taxed the energy of the younger and healthier men who accompanied him, delivering nearly fifty speeches in six weeks while covering 1,300 miles. On the eve of the election, Roosevelt invited the press to his home in Hyde Park and assured them that he was "feeling much fitter and walking much better than when the campaign began." "If I could keep on campaigning twelve months longer," he joked, "I'd throw away my canes."

He had defied the odds and won, and as the newly inaugurated governor rose from his wheelchair at forty minutes after twelve on the afternoon of January 1 and slowly made his way to the rostrum of the assembly chamber, leaning for support on his cane and the arm of his eldest son, James, even Roosevelt's Republican foes applauded his courageous performance. In a brief message that lasted less than thirty minutes, the governor pledged to carry forward the fight for social justice begun by

Smith—"a public servant of true greatness"—on behalf of the state's disadvantaged citizens. Roosevelt called upon the legislature to enact a measure of farm relief, a program of workmen's compensation, an eight-hour day and a forty-eight-hour week for women and children workers, state aid to the elderly, the handicapped, and the ill, and legislation providing for public ownership and development of water-power sites. Not surprisingly, this moderately progressive program did not elicit any visible signs of enthusiasm from the hidebound conservative Republican members of the chamber.

Then an artillery battery boomed forth the traditional seventeen-gun salute for the new governor, and Roosevelt and Smith rode through another flurry of wet snow under sodden gray skies and laughed their way through the ordeal of the inaugural ball at the Washington Avenue Armory. When the long day was finally over, Franklin Roosevelt slept again in the executive mansion, and Al Smith boarded a train for New York City.

In the nation's capital, lame duck President Calvin Coolidge ungraciously canceled the traditional New Year's Day public reception at the White House, one of the most eagerly anticipated events on the Washington social calendar, and one that every president for a century had honored religiously (except in extreme cases of ill health). Instead, the Chief Executive greeted 1929 by hunting wild turkey and pheasants on the Sapelo Island estate of automotive magnate Howard Coffin, off the south Georgia coast. Wearing the ten-gallon hat he had acquired in South Dakota, Coolidge stalked his prey relentlessly as beaters walked ahead, flushing the birds from cover. On his Thanksgiving hunting trip, the President had missed five successive quail, but a lesson from Secret Service colonel Sterling Starling presumably had improved his shooting skills. Now Coolidge stopped and stood rigid, raising his shotgun, sighting the turkey that obligingly appeared before him in the clearing, seemingly hypnotized by the large-hatted human with the gun. Coolidge aimed, squeezed the trigger . . . and missed. Chagrined, the President returned to Coffin's mansion to witness a holiday "rodeo" staged by the local black community, complete with spirituals in four-part harmony and diamondback turtle races. Then he boarded the private yacht *Zapela* and headed for Jekyl Island—the haunt of Du Ponts, Carnegies, and Morgans—for a New Year's masquerade party; the Secret Service contingent wore pirate hats, Mrs. Coolidge put on a Puritan bonnet, and the President himself donned a dunce cap.

On the West Coast, meanwhile, University of California lineman Roy Riegels earned his own dunce cap and ensured himself a place in sports immortality by his memorable performance in the 1929 Rose Bowl game. In the second quarter, Riegels picked up a Georgia Tech fumble and headed toward the Tech goal line. Then he cut back to elude a pair of tacklers, turned back toward the opposite sideline to avoid pursuit, collided with someone and bounced off, spun around to avoid another Tech player, and then—having completely lost his bearings—began to lumber toward the California goal, running as fast as he could, completely oblivious to the fact that the only people chasing him were his own frantic teammates. One of them finally caught up with Riegels on the three-yard line and tried to turn him around, but a wave of Georgia Tech tacklers knocked Riegels to the ground just inches away from the goal line. To make matters worse, the California coach opted to punt on the next play to escape from the hole; Riegels, naturally, was the team's punter, and Tech broke through to block the kick and score a safety. Those two points proved the margin of victory as Georgia Tech captured the Rose Bowl, 8–7. Riegels manfully faced reporters' questions after the game and refused to alibi. "I wasn't out of my head at all and I hadn't been hurt," he said. But through all eternity he would carry with him the unenviable nickname "Wrong Way" Riegels.

At the dawn of 1929, F. Scott Fitzgerald was "thirty two years old and sore as hell about it," and he was not particularly pleased with the condition of New York City, either. "Whole sections of the city," he decided, "had grown rather poisonous. . . . The city was bloated, glutted, stupid with cake and circuses, and a new expression 'Oh yeah?' summed up all the enthusiasm evoked by the announcement of the last super-skycrapers. My barber retired on a half million bet in the market and I was conscious that the head waiters who bowed me, or failed to bow me, to my table were far, far wealthier than I. This was no fun—once again I had enough of New York."

Fitzgerald had spent the past four years in a restless search for the creative inspiration that seemed to have deserted him after the publication of *The Great Gatsby* to extravagant critical acclaim in 1925. Through the bars and garrets of Paris, across the white beaches of the Riviera and the Cap d'Antibes in the south of France, from Hollywood to the cavernous mansion at Ellerslie in Du Pont country outside of Wilmington, Delaware, and back to Manhattan—Fitzgerald searched in vain. His wife, Zelda, who compared Ellerslie unfavorably to the black hole of Calcutta, was literally dancing herself toward madness, obsessed by her dream of becoming a world-class ballerina to compensate for the emptiness of her life with Scott. "I think 90% of all the trouble he has comes from her," Ernest Hemingway once said of Scott Fitzgerald. "Almost every bloody fool thing I have ever seen or known him to do has been directly or indirectly Zelda inspired. . . . I often wonder if he would not have been the best writer we've ever had or likely to have if he hadn't been married to some one that would make him waste *Everything.*"

Surely this was too lenient a judgment on Fitzgerald himself, who was quite capable of squandering his talent with no outside help. He had fallen flat on his face in Hollywood, unable to complete even one acceptable screenplay. Terrified that he could never repeat the success he had achieved with *Gatsby,* he was drinking far too much (a correspondent for *Variety* flippantly referred to him as "F. Scotch Fitzgerald"), and as his days passed in an alcoholic daze he became increasingly belligerent, regularly challenging strangers with the taunt "I'm Scott Fitzgerald, and who are you, and what do you do, and why do you do it?" In November 1928, Fitzgerald and Hemingway and their wives attended the Yale-Princeton football game, and while he waited for a train to take him home, Scott scuffled with a policeman; Hemingway tried to explain that Fitzgerald was a famous author, but unfortunately the cop had never heard of either of them. Accompanied by the family chauffeur, an unsavory former professional boxer whom Fitzgerald had brought back from France, Scott spent his evenings brooding and brawling in roughneck dives. In his growing fascination with the darker side of human behavior, Fitzgerald perceived an ominous trend among his own acquaintances:

> By this time contemporaries of mine had begun to disappear into the dark maw of violence. A classmate killed his wife and himself on Long Island, another tumbled "accidentally" from a skyscraper in Philadelphia, another purposefully from a skyscraper in New York. One was killed in a speak-easy in Chicago; another was beaten to death in a speak-easy in New York and crawled home to the Princeton Club to die; still another had his skull crushed by a maniac's ax in an insane asylum where he was confined. These are not catastrophes that I went out of my way to look for—these were my friends.

America, he believed, suffered from a disordered mind verging on nervous hysteria in early 1929, symbolized by the marathon dances where young men with blistered feet dragged their unconscious partners around the floor for hours until they, too, fainted from exhaustion. Behind it all lay a frantic urge to drive all worries and cares into oblivion. Fitzgerald, who certainly knew whereof he spoke, estimated that liquor was readily available in half the buildings in downtown Manhattan at that time. "Many people who were not alcoholics were lit up four days out of seven," he recalled several years later, "and frayed nerves were strewn everywhere; groups were held together by a generic nervousness and the hangover became a part of the day as well allowed-for as the Spanish siesta. Most of my friends drank too much—the more they were in tune with the times the more they drank."

Mostly they drank in speakeasies. Police officials estimated that there were 32,000 speakeasies of varying degrees of respectability in New York City in 1929; one writer described the way the scale of ambience descended from the "luxurious bars, which advertised in the campus publications of Yale and Princeton, to the beer gardens where the snarling face of the underworld peered through the German good nature of the entertainment, then on to strange and even more sinister localities where one was eyed by granite-faced boys and there was nothing left of joviality but only a brutishness that corrupted the new day into which one presently went out." In the glamorous heyday of Harlem ("dusky dream Harlem," sang Langston Hughes, "rumbling into a nightmare tunnel"), more than 120 establishments were crammed into a raw, jagged quadrangle that spread north from 125th Street between Lenox and Seventh avenues. When he first encountered Harlem, a wide-eyed Duke Ellington thought it looked "just like the Arabian nights!" One of the most famous watering spots was the Nest, an after-hours club where celebrities like Fanny "Funny Girl" Brice, Helen Morgan (the star of the smash Broadway musical *Show Boat*), and Bill "Bojangles" Robinson went slumming after the bars along Broadway closed for the night. Others hung out at Connie's, where jazz trumpeter Louis Armstrong made his New York debut; or Basement Brownies, with stride pianist Art Tatum; or a Fifth Avenue basement joint named Smalls' Paradise, where waiters sang and danced the Charleston as they twirled their trays laden with bootleg liquor; or the Campus, where the legendary ragtime king Eubie Blake held forth nightly. And then there was the Cotton Club.

Purchased in 1923 by a syndicate of prominent hoodlums, the Cotton Club parlayed an ersatz jungle atmosphere—complete with fake palm trees and erotic skits featuring black dancers clad in beads and feathers—into a gold mine. Every evening, about five hundred thirsty patrons crowded into the building on the northeast corner of 142nd and Lenox to dine, drink, and listen to Duke Ellington's band (featuring Cootie Williams, Johnny Hodges, and Barney Bigard) play their own patented brand of "jungle music" in two nightly shows at 11:30 P.M. and 2:00 A.M.; thousands more listened to the music over a live nationwide radio hookup, direct from the club over the CBS network. "At first I was happy," said Ellington of those halcyon days. "There were lots of pretty women and champagne and nice people and plenty of money." The shows attracted some of the biggest names in New York, including columnist and gossip maven Walter Winchell, trumpeter Bix Beiderbecke, and Mayor Jimmy Walker.

In a city that worshiped the gilded trappings of high style, sparkling wit, and irreverent cynicism, Jimmy Walker was the perfect grinning high priest. Although his Irish-American father had been a moderately success-ful New York City politician, Walker initially spurned politics to try to make his fortune as a songwriter on Tin Pan Alley; among other less memorable tunes, he penned the immortal musical question "Will You Love Me in December as You Do in May?" Even after he conceded artistic and financial defeat and moved into the more prosaic but lucrative prac-tice of law and loyal service to the Tammany machine, Walker never outgrew his romantic, often flippant outlook on life. "Jimmy was the extro-vert, the spontaneous eccentric, the sidewalk favorite, the beloved clown, the idol of those who seek companionship and mercy above and beyond justice," recalled Robert Moses, who worked loyally with both Al Smith and Walker. "He was like Scaramouche, born with the gift of laughter and a sense that the world is mad, but also the cause of mirth and gaiety in others. He struck sparks off dull metal." Impeccably dressed in a top hat and form-fitting, fancy clothes—including a four-button, double-breasted black Chesterfield coat with slit pockets and black silk facing on the collar and lapels, designed exclusively for him by the New York Custom Cutters' Club—Walker had enjoyed only limited experience as an assemblyman in the state legislature and had displayed no discernible qualifications for high office when Tammany suddenly plucked him from obscurity and made him (against Al Smith's wishes) the Democratic nominee for mayor in 1925.

"Here was a politician who could easily have been one of our top actors," wrote comedian Eddie Cantor. "He was a combination of George M. Cohan, James Cagney, and John Barrymore. He had the most charm, his was the greatest wit, he was the best off-the-cuff speaker I'd ever heard." One of Cantor's favorite Walker stories concerned the time the mayor was introduced at a dinner by attorney Louis Nizer, who described him in such glowing terms that it seemed more like a eulogy than an introduction. When Nizer finally finished, Walker got up and said with a humble expression, "After listening to your toastmaster, I can hardly wait to hear what I have to say." Jimmy was lovable, and he was charming, and he did not disappoint the Tammany chieftains who expected him to turn his head discreetly while they and their underworld allies ran the city for their own profit.

But the unsolved murder of Arnold Rothstein cast an unwelcome spotlight into the darker recesses of the Walker administration. There had been 337 murders, many of them gangland slayings, committed in New York City during 1928; in 115 of those cases the police had made no arrests at all, and when someone actually had been charged with murder, the odds were heavily against (about 11 to 2) the accused killer ever being sent to prison. (By contrast, the London police allegedly accounted for every murder in the British capital in 1927, and police in Berlin reported that they solved 90 percent of the capital crimes in their city that year.) At last the president of the New York Board of Trade demanded that Walker do *something* to keep hoodlums from using the city's streets as their private battlefields. "When the lives of innocent people are imperiled by such blood feuds," intoned the New York *Herald Tribune,* "it is time for the people to take serious thought about their safety, if the police will not."

So Walker dismissed his hard-pressed chief of police and hired a handsome, wealthy executive from John Wanamaker's department store, Grover Aloysius Whalen, to find Rothstein's murderer and clean up the mess at police headquarters. Whalen's appointment struck many of Walker's critics as a frivolous response to a serious problem; one Brooklyn judge uncharitably referred to him as "a snobbish, self-centered, would-be society Police Commissioner in high hat, long-tail coat, striped trousers, and light spats." Undaunted, Whalen assumed his new duties with a maximum of fanfare, which was precisely what Walker wanted. He formed six ten-man strong-arm squads, armed them with nightsticks and "whatever may be necessary for a policeman," and unleashed them upon the streets with explicit orders to "batter gunmen, gangsters and other criminals out of the city."

The squads' initial targets were speakeasies that sold poisoned bootleg liquor, known as "smoke" or "white mule." Nearly twelve thousand people had died of alcohol poisoning in the United States in 1928, including over a thousand in New York alone, an alarming statistic that led the city's chief medical examiner to declare that "there is no such thing as a safe drink nowadays." The epidemic was exacerbated by the federal government's policy of deliberately denaturing (and thereby poisoning) industrial alcohol, despite the acknowledged fact that 10 percent of the industrial alcohol manufactured in the country each year ended up in bootleg whiskey. Appalled by the government's callousness, the New York *Evening Telegram* undertook an independent survey of the speakeasies in the city and compiled a list of the places that reportedly offered tainted booze to their customers. After the paper's editors forwarded their findings to City Hall in the first week of January, Whalen's men swooped down upon several hundred subterranean hideaways from Washington Heights to Harlem to Greenwich Village, seizing cases of allegedly contaminated whiskey and smashing furniture, mirrors, and glassware with axes and iron crowbars. But nothing really changed. Two weeks later, most of the speakeasies on Whalen's blacklist had reopened for business.

# IV

# Other People's Money

You could talk about Prohibition," remarked a British journalist upon his arrival in New York, "or Hemingway, or air conditioning, or music, or horses, but in the end you had to talk about the stock market, and that was when the conversation became serious." On the last day of 1928, the old year had been buried under a joyous shower of confetti and ticker tape on the floor of the New York Stock Exchange. It had been "the greatest year in the history of Wall Street speculation"; despite a sharp break in prices in early December, when many investors had panicked on seeing the call-money rate rise to 12 percent, the market had recovered its poise to close the year at an all-time high. The *New York Times'* index of fifty selected stocks finished 1928 with an impressive 26 percent average gain in value for the year. "Nothing matters as long as stocks keep going up," observed the New York *World.* "The market is now its own law. The forces behind its advance are irresistible." And no man in America viewed that prospect with more satisfaction than Charles Edwin Mitchell.

As president of the National City Bank of New York, Charlie Mitchell directed the affairs of the largest financial institution—in terms of capital funds—in the world. The fact that Mitchell was not, by training, a banker at all, spoke volumes about the state of affairs in the American banking industry in the 1920s. Born and raised in the shabby Boston suburb of Chelsea, Mitchell worked his way through Amherst College by teaching public speaking; he graduated just three years after Calvin Coolidge, worked for several years as an equipment salesman for the Western Electric Company in Chicago, and then landed a position on Wall Street as personal secretary to the president of the Trust Company of America. In 1911, he struck out on his own, rented a couple of rooms in a New York office building, stenciled "C. E. Mitchell and Company" on the window-pane, and began selling investment bonds. Five years later, he was discovered by Frank Vanderlip, chairman of the National City Bank. In its ambitious quest to become the "foremost financing house in America," National City recently had purchased a nationwide bond distribution house, and Vanderlip was looking for an aggressive executive with sales experience to run the operation. He found Mitchell, whom he described as "a very well set-up, intelligent man with a good eye and keen mind." "He is," Vanderlip predicted, "undoubtedly going to prove of real strength to the whole situation."

By 1920, supersalesman Mitchell had turned the National City Company—the parent bank's bond-selling subsidiary—into the largest distributor of securities in America. When the board of directors reshuffled the slate of officers the following year, Mitchell emerged as president of National City Bank at the age of forty-three. Tall, gruff, physically powerful with broad shoulders, a barrel chest and rough-hewn good looks, Charlie Mitchell barked commands in language seldom heard in banking boardrooms. Although he had charmed his way into the proper gentleman's social clubs, and even once entertained Her Royal Majesty Marie, the Queen of Rumania (a granddaughter of Queen Victoria), at his Tuxedo, New York, estate, Mitchell was no stereotypical genteel, conservative banker, concerned primarily with the responsible stewardship of his clients' capital. "He saw himself as a man of destiny," wrote a contemporary critic. "If John D. Rockefeller had become the master of oil he would become the master of money." Someone else likened him to a second-rate actor playing the mad King Lear.

Employing the restless imagination and astonishing energy that so endeared him to the bank's profit-hungry directors, Mitchell immediately embarked upon a whirlwind reorganization and rationalization program. He streamlined and centralized the bank's management structure to place the reins of authority firmly in his own hands. To spur his executives to greater efforts, he instituted a sliding bonus plan to link their pay directly to the bank's profits. He swallowed smaller competitors through a series of mergers and expanded National City's branch network at an unprecedented rate both in the United States and abroad, adapting the marketing and advertising strategies of successful chain stores such as Woolworth's and Montgomery Ward to transform his bank's branches into mass market retail outlets—"financial department stores"—for National City's expanding range of monetary merchandise.

But the key element in Mitchell's master plan was his creation of a 350-man sales force whose prime mission was to hawk, with all the shameless chutzpah of snake-oil peddlers, millions of dollars' worth of bonds and common stocks to a naive and greedy public. "What General Motors was doing for the automobile and Procter and Gamble for household products," observed one analyst, "National City now did for financial services." Once Mitchell explained his evangelistic motivational technique to kindred spirit Bruce Barton, the most famous public relations expert of the era. Standing at a window in the Bankers' Club building, looking down at the city like an ancient general on a hilltop surveying the field of battle below, Mitchell launched into the stock speech he used to energize his salesmen: " 'Look down there,' I say. 'There are six million people with incomes that aggregate thousands of millions of dollars. They are just waiting for someone to come and tell them what to do with their savings. Take a good look, eat a good lunch, and then go down and tell them.' "

And they did. In Manhattan speakeasies, at dusty crossroads towns across the Great Plains, in railroad coaches speeding across the continent, in hundreds of small city banks, and on innumerable front doorsteps from Maine to New Mexico, Mitchell's high-powered pitchmen offered dreams of easy money and the good life to gullible clerks, housewives, and farmers. They sold stock both in National City itself and in other corporations whose securities the bank had purchased on the open market; on every transaction, the salesmen made a commission, and National City Bank made a profit. They also sold bonds issued by foreign governments, including some extraordinarily dicey Peruvian bonds whose utter worthlessness eventually lent new meaning to the term "bad risk." And if they still needed other incentives, the salesmen knew that Mitchell was always looking over their shoulder, exhorting them to push the marks harder and sell more stock. "As I see it, you fellows are not Self-Starters," he shouted at the laggards. "You cannot stand still in this business—you either go forwards or backwards."

Mitchell instituted sales contests, with prizes of up to $25,000, but his own personal monetary rewards, of course, were far greater. While his salary in 1928 was only $25,000, he reportedly earned another $1,316,634 as his share of the bank's profits. Certainly he did not consider this excessive compensation for his labors; National City Bank's deposits at the end of the year totaled a whopping $1.35 billion, with total resources more than $1.8 billion, a remarkable increase of more than 32 percent in the past two years. Not surprisingly, National City also was very active in the call-money market. At the end of 1928, the bank was carrying more than $225 million in outstanding brokers' loans on its books.

That statistic did not bother Mitchell at all on the morning of January 2, 1929, as he walked briskly along the seven-mile route from his uptown home in the east Seventies to his office at 55 Wall Street, a ritual he performed nearly every day to maintain his physical stamina. On New Year's Eve, he had issued his usual optimistic statement (not for nothing did they call him "Sunshine Charlie") regarding the future of the market:

"Business is entering the new year upon a high level of activity and with confidence in the continuance of prosperity." Such sunny predictions were the least he could do; after all, he had an obligation to National City to encourage its customers to keep purchasing ever greater mountains of securities. The only discernible cloud on Mitchell's rosy horizon was the threat that the pusillanimous crepe hangers at the Federal Reserve Board might decide to restrict credit by raising interest rates. But Mitchell knew that he would soon have the power to soften any blow from Washington. Before the month had ended, he would take his place as the new director on the board of the influential Federal Reserve Bank of New York, succeeding the late Benjamin Strong.

A chorus of less self-interested economic analysts cheerfully echoed Mitchell's bullish sentiment that "business will be fine in nineteen twenty-nine." "In the industrial world conditions seem to be on an even keel," declared the sainted Secretary Mellon. "I look forward with confidence to continued progress in the year ahead." The members of the Harvard Economic Society euphorically predicted that "the end of the general prosperity which began in 1922 is not yet in sight," and the financial editor of the New York *Herald Tribune* chortled that "the business outlook could hardly be better." "The business world enters into the new year with greater confidence and on a better employment basis than it did in 1928," observed the director of the United States Employment Service with wholehearted satisfaction. "After a careful survey of business and industrial conditions and improvements now in the offing, we predict that 1929 will be a good year." "The public is in a happy frame of mind, and that is the best reason for the strong market we have been having," explained a veteran stock market operator who had witnessed numerous cycles of boom and bust. "It is a difficult matter to shake the confidence of the people when they are flush with money."

Few of the nation's leading industrialists or financiers dared to disagree. Lawrence Fisher, president of the Cadillac Motor Car Company, recommended that 1929 "should be viewed not as a 'cashing-in' period but as a time for laying the foundations for a period of many years of prosperity." "We have reached in this country an amazing degree of general prosperity," decided steel magnate Charles Schwab. "The problem today is an entirely new one. It is what to do to make prosperity permanent." Toward that end, Schwab advanced ten suggestions to businessmen and investors, including: "Look ahead and think ahead. It is easier to avoid depressions than it is to cure them" and "Smile, be cheerful, and work upon the basis that the fundamental purpose of business is to promote the happiness of human beings." "The factors which make for prosperity are in the ascendancy," declared the president of the American

Bankers Association, "and there is every justification for reasonable optimism regarding the future. . . . American business is entering a new era."

Certainly the new year began on an auspicious note on Wall Street. As the New York Stock Exchange opened for business on January 2, an unexpected flood of postholiday "buy" orders poured in from across the country. Led by popular favorites such as General Electric, Anaconda Copper, and Allied Chemical, stocks advanced across a broad front, with many issues gaining between $5 and $20 per share. Elated brokers reported that it was the second busiest day in the history of the market; the volume of trading surpassed even the Hoover victory flurry of November 6. That night, Wall Street went to bed in a jovial mood, and amid the laughter one reporter heard many people say, "As goes the first day, so goes the year." "There is no doubt," said the *New York Times,* "that the Street as a whole expects 1929 to be one of memorable record."

Nothing so attracted public speculation as the sight of rising prices, and as the "Hoover bull market" (so named despite the fact that Hoover would not be inaugurated until March) gained momentum, a record-shattering horde of Americans rushed to get in on a good thing. "We are in the greatest of all speculative eras," observed the Boston *Herald,* a time when brokers' wires spread to every corner of the country, and people bought stocks with the expectation of selling them in a month or a year to someone else at a higher price, and not with the idea of keeping them permanently. The *New York Times* agreed that "the gambling spirit that has developed since the election has never before been exceeded. There have been bull markets before, but the present one surpasses them all, having been taken up at a time when stocks were already high, when all warnings had been disregarded, when brokers' loans had become swollen, and when stocks selling at $200, $300, and $400 a share had multiplied tremendously." "The great majority of investors," observed one veteran bond analyst, "never again will be satisfied with a maximum of security, a minimum of return, and no participation in profits."

Law-abiding citizens who never would have considered placing a bet with a bookie wagered thousands of dollars on the stock of General Motors, U.S. Steel, and the Pennsylvania Railroad. The widespread nature of the public's preoccupation with stocks was graphically illustrated when one Northwestern utilities corporation conducted a survey of its shareholders and discovered that they included loggers, ranchers, shingle weavers, game wardens, students, mill workers, postal clerks, carpenters, pharmacists, mechanics, milk inspectors, nurses, engineers, telegraph operators, and meat cutters. "Taxi drivers told you what to buy," recalled financier Bernard Baruch, who had made millions of dollars in Wall Street before 1929. "The shoeshine boy could give you a summary of the day's financial news as he worked with rag and polish. An old beggar, who regularly patrolled the street in front of my office, now gave me tips—and, I suppose, spent the money I and others gave him in the market. My cook had a brokerage account, and followed the ticker closely." Even Walt Wallet, star of the comic strip "Gasoline Alley," took a flier on ninety shares of stock in the fictitious Rubber Keyhole corporation, and soon found himself wholly preoccupied with the gyrations of the market. He drew a graph to plot his stock's progress, and decided that "when the black line crawls off the paper at the top, I'll sell." When Rubber Keyhole subsequently took a sharp nosedive, Walt consoled himself with the thought that "it was only the big boys shaking off the pikers. I knew it was going to happen all the time. Just think how ignorant I was of all this three weeks ago." Then when Rubber Keyhole righted itself and nearly doubled in value, Walt's friend Doc advised him to sell out while he could. ("Nobody ever went broke taking a profit.") "True enough," Walt conceded, "but nothing ventured, nothing gained," and in the time-honored tradition of amateur investors everywhere, he decided to stick it out a little while longer; after all, it would be a shame to sell out before Rubber Keyhole reached its peak.

In 1928–29, women—as befit their growing presence in the job market—entered the securities market in large numbers for the first time; conservative estimates placed their numbers at about 20 percent of the total investing public. Many brokerage houses opened special uptown branches along Broadway or Fifth Avenue, with elegantly decorated "women customers' rooms" (sometimes accompanied by a miniature beauty salon), where their female clientele could observe the latest progress of their stocks on a large blackboard and obtain investment advice from well-mannered graduates of the finest Eastern schools. A typical broker's list might include gum-chewing blonde stenographers, shy spinsters, aggressive businesswomen, farmers' wives, telephone operators, waitresses, housewives, cooks, and barely literate washerwomen who invested their savings on their wealthy employers' advice and parlayed several hundred dollars into modest fortunes. For the first time, noted Eunice Fuller Barnard in the *North American Review,* women "became a recognized, if minor, factor in the vast new trading capitalist class." Although there was a popular stereotype of women speculators as "hard losers and naggers" who were "stubborn as mules, suspicious as serpents, and absolutely hell bent to have their own way," investment houses found that they made wonderful clients; in fact, many brokers reported that their women customers were even more bullish than their male counterparts. "Brokers say that not one woman in ten can be persuaded to operate on the down side," reported *Literary Digest.* "They 'simply know that their stock is going up.' " So far the ride had been an easy one; it was not yet clear how female investors would react when they finally learned the painful lesson that buying stocks could lead to sudden and devastating loss. "And if, after the holocaust, she has any money left," wrote Ms. Barnard of a mythical typical woman speculator, "she has in many cases to discover for herself the gulf fixed between rational investing and stock gambling as it has been going on the last two years. After the introduction with veil and orange blossoms, in other words, can she compose herself to the dishwashing and the darning?"

Corporations discovered that one of the best markets for their securities could be found among their own employees; the number of stock-purchase plans grew sixfold from 1915 to 1929, with nearly one-third of all eligible workers electing to participate. Although they could never hope to accumulate enough shares to influence the company's decisions, these "small and developing capitalists," as Charlie Mitchell described them, had the psychological gratification of receiving an annual dividend check and the illusion of comradeship with millionaire market operators like Raskob and Durant.

Indeed, it seemed almost unpatriotic *not* to invest in the market. Wall Street had become a mirror of national confidence, a reflection of America's belief that the economy would keep expanding, that there were more big ideas and ambitious men waiting in the wings, that tomorrow would be even better than today. "We're gambling on continued prosperity, full employment and undiminished spending capacity," wrote one ebullient financial reporter, "on freight loadings, automobile output, radio expansion—on aviation development, crop yields, beef prices—on mail-order sales and sound retailing." The old rules of prudent investing were thrown unceremoniously out the window. The notion that a sound company's stocks were worth ten times the company's earnings seemed hopelessly outdated, especially after such an august oracle as John J. Raskob declared that General Motors' stock deserved to sell at fifteen times its earnings-per-share. Even this yardstick sometimes appeared inadequate; by January 1929, several highly sought-after issues, including Du Pont, Montgomery Ward, National Biscuit, R. J. Reynolds, and Sears, were selling at twenty-two to thirty-one times earnings.

Popular magazines and newspapers carried articles that enthusiastically encouraged readers to join the stock market mania. Respected financial writer Merryle Stanley Rukeyser told readers of his column in the New York *American* that it was becoming possible "for consumers to provide for their ordinary living expenditures by purchases of shares of the industrial corporations that they patronize." For instance, Rukeyser suggested that the dividends from nine shares of American Telephone and Telegraph stock would pay the annual cost of a private telephone; thirteen shares of New York Central stock would pay enough profits in a year to finance a round-trip fare to Chicago on the Twentieth-Century Limited; and sixteen shares of Consolidated Gas Company of New York would provide enough income for an average family's gas and electric bills. For those who preferred investing in bonds, *Forum* magazine presented a seemingly foolproof scheme concocted by a schoolteacher-turned-tycoon. In his article "How to Be Prosperous on a Small Salary," the enterprising educator explained how he had effortlessly parlayed a modest paycheck into a six-figure income:

> In the early stages of my financial development, I accidentally learned that with a very small "nest egg" as a foundation, it was possible to purchase a bond of much larger value, and on the bond as collateral, borrow the difference from my bank, usually at a lower rate of interest than the bond paid. That is to say, for $150 each plus $850 borrowed from the bank at 5 per cent, I could buy a $1,000 bond paying 6 per cent. I would then pay off my note in instalments as I was able to, month by month, and that done, buy a new bond in the same way.

This practice of investing with borrowed money—"on margin"—was raised to absurd heights with the appearance in the United States of a British financial innovation known as the investment trust, an early fore-runner of the mutual funds that became so popular in the mid-twentieth century. Investment trusts were professionally managed corporations formed solely for the purpose of investing the funds of their shareholders, usually in common stocks. At the start of 1929, there were more than two hundred such companies—with over $1 billion in capital—operating in America, and all of them could have collectively (and truthfully) adver-tised with the slogan "Never a dollar lost to an investor during our entire business existence." New investment trusts appeared at the rate of one or more per day; many were oversubscribed less than two hours after they offered their initial shares for sale.

By purchasing shares in one of these corporations, a speculator of modest means presumably could reduce his vulnerability, since the trust's funds were invested in a diversified portfolio of issues selected by purport-edly knowledgeable experts. One writer in the *New Republic* explained the appeal of this device by using the example of a man with $1,000 to invest. "He hates to take 4 percent [interest] and safety, and he does not quite dare to risk his all in a 7 percent security. On the other hand, if he can bring together nine other persons who each have $1,000, and the resulting $10,000 is invested by an expert in various 7 percent securities, it is very unlikely that the losses will equal the additional income." And since our hypothetical investor could use his original $1,000 to purchase

$10,000 worth of shares in various trusts by buying on margin and using the value of the stocks as collateral, the opportunities for profit seemed almost limitless. In turn, the investment trust itself almost invariably purchased stocks on margin, too, further pyramiding a very small amount of equity into a highly leveraged speculative venture.

If prices fell for any extended period, of course, the entire structure would come crashing down as the paper value of the collateral securities evaporated all along the line. But as long as stock prices kept going up, the public remained blind to the dangers inherent in such operations. Speculators shrugged off warnings of imminent collapse—and there was no shortage of red flags at the start of 1929—because the financial Jeremiahs had been proved wrong before. So no one panicked when the Washington *Post* predicted that "thousands of buyers of stocks are in for serious losses," or when the *Journal of Commerce* reported that many investment bankers were convinced that "conditions are in an extraordinarily overstrained situation and may break down at any moment." And when the chief economist of the National Industrial Conference Board declared that the Hoover bull market was nothing more than a cynical sham perpetrated on gullible investors, the result of "persistent and premature prosperity propaganda by interests seeking to unload non-interest-bearing speculative securities on the general public," his remarks were greeted with almost universal disdain. Former New York *World* correspondent and editor Herbert Bayard Swope's reaction to such pessimistic forecasts was typical. "Don't kid yourself," Swope laughed when a friend expressed reluctance to invest in the market. "We are going to take a pleasant ride, so climb up in the driver's seat."

Swope had been one of Al Smith's most ardent supporters in the 1928 presidential campaign, but now he and Raskob were drowning their sorrows by making several hundred thousand dollars apiece in the Hoover bull market. Swope's good friend Harpo Marx was playing the market, too, though not on such an exalted level. Harpo had purchased his first substantial portfolio of stocks just six months earlier on a tip provided by a Boston financier named Joseph P. Kennedy, whom he met during a vacation in Florida, and by the start of the new year Harpo was sitting pretty. "Nineteen twenty-nine was bound to be the greatest year in modern history," he thought cheerfully. "It began with a New Year's Eve party at the Swopes'. When the first day of January dawned, it was so beautiful out that we moved the whole party into Central Park and played croquet. It seemed as if the New Year's Eve party never did break up."

Harpo had another reason to celebrate his good fortune at the beginning of 1929. He and his brothers had just opened their rambunctious new Broadway show, *Animal Crackers,* to critical acclaim and capacity audiences; *New York Times* drama critic Brooks Atkinson reported that "speculators swore they could get as much as $100 for two tickets to the opening performance." A rave review in the *New Yorker* extravagantly praised the show as "the very concoction for which the word 'wow' had been coined," and recommended that audiences "relax and let the Marx Brothers thump and trample you. Every time you go you'll get more good and enjoyment from it." With this smash hit added to their previous triumphs in *I'll Say She Is* (1923) and the George S. Kaufman–Irving Berlin collaboration *The Cocoanuts* (1925), the Marx Brothers could justifiably count themselves among the elite along Broadway.

It had been a long, strange journey for the sons of Simon and Minna Marrix. Their father (whom the boys, with a marked lack of respect, later dubbed "Frenchy") was a Jewish immigrant from Alsace who, for reasons known only to himself, decided to become a tailor soon after settling in the Upper East Side of New York. Since he had absolutely no training in cutting or sewing clothes and adamantly refused to employ a tape measure, customers did not exactly beat a path to his door (though a never-ending procession of bill collectors did). His wife, Minnie, was the daughter of a traveling German magician, from whom she inherited a love of show business but no discernible talent. Their first son died of tuberculosis in infancy; their second, Leonard (who later became known to the world as Chico), thus received a double share of love when he was born in 1887, and remained his mother's favorite all his life. Another son, Adolf (Harpo), followed fifteen months later and received the lion's share of his father's attentions. So there was not a great storehouse of parental affection remaining when Julius (Groucho) arrived in 1890, and even less after sickly Milton (Gummo) was born in 1892. The fifth surviving son, Herbert (Zeppo), completed the crowded family portrait nine years later.

The Marx Brothers grew up in a three-room flat on East Ninety-third Street in the Yorkville section of New York City; until Leonard began staying out all night, the four oldest boys slept together in one double bed. Their father's stubborn perseverance in fashioning trousers with legs of drastically different lengths kept the family perpetually short of funds. "We didn't bathe often," Julius recalled later. "We never saw a shower. We had one bathroom. All we had was a tin tub." Although Julius admitted that he and his brothers never really went hungry, "there was generally some kind of brawl at the dinner table over who would get what. I distinctly remember one occasion when I almost lost an arm over a sweet roll."

To make ends meet, the boys earned money at various odd jobs. Adolf, who had dropped out of school after the second grade, earned $12 a month as a bellboy at the Hotel Seville; Julius, the bookish brother, sang in the boys' choir at the Episcopal Church on Madison Avenue for $3 a week (the rector either did not know or did not care that young Marrix was Jewish); and Leonard—well, Leonard was a problem, even for his doting mother. As the eldest son, he had been chosen to receive the precious gift of music lessons, and he dutifully employed his talent as a piano player in nickelodeons and neighborhood saloons. But after falling in with a gang of street toughs at the age of eleven, he became something of a delinquent and a compulsive gambler, and frequently frittered away his wages in back alley crap games. By the time he was sixteen, Leonard had left home for good.

Although it was Julius' dream to become a surgeon, he was unceremoniously yanked out of school after completing the seventh grade when his mother pressed him into show business as part of a traveling vaudeville act. For the next four years, he shuffled in and out of a succession of undistinguished troupes, until Minnie finally teamed him with brother Milton and a cross-eyed young girl singer named Mabel O'Donnell in a vocal act called the Nightingales. Shortly thereafter, nineteen-year-old Adolf joined the group, much against his will. "The only ambitions I ever nourished," Harpo admitted near the end of his career, "were to be left fielder for the New York Giants, a full-time tin-can swinger for an umbrella mender, or a piano player on an excursion boat." Instead, he became an entertainer, though "nothing that I could have done could have frightened me more."

The indomitable Mother Minnie dragged the Four Nightingales and their twenty-minute musical act up and down the East Coast on a hectic tour of small-time vaudeville theaters from Pennsylvania to Massachusetts. After wearing out their welcome in the East, they moved to Chicago and toured the Midwest and the South, finally changing their name to the Marx Brothers and Company (the better to disguise themselves from anyone who had already heard the Nightingales). But a trio of young Jewish men singing harmony with an Irish girl did not always play well in the less sophisticated cow towns of southern Texas; catcalls and rude behavior from the crowds grew increasingly bothersome, and when the entire audience at a matinee in Nacogdoches walked out on the Marx Brothers' performance to watch a runaway mule cavort in the street, something snapped. As the customers returned to their seats half an hour later, Julius began throwing out insults about Texas in general and Nacogdoches in particular, such as "Nacogdoches is full of roaches," and "The jackass is the finest flower of Tex-ass." Surprisingly, the audience loved the abuse, and the brothers began receiving offers from theater managers in search of new comedy acts.

So they developed a juvenile act, known as "Fun in Hi Skule," filled with slapstick and rapid-fire dialogue. Julius donned a frock coat and a black mustache to play the part of the schoolmaster; Adolf, who played a simple-minded country bumpkin, wore an unruly wig made of old rope and a hat that resembled an upside-down bucket. Everything seemed to be running smoothly until one night in Waukegan in 1911, when Julius looked down into the orchestra pit and saw, to his amazement, Leonard (remember Leonard?) sitting at the piano. Adolf's initial reaction was to launch an apple in anger at his prodigal brother, who promptly threw the missile back at Julius, who turned and threw it at Milton; soon smashed bits of fruit were flying furiously across the stage, and though the curtain fell before the performance ended, the audience whooped and howled for an encore.

Leonard had returned to the fold after spending the past nine years working as a professional wrestler in a circus, a flyweight prizefighter, a pool shark, a pianist in sundry whorehouses, a song plugger for a music publisher, and the piano-playing half of a two-man musical act known as Marx and Gordoni. Along the way, he had developed a comic Italian accent, which he reportedly picked up from his barber. Upon his reconciliation with the family, Leonard—who was a much tougher negotiator than Minnie—took over management of the act and immediately began steering his brothers away from the dying vaudeville market, in the general direction of the legitimate theater. And during a backstage poker game in a small town in upstate Illinois, a show business colleague blessed them with nicknames to go along with their stage personalities: Leonard, the most accomplished ladies' man, was christened "Chicko" but later dropped the "k"; Adolf, who had changed his name to the less Teutonic Arthur during the war, had taught himself to play the harp and so became "Harpo"; and Julius' sober, glowering persona—both on- and offstage—earned him the unenviable appellation "Groucho." ("I hate it," he once said. "It's terrible. It makes me sound like I'm the kind of guy who goes around whipping little children.") The hypochondriac Milton, who inevitably wore galoshes, or gumshoes, to ward off colds, was dubbed "Gummo." Perhaps because he came last, the others named Herbert "Zeppo" when he replaced Milton after the war.

The Marx Brothers broke into the big time with a show entitled *I'll Say She Is,* which opened in Philadelphia in the summer of 1923, moved on to Boston and Chicago, and gradually made its way back to New York in May 1924. This was a pattern that *The Cocoanuts* and *Animal Crackers* repeated profitably; because so much of their act was developed in ad-libs and impromptu shenanigans onstage, the Marxes needed the help of out-of-town audiences to tell them which bits were funny and which were not.

*I'll Say* was an immediate hit on Broadway, aided in no small part by an enthusiastic review in the New York *Sun* by drama critic Alexander

Woollcott, who fell in love with Harpo's "wild and silent face." When the show finally closed after a thirty-eight-week run, the Marx Brothers began rehearsals on *The Cocoanuts,* a satire on the ill-fated Florida real estate boom of the mid-1920s; the musical comedy opened to a standing-room-only audience at the Lyric Theatre on December 8, 1925. For the next two years it set box-office records on the Great White Way. During its 377 performances, all sorts of celebrities—including the Prince of Wales and Al Smith—stopped by to enjoy the fun. Groucho usually obliged them by hurling insults from the stage. "I see we have the Honorable Mayor Walker with us," he said during the performance on the night before the city elections of 1927. "I wonder why he isn't home stuffing ballot boxes." And when he spotted President Coolidge in the audience on another evening, Groucho stopped, walked to the edge of the stage, peered closely at the dour Coolidge, and asked, "Aren't you up past your bedtime, Calvin?"

In early 1929, the Marx Brothers began filming a movie version of *The Cocoanuts* for Paramount's Adolph Zukor, who paid them $100,000 for their services; they were also earning about $2,000 a week from the performances of their new play, *Animal Crackers.* Added to their income from their previous Broadway successes, the Marx Brothers should all have been fairly wealthy men in early 1929. Chico, however, still could not resist the temptations of high-stakes poker games, fast horses, and easy women, and managed to gamble away almost all his considerable earnings. Harpo, too, wagered heavily on occasion—especially at chemin de fer and croquet, his newfound passion—but was far less of a compulsive gambler than Chico. Since his canonization by Woollcott, the forty-year-old Harpo was spending most of his time either at Lindy's Restaurant, where he had a special table not far from Arnold Rothstein's, or in the company of the Thanatopsis Literary and Inside Straight Club, a poker-playing offshoot of that unique aggregation of New York literary and theatrical personalities known as the Algonquin Round Table. There he consorted on equal terms with humorist Robert Benchley, the caustic poet and short story writer Dorothy Parker, novelist Edna Ferber, journalists such as Heywood Broun and Herbert Swope, *New Yorker* editor Harold Ross, columnist Franklin P. Adams, and occasionally actress Helen Hayes, Wall Street wizard Bernard Baruch, Irving Berlin, financier and patron of the arts Otto Kahn, and Will Rogers. Harpo was showered with invitations to the Long Island estates of Whitneys, Pulitzers, Guggenheims, and Kahns, and when the Thanatopsis Club migrated to Cap d'Antibes for the winter, he enjoyed the brilliant company of George Bernard Shaw and Somerset Maugham. No one condescended to Harpo because he had never passed the second grade; in fact, most of his new friends found his unpretentious charm immensely refreshing. Besides, he was one of the few members of the club who did not feel compelled to constantly utter tiresomely witty remarks. "Until I came along," he said, "there wasn't a full-time listener in the crowd. I couldn't have been more welcome if I had had the power to repeal Prohibition."

Groucho, on the other hand, was far too insecure and aware of his educational shortcomings to mix with such a lofty crowd. He much preferred the company of his family and a few close friends from the old vaudeville days. And unlike his two elder brothers, the frugal Groucho was the soul of financial prudence; he was so obsessed with the fear that the good times might suddenly come to a screeching halt that he refused to buy a house until he could pay for it in cash. "Groucho may have given the impression that he was perpetually thumbing his nose at the established order," remarked Chico's daughter Maxine, "but no one yearned for the security of wealth more than he." After he finally purchased an estate on Long Island, in the writers' and artists' colony at Great Neck, Groucho's only two major indulgences were a 1929 Runabout Packard convertible with a rumble seat and crimson wire wheels, and membership in the exclusive Lakeville Golf Club. He took the rest of his savings— nearly $250,000 at the start of 1929—and invested it in the stock market.

"Knowing how wary Father has always been of schemes where you can make money without working for it," wrote his son Arthur, "I'm amazed that he ever let himself get sucked into Wall Street. . . . Never— even in the most prosperous times—did he stop looking for ways of keeping unnecessary expenses down around the house. He was as conscious of the price of pumpernickel in 1929 as he had been before *I'll Say She Is* put him in the high-income bracket. Yet when it came to tips on the stock market, he was as gullible as everyone else. He'd accept the word of a total stranger and invest thousands of dollars in a stock that he knew absolutely nothing about." Like many other amateur investors in 1929, Groucho Marx simply chose not to acknowledge the risks inherent in playing the market. "He was in it," explained Arthur, "because, like everyone else, he was convinced that it was a sound, money-making venture. You were in partnership with big business. Financiers had been on to this for years. Did J. P. Morgan, the Whitneys and the DuPonts bury their money in banks that only paid two and three percent interest? Of course not. They put their money to work for them. That's why they could afford yachts like the Corsair. It was amazingly simple. Father could never get over the wonder of it."

Groucho was so mesmerized by the tangible vision of appreciating assets that he began spending more time in his broker's boardroom than on the stage. (Even when he was on the movie set of *The Cocoanuts,* his mind was elsewhere; he invariably carried a copy of the *Wall Street Journal* in his pocket and frequently interrupted script conferences to discuss points and margins.) Every day, Groucho drove down to the branch office of his broker, Newman Brothers and Worms, on Main Street in Great Neck and sat there for hours, in a transport of ecstasy, as he scrutinized the ticker tape and watched the office boys chart the upward progress of his stocks. "He was not alone," remembered Arthur, who often was dragged along unwillingly when his father wanted to take "just a quick look" at the latest quotations on the way to the beach or a baseball game: "He'd meet all his friends and neighbors and the local tradesmen in the place, and they would exchange tips and discuss the latest financial trends, as if they really knew what they were talking about." Often the neglected Arthur ended up walking home alone; when Groucho finally returned, he would gloat over his good fortune. "What an easy racket," he'd say. "RCA went up seven points since this morning. I just made myself seven thousand dollars."

Groucho was willing to act on a stock tip from almost any source. Once an elevator boy at the Ritz Carlton Hotel in Boston suggested that Union Carbide was an attractive buy because he heard it had just dropped two points; Groucho rushed to his broker and bought $9,000 worth of shares. Then he passed the tip along to Harpo, who invested nearly ten times that much in the stock. On another occasion, Eddie Cantor telephoned Groucho and said, "Julius, get yourself two hundred shares of Goldman-Sachs immediately." (Goldman-Sachs was an investment trust formed by one of Wall Street's more conservative banking houses in December 1928.) "It's selling for one hundred and thirty-seven," Cantor chortled, "and I just got word from Herbert Swope that it's sure to go to one hundred and fifty by the end of the week."

An innocent observer might legitimately have wondered exactly how the indefatigable Mr. Swope knew that the price of this particular stock was going to rise, and by precisely how much. Had Mr. Swope consulted the nation's most famous astrologer, Miss Evangeline Adams, who regularly cast celestial charts for clients who dabbled in stock speculation or wagered on horse races and prizefights? Probably not; Miss Adams' own stock had recently suffered a serious blow from her widely publicized prediction that Al Smith would win the presidential election. Had Mr. Swope developed his own idiosyncratic system of choosing stocks, like the investors who closed their eyes and pushed a pin through the financial page of the newspaper, or the gentleman who professed to discern a revealing pattern in the tiny dots that appeared between quotations on the ticker tape? Or did Swope, like Groucho Marx, know a knowledgeable elevator operator or shoeshine boy?

No, no, certainly not. As the confidant of corporate executives and millionaire financiers and a friend of the famous, the wealthy, and the powerful, Mr. Swope received a steady supply of "inside information," that most precious Wall Street commodity sought by every speculator but obtained by few. This was the meat upon which professional market operators fattened; in the words of one disenchanted commentator, it turned speculation into a game "played by some three or four thousand insiders and some half a million outsiders on terms of complete inequality." While the multitude of ordinary investors were "permitted to see only a part of their own cards . . . their professional adversaries have access to the cards of all the players as well as their own."

The favorite device of Wall Street insiders in early 1929 was the stock pool or syndicate, a form of price manipulation that could net millions of dollars for the lucky participants in a very short time. A typical pool began with an agreement among a limited number of players to purchase a large block of stock in a single corporation, preferably one of the more glamorous issues like RCA or General Motors, which could easily attract public attention. As they quietly accumulated their shares, or at least an option to purchase shares at a certain price, they confided their intentions to the trader on the exchange floor who specialized in buying and selling that corporation's stock; to secure his cooperation, the specialist usually was invited to become an active partner in the maneuver. The players then selected someone—possibly the trader himself—to direct the operation as the pool manager.

Once the options or shares were firmly in hand, the manager began trading the stock back and forth between members of the pool, gradually stepping up the pace to draw attention to the steadily increasing flurry of activity. In the boardroom at Great Neck, Groucho Marx and his friends would see from the tale of the ticker tape that the stock was "active and higher," and as it rose they decided that they, too, would buy shares to get in on the profits. Concurrently, pliable journalists—including reporters from the *Wall Street Journal,* the *New York Times,* and the New York *Daily News* who were willing to act as shills—planted stories and tips inspired by the pool manager to stimulate interest in his stock. And amenable brokers might offer suggestions to their clients that "we hear that Mr. So-and-so [fill in the name of a prominent stock speculator] will make his main campaign this year in the following stocks." None of this would have worked, of course, if a majority of investors had shunned pools as illegal or unethical. In 1929, they certainly were not illegal, and the issue of morality of trading on inside information never bothered most investors.

As an avalanche of purchase orders from greedy outsiders boosted the price of the stock far beyond its intrinsic worth, the pool manager "pulled the plug." Quietly, surreptitiously, trying not to spook the market, he started to sell off his partners' shares at the prearranged peak, cashing in on the profits before the stock began the inevitable downward spiral. Eventually, of course, the pool's selling operations accelerated the price decline, but by the time the public realized that the tide had turned, the syndicate had disposed of its holdings and earned a tidy profit. These were bull market pools, dedicated to inflating the price of a stock. A bear market pool would work in precisely the opposite manner to drive prices down so insiders could pick up extraordinary bargains; but in the heady atmosphere of the late twenties, it was almost impossible to convince the public to sell any prominent stock short.

As business historian John Brooks has pointed out, the management of a successful pool operation required finesse and a sure sense of timing. "There *was* an element of risk," Brooks argues. "Sometimes the suckers refused to play their assigned role, some pools failed and lost money." But not often. Between mid-October and late November 1928, the automotive Fisher Brothers—who had nearly $400 million at their disposal for speculative ventures—reportedly made between $30 and $50 million in two pools in Montgomery Ward and RCA stock. And in the four months from December 1928 through March 1929, Charlie Mitchell's National City Bank participated in three separate pools involving the stock of Anaconda Copper subsidiaries. These represented, perhaps, the ultimate in price manipulation by insiders, for National City's partners in the pools included John D. Ryan, chairman of the board of Anaconda, and Anaconda's president, Cornelius Kelley. The pool managers drove up the price of the stock from $60 to $125; at the conclusion of their operations, National City was richer by $167,000 in cash and $9 million worth of Anaconda stock. By using the bank's money (that is, the money of the bank's customers) to purchase the copper stocks, the element of personal risk to the operators themselves was reduced virtually to zero; but the extravagant profits, of course, were distributed almost exclusively among the officers of the bank and the corporation. And then Sunshine Charlie Mitchell's salesmen went out and peddled the Anaconda stock to suckers at the artfully and artificially inflated price of $125 per share.

There were even less scrupulous variations on the theme. As the bull market of 1928–29 gathered steam, con men began to publish "advisory service" newsletters, using well-tempered prose and dignified stationery, which they mailed to credulous investors. After acquiring shares or options of a stock with relatively small distribution, the tipsters enthusiastically recommended that issue to their readers as a hidden bargain. When investors acted on the tip, the price of the stock naturally began to rise, stimulating further interest. The operator then sold his original shares at a profit, and as the artificial stimulus of the "advice" wore off, the price fell back to its normal level. Ironically, this procedure strengthened the reputation of the operator/con man, because it appeared that he had indeed accurately predicted the price rise, and those who lost money in the subsequent decline usually blamed themselves for jumping into the market too late.

Perhaps the most famous bull market pool operator in America in 1929 was automobile entrepreneur William Crapo Durant. Born in Boston in 1861, young Billy Durant grew up among the blacksmith shops, factories, and paper mills of the vigorous industrial town of Flint, Michigan. Although his drunkard father deserted the family when Billy was in his teens, his ancestors on the maternal side were considerably more distinguished: his grandfather, Henry Howland ("Howlin' Henry") Crapo, served as governor of Michigan during the Civil War, and his Uncle James was a prominent businessman and longtime congressman from Massachusetts.

A former business competitor once described William Durant—and it was not entirely a compliment—as "a born optimist." When he was nine years old, his family thought he might become an evangelistic preacher; instead, he became a salesman. He sold patent medicines, cigars, and fire insurance, and his soft voice and sober demeanor made him a refreshing presence in an era of high-pressure, backslapping drummers. "Assume that the man you are talking to knows as much or more than you do," Durant once said. "Do not talk too much. Give the customer time to think. In other words, let the customer sell himself." That seemingly serene philosophy masked a host of restless ambitions inside the young promoter. In 1886, Durant went into business for himself by purchasing a very small but promising carriage-making factory, and quickly turned it into one of the largest and most profitable manufacturing concerns in Flint. But horse-drawn carriages would not take William Durant where he wished to go; for that he would need the automobiles that Henry Ford, Leland Olds, and the Dodge brothers were building in Detroit and nearby cities. So when a representative of the Buick Motor Company approached him in 1904 to see if he would take over and reorganize the troubled firm, Durant accepted with alacrity.

Directing the company's affairs in a dictatorial, freewheeling style, Durant tripled Buick's capitalization base, launched an aggressive sales campaign that brought in orders for more cars than the company had ever produced, and increased the amount of Buick stock twentyfold from $75,-000 to $1,500,000. By the end of 1908, the Buick Motor Company reported a net worth of $3,417,142. But the field of auto manufacturing was littered with far too many cutthroat competitors—nearly fifty separate companies in 1908—producing far too few cars, fewer than forty-five thousand per year. So Durant and Buick began swallowing other automotive corporations: the struggling Olds Motor Company, the Cadillac Motor Company, the Marquette Motor Company, Reliance, Oakland, and the Welch Motor Car Company of Pontiac. "I was for getting every car in sight," Durant admitted candidly. He almost got Ford, too, at a moment when Henry Ford was uncharacteristically despondent over the future, but no banker was willing to lend Durant the $8 million in cash Ford demanded as his price. This ambitious program of acquisitions was financed primarily by Durant's adroit manipulation of stock issues and dividends; by the time he was finished, he had spent less than $6 million in cash to acquire companies worth $54 million. Confident that he could single-handedly forge these disparate elements into a giant corporation that would dominate the auto industry, Durant called his new corporate entity General Motors—and immediately fell flat on his face.

Obsessed by a vision of a nation on wheels ("Durant sees—actually sees—90,000,000 people just aching to roll along the roads of this country in automobiles," wrote an amazed automotive industry journalist), Durant enthusiastically bounded far ahead of conventional wisdom and the existing marketplace. In the deflationary decade before the war, when a phalanx of conservative Eastern financiers led by J. Pierpont Morgan, Sr., held the purse strings of American industry, visionaries like Durant were considered irresponsible at best, and downright dangerous when the stakes were high enough. Thus when General Motors invested $30 million in new supplies and another $8 million in plant expansion in 1910, Durant's bankers nearly fainted. They refused to believe that even General Motors could increase its business sufficiently (about 500 percent would be required) to justify such exorbitant expenditures. Considering Durant's disorganized management style—he refused to delegate responsibility to subordinates, or establish clear lines of authority or communication—and the amount of dead weight and fixed costs that needed to be pruned from some of his less efficient acquisitions, the bankers' skepticism seemed entirely justified. Desperate for funds when the bottom suddenly dropped out of the auto market, Durant finally convinced a New York financial syndicate to issue General Motors a loan of $15 million—but only on the condition that Durant relinquish control of the corporation to the bankers' trustees for the life of the five-year loan, from 1910 to 1915. He had no choice but to concede.

Hurt but not defeated, Durant promptly formed another corporation, which he named after the famous French racing driver Louis Chevrolet, who helped Durant design a new six-cylinder touring car. Then Durant set out to avenge his humiliation at the hands of the bankers. Aided by Du Pont financial executive John Jacob Raskob, who convinced his superiors to invest the war-swollen profits of the Du Pont chemical and explosives empire in the automotive industry, Durant won a hotly contested proxy contest with the reigning leadership of General Motors at the end of 1915. When the dust had settled, William Durant once more sat in the president's office at General Motors, this time under the chairmanship of Pierre S. Du Pont. Once more Durant embarked upon an ambitious scheme of mergers, pulling in Fisher Body Corporation (for $5.8 million in cash and $21.8 million in securities), Delco (the acronym for Dayton Engineering Laboratories), Frigidaire, and the Dayton Wright Airplane Company. And once more Durant foolishly overreached himself, though this time he had help from Raskob, who encouraged and promoted expansion schemes during the wartime boom and then nimbly dodged the consequences when the postwar recession that began in the winter of 1920 exposed the cracks in the hastily constructed foundation.

Cracks became fissures in the summer of 1920 as auto sales declined precipitously and the price of General Motors stock dropped from $40 to $25 and kept on falling. Durant tried to maintain its value artificially by organizing pools to bid up the price of G.M. stock, but nothing worked until Raskob and Pierre Du Pont convinced the nation's leading investment banking house, J. P. Morgan and Company, to underwrite $1.4 million worth of G.M. securities. The relief was only temporary; investors continued to unload their General Motors stock, and Durant scrambled to purchase as much as he could—on margin, of course, using the rest of his G.M. stock as collateral—to protect the funds he had already invested in the company. But he succeeded only in tumbling further into a bottomless abyss of indebtedness. By October 1920, several Morgan partners were convinced that the beleaguered Durant was far too heavily in debt—their estimates ranged as high as $27 million—to continue in office. When Durant admitted that the actual total was closer to $34 million, he was gone. By that time, General Motors stock had dropped all the way to $13 per share. It was obvious Durant would not be able to meet his obligations; it was equally certain that had he defaulted, a catastrophic wave of liquidation might have engulfed both General Motors and the banks and investment houses that had loaned millions of dollars to him. To avert such a debacle, Morgan partner Dwight Morrow negotiated an arrangement whereby Morgan and Du Pont bailed Durant out of his personal financial embarrassment in return for the surrender of most of his G.M. stock. Morrow also insisted on Durant's resignation. Grief-stricken, Durant walked away from General Motors for the second and last time.

Although his downfall stemmed directly from an insatiable drive to manipulate securities and speculate in stocks, Durant promptly plunged right back into the market by forming the Durant Motor Company. Between 1921 and 1929, the Durant Company succeeded in soliciting nearly $80 million from the public; available to investors of modest means through various installment plans, the company's stock debuted at $10 per share and finally peaked at $80. One year after its formation, Durant Motors reportedly had more stockholders than any American corporation except American Telephone and Telegraph. It was a remarkable tribute to the public's unshaken confidence in William Crapo Durant, who gloried in his popular nickname of "the Dream Maker." Actually, the Durant Motor Company never became much more than "a money collecting machine of huge proportions," as one historian described it, because very few cars ever rolled off its assembly lines. Durant himself took little interest in the day-to-day management of his own company; instead, the Dream Maker devoted his attention during the 1920s to his first love, the stock market, where he soon was crowned "King of the Bulls."

From his office high above the corner of Broadway and 57th, Durant reportedly commanded over $1 billion worth of funds entrusted to him by friends and business associates (including the ubiquitous Fisher Brothers). He liked to say that "success in the stock market comes from finding out a stock selling at $50 that should be selling at $100, or one selling for $100 which should be selling at $150 or $200," and if he could elevate a stock to its rightful level and make money on the deal, so much the better. Rumors that Durant was bidding up the price of a stock or managing a bull pool invariably sent a buoyant tremor through Wall Street. "Acting as a sort of market commissioner of police," wrote one contemporary observer, "he watched for weak spots in the market and whenever he found one, plugged it with millions of dollars. He placed other millions behind key stocks which, in rising, would drag the whole market upward in sympathy. Nothing like that had ever been tried before." Durant's motives were not entirely altruistic, of course. Early in 1928, he accumulated 100,000 shares of Anaconda at an average price of $60, advanced it to $71, and then sold all of it at an average price of $69 and cleared about $800,-000 on the deal. That transaction, however, paled beside his purchase of 623,000 shares of General Motors, which he subsequently cashed in for an $8 million profit.

By 1929, Durant had accumulated a personal fortune estimated at more than $100 million; in January, *Collier's* magazine noted that "in Wall Street it is believed that he has made more money out of this market than any other operator." When the new year began, the King of the Bulls had recently returned from a European vacation to his American estate, Raymere, the opulently baroque New Jersey mansion he had purchased from the Rothschild family. While in Europe, Durant had issued a formal announcement that he would sponsor a nationwide contest, with $25,000 in prize money, for suggestions to improve the enforcement of America's prohibition laws. The nation's business executives, Durant charged, had brazenly flouted the law themselves and encouraged others to follow their irresponsible example: "Instead of using their wealth and influence to create public opinion demanding law enforcement, our business men of character and position are the chief support of the master criminal class, the bootlegger." Newspaper publisher William Randolph Hearst mockingly responded to Durant's challenge by offering an identical prize for the best suggestion on how to make prohibition disappear altogether.

On January 10, 1929, Durant finally stepped down as head of the Durant Motor Company. At a melodramatic meeting in Manhattan of five hundred Durant Motors dealers and distributors, he asked his audience, "Do you believe in W. C. Durant?" "Yes! Yes!" they screamed in unison, leaping out of their chairs to shout their approval. "Do you believe that W. C. Durant would be unfair or unjust," he went on, "to men who have been loyal to him for years . . . through every trial?" "No! No!" they shouted. Then Durant calmly announced that he was relinquishing management of the Durant Motor Company to devote his time to other interests, and the Dream Maker walked away from the corporation that bore his name. He immediately began making plans for a journey to Washington.

Durant was an old friend of Herbert Clark Hoover, and the President-elect had arrived in the nation's capital just a few days earlier.

# V

# A Noble Order of Ostriches

"Damn you, what the devil are you doing here?"
—KING GEORGE V

Herbert Hoover welcomed the year 1929 on board the battleship USS *Utah,* about six hundred miles east of Santo Domingo, bound for Norfolk. Fifteen days after his election day triumph, Hoover had embarked upon a six-week goodwill tour of Central and South America. He told reporters that he wanted to smooth over relations with the Latin republics in the south, dispel allegations of "Yankee imperialism" which had surfaced during the Coolidge regime, and safeguard U.S. trade interests in the Southern Hemisphere. He also wanted desperately to escape from the importunate politicians who had begun to pressure him for patronage or favors.

Coolidge suggested that Hoover make his journey on a cruiser, which would have been cheaper, but Hoover insisted that only a full-fledged battleship befitted his dignity. So the President-elect left his home in Palo Alto, carrying with him fifty first-run movie features and shorts donated by Cecil B. De Mille (all fifty were silent films, mostly documentaries and mysteries—Hoover hated the newfangled "talkies" because they demanded too much attention), and headed out to sea aboard the USS *Maryland,* flagship of the United States Pacific Fleet. Eighteen reporters came along for the voyage; Hoover asked them to refer to his ship as "the friendship *Maryland*" instead of "the battleship *Maryland,*" but they just laughed.

Down the Pacific coastline steamed Hoover and his entourage, holding spelling contests to pass the time. (Hoover and his wife usually won.) The journalists grumbled over Hoover's insistence that all stories filed from the ship had to be cleared through one of his secretaries, to avoid any misunderstandings with the "very sensitive" South American governments and people. In practice, virtually everything they wrote was permitted to pass, but the fact that Hoover attempted even a mild form of censorship exacerbated an already hostile relationship between the President-elect and the press.

When the *Maryland* reached Santiago, Chile, the troupe disembarked and headed eastward across the continent by rail and steamer. Preceded by five railway cars full of heavily armed Argentine soldiers, Hoover's special train rumbled down through the snowy Andes and across the wheat fields of the pampas. At every official reception, Hoover tried to say all the right things—"There are no older and younger brothers of the American continent. . . . The fear of some persons concerning supposed intervention ideas of the United States are unfounded. . . . I see a group of friends as friendly, or more so, than brothers with similar ideals, which lead in new directions to new purposes, all close together and all at equal levels"—and for the most part he was welcomed with cheers from the people, booming twenty-one-gun salutes from the artillery batteries, and signs that read, "Welcome to the successor of Washington. Welcome to President Hoover." At every stop, he left behind him scores of newborn babies christened "Herbert" or, even more traumatically, "Hoover."

But when Hoover reached Montevideo, he heard more clearly from the crowd the angry, insistent chants that had pursued him faintly across the continent: "Down with imperialistic America!" "Down with the American marines!" and, especially, "Viva Sandino!" Assured by his hosts that the protesters were nothing more than scurrilous, rabble-rousing agitators from the local Communist organization, Hoover continued his tour unperturbed; after a three-day stop in Rio de Janeiro, he boarded the battleship *Utah* and headed for home, omitting Venezuela and Cuba from his itinerary at the last moment.

Nor did he stop in Managua, the capital of Nicaragua, the unhappy land where five thousand American marines were engaged in a military mission "to maintain law, order and peace," a lofty objective the Nicaraguan government had decided could only be fulfilled by the capture and detention of one General Augusto Cesar (Calderon) Sandino. By January 1929, the armed revolt of General Sandino and his ragtag band of guerrillas against the U.S.-backed government in Managua had transformed Sandino, the illegitimate son of a prosperous Nicaraguan landowner and an Indian servant girl, into the leading symbol of anti-American sentiment throughout Latin America. It was not a distinction Sandino had deliberately sought.

The roots of both Sandino's predicament and the American involvement in the domestic affairs of Nicaragua lay in the tangled and often sordid political squabbles that had plagued the thinly populated Central American republic since it gained its independence from Spain in 1821. Throughout most of the nineteenth century and the early years of the twentieth, Nicaraguan public life was dominated by two political parties, the Conservatives (primarily affluent landowners) and the Liberals (primarily businessmen and merchants), whose philosophical differences were limited largely to a disagreement over the proper influence of the Catholic church in secular affairs. As one perceptive historian recently pointed out, the interminable and frequently violent conflict between the Liberal and Conservative parties was not, for the most part, related to these differences in philosophy at all: "Rather, it was about power and the possibilities that power offered for enrichment. The two groups functioned more like tribes or armies than political parties, and those who aspired to public office needed the talents of a warlord more than those of a political thinker."

Often their hostility flared into open warfare. In 1855, a faction of Liberal politicians invited an American mercenary named William Walker to lead a military expedition against their Conservative foes. Although Walker brought fewer than sixty troops with him to Nicaragua, within the space of a few months the former Tennessee lawyer had managed to conquer the country, elect himself president, introduce slavery, seize the Vanderbilt Transit Company's railroad, and antagonize the British government as well as his Central American neighbors. After Walker's ouster at the hands of a British-supported and Vanderbilt-financed force in 1857, Nicaraguan political affairs remained relatively placid until the early years of the twentieth century, when a particularly harsh Liberal dictatorship sparked a Conservative revolt (in 1909) supported by a force of four hundred American marines, who were dispatched by President Taft primarily to ensure the safety of the ports and customs houses, and to protect American and European investments through the establishment of a stable, friendly government. Though the marines quickly departed, they returned in far greater force in 1912 to suppress another armed rebellion. This time they stayed for thirteen years.

In 1926, shortly after the marines finally left, the two parties began shooting at each other once again. This time, however, the Republican administration in Washington professed to discern a Communist conspiracy behind the activities of several insurgent Liberal factions; Coolidge claimed that he had documentary proof that the leftist government of Mexico was furnishing arms to the Liberal rebels, and the President lost no time in sending several thousand marines to restore order and defend American interests (including the treaty right to construct a proposed Nicaraguan Canal). At the same time, he dispatched former secretary of war Henry Stimson to Managua as his personal representative to negotiate a settlement. Though the lengthy and acrimonious discussions nearly broke down several times, Stimson finally hammered out a settlement by threatening to unleash the marines against anyone who refused to sign. (Since Stimson spoke no Spanish, he employed an interpreter named Anastasio Somoza Garcia, a Liberal general and future dictator who had learned English while attending business school in Philadelphia.) Stimson's plan permitted the Liberals, who had been winning the civil war, to retain control of six provinces until new national elections—supervised by the United States—could be held in 1928. The United States also promised to organize and train a purportedly nonpolitical police force, the National Guard, which could preserve order after the marines departed. Everyone in both camps agreed to the compromise, save for a stubborn thirty-two-year-old Liberal general named Augusto Sandino, who took thirty loyal men and retreated to the northern mountains to continue the fight.

At this point, Sandino's outrage was directed less against the Americans than his Liberal colleagues, whom he accused of selling out to the despised Conservatives; in fact, he reportedly implored the American marine commander to install an interim U.S. military regime to govern Nicaragua until the election. But because he opposed the American-inspired settlement, the marines—accompanied by an ineffectual unit of the fledgling Nicaraguan National Guard—launched an assault upon Sandino's isolated mountain fortress of El Chipote in May 1927. Sandino lost that battle, due to the incontrovertible fact that the marines possessed dive-bombing airplanes and he did not, but he refused to surrender, and after several more inconclusive battles in the summer and autumn of 1927, he began to reconsider his original willingness to entrust his country's fortunes to the representatives of American democracy. Soon General Sandino was issuing blustering, radical anti-imperialist proclamations at every opportunity, insisting, "I will not abandon my mountains while even one Gringo remains in Nicaragua; I will not abandon my struggle as long as my people are denied even one right. My cause is the cause of my people, the cause of America, the cause of all oppressed peoples."

Leftist intellectuals in Latin America and the United States lionized Sandino as a romantic symbol of popular revolution, despite the fact that he and his men frequently acted more like bandits, thieves, and murderers than idealistic, socialist saints. The Sandinistas employed the tactics of modern guerrilla fighters, living off the land for greater mobility, traveling light, and striking from ambush with massed forces that dispersed after every attack. Sandino sought to control one area at a time, convincing the local populace that while he and his men might retreat in the face of superior force, they would return after the foreign invaders had gone. It was a formidable combination of intimidation and fervent appeals to nationalist pride.

Sandino himself impressed foreign visitors as an almost reluctant hero who alternated between moods of swaggering bravado and deep melancholy. He was a remarkably ordinary looking man, slight, dark-haired, with more Indian than European blood; but there was a disquieting intensity about his presence that invariably impressed strangers when they saw him for the first time. "His prematurely lined face reflected an expression so peculiarly his own, somewhere between profound reflection and intimate sadness," wrote a sympathetic Basque journalist. "More than on the privation-worn soldiers who passed before him, his attention seemed to be fixed on something remote and invisible. There was about him none of the fierce air of a battle-hardened soldier with nerves on edge from war's dangers and inevitable cruelties. Rather was it the face of a man born to think and fantasize, a spiritual man cast by fate in the role of ringleader."

To Nicaraguan President Jose Maria Moncada, however, Sandino was a lunatic and a traitor. Moncada, formerly the foremost commander of the Liberal armies, had won the American-supervised election of November 4, 1928. While it was true, as his supporters claimed, that the people of Nicaragua (about three-fourths of whom were illiterate) had been allowed to cast their ballots free from coercion or threats of violence, it was also true that both the Liberals and Conservatives had openly expressed their approval of the American military presence in Nicaragua, while the Nationalists—the only party to openly condemn American intervention— had not been allowed to place their candidates on the ballot. After the election, Coolidge sent his congratulations to Moncada for returning stability to the strife-torn nation; Sandino's mother sent her son a letter begging him to give up his hopeless fight; and the commander of the American marine contingent reported from brigade headquarters that "the entire country is in the most peaceful state it has ever been, not withstanding some local rumors and reports to the contrary."

Predictably, Sandino condemned Moncada's election as a contemptible farce, and renewed his insistence upon the immediate American military evacuation of Nicaragua. "Patriotism compels me to repel force by force," he wrote in a defiant message to the American marine commanders on January 1, 1929, "and I must absolutely reject any interference by your Government in the internal affairs of our country and demonstrate that the sovereignty of a people cannot be discussed, but only defended by arms in my hand. . . . To arrive at an effective peace settlement, we propose as the first condition that it is indispensable that the American forces withdraw from our country." The marines responded by chasing Sandino farther into the jungle, reporting every week that his followers were deserting him in droves; in fact, the alleged desertions far outnumbered the total number of men Sandino ever commanded.

Privately, a marine lieutenant confided that "by the beginning of 1929 it was becoming more and more evident that the marines in Nicaragua had been called upon to perform an impossible task." They were expected to maintain order, he complained, without any effective control over the civilian population: "Neither the people nor their officials stood behind the marines in their attempt to put down lawlessness. . . . Notwithstanding all of their vigorous efforts, officers conducting the campaign were practically unanimous in the opinion that the military situation had reached a stalemate. So long as the people would not assist the marines, the bandits could continue to operate in small groups and carry on their depredations in spite of everything the marines could do." And marine commander Oliver Floyd reported bluntly to his superiors that

> further progress will be accomplished only as follows under present conditions:
> a. I will have to wage a real blood and thunder campaign and I will have casualties every day.
> b. I will be involved in a small real war.
> c. These people will shoot it out with small arms opposition for at least a while.
> d. All people encountered are unquestionably strong for Sandino.

So the bloody fighting continued. On January 21, three marines were butchered in a Sandinista ambush. Government forces responded by capturing one of Sandino's top lieutenants; the prisoner was then summarily executed by a squad of National Guard volunteers supervised by an American officer. In Washington, a growing number of senators began to wonder whether the price of American involvement in Nicaragua had not already become too dear.

For the first two weeks following his return to the United States, Hoover sat in a suite in the Mayflower Hotel in Washington and endured a grueling round of conferences with Republican leaders and job seekers. Speculation in the press centered around his prospective cabinet choices. The odds-on choice for secretary of state appeared to be Dwight Morrow, the erstwhile Amherst classmate of Calvin Coolidge who had resigned his position as a partner in J. P. Morgan's Wall Street firm to serve as Coolidge's ambassador to Mexico; in less than two years, Morrow had earned almost universal admiration for his diplomatic prowess in easing the tensions that had arisen from the Mexican government's confiscation of the lands of American oil companies. Although there was less of a clear-cut favorite for the second most important cabinet job as head of the Department of Justice, Hoover was under considerable pressure to select William J. "Wild Bill" Donovan, the able assistant attorney general who had first captured the public's imagination as a flamboyant army commander in the Great War. But Hoover decided to pass over both men; his cabinet would have no strong personalities to challenge his own dominance.

Coolidge, meanwhile, was amusing himself in his last months in office by playing practical jokes on the Secret Service. One sunny January afternoon, the President crept up to the north portico and pressed the bell that allowed the guard on patrol duty to summon the full company of White House Secret Service men in case of emergency. Then Coolidge scampered away and hid. When the guards arrived, they asked the patrolman on duty why he had pressed the button; mystified, he naturally denied any knowledge of what had happened. When everyone departed, Coolidge emerged and pressed the bell again, and then again ran away. After several repeat performances, the Secret Service guards finally realized who the culprit was, and so they installed another emergency buzzer and refused to tell the President where they put it.

Coolidge took time out from these adolescent pranks on January 10 to meet with Owen D. Young, the chairman of General Electric Corporation, who had been chosen to head the American delegation to the international conference of financial experts gathering in Paris to discuss the tangled questions of German reparations and Allied war debts. In a singularly unhelpful but not uncharacteristic discussion, Coolidge informed Young that the U.S. government intended to maintain "a detached position" on the reparations problem and encourage the European statesmen to work out a solution by themselves, as if the United States did not have a vital stake in the outcome of the negotiations.

Fortunately, Coolidge's stricture was not binding on Young, since he would be attending the negotiations at the request of the European governments, and as a private citizen rather than an official representative of the American government. During the previous reparations conference which had fashioned the Dawes Plan in 1924, Young had impressed his European colleagues with his impartial goodwill and his unerring grasp of complex financial and diplomatic issues; as Dawes readily admitted, the reparations settlement that emanated from that conference rightly should have been named the Young Plan, in recognition of his partner's role in steering the negotiations to a successful conclusion. Young himself had little desire to return to Paris in 1929 to take up the burden again, but he reluctantly accepted the challenge. "I did everything in my power to escape this job both for personal and business reasons but it seemed inevitable," Young wrote to a colleague at General Electric in January; and, to a friend of his daughter: "The bloom is off the rose on this reparations business for me so I am approaching it in the spirit of a disagreeable thing to be done rather than with the anticipation of a new experience."

A tall, lanky man with thinning black hair parted in the middle and the hollow, deep-set eyes of an ascetic, Young was temperamentally incapable of refusing an appeal to his conscience or sense of duty. More than any other prominent American businessman of the era, Owen D. Young devoutly believed and acted on the conviction that business leadership imposed certain social and moral obligations upon corporate executives—a notion strikingly similar to the concept of Christian stewardship to which Franklin D. Roosevelt pledged allegiance. (Both men were also Democrats.) The only child of deeply religious parents of Dutch and German descent, Young was born in 1874—the same year as Herbert Hoover—and grew up on a farm near the town of Van Hornesville in Otsego County, just south of the Mohawk River in central New York State. At an early age, his parents brought him into the faith of the Universalist church, a humanist sect that preached the brotherhood of man, a wide-ranging intellectual freedom, the paramount virtue of human kindness, and strict standards of social accountability.

These were doctrines Young sought to keep firmly in mind when he embarked upon a career as an attorney, first as a member of a small firm specializing in utility and electric power cases, and, after 1913, as vice-president and chief counsel of the General Electric Company. In 1919, at the end of the Great War, President Wilson and his ambitious assistant secretary of the navy, Franklin Delano Roosevelt, decided that the commercial and military interests of the United States required the establishment of "an American-owned, world-wide radio-operating company" to coordinate the nation's research and development of wireless communications technology. (The navy's interest stemmed from the fact that radio communications at that time were employed primarily between ships at sea and transmission stations on land.) To efficiently mobilize the nation's resources and avert American dependence on British-dominated cable communications, Roosevelt encouraged the formation of a private corporation that would share access to some of the navy's wireless patent rights; since General Electric also held certain patents in this area, nothing seemed more natural than the active cooperation of G.E. and the federal government in the formation of the Radio Corporation of America in October 1919. To avoid violating antitrust regulations, RCA was not established as a subsidiary of General Electric, but G.E. was a major shareholder in the new venture right from the start, and Owen Young became the fledgling corporation's first chairman.

Young also ascended to the chairmanship of General Electric in 1922 and continued to hold both positions simultaneously for the next decade. With the active cooperation of G.E. president Gerard Swope, brother of New York *World* editor and dedicated stock speculator Herbert Bayard

Swope, Young moved to put General Electric in the forefront of a revolution in labor-management relations by implementing an expanded program of benefits for the corporation's employees and granting workers what he called a "cultural wage" (as opposed to the traditional "living wage") that purportedly permitted them to more fully realize their human potential. He further enhanced his image as a visionary and unorthodox member of the business community by openly calling for the adoption of draconian inheritance tax laws, recommending close cooperation between the public and private sectors in the generation and distribution of water power (a highly controversial issue in New York state politics in the 1920s), and making statements that struck some observers as downright socialistic. "I hope the day may come when these great business organizations will truly belong to the men who are giving their lives and their efforts to them, I care not in what capacity," he declared in 1927. "Then they will use capital as a tool and they will all be interested in working it to the highest economic advantage. . . . Then, in a word, men will be as free in cooperative undertakings and subject only to the same limitations and chances as men in individual businesses. Then we shall have no hired men."

As director and then deputy governor of the Federal Reserve Bank of New York, Young sought to turn even something so seemingly straightforward and prosaic as the formulation of the bank's interest rate into an exercise in moral philosophy. "The bank rate," he explained, "affects credit; increases or diminishes the value of money; gives every aged person dependent upon his savings more or less of good things to eat. That is why it is a high moral responsibility to fix the bank rate."

Young's well-advertised sense of social responsibility, the remarkable growth and profitability of both G.E. and RCA under his leadership, and his crucial role in forging the Dawes reparations compromise in 1924 vaulted him into serious consideration as a viable Democratic political candidate. In 1926, Eleanor Roosevelt pressed him unsuccessfully to run for the United States Senate, and in 1928 his name surfaced as a possible successor to Al Smith in the executive mansion in Albany. Young at once squelched all such speculation. With his reputation intact, his ambitions largely achieved, and his future financially secure—his salary and dividends from G.E. and RCA stock earned him approximately $375,000 per year, much of which he spent acquiring rare first editions for his library and raising prize Holstein cattle on his Van Hornesville farm—Young truly had no wish to hold public office or return to Paris to plunge into the maelstrom of Continental jealousies once again. And with equal candor Coolidge attempted to discourage his appointment as one of the American delegates to the financiers' conference, fearing that the wily Europeans would make Young chairman of the assembly and thus draw the United States further into the snarled reparations controversy. But under intense pressure from Treasury Secretary Mellon, the Allied nations (Britain, France, Italy, Belgium, and Japan), and the German government, and most of all the dictates of his own conscience, Young reluctantly consented to undertake the assignment.

On January 19, British ambassador Sir Esme Howard formally extended the conference invitation to Young amid the solemn and secluded splendor of the Pierpont Morgan Library on Murray Hill, just east of Madison Avenue. Here the blazing hearth was flanked by ancient columns of lapis lazuli, and the walls tiered with priceless manuscripts from medieval monasteries, Byzantine physicians, and ancient Arab scholars; on the desk in Morgan's library sat a paperweight made of pure gold. And here John Pierpont Morgan, Jr., the most powerful financier in America, accepted Ambassador Howard's invitation to serve as Young's colleague at the reparations conference. The formalities took just three minutes; for the rest of the evening, the men sat around discussing the esoteric virtues and values of fine, rare books.

Morgan's decision to join Young at the proceedings at Paris portended a far greater American involvement than Coolidge might have preferred, for one of the conference's main tasks would be to commercialize the German government's debt; that is, to transform it into a private debt by selling German bonds to foreign bankers. In any such endeavor, the active cooperation of the House of Morgan—whose vast prestige and immense resources gave it access to a larger pool of capital than any other private investment banking firm in the world—would be of incalculable value. So powerful was the Morgan firm that the granite building that housed its offices at the corner of Wall Street and Broad, directly across from the stock exchange, was known simply as "the Corner," and when people referred to the Morgan partners, they spoke in hushed, awestricken tones and used the generic pronoun "they"—everyone knew who "they" were. "Here," said one American newspaper upon learning of Morgan's selection as a conference delegate, "is the ace of spades himself."

Everything about the son of the legendary Pierpont Morgan—his bluff manner and melodramatic gestures, his imposing physique and arrogant dignity, his unshakable faith in the moral supremacy of the Morgan way of life, even his round, studiously cultured English accent—seemed larger than life to his contemporaries in the 1920s. Dwight Morrow's daughter Anne first encountered the imperious Morgan presence in 1926 at the great man's British estate, Wall Hall, in Hartfordshire: "He greeted us at the door: a great, massive, overpowering sort of man. Shaggy eyebrows, almost a fierce face. A hearty and generous host—very much a host.

We walked across the lawn, down walks and through the garden. He took great pride in it all and showed it off with a kind of formal playfulness. . . . Then tea on the lawn. I felt quite overawed, and even Tom [Cochran] and Daddy were a little subdued, not exactly at their ease. Just subdued a little, not in high spirits." Yet by the end of the visit, Anne was moved to remark on the vulnerable, human side of Morgan, whose wife had died suddenly a few months earlier. "The atmosphere, although of perfect comfort, luxury, is somehow cold and lonely—empty," she wrote in her diary. "He must be very lonely."

Few other people felt J. P. Morgan, Jr. ("Oh hell, call me Jack"), needed their sympathy. Educated at St. Paul's and Harvard, he had been received into the Morgan partnership in 1892, and served as the firm's British representative from 1896 to 1906. From that time on, he considered Britain his spiritual home; he was far more comfortable shooting grouse with the Prince of Wales on the Scottish moors, or sailing on his magnificent yacht with the archbishop of Canterbury, or watching the races at Ascot from the royal box, than attending baseball games or discussing the sordid realities of American politics. Lewis L. Strauss, who later became a partner in the rival investment firm of Kuhn, Loeb and Company, recalled his first glimpse of Jack Morgan when the financier visited Richmond, Virginia: "For that brief visit, he had taken one of the stately houses of the city, staffed it, brought down his own transportation—a barouche and horses, complete with top-hatted coachman and footman on the box. I remember standing goggle-eyed with a crowd of other small boys along the curb across Franklin Street to see the great man arrive and depart, with the footman hopping down to open the carriage door for him and unfold the little iron steps." Morgan would have made a wonderful eighteenth-century English country squire, except for the fact that he was also something of a prude and just a mite too fastidious. "I do like girls to be ladylike," he confided to his mother while he was in college, and the violent world of intercollegiate football struck him as hopelessly vulgar and barbaric. When Harvard asked him for a contribution to its athletic program, Morgan brusquely replied, "I cannot too emphatically say that nothing would induce me in any circumstances to do anything that would further the game of football in any manner. I have a complete and supreme dislike for the game in every aspect, and, had I any power in that direction, I should use whatever I had to stop the game being played at all as being (1st) immoral, (2nd) dangerous, (3rd) brutal."

When his father, Pierpont Morgan the elder, died in Rome in 1913, Jack inherited the lion's share of an estate valued at $77.5 million, along with the leadership of J.P. Morgan and Company. He was the quintessential puritan man of business, sanctimonious and rigidly scrupulous—always fair but never overly generous—in his dealings with God and his fellow man. He studied the Bible almost every day, and delighted in studding his conversations with obscure scriptural allusions. His oft-repeated motto was "Do your work; be honest; keep your word; help when you can; be fair; be a good straight fellow." "It would be difficult to think of Mr. Morgan as being involved in anything of a petty nature," acknowledged a contemporary observer who otherwise had little love for the House of Morgan. "The tricks and equivocations that have been employed too often by some of the gentry of the financial world are foreign to his character. His personal probity is above question."

So were his distasteful attitudes toward Jews and Roman Catholics (although he did make an exception in the case of his personal friend, Pope Pius XI). He did not hate these unfortunate creatures; he simply despised them, and he did not want them crawling around him. Not a single member of either untouchable group had ever been a partner in that exclusively Anglo-Saxon, Protestant gentleman's club known as J.P. Morgan and Company. He opposed their appointment to the board of overseers of Harvard University, and "the Morgan" (as his family knew him) preferred not to have any of them on board the same ship during his frequent journeys across the Atlantic. Nor were these his only prejudices; he once referred to investigative attorney Ferdinand Pecora of New York as a "dirty little wop," and he was only slightly more charitable toward the scurrilous ranks of newspaper photographers and reporters. He permitted none of his partners (whom he could dismiss at will) or his employees to obtain a divorce. But his bigotry, though reprehensible, was not uncharacteristic of his social class in the early decades of the twentieth century, and it certainly paled in comparison with the rabid anti-Semitism of Henry Ford, who swore that Morgan, as an international banker, was dominated by Jewish interests, and that Jack had some of those "dark-skinned fellows with the big noses" hidden in an upstairs enclave at Morgan and Company's offices at 23 Wall Street. (Incidentally, Ford also numbered his fellow automaker William Durant among the "kosher robber barons" of Wall Street, ostensibly because Durant took such an unmitigated delight in financial operations.)

Though Ford's charge was ludicrous, it was true that Morgan had guided his firm into the troubled waters of international finance where his father—who always focused his attention on the course of domestic American economic affairs—had feared to tread. Several hours after Great Britain entered the war against Germany in August 1914, the British ambassador in Washington telephoned Jack Morgan and requested a meeting. By the time the ambassador walked out of the famous library on Murray Hill, Morgan had pledged the full power and force of his firm unequivocally to the British cause. In typical Morgan fashion, the gentleman's agreement was sealed with a word and a handshake; no legal documents were signed until many months had passed and millions of dollars had changed hands. The following year, Morgan and Company floated loans totaling $500 million for the Allied cause. In the postwar decade, Morgan helped arrange a $200 million loan for Germany as part of the Dawes agreement, and assisted both Britain's Conservative government and Italy's Fascist regime in their quest to stabilize their respective national currencies and return to the gold standard. Much to Coolidge's disgust, Morgan was a firm believer in the forgiveness of Allied war debts to the United States. "Those debts should be canceled," he once explained:

> As a practical proposition they can never be paid, but they should be canceled for another reason. This money was loaned our allies after we entered the war, at which moment we pledged all our strength and resources to winning it. When we entered the war in April 1917, we could not send soldiers because we did not have them ready. We sent dollars in the form of loans to our allies. While we were sending dollars, our allies were sending soldiers until ours got there. I look upon these loans as being the same sort of contribution to victory as our sending 2,000,000 troops.

No wonder the French press welcomed his appointment to the Paris reparations conference. "Of all American business men and bankers, Owen D. Young and J. P. Morgan are considered to be the most favorably disposed toward Europe," declared the columnist "Pertinax" in an editorial in the *Echo de Paris.*

But as Morgan prepared to accompany Young to Europe, his firm was starting to drift in a new and far more dangerous direction at home. Although Morgan and his partners dominated the boards of directors of some of the largest corporations in the United States—eighteen Morgan partners held ninety-nine directorships in seventy-two corporations worth approximately $20 billion, and Morgan himself served as chairman of the board of U.S. Steel—and though Charles Mitchell's National City Bank was one of Morgan's leading business allies, Morgan and Company had long disdained active participation in the slightly tainted world of speculation and stock manipulation; its Olympian attitude was aptly symbolized by Jack's adamant refusal to sully himself by ever setting foot onto the floor of the New York Stock Exchange. In the early winter of 1929, however, the firm agreed to distribute $180 million in debentures and 4.5 million shares of common stock in the Allegheny Corporation, a dangerously leveraged holding company formed by the Van Sweringen brothers, a high-rolling pair of adventurers from Cleveland whose chronic indebtedness and highly speculative ventures in railroad properties were notorious even in the amoral atmosphere of Wall Street in the late 1920s. In return for their assistance, the Morgan partners received 250,000 shares of Allegheny stock at $20 per share; some they kept, and some they offered to their "preferred customers," an exclusive group that included Coolidge, Raskob, Owen Young, Charles Lindbergh, Bernard Baruch, former president of the New York Stock Exchange Richard Whitney, and Senator William G. McAdoo. ("Many thanks for your trouble and for so kindly remembering me," wrote Raskob from his winter home in Palm Beach as he sent Morgan and Company his check for $40,000 worth of Allegheny stock at the bargain price. "I appreciate deeply the many courtesies shown me by you and your partners, and sincerely hope the future holds opportunities for me to reciprocate.") The remaining shares of Allegheny stock opened on the market at $37, and soon reached a peak of $56. Not even the venerable headquarters of the old-stock financial gentry in America could resist the lure of the Hoover bull market.

At the end of January, Will Rogers gave Young and Morgan an appropriate send-off to the Paris conference: "We are loaning Europe two financiers to show 'em how to pay each other off without any money," he said, "by just reorganizing and issuing more stock like we do." Shortly before midnight on the evening of February 1, Owen Young and his team of financial experts and advisers gave reporters a final brief statement before disappearing into their staterooms on the luxury ocean liner *Aquitania* as the ship prepared to depart New York harbor for Cherbourg. Protected by several bodyguards from his firm, the publicity-shy Morgan evaded photographers by boarding via his customary private gangplank that led to an open port low on the *Aquitania*'s side. Young told the press he expected to be gone for two months, or ninety days at the most. He would not return to the United States until the middle of June, and by then he seemed to have aged five years.

Britain welcomed 1929 with solemn celebrations and an ominous sense of foreboding. Newspaper reports told the people that their king was dying. In the late autumn of 1928, George V, then sixty-three years old, had contracted streptococcal septicemia, which rapidly developed into a case of severe toxemia and a generalized infection of the blood; he endured periods of delirium, labored breathing, and exhaustion, and on December 12 his temperature suddenly rose precipitously and his skin turned blue from lack of oxygen. As a last resort, one of his physicians plunged a needle into the King's chest and fortuitously struck a pocket of pus and drained off the poison. From that time on, recovery continued through an irregular series of advances and declines. By New Year's Eve, however, the King was by no means out of danger, and so a respectful crowd of Londoners—attired in evening clothes and fancy costumes on their way to or from the holiday revelries—gathered outside Buckingham Palace shortly before midnight. As Big Ben chimed in 1929, they sang together "God Save the King" in subdued tones, and "Auld Lang Syne," and then they went away.

Loyal subjects inundated the royal court with their favorite patent medicines, until the palace was nearly buried under an avalanche of bottles of multicolored liquids, jars of chest paste made from flour and fruits, and centuries-old protective amulets. One elderly woman sent a jar containing a mixture of linseed, aromatic herbs, and toad's blood that she had religiously stirred for twelve hours in accordance with strict instructions handed down by her great-great-grandmother. Another old lady sent a pair of doves in a wooden cage for the King's bedroom because, she said, "their breathing purifies the air."

All of these home remedies were properly disposed of (or, in the case of the doves, released into the garden), but there was another sort of medicine that seemed to work wonders. Although most Englishmen were unaware of it at the time, King George's recovery was hastened immeasurably by his manifest unwillingness to leave the British Empire in the demonstrably irresponsible hands of his eldest son, with whom he had never enjoyed particularly close relations. When the King first fell seriously ill, the cabinet had summoned the heir to the throne—Jack Morgan's good friend Edward, Prince of Wales—to return to England from a safari in East Africa, where he had been having a smashing good time playing golf, entertaining beautiful women (some of them married, though he had not yet met Wallis Simpson), and shooting elephants. Prime Minister Stanley Baldwin met the young man at Southampton and escorted him to London; when they arrived at Buckingham Palace, Baldwin recalled that the prince "was told that he might not on any account go *near* his father, who was, we all thought, near death, for at least 48 hours. He simply took no notice, damned everybody and marched in. The old King, who had for nearly a week been practically unconscious, just opened half an eye, looked up at him and said: 'Damn you, what the devil are you doing here?' And from that moment on he turned the corner and began rapidly to get better. It was exactly like the scene in 'Henry IV' when Prince Henry tries on the crown."

More than a few Britons were beginning to wonder whether the Prince of Wales (whom they called "the young guv'nor") would ever grow up. He frequently performed his official duties with a scowl (people spoke of his "grey, sullen visage") and ill grace; sometimes he refused to perform them at all, with no apologies or excuses. He freely indulged his passions for hunting, jazz, nightclubs, and steeplechasing with abandon, though his family forced him to give up riding while the King was seriously ill. (Though he was not a poor horseman, the prince often rode his mounts so violently that horse and rider both ended up on the ground far too often for either's well-being.) "There is a feeling that there is a lack of seriousness, which, excusable and even natural to healthy youth, is disquieting in the mature man," noted British journalist and historian A. G. Gardiner. "This implies no disapproval of the Prince's love of sport, of fun and of innocent amusement. Nor does it imply a demand that the heir to the throne should have intellectual tastes that nature has not endowed him with. . . . But it does mean that the public would be relieved to read a little less in the encomiums of the Press about the jazz drum and the banjo side of the Prince's life."

Only in two areas did he evince serious interest in public affairs: the plight of his fellow ex-servicemen, many of whom had returned to find the promise of "a land fit for heroes" a cruel sham, and the distress of the unemployed, whose numbers had grown alarmingly in the later months of 1928. "Unemployment is not yet, but bids fair to be, the greatest of British industries," the *Manchester Guardian* had warned in November. By the end of the old year, 1.2 million Britons were out of work; the national unemployment average had reached 12.2 percent, though in Wales and the northern counties the number was far higher, surpassing 60 percent in some ravaged districts. The hellish cost of four and a half years of war had been far greater than anyone had anticipated, and ever since the conflict ended, practically the entire British economy had been drifting aimlessly through the doldrums. The outlook was bleakest in the stagnant basic industries: textiles, coal, shipbuilding, and iron and steel. British exports had fallen off drastically since 1920, as a result of the combined influence of antediluvian management techniques, increased competition from abroad (including emerging industrial nations such as Egypt and India, where wages were drastically lower), and the Baldwin government's ill-advised return to the gold standard in 1925, a rash move that deflated the pound and priced British exports out of many foreign markets. Income in Great Britain was even more poorly distributed than in the United States: 1 percent of the population owned nearly two-thirds of the national wealth. The once-robust British labor movement had been demoralized by the collapse of the General Strike of 1926 and the single-minded determination of employers to reduce wages throughout the 1920s, and as the level of unemployment rose inexorably, few workers cared to risk their jobs by striking for improved conditions. Agriculture remained depressed for the entire postwar decade, reviving the pre-1914 movement of farm workers to London and the other cities of the south, where the presence of more technologically advanced industries kept unemployment in the relatively tolerable range of 5 to 7 percent. In a very real economic sense, England already was breaking into two separate nations: the prosperous southern counties and the perennially depressed north country.

London had lost her position of international financial preeminence to Wall Street during the war, and in 1929 the British government still owed the United States the upsetting sum of over $4 billion in war debts, which translated into interest payments that exceeded £30,000 per year. Although the London stock exchange had remained relatively stable since 1925, the British financial community was disturbed by the increasing outflow of gold from the Bank of England to the United States; to no one's surprise, much of the precious metal was headed directly for Wall Street to fund high-profit, speculative ventures in the Coolidge-Hoover bull market. "While Wall Street continues to boom," mourned the *Manchester Guardian,* "there can be no assurance that the loss of gold may not become so large that the authorities may deem it prudent to raise the Bank [interest] rate." And any decision by the Bank of England to increase the cost of money was, of course, likely to depress British industry still further.

Prime Minister Baldwin and his chancellor of the Exchequer, Winston Spencer Churchill (who freely admitted when he took the job that he was no financial expert), tried to allay the nation's concern by explaining patiently that the British economy was undergoing a necessary, albeit painful period of reconstruction and readjustment. But they and their Conservative colleagues in the cabinet and the Commons steadfastly refused to acknowledge the possibility that the national government was qualified to interfere in the impersonal and impenetrable workings of the normal business cycle. In an address to the Manchester Chamber of Commerce on January 21, 1929, Churchill acknowledged that he was "strongly of the opinion that it was no use exaggerating what Governments could do to help commercial and industrial development. They could do a great deal to hinder and hamper, but to help and foster was most difficult and doubtful." "Why should we blame one another," the chancellor asked the House on another occasion, during an emotional debate on the distressing unemployment figures, "for the appalling conditions which prevail in the coalfields?"

The answer to Churchill's characteristically flip query lay in the heartbreaking misery of Britain's coalfields. More than a quarter of the nation's unemployed were miners, many of whom had been out of work for three years or more. They had long ago exhausted their meager savings and the dole from government benefits and the miners' union funds; often they had sold nearly all their furniture to purchase food, and by the winter of

1929 many were wholly dependent upon charity or parish relief. The miners were so destitute that there was not even a spark of revolution left in them. "Most of these people have not had a stitch of new clothing or a new pair of shoes since the General Strike," remarked a schoolteacher in the Rhondda Valley in eastern Wales. "Maybe they listened a bit to the Bolshevik then, but that's all over now. . . . There's no fight left in any of them. All they want is a chance to work so they can eat. . . . Nobody steals around here. There's nothing to steal. Half the people haven't a table or a chair—had to sell them to buy bread and tea."

On January 28, the Prince of Wales left London on the night express to begin a three-day tour of the north country to publicize the distress of the coalfield villages. It was wretched weather for a journey; when the prince emerged from his sleeping car at Newcastle-on-Tyne the following morning, he stepped into slush that stood several inches deep along the roadway. But he pressed on, slogging through the ice and mud in his galoshes, fortified against the cold by a gray overcoat, a great black ulster with an astrakhan collar, and a black bowler perched precariously on his head. At the first village on his list, he saw children with deathly pale skin and legs as thin as sticks, and running sores on their faces from malnutrition and the cold. The prince looked into the cottage of a miner who had written to tell him of the misery in this town; as he entered, he saw a gray-haired woman lying motionless on a bed, surrounded by weeping children. It was the wife of the miner—his late wife, for she had died just hours before, and her husband had gone to fetch a coffin. "Cheer up," the prince said to the bereaved children, "cheer up."

He sloshed through the gathering crowd to his waiting limousine and sped toward the next hamlet. In Northumberland, where unemployment ranged as high as 70 percent in some areas, he saw miners' families living in hovels that had been condemned as unsanitary years before, ramshackle piles of dirty brick surrounded by a sea of mud and refuse. He met a widower with eight children living in one room where the only furniture was a single bed; the sole employed member of the family was a fifteen-year-old boy whose boots were falling to pieces. When the prince asked him how he managed to work in boots such as those, the boy replied that he had no choice; his family had to spend every penny he earned for food. "We have not been able to buy clothes or boots for many a long day," he said. The prince met a veteran of the Great War who had been gassed and had not held a steady job for five years. "Aa want a job," he kept repeating over and over again to the royal visitor. The prince went into the home of a miner who was going blind and whose wife had been crippled in an accident, and heard how they had just received an eviction notice that would be carried out in three weeks. In another town, where the dilapidated cottages reminded one witness of a shell-ravaged French village on the western front, a woman told the prince, "There's many a time now when we have nothing to eat. We have gone days without anything to eat. The children sometimes have to go to school with half a slice of bread, and sometimes not that."

One elderly housewife startled the prince by asking, "How is your dad, sir?" "He is getting on as well as can be expected," he replied. "Thank you very much for your kind inquiry." "I do hope he will soon be all right," she said. "Many of us have sent up our prayers for him and the Queen in these dark days."

By the third day, the magnitude of the disaster had begun to make an impression on the prince. He asked to see the books and pay sheets of several mine owners, and appeared stunned to learn that a team of four able-bodied men, working five shifts, received only 29 shillings at the end of the week.

"For each man, surely!" he exclaimed, incredulous.

"No, for all four," they told him.

"What causes all this?" he asked.

"Management."

"Bad management?"

"No, just hard management."

At the end of the tour, reporters noticed that the young man who had left London so gay had a pale and haunted look about him. "This is ghastly," he kept repeating to his aide. "Positively damnable . . . enough to chill the blood. I never thought things were so bad. A ghastly mess."

"I have been deeply touched at what I have seen," he announced to the press, "the bravery and patience and hopes of all those poor people. It is very difficult to know what to do to solve this most pressing problem. I am sure things will be righted, but I am afraid it must take time." Then the prince hopped aboard a local train for his favorite hunting center of Melton Mowbray, and the next day he seemed like his old carefree self again.

But Baldwin's government could not escape the problem so easily, especially after the prince's visit had thrown an unwelcome spotlight of publicity upon the heartbreaking poverty. Baldwin's cabinet, distinguished by the brilliant talents of the Chamberlain brothers (Austen and Neville), Winston Churchill, Lord Birkenhead, and Leo Amery, had governed Britain for four years, ever since the October 1924 general election forced by the collapse of the tenuous alliance between the Labour party (led by Sir Ramsay MacDonald) and the Liberals (led after a fashion by Sir Herbert Asquith). Rebounding from their short-lived postwar decline, the Conservatives had captured 419 seats in the Commons to Labour's 151 and the fading Liberal party's 40. But between 1925 and 1929, Baldwin's government had signally failed to solve the nagging problem of chronic unemployment—the so-called "intractable million"—or provide any sort of inspiring vision of the future. Former supporters who had expected Baldwin to lead the nation into a new era of prosperity were bitterly disappointed by the reality of British life in the winter of 1929. "A ruling class living on dividends, masses of the people on the dole, and a Government trying to maintain an uneasy status quo," wrote one disillusioned critic, "is a picture which fills thinking people with despair."

The government's foes were even less charitable. In a comprehensive indictment of the "colossal failure" of Baldwin's cabinet to remedy any of the nation's most pressing ills, Liberal leader Sir Herbert Samuel charged that "the complacency of the present Government in face of the poverty of its achievement is remarkable." Samuel sarcastically likened Baldwin to Mr. Pecksniff's unfortunate horse in Dickens' comic novel *Martin Chuzzlewit:* "He was full of promise, but of no performance. He was always, in a manner, going to go and never going. . . . He was a kind of animal who infused into the breasts of strangers a lively sense of hope, and possessed all those who knew him better with a grim despair."

Since the government had called a general election for May 1929, the Conservative party badly needed some bold initiative—and needed it quickly—to capture the voters' imagination. But the best it could offer was Churchill's dull, plodding call to duty: "We have to march forward steadily and steadfastly, along the highway. It may be dusty, it may be stony, it may be dull; it is certainly uphill all the way, but to leave it is only to flounder in the quagmires of delusion and have the coat torn off your back by the brambles of waste." By adopting the stodgy electioneering slogan of "Safety First," the party practically ensured its own defeat. "There is no non-partisan indignation against the government," noted J. L. Garvin, editor of the *Sunday Observer,* as the electoral campaign got under way in earnest in February. "The peril to Ministers—and it is a very real one—is of quite another kind. They arouse no enthusiasm. They are regarded in an odd mood of benevolent boredom. Another four years of them on similar terms does not appear to the plain man a very appetizing prospect. . . . The government and their party seem to have resolved themselves into a noble order of ostriches."

One influential Conservative faction suggested that Baldwin rally the electorate behind some bold imperial initiative, but the cabinet already had enough on its plate trying to hold together the empire as it was. Recently there had been rumblings of discontent from India, where the saintly Mohandas K. Gandhi was returning to politics after an absence of seven years. In 1922, Gandhi had been sentenced to six years' imprison-

ment by a British court for writing a series of purportedly seditious articles; released prematurely in 1924 because of ill health, the *mahatma*
(great soul) had spent most of the next four years at his ashram near
Ahmadabad, fasting to purify his body and spirit, writing articles to spread
his gospel of a united and casteless India, and spinning and weaving rough
native khaddar cloth to dramatize the virtues of Indian self-sufficiency.

Gandhi returned to the struggle for Indian independence at the request of Motilal Nehru, president of the Congress party, easily the largest
and most influential native political organization in India. Angered by
incontrovertible evidence that the Baldwin government had absolutely no
intention of granting even the limited concession of dominion status to
India in the foreseeable future (Lord Birkenhead, secretary of state for
India, left no doubt that he considered it "frankly inconceivable that India
will ever be fit for Dominion self-government"), Nehru had devised a
seven-point proposal for a new constitution for India. Because Nehru's
plan called for the immediate bestowal of dominion status, it was far too
radical for British opinion; but because it temporarily abandoned the goal
of full independence, it came under fire from radicals—including Motilal's
son, the Cambridge-educated and wholeheartedly socialist Jawaharlal
Nehru—at the annual convention of the All-India National Congress in
Calcutta in December 1928. And, most ominously, because the Nehru
plan failed to reserve a certain minimum number of seats in the Indian
legislature for minority religious groups, Moslem leaders stormed out of
the convention, vowing never again to participate in a unified nationalist
movement.

Gandhi arrived at the Congress meeting on December 31. Contemptuously dismissed by Winston Churchill as a half-naked, seditious fakir, the
frail, bespectacled mahatma was dwarfed by the massive figure and florid
oratory of Motilal Nehru as the two men stood together on the platform.
The impression of vulnerability was strengthened when the loudspeakers
in the hall failed just as Gandhi began his speech in a thin, almost inaudible
voice. But those near the platform could hear the words of the most
revered man in India: "I have got full faith. If you will follow me and follow
the programme I have suggested honestly and intelligently, I promise that
Swaraj [self-determination] will come within one year." He believed he
had drawn the measure of British public opinion. "An Englishman," he
liked to say, "never respects you till you stand up to him. Then he begins
to like you. He is afraid of nothing physical; but he is very mortally afraid
of his own conscience if ever you appeal to it, and show him to be in the
wrong." Hence Gandhi's plan included a resumption of *satyagraha*, the
nonviolent movement of political protest he had first devised and employed against the raj in 1919. "Either grant to India full and free Domin-

ion Status before December 31, 1929," he warned the British government, "or from that day forward the Congress will declare a non-violent but absolute boycott of British goods, British officials, British schools, and British taxes." In London, the liberal *New Statesman,* no bastion of reactionary imperial sentiment, immediately branded Gandhi's resolution as "palpably insane."

Affairs in the Union of South Africa were only slightly less troubling to Whitehall. There the powerful Afrikaan Nationalist party, dominated by South Africans of Dutch descent who had never reconciled themselves to their nation's status as a dominion of the British Empire, had resumed its agitation for full independence, accompanied by blatant appeals to racial hatred. "We have paused on the brink of a sure and certain abyss," thundered Prime Minister James Barry Munnik Hertzog, "and the question is: Shall the white race in Africa plunge down to final destruction?" Judging by the vicious inequalities in law that existed between the white and colored races in South Africa, General Hertzog had little to fear from that quarter for the foreseeable future.

There was an old saying in Pretoria that "justice may be blind, but she is certainly not colour-blind," and the findings of an investigation led by a team of attorneys and academics from Transvaal University College demonstrated precisely how the discriminatory system operated in practice, specifically over a two-year period in Transvaal Province, where, two decades earlier, Gandhi had led the fight to end discrimination against Indian nationals. First, the inquiry found that the Transvaal police force—most of whom were of Dutch extraction—regularly resorted to brutal methods of coercion to obtain statements from native witnesses. Second, bewildered natives, many of whom spoke not a word of English, were routinely "hustled" through the court system without receiving sufficient opportunity to explain their story to a magistrate. Third, juries in criminal trials (all jurors were white, of course) clearly appeared to base their legal judgments upon several tacit, shared assumptions:

> In the first place, a white man will naturally use a considerable amount of force in dealing with a native with whom he has had a difference. Should the native die thereafter, it may be presumed that he has not died as the direct result of the assault unless there is irrefutable evidence to the contrary. Secondly, no white man should ever be hanged because he has killed a native. Hence, as hanging is the only possible sentence for a murder, a jury ought not to find a white man "Guilty" if he is charged with the murder of a native. Thirdly, if the verdict is such that the white man in such a case is sentenced to a short term of imprisonment, the jury has performed a laudable action and one calculated to meet amply the

ends of justice. Finally, native evidence is frequently unreliable. Hence, in the case of direct conflict between native evidence and European evidence, the latter should prevail.

Verdicts handed down by South African juries exhibited extraordinary discrepancies, depending solely upon the color of the defendant. For instance, a white man convicted of raping a fifteen-year-old native girl was sentenced to eighteen months' imprisonment with hard labor. But a black man convicted of *attempted rape* received seven years' imprisonment with hard labor and seven lashes. "Had you succeeded," the judge warned the latter defendant, "I would certainly have sentenced you to death." (As the Transvaal report suggested, the solution lay not in protecting white women less, but in protecting black women more.) In cases of murder, the color bar was drawn even more rigidly. A European charged with culpable homicide actually admitted that he had killed his native servant by striking him with a pickax, but the jury obdurately found him not guilty; another white man was convicted of common assault after kicking a black man to death and was sentenced to two weeks' imprisonment without hard labor. But when two native servants accused of the attempted murder of their master were convicted, they were each sentenced to three and a half years in prison. And a black man accused of murdering his master was found guilty, condemned to death, and hanged.

Egypt, the third linchpin of the British Empire, witnessed no outbreaks of nationalist violence at the outset of 1929, but across the eastern border, on the other side of the Suez Canal, rebellious bedouin tribesmen were threatening the regal authority of Abdul Aziz ibn Abdul Rahman, more frequently known by his formal title of Ibn Sa'ud (the name means "Son of Sa'ud"), King of the Nejd and the Hijaz. The British government wanted stability on the Arabian peninsula, and Whitehall decided late in 1928 that Ibn Sa'ud's demonstrated ability to command the religious and national loyalties of the Arab peoples made him their best bet to keep the region under control. But in December of that year, a tribe of fractious and quite irrational Muslim zealot-warriors known as the Ikhwan, heretofore the faithful core of the Sa'udi armies, had launched a series of murderous assaults against foreigners and Arab traders along the Iraqi border. Although the specific grievance that provoked the anger of the Ikhwan was the presence of British forts along the frontier, the raids were really the outward symbol of their deep-seated, fanatical hatred and fear of Ibn Sa'ud's progressive campaign to introduce the supposed benefits of twentieth-century civilization (such as cities, telephones, and motor cars) into a primitive, traditional society of nomadic shepherds and warriors. "You have also prevented me from raiding the Bedouins," wrote the leader of the Ikhwan to the son of Ibn Sa'ud, "so we are neither Moslems fighting the unbelievers, nor are we Arabs and Bedouins raiding each other and living on what we get from each other. You have kept us away from both our religious and our worldly concerns."

No matter the motives of the men whose swords had placed him on the throne, Ibn Sa'ud could not tolerate any open challenge to his authority, particularly since that throne (which, in fact, he had occupied for less than a decade) was still dangerously vulnerable to threats from within. So in the late winter of 1929, he left his capital of Riyadh at the head of a force of motor cars and machine guns to subdue the camel-riding Ikhwan. He caught up with them at Sabillah. Outnumbered three to one, the Ikhwan were torn to shreds in a cross fire of bullets from camouflaged guns. Although Ibn Sa'ud granted leniency to the survivors, he demolished their fortress and arrested their leaders. Yet the rebellion continued to smolder until the summer, when it erupted into open flames once again.

Still further to the east, in Palestine, where the Transjordanic Locust Service had borrowed flamethrowers from local military commanders to repel an invasion of locusts outside the walls of Jericho, the British government had its hands full quelling the latest round of riots between Jews and Arabs in Jerusalem. The disorders were sparked by an incident at the sacred site of the Wailing Wall, the sole remnant of the ancient glories of King Herod's Temple, where devout Jews still gathered to pray and place *kvitlach*—petitions to the Almighty—between the crumbling gray stones. In a calculated bid to provoke open conflict, the extremist Arab mufti of Jerusalem had authorized the addition of several new levels of stone to the wall, an act of sacrilege that drew anguished complaints from the Jewish community. Efforts to halt the construction disintegrated into violence that spread throughout the old quarter of the city, resulting in scores of casualties before the Anglo-Arab police finally managed to restore order.

Since September 1923, Britain had governed Palestine under a mandate from the League of Nations. British interest in the region had been dramatized during the late war, when Foreign Minister Arthur Balfour issued the famous declaration in 1917 that appeared to grant diplomatic sanction to the notion of a Jewish national homeland; and though Balfour's statement had been motivated in part by other, less altruistic concerns (such as a desire to advance British security and economic interests in the region), there was a formidable body of opinion in Europe and the United States that strongly supported the establishment of an independent Jewish state. But by 1929, the Zionist dream appeared to be dying under the weight of economic stagnation and the recent decision of the British civil administration to severely restrict Jewish immigration into Palestine. "You Jews wanted to own a national home," a cynical Englishman told

Golda Meir, who had arrived in the Holy Land eight years earlier, "but all you are getting is a rented flat!"

Over the previous decade, approximately 80,000 Jews—mostly from central and eastern Europe—had left their homes to settle in Palestine, increasing the total Jewish population to 146,000, against 645,000 Arabs and fewer than 77,000 Christians. At a time when the region's main export was still the annual crop of Jaffa oranges raised in plantations along the coast, the severely underdeveloped local economy buckled under the weight of the immigration burden; there simply were not enough industrial enterprises to sustain so many new workers, particularly since Jewish wages, though low by European standards, were still far higher than the pittance accepted by Arab laborers. To make matters worse, donations from the United States to support Jewish settlement in Palestine had fallen off sharply in 1927 and 1928. Although the British administration instituted a program of public works to help meet the crisis, the dismal unemployment situation might have become intolerable had not thousands of Jews opted to leave Palestine and return to Europe or the United States. "The late 1920s were depressing years throughout Jewish Palestine, not just for me," recalled Meir. "It was almost as though Zionism, in its great zeal, had overreached itself. . . . On those rare visits to Tel Aviv I was always depressed and shocked by the sight of unemployed men on the street corners and the desolate look of half-finished buildings all over town. It was as though a huge burst of energy had worn itself out."

But outside the cities, in the kibbutzim, the job of forging a nation out of the wasteland went on. There in the fields, schoolteachers from America worked side by side with the sons of German businessmen and pioneer girls from Zionist training farms in Lithuania. In the winter the kibbutz swam in a sea of mud; during the long, terribly hot summer days, swarms of mosquitoes, gnats, and sand flies tormented the settlers mercilessly, and the wind and sun scorched their skin. Epidemics of malaria and dysentery periodically swept through the settlements. At the kibbutz of Merhavia, the staples of the settlers' daily diet were (according to one member) "sour cereals, unrefined oil (which we bought from the Arabs in goatskin bags, making it as bitter as death), a few vegetables from the kibbutz's own precious vegetable patch, canned bully beef that came from British military supplies left over from the war and an incredible dish made up of herring preserved in tomato sauce" which was served every morning for breakfast. Women insisted on sharing the burdens of manual labor equally with the men, and complained strenuously when they were assigned to kitchen duty or the sewing room.

Why did intelligent young men and women subject themselves to such hardship? "Because the soil gives people something that nothing else can give them," explained one sunburned farmer who had forsaken his wealthy family in Poland to till the earth at the settlement of Geva.

> Working on the land is different from any other kind of work. You can work hard, you can give your whole strength to the soil, but you can't impose your will on it as you can on a machine. You sow the seed and you water it but can't pull at the shoots to make them grow. You have to be patient. You have to wait on the seasons, on the weather. The land has a will of its own, you have to win it over and this is good for you. It makes you know that it's nature that creates—or God if you like—and all you can do is to help it by your work. It's a living relationship. You need the land, the land needs you.

And poverty, he was asked—why does poverty seem to make these people so happy? After a few moments of silence, he replied:

> Well, you live among rich people—are they or their children happier? Our people are happy because they don't care for money or for what it gets. Of course a time may come when they'll begin to care how much the community has, and then even if they have nothing of their own, they will be beset with dangers. But at the moment they care for nothing but the land and the good life. That makes them happy and it's good for them. . . . Poverty is a freedom. And we needed to be set free, not only from the servitude to masters, but also from the servitude to fear which makes people chase after wealth. . . .
>
> Of course I don't mean that poverty which is imposed on you is good for you. You're no better just because you are poor. You can worry about material things as much if you are poor as if you are rich. Not knowing where your next day's breakfast is coming from can be as bad for you or as good as gambling on the stock exchange. Real poverty means giving oneself and one's work all the time—giving up even anxiety. Everyone has this need. It takes different people in different ways.

# VI

# Enter the Fed

"Administration policies have made for a substantial
and increasing stability in business for several years. . . .
If these conservative, constructive policies of the government
are maintained, then there would seem to be no reason why the
present economic situation should not continue."
—SECRETARY OF COMMERCE ALFRED WHITING,
*February 1929*

**W**inter brought the tourists to Palestine. In the early months of 1929, seven out of every ten visitors to Jerusalem were Americans eager for a glimpse of the Holy Land. There were sparkling new first-class hotels to shelter them, shops full of glittering Oriental souvenirs to amuse them, and American-made automobiles to carry them across the arrow-straight paved thoroughfares the British administration had recently constructed between the region's major cities. Instead of a ten-day journey by camel or coach, tourists could now ride in comfort from Dan to Beersheba, the entire length of Palestine, in a single day.

And if you happened to be John Davison Rockefeller, Jr., the government would even build a highway specially for you. Rockefeller, accompanied by his wife and their son David, arrived in Jerusalem in February, and set out on a tour that included the ancient sites of the Church of the Holy Sepulchre and the Dome of the Rock. Rockefeller graciously acknowledged that the magic atmosphere and the modern conveniences of the city had quite overwhelmed him; it all seemed far more agreeable and charming than he had anticipated. Then he rode across a thirteen-mile asphalt highway—constructed for his convenience by 1,200 local laborers working in record time—to view the archaeological excavations at the ancient fortified city of Megiddo, a project toward which the Rockefeller-sponsored Oriental Institute already had contributed more than $60,000.

In his father's heyday at the turn of the century, the names of John D. Rockefeller (Senior) and the Standard Oil Company had been virtually synonymous with the term "malefactors of great wealth" in the American press. The fact that Rockefeller was a devout Baptist who sincerely believed that his personal business ethics reflected the dictates of his uncompromisingly austere Christian faith did not deter muckraking progressive reformers from regularly flaying the Rockefeller petroleum trust with all the zealousness of revivalist preachers denouncing Satan. Their protests bore fruit in 1913, when the federal government, in the most spectacular antitrust prosecution of the era, ordered the dissolution of the massive Standard Oil monopoly into four separate corporate entities: Standard of California, Standard of Indiana (which was actually little more than a marketing organization at that time), Standard of New York, and Standard of New Jersey. As it turned out, the government's action was only marginally effective, since the four Standard companies promptly divided up the United States into geographical domains that paralleled one another, thereby precluding effective competition.

By the late 1920s, however, the passage of time and the talents of a gifted public relations agent named Ivy Lee had turned the senior Rockefeller into an elder statesman of American industry, and a venerated philanthropist who every day distributed several rolls of dimes (accompanied by an occasional encouraging pat on the head) to enterprising children and young people he met. At the outset of 1929, the senior Rockefeller was eighty-nine years old; for the past ten years he had made no public statements at all, and he had long ago turned over management of the family's business affairs to his son. He retained most of his money, however; his fortune in oil, coal, railroads, and metals reportedly was twenty times as great as the inheritance of King George V of England.

For his part, John D., Jr., adored the old man. Some said the son got down on his knees every night and asked God to make him more like his father. "From the time I entered my father's office until the day of his death," he once said, "my one desire was to help him in every way in my power. I was always as glad to black his shoes, to pack his bag, to act as the courier of family travels . . . and handle his mail and callers, as I was later to represent him in various of his interests, business and philanthropic." And, in a letter to his father:

> I have tried to do what I thought you would have me do. I have striven to follow in your footsteps. I have endeavored to use wisely and unselfishly the means that you have so unselfishly placed at my disposal. . . . In all these years of effort and striving, your own life and example have ever been to me the most powerful and stimulating influence. What you have done for humanity and business on a vast scale has impressed me profoundly. To have been a silent partner with you in carrying out these

great constructive purposes and benefactions has been the supreme delight of my life.

Born in 1874—the same year as Herbert Hoover and Owen D. Young—John D., Jr., grew up in a sheltered environment dominated by his mother and sisters, a circumstance that might explain the marked strain of prissiness some contemporaries discerned in his character. From early childhood, his parents vigilantly molded the boy into a model of their own Midwestern Baptist faith, eschewing such worldly temptations as dancing, card playing, drinking, and the theater for a life of self-discipline, family outings, music lessons (little John earned five cents an hour for practicing the violin), and wholesome, church-centered entertainment. They succeeded only too well; by the time he graduated from Brown University, the dour young man with the square jaw and cold gray eyes had earned himself the affectionate but not entirely flattering nicknames of "Johnny Rock" and "Old Ice Wagon." Shortly after entering the adult world, he financed a not very successful campaign to eliminate prostitution in New York City, and threw his financial and moral support behind the Anti-Saloon League's drive to enact prohibition. Even old friends from his undergraduate days occasionally found Junior too sober and high-minded for his own good. "You are altogether too grumpy, too morose and gloomy, John," wrote a former classmate in July 1898. "You are thinking too much of yourself not *selfishly,* you understand, but introspectively. . . . I truly think it would do you good, for instance, to take up smoking an occasional cigarette, or something of that sort. I am not joking. Just try being a shade more reckless, or careless as to whether or not you reach perfection within five years, and see if you don't find more happiness."

It was no use. Although his father always allowed him to make his own executive decisions without interference (and usually without so much as a hint of the old man's wishes), John D., Jr., constantly suffered feelings of inadequacy from his privileged position in the business world; he mourned the fact that he never had a chance to prove that he deserved his commercial worth. He was perfectly capable of spurning a $1,000 raise from his father in 1907, with the explanation that "I have always wished, simply as a matter of satisfaction to myself, that my salary might represent the real value of my services to the office, while as it is, and has been in the past, it represents rather your generosity." At the same time, however, he was one of the few mortals who possessed sufficient self-assurance and courage to deal face-to-face with the fearsome J. Pierpont Morgan, Sr., without flinching.

The younger Rockefeller inherited his father's fanatical abhorrence of waste. No detail was too small to escape his attention in questions of thrift and economy; no extravagant expenditure could withstand his rigorous scrutiny. He contributed $80 million to endowments to improve the physical and spiritual welfare of humanity, but quibbled over the installation of a $2,000 fence at a rundown Southern seminary.

Nor did his concept of stewardship permit the Rockefeller money to remain idle, for that, too, was a form of waste. Although John D., Jr., was far too prudent to engage in stock speculation himself—he never forgot that his father had lost a considerable portion of his investments in the Panic of 1907—by 1929, the Rockefeller corporations had become deeply and irresponsibly involved in the Wall Street boom by loaning nearly $100 million to brokers on the call-money market. Neither Rockefeller father nor son ever issued any public warning to discourage the frenzy of stock market gambling in 1929, nor did they take any steps to curb the flood of easy credit from their companies.

Calvin Coolidge seemed to be sleepwalking through his final days in the White House. Depressed, restless, he spent his working hours—and sometimes his evenings—alone in the Executive Office, sorting through his papers, methodically cataloguing his correspondence, and occasionally falling asleep when overcome with ennui. Silently he prowled through the kitchen and pantry storerooms. He complained to friends about the loneliness and terrible responsibility of the presidency. His ill-concealed discomfort cast a pall over the final social events of his administration; the annual army and navy reception was over in less than an hour and a half, as Coolidge rushed visitors through the receiving line at the rate of thirty-two per minute, and the dancing lasted for only fifteen minutes. At a ceremonial dinner in honor of the Supreme Court, Coolidge neglected to provide either music or entertainment. "Nine aging lawyers and their middle-aged wives sat around the table," recalled William Allen White, "politely waiting for a decent time to go home and go to bed." The President and his wife continued to pack their belongings for consignment to Northampton: china, objets d'art, books, stag antlers, whittling knives, even the fabled White House electric horse were crammed into the 150 boxes, 16 trunks, and assorted barrels and crates bound for Massachusetts. "It is easier to get into the White House than out of it," Coolidge sighed sadly.

He received offers of employment from scores of corporations, but refused them all for the present. "These people are trying to hire not Calvin Coolidge, but a former President of the United States," he explained to a friend. "I've had banking offers, but banks sell securities, and securities sometimes go bad. I can't do anything that might take away from the Presidency any of its dignity, or any of the faith people have in it."

Despite his evident dislike for the President-elect, Coolidge promised to refrain from criticizing his successor: "The best thing I can do for the Hoover administration is to keep my mouth shut." Before he left Washington, however, Coolidge recalled with pride his prudent stewardship of the public treasury: in his five and a half years in office, he had reduced the federal debt from $24 billion to slightly over $17 billion, and cut annual expenditures from $5 billion to $3 billion. The departing President made it clear that he was leaving Hoover a legacy of unprecedented national prosperity—"The closing months of 1928 and the opening weeks of 1929," Coolidge boasted, "have seen American industry and commerce at the highest point ever attained in time of peace"—and he urged continued thrift in all branches of government. But, he warned darkly, "peace and prosperity are not finalities; they are only methods. It is too easy under their influence for a nation to become selfish and degenerate. This test has come to the United States."

Hoover departed Washington at ten-thirty on the morning of January 21, after a tiresome two weeks of nonstop conferences at the Mayflower Hotel. As he strode across the platform to his train at Union Station, reporters noticed deep lines of fatigue across his face. About three hundred well-wishers bade him farewell; they clapped politely, but there were no other overt displays of public affection. All along the route south, through Virginia, North Carolina, Georgia, the future President could see scattered groups of people standing patiently on train platforms to watch and wave as his twelve-car special sped past along the Atlantic coastline. Early the next morning, he crossed the line into Florida, and continued on to Miami, where a reception committee of Governor Carlton, former heavyweight champion Jack Dempsey, and a score of local politicians welcomed him to the playland of millionaires that had come to be known as Tycoon's Coast.

One of those millionaires, chain store magnate J. C. Penney, had offered his palatial manor on Belle Isle, just across the causeway from Miami Beach, to Hoover as a winter vacation home. It was a magnificent white limestone villa of Italian Renaissance design, with a low roof of peach-colored tiles. From the front balcony, Hoover could peer across the calm blue-green waters of Biscayne Bay to see the Palm Island estate of Al Capone, the nation's most notorious gangster. Farther to the south and west, novelist Ernest Hemingway was completing the final revisions to the manuscript of A Farewell to Arms on January 22, the day Hoover arrived at Belle Isle. Admittedly "pooped" by the strain of writing, Hemingway— who was still recovering from the shock of his father's suicide in December—spent the rest of the winter fishing, playing tennis, and trying to scrape together enough cash to invest in the bond market. He implored his editor, Maxwell Perkins, to come down and join the fun. "The Gulf Stream is alive with fish," Hemingway chirped. "Now—really—it's like the old wild pigeon and Buffalo days. I've fished every Sunday—we got a 8 ft. 6 inch sailfish a week ago. Last Sunday—day before yesterday—were out salvaging liquor from a [rumrunner's] boat that went on the reef coming from the Bahamas—got 14 bottles of Chateau Margaux among other things. Boat had about $60,000 worth of liquor on her but everybody else was salvaging too. We got caught in a storm and I was afraid I might Shelley-out on you for a while."

Herbert Hoover, too, was an avid and expert fisherman (though not as enthusiastic a drinker as Hemingway). He had brought a new rod and deep-sea tackle with him from Washington, and on January 24 he climbed aboard the luxury yacht of Manhattan banker Jeremiah Milbank and headed for the Keys on a three-day deep-sea fishing trip, in search of the elusive sailfish. Wearing a battered slouch hat and rumpled old clothes (and, incongruously, his trademark white starched collar) while puffing on an old briar pipe, Hoover reclined in a wicker armchair on a small motorboat with only one or two companions—usually either journalist Mark Sullivan or Associate Supreme Court Justice Harlan Stone—and cast his lines baited with shreds of bonita and a red wood and aluminum decoy. Banished to a nearby Coast Guard cutter, Secret Service agents had to watch the President-elect through binoculars. (Reporters were banned from the trip altogether, and were forced to stay behind at Belle Isle to feed off bland statements released by Hoover's secretaries.) After reeling in plenty of tuna and barracuda, Hoover finally landed a small, stubborn, forty-five-pound sailfish; with honor satisfied at last, his face burned a deep red by the wind and sun and his hands covered with blisters, Hoover headed for home.

Although a record number of Americans spent their profits from the stock market for first-class berths on luxury passenger liners to Europe or the Near East in the winter of 1929, there was no shortage of glittering entertainment along Tycoon's Coast for those who remained behind. The millionaires' paradise stretched from the venerable Georgetown, South Carolina, estate of renowned financier and sometime government adviser Bernard Mannes Baruch, southward past Henry Ford's hideaway outside Savannah and the Jekyl Island mansions of the Morgans, Du Ponts, and Goulds off the Georgia coast, down along the shore of the fabled Fountain of Youth, to the Miami Beach homes of Harvey Samuel Firestone, John Hertz, William L. Mellon, S. S. Kresge, and Carl G. (Body by) Fisher.

Al Smith, too, spent the winter in Florida, in the company of John

Raskob and William F. Kenney, the Tammany-connected head of a multimillion-dollar New York construction firm. Before leaving New York
City, Smith had completed his metamorphosis into a full-fledged corporate executive by joining the board of directors of the County Trust Company, the bank that had accepted the note for $1 million that Raskob had
persuaded Smith's inner circle of supporters to sign in the closing days of
the presidential campaign. Now, between rounds of golf and gala Palm
Beach dinner parties with the likes of Prince Cyril of Bulgaria and the
grand duke Alexander Michaelovitch of Russia, Smith and Raskob discussed the details of another grandiose scheme: the demolition of the
aging Waldorf-Astoria Hotel on the corner of Thirty-third Street and Fifth
Avenue in Manhattan, and its replacement by a new landmark of concrete
and steel, a towering, thirty-six-million-cubic-foot office building they
planned to call the Empire State Building.

One man who did not receive invitations to any parties hosted by the
doyens of the southland social register was America's most famous songwriter, Irving Berlin. Born in the tiny Siberian village of Temun in 1888—
his real name was Israel Baline—Berlin and his family fled to America four
years later to escape the ravages of a Russian pogrom. Like Al Smith (for
whom he later penned the immortal campaign ditty "We'll All Go Voting
with Al"), Berlin grew up on the Lower East Side of New York; between
his family's musical heritage (his father was a deputy cantor in the local
synagogue) and the ethnic groups that jostled one another for space in the
teeming tenements, Berlin assimilated a rich mixture of musical tradi-
tions. He worked his way through the music halls and the night spots of
the Bowery, earning tips as a singing waiter in a Chinatown restaurant,
until he finally received his big break when a music publishing firm in Tin
Pan Alley hired him as a staff composer. Although he could play music in
only one key (F-sharp major)—he later designed a special piano keyboard
that automatically transposed the songs into different keys—Berlin
quickly captured the nation's imagination with his quirky syncopated
rhythms ("Alexander's Ragtime Band") and lyrics that ranged from the
suave, sophisticated "Puttin' on the Ritz" to the cheerful insouciance of
"Everybody's Doing It" and the unabashedly corny patriotism of "God
Bless America."

In 1926, at the height of his fame, Berlin eloped with Ellin Mackay,
daughter of Clarence Mackay, chairman of the Mackay Radio and Telegraph Corporation and heir to the Comstock Lode silver mine fortune.
Unfortunately for Mr. and Mrs. Berlin, Mr. Mackay was one of the most
pigheaded bigots in America. He never forgave his daughter for marrying
a "kike," and he had only hatred and contempt for the immigrant Jew who
had crawled out of the Lower East Side and into the bed of his daughter.

From his ersatz French château of Harbor Hill, situated on a thousand-acre estate on Long Island, Mackay instructed his society friends to ignore the Berlins completely, to freeze them out without exception. He refused to visit his daughter when her second child died shortly after birth on Christmas morning 1928, nor did he console her in the winter of 1929 when the Berlins journeyed to Florida to recover from the tragedy. While Ellin recuperated in the South, Irving tried to forget his troubles by forming a new theatrical producing partnership that would specialize in musicals; his first project was a comedy called *Fifty Million Frenchmen,* with music and lyrics by a young and still relatively unknown songwriter named Cole Porter.

There was only one thing that Berlin and his obstreperous father-in-law had in common: both had committed a substantial portion of their fortunes to the stock market. Mackay, who had sold his telegraph and cable properties to International Telephone and Telegraph in return for a large chunk of stock in that rapidly growing communications concern, relied on the market to provide him with the ready cash he required for his personal comfort—he reportedly managed to spend over a million dollars in 1928 alone—while Berlin was banking on his invested savings to provide all the money his family would need for the rest of his life. And that prospect reassured Berlin immensely, for his creative output had declined badly in recent years, and he had already begun to entertain serious doubts about his future creativity.

Ebullient brokers on Wall Street reported a deluge of purchase orders from Palm Beach, Miami, and Havana that glorious winter. In the Florida branch offices of brokerage houses, customers were "hanging over their tickers from 10 A.M. to 3 P.M.," observed a *New York Times* correspondent, "and some of the orders which have come through have fairly burned up the wires." Tips flew thick and fast between guests at society luncheons; Herbert Bayard Swope, comfortably ensconced in Palm Beach, gave his secretary standing orders to pester Bernard Baruch by telephone every weekday at noon to obtain the latest nuggets of inside information. Sometimes an investor succumbed temporarily to nagging doubts about the market's stability; as he departed for a European vacation at the end of January, steel magnate Charles Schwab declared that he was worried, "as all good business men are," about inordinate public speculation and the possibility of an imminent crash. But when he returned five weeks later, Schwab cheerfully admitted that he had revised his "old-time point of view." "Today, I do not feel that there is any danger to the public in the present situation," Schwab announced. "As long as the people remain enthusiastic and interested the market will hold up."

The glamour stocks continued to bound merrily upward through the first month of the year, though numerous brokerage houses admitted in their market advisory letters that the rest of the market "acted tired" and appeared "stale and listless." Pools had been especially active in January, bidding up prices of selected issues such as Warner Brothers, Curtiss Aero, Studebaker, Anaconda Copper, and IT&T. The *New York Times'* index of fifty industrial and rail stocks reached an all-time high on January 23; the sweeping upswing since the sharp break of early December marked the largest gain ever recorded in such a short time. Yale economist Irving Fisher reported that his own index of the fifty most active industrial stocks had jumped nearly ten points in one week. The Fisher formula was pegged to a 1926 average stock price of 100; at the end of January 1929, it had soared to the phenomenal figure of 705.

No wonder brokers reported that their customers were completely uninterested in conservative, "safe" securities that were likely to resist any violent break or selling spree in the market. Such stodgy stocks—which, it must be remembered, still represented a substantial portion of the issues offered on the exchange—generally remained stagnant in January. Instead, investors insisted upon the "fast-steppers," the industrial giants and the pioneers of advanced technology that promised fireworks, spectacular profits, and dividends that seemed to increase with almost magical speed. "It is the phenomenal growth of these vigorous firms that has aroused the present public enthusiasm for speculation," explained Colonel Leonard P. Ayres, vice-president of the Cleveland Trust Company and one of the nation's most respected market analysts. "Every one knows that if he could only have put a few dollars into the stock of one of them a few years ago he could have fabulous profits now. Every one suspects that similar opportunities are available at present if he could but have the insight to discern them. The result is that speculators are buying on expectation and almost without regard to present earnings, dividends or asset values." Colonel Ayres' point was well illustrated by the case of Mrs. Amy Boulter of West Eighty-third Street in Manhattan. In 1923, Mrs. Boulter had purchased two hundred shares of RCA stock at $2 per share; through a clerical error, her stock certificates were misplaced and then lost in the mail. By the time all the red tape was cleared away and duplicate certificates issued in early 1929, her shares were worth $18,000.

Even by traditional standards, there was an abundance of good economic news at the start of 1929. Stock values had leaped from $75 billion in January 1927 to $100 billion in January 1929. Cash dividends from American corporations paid in 1928 reached the unprecedented total of $3,440,502,549. General Motors reported the highest annual earnings ($276,468,108) in its history, and its nine-month earnings established a new record for any corporation in the United States; United States Steel, operating at virtually 100 percent capacity, recorded its highest quarterly earnings in two years; Standard Oil of New York's 1928 earnings were more than three times its 1927 net; and Du Pont and Standard Oil of California together awarded nearly $20 million in additional dividends to their stockholders. American exports reached their highest level since 1920, providing a trade surplus of over $1 billion. Spurred by demands from railroads, building construction, and automobile manufacturers, the nation's steel mills had set a new production record of approximately fifty million tons in 1928, though the pace appeared to be slowing, and industry executives kept insisting that they still needed greater protection from foreign competition. (Certainly American steelworkers enjoyed considerably higher wages than their counterparts in Europe; rolling mill laborers earned an average $3.28 a day in the United States, compared with $1.62 in Great Britain and about $1.50 in Germany.)

The bad news was that these wages still left far too many American workers on the edge of abject poverty. The average yearly wage for the entire American labor force (industrial and agricultural workers together) stood at only $1,280, a shameful figure that, in the words of one angry critic, "doomed the worker who is the father of dependent children to chronic want, forcing him into an acceptance of public or private charity in the event of any of the ordinary disasters of life—unemployment, sickness, death." Contrary to the euphoric rhetoric of prosperity, a study published by Harvard University revealed that workers' savings accounts were actually declining, partly because installment purchases were leading them to live beyond their means. Worse, there were still four million unemployed workers in America, an ominous statistic that convinced actor Charlie Chaplin (who had just read a book citing joblessness as a critical barometer of economic activity) that the storm clouds of financial catastrophe loomed just over the horizon; by January 1929, Chaplin had sold all his stocks and was completely out of the market.

Overproduction continued to plague both industry and agriculture. The president of the National Association of Manufacturers declared glumly that "the most ominous problems which I see are those which appear to have resulted from the general loss of balance between production and distribution. Of practically all commodities which America can produce, it is producing regularly from 15 to 30 percent more than it has the capacity and power to consume and dispose of profitably in other available markets. . . . It is safe to say that a general average of 40 percent of all the factories that are operating at all today are doing so at a loss," a loss disguised, of course, by the booming stock market. For the thirty million Americans who made their living by farming, the situation was even worse. Prices had been falling since the postwar European recovery, and the subsequent worldwide overproduction of wheat, cotton, and other staples had knocked the bottom out of the agricultural market in 1920–21. Technological improvements only made matters worse by further increasing output and glutting the market. Since 1925, the combined average price of leading agricultural commodities had declined by nearly 30 percent. Many farmers struggled each year to earn enough just to pay their taxes or the interest on their mortgage. As a farmer friend told Will Rogers in a gloomy New Year's prediction, "1929 just brings on 365 more days to pay interest to the people who are prosperous."

Meanwhile, conservative members of the banking community kept insisting that a debilitating crash was near at hand. "The cycle will turn and I want to issue the warning now," declared prominent investment banker Edward C. Bendere in an address to the Philadelphia Bankers' Association at the outset of 1929. "In 75 percent of the cases the market is reaching a point where it is beyond itself. . . . The greatest opportunity for investment has passed, until there is a complete reconstruction." Bendere accused bankers of being sucked into the market so completely that they had lost the ability to render objective judgments to their clients: "You haven't the courage to tell others to keep out, because the more people in the market the more bullish it will be. . . . People are going crazy and mortgaging their homes. The reaction is coming and to some it will be too late."

But the irrepressible bulls on Wall Street nonchalantly shrugged off the bad news and the predictions of doom. For the past two years, a host of Cassandras had regularly issued dire threats of impending disaster, but the market kept spiraling gaily upward in defiance of all portents. By the start of 1929, the pessimists had cried wolf too often and lost all credibility with investors; each new round of warnings brought only derisive laughter from the customers' rooms in brokerage offices. Led by public utility and railroad stocks, a group of 217 representative issues on the New York Stock Exchange increased in value by over $1 billion during the first month of 1929, though automobile and retail stocks generally declined. The volume of transactions on the exchange in January set another new record for a single month. The extra commissions meant that brokers' incomes kept climbing, too; at the start of the new year, the average annual income for those with seats on the New York Stock Exchange was $367,000, exclusive of profits from their own speculative ventures. Business was so brisk that the governing committee of the exchange decided to authorize the creation of 275 additional brokers' seats on the floor—the first increase in membership since the limit of 1,100 seats was established in 1879—and to install a speedier ticker system to handle the deluge of orders that threatened to overwhelm the existing technology. And the surging flood of brokers' loans, fed by the influx of gold from abroad, grew by nearly $500 million between December 28 and February 5, to a new record total of $6,736,164,242.

One day early in February, Herbert Swope received a disquieting message from his financial guru, Bernard Baruch: "UNDERSTAND CORNER PEOPLE [J.P. Morgan and Company] THINK MARKET IS OVER. PERSONALLY SITTING TIGHT BECAUSE I THINK FEDERAL RESERVE DOES NOT UNDERSTAND CONDITIONS AND STILL HAVE BELIEF IN MY INDUSTRIAL RENAISSANCE."

In truth, the Federal Reserve Board understood conditions perfectly well. Established in 1913 as a response to the recurring panics and deflationary spirals that struck the American economy with depressing regularity, the Federal Reserve System was designed to provide all segments of the nation's banking and business community with a reliable, elastic supply of credit on fair and reasonable terms. The system consisted of a three-tiered structure: at the top was the board of governors; then came the twelve Federal Reserve Banks, one for each district within the system; and finally, there were the member institutions, approximately nine thousand national and state banks. In theory, the member banks pooled their resources to form a virtually inexhaustible reserve upon which any individual member could draw in a crisis. In practice, the board regulated the flow of credit to the economy through a variety of monetary devices, including the sale of government securities on the open market. But the most significant weapon at its disposal in 1929 was the rediscount rate: the interest rate charged by each of the twelve individual Federal Reserve Banks for loans to the member banks in its district. By raising the rediscount rate, the Federal Reserve discouraged the extension of credit by making borrowed money more expensive; by lowering the rate, it naturally encouraged an expansion of business activity.

What bothered the board most about the unrestrained speculation in Wall Street in early 1929 was the likelihood that the irresistible lure of easy profits on the stock market would soon divert a dangerous amount of credit from industrial and agricultural enterprises that were more productive in the long run, but less immediately remunerative. "So far as the Board is concerned, it does not view the broker loans themselves as dangerous," explained one sympathetic financial writer. "But the diversion of funds to speculative channels which ought to be available for the normal needs of the country, especially in harvest seasons and in periods of necessary constructive activity, is regarded as a menace to the whole economic structure."

After irresponsibly lowering the rediscount rate in the summer of

1927, a move that had revived the faltering Coolidge bull market, the board had reversed itself and attempted to discourage speculation in 1928 by raising the rate slightly to 5 percent; in fact, the New York Bank raised its own rediscount rate three times within the space of twelve months. Unfortunately, this action, however well intentioned, came squarely under the heading of locking the barn door after the bulls had escaped. It simply did not work because it was not sufficiently drastic.

Thus the Federal Reserve Board found itself facing an extremely difficult dilemma at the outset of 1929. Should it raise the rediscount rate still further, to prohibitive heights, and deliberately invite a violent reaction that might send the entire economy into a tailspin? Or should it wait for the raging speculative fever on Wall Street to play itself out and risk an almost certain depression in the long run—for prosperity could not continue indefinitely if such an extensive portion of the nation's credit was imprudently diverted from the actual production and exchange of goods and services. Indeed, many sectors of the American economy already had ceased to expand; and sooner or later the speculators would realize, to their shock and dismay, that the future corporate profits they anticipated—and upon which buyers had based the exorbitant prices they paid for stocks—simply were not going to appear because industry had forsaken productive investment for the speculative market. As the *New Republic* remarked sarcastically, "A village whose members live by taking in each other's washing is nothing compared with a nation all of whose citizens should try to live solely by speculating on each other's production."

It was a puzzle that called for the bold wisdom of Solomon; but the Federal Reserve Board possessed only a timorous Mellon. So the board decided to adopt neither alternative—at least, not exactly. In a February 2 letter to the twelve Reserve Banks, the board stated that it wished to reduce the prodigious volume of funds absorbed in stock market speculation without formally raising the discount rate. "The Federal Reserve Act does not, in the opinion of the Federal Reserve Board, contemplate the use of the Federal Reserve banks for the creation or extension of speculative credit," the board explained. "A member bank is not within its reasonable claims for rediscount facilities at its Federal Reserve Bank when it borrows either for the purpose of making speculative loans or for the purpose of maintaining speculative loans." In other words, member banks were advised in the strongest terms to reject loans for speculative purposes while granting requests for legitimate commercial loans. They had the right to loan their own money for speculation if they wished, but they could not remain permanently in debt to the Federal Reserve Banks for that purpose.

Four days later, while Treasury secretary Mellon was closeted in conference with the governor of the Bank of England, the estimable Montagu Collet Norman (who was seeking American cooperation to stem the outflow of gold from Britain to Wall Street), the board made public the text of its February 2 letter and issued a formal statement elaborating upon its decision. "The United States," it began, "has during the past six years experienced a most remarkable run of economic activity and productivity. The production, distribution and consumption of goods have been in unprecedented volume." So far, so good. "During the last year or more, however, the functioning of the Federal Reserve System has encountered interference by reason of the excessive amount of the country's credit absorbed in speculative security loans. The credit situation since the opening of the new year indicates that some of the factors which occasioned untoward developments during the year 1928 are still at work. The volume of speculative credit is still growing." Although the board scrupulously denied that it sought to establish itself as the arbiter of security values, it insisted that it had a duty "to restrain the use, either directly or indirectly, of Federal Reserve credit facilities in aid of the growth of speculative credit." At the same time that the board released its statement (which was deliberately timed to come after the New York Stock Exchange had closed for the day), the Bank of England announced that it had decided to raise its discount rate by one percentage point—to its highest level since 1921—to conserve its gold supply.

Reaction followed swiftly. The following day, Thursday, financiers in London freely expressed their fears that the increase in the bank's rate would further depress British trade and boost unemployment another notch. Berlin and Paris both reported general declines on their stock exchanges. On Wall Street, the combination of the Federal Reserve Board's statement and the Bank of England's action created intense anticipation at the opening of the day's session; brokerage houses reported crowds of nervous clients hovering anxiously around the tickers in their customers' rooms. Those who had purchased most of their portfolios on margin—on borrowed money—were especially worried, for if stock prices should start to fall (or even rise at a slower pace) while interest rates rose, they would be caught in a nasty squeeze.

In the first thirty minutes of business, the market was battered by a flood of selling. Some speculators feared that this time the Reserve Board finally would succeed in stemming the flow of easy money that had permitted the market to soar so high for so long; in that case, they deemed it better to cash in their profits now, before the bottom dropped out of the market altogether. As prices declined suddenly and sharply, the break triggered a large number of stop-loss orders—orders that investors had left with their brokers to sell stocks automatically if prices fell to a certain level, to cut their losses as much as possible; accordingly, a second violent wave of liquidation swept over the beleaguered market, sending prices tumbling even lower. The ticker fell behind by nearly half an hour as shares were sold in blocks of twenty thousand or more. The speculative favorites led the decline: General Electric, Du Pont, U.S. Steel, Westinghouse, all fell by six to seventeen points.

Prices rallied slightly in the afternoon, particularly after newspapers reported that Congressman Louis T. McFadden, chairman of the House Committee on Banking and Currency, had blasted the Federal Reserve Board's statement. "I do not think that the assumption is warranted that brokers' loans are depriving business of funds, nor that all of the security loans are unproductive," McFadden proclaimed. "It seems to be rather far-fetched to endanger the pay envelope of the working man and the profits of the business man because some one gets the notion that there is too much stock speculation or that stocks should not sell as high as they are now." Wall Street also buzzed with the rumor, attributed to reliable sources, that Secretary Mellon was unalterably opposed to any further steps by the Federal Reserve Board to curb speculation.

But even this gratifying news could not keep the market from closing the day sharply down. One popular journal's index of fifty representative stocks showed the largest single-day decline in the history of the stock exchange. RCA led the losers with a decline of 35 points, nearly 10 percent of its value; G.E. dropped more than 12 points, from 247 to 235. After the closing bell rang, the governing committee of the stock exchange announced that the usual half-day of business on Saturday would be canceled owing to an influenza epidemic that allegedly had left many brokerage houses with a shortage of healthy employees. (Actually, medical authorities reported that the flu epidemic had reached its peak several weeks earlier, and was now on the wane, but it served as a good excuse anyway.) "Called off on account of the 'flu,' " chuckled Will Rogers. "And a funny thing it was on account of the 'flu.' If it had 'flu' up they wouldn't have had to call it off on account of the 'flu,' but as it 'flu' downward, why everybody has to 'flu' around Saturday and get ready for not only the 'flu' Monday but maybe pneumonia."

A flurry of recriminations descended on the Federal Reserve Board for its role in causing the market break. "Any sudden drop in the stock market has a disastrous effect upon the psychological stability of our entire economic structure," charged Michael H. Cahill, president of the New York State Bankers' Association. "Neither the federal Reserve Board nor any other agency has any moral or legal right to take any public action which will create a panic in the minds of the people and thus jeopardize the investing public's money." Theodore Prince, head of the brokerage firm that bore his name, claimed that the board's intrusion into Wall Street's affairs "has simply resulted in the rich man keeping his stocks and the man not so rich selling them to his loss." "The time is still to come," swore Prince, "when this country by edict or commission has seen fit to dictate what any one should do with his surplus money." The xenophobic Representative Loring Black of New York, who suspected that Britain had pressured the Reserve Board into making its public statement, introduced a resolution to investigate the board's decision and prevent it from ever interfering in the stock market again. "The credit situation is too delicate for such heavy-handed statements as the board issued Wednesday," Black warned. "Its action represents a government thrust at American prosperity." If Britain wanted gold, he suggested, the United States might be willing to trade it for British naval bases in the Western Hemisphere. And as far as the *Wall Street Journal* was concerned, "checking stock speculation is none of the Federal Reserve's business": "The country is apparently expected to believe that the Federal Reserve System was organized to regulate Wall Street, stabilize farm prices, control prize-fighting at Madison Square Garden, ameliorate the traffic congestion on Broadway, and wash the baby, in its spare time. May it be humbly suggested that the business of the Federal Reserve Bank is banking?"

Yet most of the nation's newspapers, from the *New York Times* to the Topeka *Capital,* praised the board for its courage in trying to restore a modicum of sanity to Wall Street. Sentiment in Congress also ran heavily against the wounded speculators. The Senate quickly passed a resolution introduced by burly Tom Heflin of Alabama asking the Federal Reserve Board to provide it with information and recommendations for legislation to check "illegitimate and harmful speculation." Wall Street, roared Heflin, was "the most notorious gambling center in the universe," "the hotbed and breeding place of the worst form of gambling that ever cursed the country," and he blamed the sinful lure of the stock market for driving hundreds of thousands of Americans to poverty, vice, and even insanity. "The government," Heflin concluded, "owes it to itself and to its people to put an end to this monstrous evil." Senator William H. King of Utah suggested that since 85 percent of stock speculation was done on margin, Congress should forbid marginal trading. Iowa's Senator Smith Wildman Brookhart went one step further and recommended that the federal government prohibit any loan by any bank to any borrower who might conceivably use the loan for speculative purposes. "It is preposterous," argued Brookhart, "to claim that the Government of the United States or of the various States should be called upon to furnish a banking system to sustain an institution of stock gamblers."

The Senate's leading authority on banking practices was the urbane and irascible Carter Glass of Virginia, one of the fathers of the Federal Reserve Act of 1913, and a dedicated foe of stock market speculators. "There is not a thing in the world constructive in their operation," Glass growled in the aftermath of the latest evidence of speculative excess. "It is a matching of the gambling wit against gambling wit. They do not produce a thing on earth that contributes either to the happiness or to the prosperity of legitimate businesses." Glass reminded his Senate colleagues that he had "often pointed to the absurdity of States and communities and the nation enacting laws making it a criminal offense for a company of gentlemen to sit around the table and wager at poker, or go to a race track and bet on a race, and then legalize a system of pure gambling that menaces the entire commercial and financial fabric of the nation. It is an absurdity . . . and laws should be enacted to put these people out of business." But Glass conceded that it would be almost impossible to establish a statutory distinction between "investment" and "speculation." And, he added, the Federal Reserve Board already had waited far too long to successfully check the current wave of speculation.

Indeed, the board soon learned that it was no easy task to stop a raging bull market that had nearly four years' momentum behind it. Although the Reserve Banks dutifully began to tighten their control of the money supply by selling government securities and pressuring their member banks to abjure loans for speculative purposes, there was absolutely nothing they could do to stop the surging flow of bootleg credit from corporations to Wall Street. In fact, since the banks' restrictive policies drove the call-money rate up to 10 percent, the net effect was to render loans to brokers an even more attractive investment for corporations with surplus capital (which, in turn, meant that those corporations would dedicate even less of their available funds toward productive investment). "The real trouble," concluded the *New Republic*, "is not that the Federal Reserve authorities have attempted to put the brakes on speculative credit, but that they have not had four-wheel brakes to put on. They probably were not able to slow the car down soon enough. A moderate speed is better than a joy-ride ending in a crash."

Still the board did not give up. On February 15, the Federal Advisory Council, a body of businessmen and bankers appointed by the directors of the twelve Reserve Banks, plunged into the tussle with an unexpectedly stern statement that strongly supported the board's actions and explicitly requested the member banks to support the board's antispeculative policy.

So the market drifted raggedly through the rest of February, advancing almost reluctantly one day and retreating the next; the volume of trading remained low as cautious investors waited to see whether the infinitely resourceful bulls could outmaneuver the Reserve Board.

Charlie Mitchell was certainly doing everything in his power to thwart the board. In an unprecedented five-hour meeting on the afternoon of February 14, the board of directors of the Federal Reserve Bank of New York debated a proposed increase in the rediscount rate for their district. Mitchell, the newest member of the board, argued furiously against the measure. He told them that an imaginative businessman could always find ways to expand production without withdrawing money from the stock market; his own bank, for instance, had just developed an innovative (and somewhat fantastic) plan to finance building construction through the sale of stock instead of traditional mortgages. But Mitchell's creative schemes were far too radical—and provided far too much opportunity for chicanery—for a majority of his colleagues. Although the board was reluctant to take strong measures on its own, it decided to ask Washington for permission to raise the rate. Fortunately for Mitchell, he had already discussed the question privately with Secretary Mellon, who had assured him that the administration had absolutely no intention of intruding further into Wall Street's affairs. So Mitchell was not surprised when the answer came back from the Treasury Building: permission denied. When the meeting finally ended at 6:50 P.M. and the directors filed out of the room, reporters noted that the bank's harried governor, George L. Harrison, appeared on the brink of nervous exhaustion.

Back in his office at National City Bank, Mitchell began calling his contacts on newspapers and financial journals to plant stories discrediting the notion that events on Wall Street were of any concern to Congress or the Reserve Board. He also telephoned Billy Durant in Michigan on February 16 to suggest that Durant schedule a meeting with his buddy Herbert Hoover—who, according to well-founded rumor, viewed excessive stock market gambling with Quakerish distrust—to explain the dangers of government interference in the market. Durant, who earlier had decided to postpone his trip to Washington until after Hoover's inauguration on March 4, assured Mitchell that he would take whatever steps he deemed appropriate. To lay the groundwork for his mission, Durant issued his own statement blasting the Reserve Board's "lack of tact and judgment": "Any group of eight men, vested with or assuming power which, by careless or intentional action, succeeds in destroying credit and confidence—the basis of our great prosperity—will be subject to criticism by every sensible business man."

Henry Ford had absolutely no use for Wall Street. Unlike fellow automobile magnate Billy Durant, who never could have assembled the General Motors empire without using other people's money, Ford considered stockholders "useless parasites in enterprise." "They put in their money to gamble on the other fellow's brains," Ford complained, "and it was as they deserved when they lost their money." "I doubt if he knows what hour Wall Street opens or closes," wrote Will Rogers of his friend Henry. "He thinks Margins are the things you leave around the edge of anything. He knows what calling Hogs is; but Call Money would be Greek to him. He never did merge two or more companies together and sell stock. He has had to make what little he has out of just what little he had to work with."

Even so, Henry had done all right. According to a survey conducted by journalist Stuart Chase in 1926, Henry Ford and his son Edsel were the wealthiest individuals in America. Henry ruled the Ford Motor Company as his private fiefdom, and gathered the profits as tribute to his unique genius. Lately, the profits had fallen off a bit, as the Ford manufacturing plants passed through a period of transition occasioned by the discontinuance in 1927 of the fabled Model T, the inexpensive and reliable "Tin Lizzy" that had changed forever the lives of millions of Americans. ("It was the miracle God had wrought," wrote E. B. White in a tender eulogy to the faded glory of the Model T. "And it was patently the sort of thing that could only happen once.") It was due largely to the force of Ford's success that the U.S. automobile industry provided consumers with cars so affordable that 1 out of every 6 Americans owned a car at the beginning of 1929; in the rest of the world, only 1 out of 64 people owned an auto, and in China the figure was 1 out of 21,257.

After considerable bickering (Henry was a stubborn man), Edsel finally had convinced his father that the American public of the late 1920s wanted a sleeker, more powerful, and more sophisticated car, and so the Model A was born. Unveiled in Ford showrooms across the nation on December 2, 1927, the Model A's rounded body, powerful four-cylinder engine (it could cruise at a speed of 55–65 miles per hour), economical fuel consumption (20 miles per gallon), and affordable price (between $395 and $625 depending upon the options selected, or about $100 less than comparable Chevrolet models) proved an immediate hit with consumers. Douglas Fairbanks promptly bought one for Mary Pickford as a Christmas present. "The new Ford is more than a new automobile," bragged the advertisements that seemed to be everywhere. "It is the expression of an ideal—an ideal that looks to bringing the benefits of modern transportation to all the people." But production lagged until the end of 1928, while Ford's plants were painstakingly reconstructed to handle the nearly six thousand parts—most of them new—that the Model A required. One reliable estimate placed the cost of the transition at $250 million in lost profits, a horrifying figure that surely would have toppled someone like Durant from the leadership of a publicly held corporation.

Fortunately, Henry Ford needed to answer to no one except himself. He still kept the thirty-six-year-old Edsel on a short leash; unlike John D. Rockefeller, Ford refused to relinquish control of the family business to his son and heir. Henry made all the important decisions himself, and in the early months of 1929 he decided to expand Ford's production of aircraft to the rate of one plane per day, and to put his auto assembly lines on a six-day-a-week basis to boost production by 20 percent above the prevailing pace of six thousand cars per year. Because each employee worked only five days, Ford announced plans in January to hire another 30,000 men, bringing his total work force to 150,000. The resulting stampede of shivering and desperate unemployed laborers to the doors of Ford's plant at River Rouge belied the comfortable slogans of unalloyed national prosperity. Although Ford had said that local workers would have preference over outsiders, a quick survey of automobile license plates in the Ford parking lot (South Carolina, Missouri, Louisiana, Kentucky, New York, and others) revealed that hundreds of job seekers had defied his edict. "We are from other states," some admitted, "but if we are asked about it, we've been in Detroit all our lives. What we want is a job."

It was also Henry's decision to launch an intensive drive to extend the company's presence in Europe, Africa, and the Middle East, to recapture ground lost to competitors while the Model A had been in embryo. Ford's most dangerous competition on the European continent came from France, where Citroën had developed a four-cylinder, mass-produced model that cost no more than the cheapest Model A (which was known in Paris as the "Henri"). To manufacture and sell cars for the foreign market, Ford took the highly uncharacteristic step of establishing a publicly held corporation, the Ford Motor Company, Ltd., based in London. Henry, of course, kept 60 percent of the company's stock in his family's hands and intended to sell the rest to the British public, but he was surprised and chagrined to learn that most of the other 40 percent had been gobbled up by the detestable and insatiable scavengers of Wall Street. Henry was also negotiating with the government of the Soviet Union to construct a Ford plant in Moscow, to turn out one hundred thousand cars annually, but he found the Communists to be difficult partners. "It seems that the Russian government gained the impression that we wanted a slice of Russia or something like that," he said with a tone of injured innocence. "As a matter of fact, we want to help Russia. We want to help *all* foreign countries."

Probably the Communists were not quite sure what to make of Henry. A man of decidedly unconventional beliefs, Ford often befuddled unwary observers by spouting epigrams that trod the thin line separating simple wisdom from foolish simplicity. Someone once said that Ford thought "in dots and dashes," that he possessed "a busy, scattered mind" which dealt only in certain universal laws that purportedly governed human existence. He firmly believed that mankind was on the road to international harmony and understanding ("Political boundaries and political opinions don't really make much difference. It is the economic condition which really forces change and compels progress") through the steady advance of material civilization ("Machinery is accomplishing in the world what man has failed to do by preaching, propaganda, or the written word"). He had convinced himself that mysterious races lost in the mists of antiquity had previously possessed the blessings of advanced technology: "I am sure they had the automobile, the radio, the airplane—everything that we have, or its equivalent, and perhaps many things that we have yet to discover."

A devout vegetarian, Ford exhorted American religious leaders to teach their congregations the evils of eating meat. "Instead of cluttering up religion with a lot of things that do not belong to it," he suggested, "why doesn't the clergy teach people how to eat?" Although he exercised vigorously upon rising and before going to bed, and often ran several miles a day, the sixty-five-year-old Ford blamed the game of golf for causing more heart trouble among his contemporaries than any other single factor. "I own a golf course," he admitted, "but never play. The American people drag themselves over the courses at slow speed, then, completely fatigued, they sit down and eat hearty meals." And, contrary to John D. Rockefeller's gospel of saving every possible dime, Ford advised young men to "invest in yourself until you are forty." "No successful boy ever saved any money," Henry insisted. "They spent it as fast as they could for things to improve themselves." As outstanding examples of this philosophy, Ford offered himself and Thomas Alva Edison, the world's most famous inventor; both men had been more than forty years old before they got their financial heads above water.

Ford had begun his career as the chief mechanic for the Edison Illuminating Company's plant in Detroit, and for the past twenty years he, Edison, and automobile tire manufacturer Harvey Firestone had taken their winter vacations together. In fact, Edison had installed a special workshop for Ford (who never stopped tinkering) in his Florida laboratory, and Ford had set aside part of his twenty-two-thousand-acre Georgia plantation for Edison's experimental work in cultivating rubber plants. So when Ford arrived at his winter home in Fort Myers on the west coast of Florida on February 7, he did not even stop to unpack his bags before walking the two miles to Edison's estate to greet his inventive crony.

Ford returned to Edison's estate four days later with an equally distinguished guest. At ten-thirty on the morning of February 11, Herbert Hoover stepped off a yacht onto Edison's pier and heard the inventor welcome him with a high-pitched shout, "Hello, fisherman!" The President-elect, along with Firestone and Ford, had journeyed to Fort Myers to help Edison celebrate his eighty-second birthday. Hoover strode jauntily through the mangoes and orange trees to shake the inventor's hand. "Congratulations," chirped Hoover, who was almost never at a loss for words. "Thanks," replied Edison, who was almost completely deaf. As the movie cameras whirred, Hoover started to back out of the picture, but Edison grabbed his elbow and held on for dear life.

After a parade through Fort Myers and a luncheon of wild turkey and trimmings, Henry Ford presented Edison with his birthday gift: a $5 million contribution to the Edison Institute of Technology and the Museum of American Industries, where Edison's old tools were kept in perfect working order. At the party, Edison announced to the press that he envisioned even greater national prosperity for America under the inspired leadership of a Hoover administration. But then a reporter asked him (in writing, since Edison didn't want to look foolish by misunderstanding a question) what he foresaw as the dangers of the current wave of stock speculation. "Ultimate panic," replied the inventor tersely. "Loss of confidence."

# VII

# The Spider in the Center
# of the Web

"We can no longer wonder why we are faced with such a
large number of crimes today. Instead we should be amazed
that there is not more crime in existence. When people of
high standing in society choose to risk their fortunes
in order to get big returns in a quick and easy manner,
it is not surprising that others will turn to crime
and an even quicker and easier method of increasing
their earnings with just a little more risk."
—RABBI STEPHEN S. WISE, *April 1929*

On a raw, dreary morning in the late winter of 1929, the Twentieth-
Century Limited sped smoothly through the slatternly towns and somber
blackness of the Indiana prairies. Through the drifting showers of snow
and soot outside their windows, early-rising passengers could recognize
the unmistakable and immeasurably tedious progression of sights that
signaled the approach into Chicago: mile after mile of ramshackle wooden
frame houses barely visible in the distance above the deserted plains;
mournful grain elevators, rusting in disrepair from half a decade of Coolidge prosperity; vacant factories with rough, gaping holes in their windows; and the cheerless freight yards and warehouses in mist-covered
ports where thick-bodied lake steamers unloaded their cargoes of coarse
iron ore.

Then the city loomed sharp against the horizon—a vast, fantastic,
jagged mass towering above the prairies, the menacing embodiment of
that relentlessly acquisitive and brutish spirit Ford Maddox Ford once
denounced as the "pitiless, ironic and harsh-voiced" deity of the Middle
West. "I fear Chicago," admitted critic Lewis Mumford, a confirmed lover
of Manhattan; to him the city on the shores of Lake Michigan seemed "an
imbecile colossus," a "nightmare of magnificent energy and raucous imbe-
cility" overladen by an atmosphere of "murk, gore, horror." "That Chicago is dirty is indisputable," said Mumford:

That it dominates a vast swamp of bad housing and mean civilization is obvious. That its chief newspapers are fourth-rate provincial sheets, poorly edited and composed, is plain, too, to anyone who can read. Even its great drives and parks have about them something of the sinister sweep and energy of Peter the Great's city on the fens; the same blackness, the same fake classic exterior, the same stubborn monotony. The city plan is staggering, grandiose; but the quality of mind exhibited in these efficient dreams is not, for all their audacity, a thoroughly civilized one—one that values life, your life, my life, everyone's life, and that respects individuality.

"The secret to survival in Chicago," concluded Mumford, "was to maim and kill with more expert precision than one's neighbor."

At number 2122 North Clark Street, less than a mile from the Loop (the city's business and financial center), and just one block from Lincoln Park and its exquisite residential palaces, there stood a squat, ugly, one-story warehouse fashioned from plain red brick. It used to be a garage. The glass on the front door and the front window had been swabbed with black paint to discourage curious passersby. In the window there was a sign that read, "S-M-C CARTAGE-CO," but there really was no such company.

From a pair of rooms across the street, the lookouts saw their prey enter the warehouse on the morning of February 14, St. Valentine's Day. They grinned because one of the men who walked inside looked like George "Bugs" Moran, kingpin of the old O'Banion gang, which ruled the liquor and vice rackets on the North Side of the city. The lookouts picked up the telephone and gave a prearranged signal to the party at the other end.

Inside the warehouse, six men sat huddled around a small portable electric stove, drinking hot coffee and eating crackers. They all wore overcoats and hats, because the temperature outside had dropped to eighteen degrees above zero, there was a bitterly cold west wind gusting against the window and the doors, and the only heat in the building came from the hot plate and the bare lightbulb that shone above them. Outside, a light snow was falling. The six men had gathered to receive and pay for a truckload of hijacked liquor that had been offered to Moran the previous evening by an anonymous tipster over the phone. Two of the men in the warehouse were brothers, Frank and Pete Gusenberg, whom Moran liked to employ as executioners; a third was Adam Heyer, alias John Snyder, a professional accountant who allegedly kept the books for the Moran gang's transactions—a police spokesman later called him the "brains" of the Moran "mob." Moran's brother-in-law, James Clark, a convicted robber and burglar, was present, too, along with a strong-arm thug named Albert Weinshank whom the watchers apparently mistook for the burly Moran. The least likely member of the group was a thirty-year-old optometrist named Reinhard Schwimmer who apparently was not a criminal at all, but a braggart friend of Moran who liked to boast that he was in the booze business and could have anyone who hassled him "taken for a ride"; it was Schwimmer's misfortune that he just happened to stop by the warehouse that morning to chat with his friends. A seventh man, a mechanic named Johnny May, was repairing a wheel on a beer delivery truck. His German shepherd dog was chained nearby.

Moran himself was on his way to the warehouse, but he was late. He turned the corner onto North Clark Street shortly after ten-thirty, just in time to see five men—two in blue police uniforms with brass badges, three in plain clothes—pull up in front of number 2122 in a black Cadillac touring car that bore a striking resemblance to an official detective bureau vehicle, right down to the gong attached to the running board. Moran backed away and began to retrace his steps. The men inside heard the sound of what they thought was a police gong and decided to open the door.

Four of the visitors swaggered in, swinging submachine guns and sawed-off shotguns at their side. The two who wore police uniforms ordered everyone inside to surrender their weapons and line up with their faces toward the whitewashed wall. Apparently believing that they were the victims of a shakedown by corrupt cops angling for a bigger percentage of the gang's profits, the Moran men docilely obeyed. Then the visitors deliberately opened fire at point-blank range, shattering the morning calm with a violent explosion of bullets and shells, systematically aiming the first round at their victims' heads, then another round at their chests as the wounded men slumped against the wall, then a final round at what remained of their waists. The butchery lasted for nearly two minutes. Almost all of the bullets found their mark: police later recovered nearly a hundred spent shells and only eight stray slugs lodged in the wall. Their bodies riddled with lead, May and Clark desperately tried to crawl away; their faces were blown off by shotguns fired from less than six inches away.

Then the killers walked quickly out of the warehouse; to complete the charade of an arrest, the two uniformed men kept their guns pointed at their accomplices. They all climbed back into the Cadillac and drove away at high speed on the wrong side of the street, swerving to avoid a passing trolley car. They dumped the car in a garage about a mile away.

Mrs. Jeanette Landesman, the wife of an investigator in the city prosecutor's office, lived in an apartment next door to the warehouse, at 2124 North Clark. She heard the fusillade of shots and the furious howling of the dog and ran downstairs to the front door. "I tried to look into the garage, but the door was stuck. I got excited and ran back up-stairs. I told a couple of men about it and they told me to call the police. I did that, and when the first policeman arrived he got in and I followed him. One of the men was moaning a little but the six others were dead."

Frank Gusenberg was still alive, though just barely. By coincidence, the detective summoned by Mrs. Landesman had grown up in the same neighborhood as Gusenberg. He accompanied the wounded man to the hospital, and when Gusenberg regained consciousness for a brief moment the detective asked him softly, "Frank, what happened? Who shot you?"

"Nobody shot me," murmured Gusenberg.

The detective told him that his brother was dead, and that he was dying. There was no one left to protect.

"I ain't no copper," the gangster replied, and minutes later he, too, was dead.

Bugs Moran had no doubt about the identity of the man who had ordered the cold-blooded St. Valentine's Day Massacre. "Only Capone kills like that," he said.

The next day a reporter who was acquainted with Capone asked him if he had ordered the executions. "The only man who kills like that," Capone answered smoothly from his Florida hideaway, "is Bugs Moran."

Other wild theories pointed an accusing finger at the notorious all-Jewish Detroit Purple Gang, or an execution squad financed by a mysterious "Mr. X," the purported ringleader of a Canadian distillery empire engaged in a war with an equally ruthless competitor for the liquor trade of the entire western United States. As far as Major Fred D. Silloway was concerned, however, the killers really *were* Chicago policemen. Silloway, the deputy prohibition administrator for the Chicago district, announced on the day after the massacre that he believed the murders were retribution for Moran's sudden decision to cut off payments for police protection of his illicit liquor shipments. Silloway later backed away from his accusation and claimed he had been misquoted, but other equally outraged prominent citizens of Chicago left no doubt that they believed the ultimate if not the proximate blame for the killings could be laid squarely at the doorstep of the extravagantly corrupt city administration of Mayor William Hale "Big Bill" Thompson, Jr. "Chicago is on a volcano," charged Frank J. Loesch, first assistant state's attorney and president of the Chicago Crime Commission. "The massacre and other killings can be traced right to City Hall."

Thompson, a flamboyant buffoon who affected cowboy garb and did more than his fair share to make Chicago "the worst governed city in the world," had settled into the mayor's office for a third term in 1927 following a campaign distinguished (even by Chicago's own peculiar standards) by excessive violence, vicious mudslinging, and unabashed bribery. Even without the hoodlums' guns and the dirty money, however, Thompson remained an accomplished demagogue who rolled up huge majorities by flimflamming the public with his fantastically outlandish antics and minority-baiting rhetoric. "He may not be too much on brains," a friendly congressman once said of Thompson, "but he gets through to people." His platform certainly appealed to Al Capone. After Thompson publicly vowed to reopen all the speakeasies which had been shut down by the reform administration that had ousted him in 1923, Capone reportedly contributed $260,000 to Wild Bill's campaign coffers and instructed his goons to "vote early and vote often." "Thompson is a buffoon in a tommyrot factory," declared a disgusted *Tribune* editorial writer, "but when his crowd gets loose in the City Hall, Chicago has more need of Marines than any Nicaraguan town."

The immediate result of Thompson's return to power following the 1927 municipal election was a shocking epidemic of fatal violence: in 1928, Chicago recorded 527 murders in a city of four million inhabitants, compared with 337 in more populous New York. The nauseating rash of slayings awakened voters to the cost of Wild Bill's suzerainty and inspired them to oust Thompson's henchmen in the state and local elections of 1928. A partially reformed police force proceeded to gun down thirty gangsters in the last five months of that year before launching a series of sweeping drives in early January 1929 that brought nearly three thousand criminals into custody during a single weekend. But the voters had waited too long, and the crusaders were forced to wage an uphill battle with inadequate resources; while New York had one policeman for every 360 inhabitants, there was only one cop for every 650 Chicagoans. Graft was too deeply entrenched in the city's government to admit of easy or quick solutions ("Chicago is unique," said one of Thompson's former rivals—"It is the only completely corrupt city in America"), and the profits from bootlegging and racketeering were far too enticing to allow a few casualties or jail terms to discourage the city's rival gangs.

For most of Chicago's well-connected hoodlums, the most dangerous threat came not from the police (60 percent of whom were said to be on the take anyway) nor from civic-minded reformers, but from executioners in rival gangs. Gang warfare on the shores of Lake Michigan erupted in earnest in November 1924, when Dion O'Banion, an ex-safecracker who ruled the rackets on the North Side of the city, was slain in his own florist shop by gunmen from Johnny Torrio's gang who were seeking revenge for the hijacking of several liquor shipments belonging to Torrio's lieutenants. No one was ever convicted for the murder. O'Banion's successor, Little

Hymie Weiss, vowed revenge; two months later, four thugs attacked Torrio in front of his apartment house and left him for dead with four bullets in his body. Torrio recovered, however, and soon thereafter judiciously decided to retire from active management of the empire of organized crime (booze, brothels, and gambling dens) he had built with the organizational skill and fine calculating judgment of a multimillionaire business executive, which is precisely what he—like Arnold Rothstein— was. But before he departed for the less turbulent environs of Sheepshead Bay, New York (where the average life expectancy was far longer), Torrio relinquished control of his widespread enterprises to the man he had imported from the East as a bodyguard and chauffeur in 1919: Alphonse "Scarface" Capone.

The son of Gabriel Caponi, a Neapolitan immigrant who became a barber in the New World, Al Capone was a member of that first generation of Italian-Americans who refused to be shut out, as their fathers had been, from a share in the Good Things that America offered to enterprising young men. Some sought their fortune in the world of business and finance, others fought and cajoled their way to the top of powerful urban political machines, and a few, who were more notorious than numerous, turned to crime. Born in 1899, Capone grew up in the slums of Brooklyn, in the shadow of the navy yard. A graduate of the vicious Five Points street gang, he got his first break when Francesco Uale, alias Frankie Yale, head of the fraternal (and allegedly criminal) Italian-American association known as the Unione Siciliane, hired Capone as a bouncer and bartender for one of his Coney Island clubs. It was there that Capone one evening impetuously insulted a knife-wielding patron's girlfriend and received in reply the three scars on the left side of his face that left him disfigured for life and gave him the sobriquet he loathed so violently.

Physically Capone resembled a gorilla. He stood five feet ten, weighed 255 pounds, possessed powerful, meaty hands, walked with his shoulders sloping slightly forward, lacked any discernible neck, and had thick, dark eyebrows that met in the middle of his forehead. "His face looked congested," wrote one perceptive observer, "as if too much flesh had been crammed into the available frame." A half decade of loyalty and resourcefulness in the service of his boss carried Capone to the top rung in Torrio's organization, but when he inherited the mantle of leadership upon Johnny's hasty departure in 1925, he also fell heir to the unslaked enmity of Hymie Weiss. Twice Weiss attempted to perforate Capone (one of Weiss' gunmen in the first assault was Bugs Moran) and twice he failed, though he did eliminate several of Capone's thugs along the way. Inevitably, Capone struck back. Weiss was shot to death in front of Holy Name Cathedral on North State Street in October 1926; his successor,

"Schemer" Drucci, suffered an inglorious demise at the hands of an angry policeman while resisting arrest.

Leadership of the North Side gang then passed to the Irishman Moran, and the underworld conflict that had begun as a blood feud between Weiss and Torrio erupted into full-scale warfare. Between January 1927 and February 1929, ninety-one gang members ("soldiers," in contemporary parlance) were slain in Chicago in the battle between Moran, Capone, and splinter factions like the hot-headed and trigger-happy Aiello family. Frankie Yale himself was gunned down by Capone's men while riding through the streets of Brooklyn in his flashy sports coupe on July 1, 1928, after Capone received evidence that Yale had double-crossed him on a liquor deal.

The sight of fully armed mercenaries shooting one another in broad daylight in the middle of America's second largest city struck some observers as a surrealistic imitation of the late Great War. Chicago's gangsters, noted Lloyd Lewis in the *New Republic,* "are marshalled in opposing armies, live in armed fortresses, travel in cars that are armed if not armored, plan their strategic raids, surprises, ambushes, and defenses, like professional soldiers. They enlist for the loot that awaits them, live in plenty while they live, and obviously enjoy the life. . . . If they take each other for 'a ride,' shoot each other in the back, spray rivals with machine-gun bullets—perhaps poisoned—or slash suspected traitors with knives, they do so because they are at war. And," added Lewis, a bit disingenuously, "it is a war in which the non-combatants are safer than they were in Belgium. . . . It is hardly an accident that, in all this warfare, no citizen, living his normal life, has been harmed. The bootleg soldiers have no grudge against the general public, and take the cursings of the newspapers with cynical indifference."

The mercenaries risked their lives for the glittering strategic prize of the Chicago illicit liquor market, and the rights to distribute across the northern United States the millions of gallons of bourbon and ale smuggled in annually across the Canadian border in steamers, airplanes, freight cars, and automobile trunks. "It is this matter of important money that makes Chicago gang wars so bloody," one astute columnist explained. "The city holds the key to the rich trade of the West and Northwest in whiskey, wine, gin and beer, exactly as it does in wheat, hogs, furniture, and more staple commodities . . . and the control of such fabulous wealth makes life itself unimportant to the gangster who rides upon the flood of gold."

By forcing the nation's liquor trade into illegal channels, prohibition unwittingly had paved the way for the rise of organized crime syndicates in the United States. As the president of the American Bar Association put it, the bootlegger was "the spider in the center of the American web of crime." "Ever since Prohibition came in," charged the New York *Evening Post,* "we have seen the old 'corner gangs' rise in power till they controlled cities or battled with each other for district liquor privileges that meant the income of many an ancient empire. Their wealth grew. They had influence in their neighborhood banks. They could buy and sell Aldermen and policemen. They could, in ordinary times, make and break city-wide elections. They could elect their own State's Attorneys, or even judges. And they could hire the most expensive legal talent to cheat, to delay, and to get them off." Capone, the outstanding example of a crime lord, had nearly a thousand enforcers at his command, along with a network of police and politicians eager to do his bidding, and a financial wizard—a portly Russian immigrant named Jake "Greasy Thumb" Guzik—who managed Capone's investments in scores of speakeasies, gambling clubs, racetracks, labor unions, whorehouses, protection rackets, and commercial associations.

But the foundation of the empire that brought Capone $100 million worth of profits annually (in 1928, his syndicate reportedly grossed $105 million) was always booze, and he tolerated no intrusion onto his turf from any quarter, as the seven unfortunate victims at 2122 North Clark Street learned at the cost of their lives. "Remove Prohibition and its attendant high prices for low-priced liquor," said recently appointed Chicago police commissioner William F. Russell on the day after the St. Valentine's Day Massacre, "and these gang killings will cease, because they won't pay. We had no such outrages as this 'massacre' before Prohibition. Don't misunderstand me—we had plenty of crime and, in those days, a lot more vice than we have to-day. But there was no crime, no vice in pre-Prohibition days that was worth a 'massacre.' . . . No other crime—except, perhaps, dope smuggling and peddling—would be worth it."

So long as contraband liquor remained a Big Business, however, in which the demand for goods exceeded the available supply, no officials, however well-intentioned, could ever hope to control organized crime in Chicago or any other metropolis. Men like Capone and Moran and their counterparts across the United States appeared untouchable because they supplied American consumers with a reliable product at a reasonable price, and they guaranteed delivery. "From Big Business in more admired fields," wrote one journalist, "the gangsters have learned that the 'important money' is to be gained by keeping the customer happy and satisfied." In fact, the price of bootleg liquor in Chicago had declined since the trade had been monopolized by well-organized syndicates whose executives applied proved techniques of modern management to their enterprises. "The so-called 'insolence' of the Chicago gangster is merely an assurance that society is with him rather than against him," argued the *New Republic*'s Lloyd Lewis, perhaps overstating the point. "He attends opening nights at the theater in evening clothes, occupying front-row seats while his bodyguards sit a row or two behind. He behaves quietly in the lobby between acts while these same shadows brood over him near by. His guards are not to protect him from the populace or the police but from snipers of the enemy's camp. His only enemies are his rivals."

Certainly Capone considered himself an exemplary man of American business. "I give the public what the public wants," he told reporters. "I never had to send out high pressure salesmen. I could never meet the demand." Capone openly admitted he violated the Volstead prohibition laws, but, he added, "Who doesn't? The only difference is I take more chances than the man who drinks a cocktail before dinner and a flock of highballs after it. But he's just as much a violator as I am." Gangsters had feelings, too, Capone reminded his audience, and constant criticism in the press wounded his sensitive pride. "I've been spending the best years of my life as a public benefactor," he huffed. "I've given people the light pleasures, shown them a good time. And all I get is abuse—the existence of a hunted man. I'm called a killer. Ninety percent of the people of Cook County [Illinois] drink and gamble and my offense has been to furnish them with those amusements. Whatever else they may say, my booze has been good and my games have been on the square. Public service is my motto. I've always regarded it as a public benefaction if people were given decent liquor and square games."

Well, not quite everyone shared Scarface's intriguing system of ethics. When he visited Los Angeles in December 1927, he was unceremoniously evicted from his room at the Biltmore by the hotel manager and the chief of police. ("I thought you people liked tourists," Capone complained angrily. "Whoever heard of anybody being run out of Los Angeles that had money?") So he journeyed—incognito, using his favorite alias of Al Brown—to Florida, finally settling in Miami Beach, where he rented a bungalow for one winter and then purchased a fourteen-room, two-story Palm Island estate originally owned by St. Louis beer magnate Clarence M. Busch. Naturally Capone modified the house and grounds to meet his own peculiar requirements. He erected a barrier of concrete blocks around the perimeter of the estate and stationed armed guards behind the solid oak and iron entrance gate. Because he was a physical fitness fanatic, Capone ordered architects to build him the largest swimming pool in all of south Florida, so he and his guests could frolic in a sixty-by-forty-foot pool that stretched between the house and Biscayne Bay. At the pier he kept a cabin cruiser, *Arrow,* and a speedboat, *Sonny and Ralphie,* for fishing trips and perhaps a rapid getaway in case of emergency. He rode in a seven-ton, custom-built Cadillac limousine with bullet-proof glass in the windows and steel-plated armor covering the body and the gas tank; a built-in gun rack and a sliding rear window allowed Capone and his bodyguards to fire at any cars following them.

He affected boxer shorts made of Italian silk, monogrammed royal blue and gold silk pajamas which he ordered by the dozen, and custom-made suits, powder blue and sunshine yellow, fashioned by the tailors of Chicago millionaire Marshall Field. (The right-hand pockets of Capone's jackets had to be reinforced to accommodate a loaded pistol.) In the proper light, Capone seemed to glitter; oversized diamonds adorned his tiepin, his platinum watch chain, and his stubby middle finger. In typical arriviste style, he surrounded himself with fawning sycophants. "Capone hires nothing but gentlemen," boasted Harry Doremus, a former lieutenant in Al's Florida beer-running business. "They must be well dressed at all times; they must have cultured accents; must always say 'Yes Sir' and 'No Sir' to Capone when he addresses them. He hires his men with great care and takes pains that they are of his own type in dress and conduct." Part of that conduct included raucous sex; Capone liked to test his employees by throwing beautiful, lascivious women at them, and any man who failed to perform in the expected manner was summarily demoted.

"Capone is living the life of a country gentleman, with all the luxuries that a gentleman should have," acknowledged a district attorney who visited the gangster in Miami. But there were two things Capone did not have: a life insurance policy—every company to which he applied turned him down flat—and a stock portfolio. "It's a racket," Capone said scornfully of the gambling mania that had seized Wall Street. "Those stock market guys are crooked!" He prudently kept his own money in banks or in padlocked wooden chests in his bedroom and offices.

On the morning of February 14, 1929, St. Valentine's Day, Al Capone was sitting conspicuously in the office of the Dade County solicitor, flippantly answering (or not, as he chose) pointed questions about his business activities in south Florida. It was true that he had talked on the telephone with Jake Guzik in Chicago nearly every day for the past few weeks; Guzik allegedly made a call to Capone's Palm Island residence thirty minutes after the massacre. It was also true that Chicago authorities quickly obtained murder indictments against two of Capone's top executioners, John Scalise and Jack "Machine Gun" McGurn (whose real name was Vincenzo De Mora) for their role in the massacre. "We got a 'cold bang' on McGurn," boasted the detective in charge of the investigation, after a teenaged boy—who had testified that one of the men who had come out of the garage on North Clark Street had been missing a finger from his right hand—picked McGurn out of a lineup. McGurn was not amused.

"The police probably did it themselves," he snarled. Actually, McGurn—whom the Gusenberg brothers twice had tried to kill—and Scalise probably were innocent; either the authorities arrested them to put pressure on Capone, or else they had not yet learned that Capone (who had studied under the obsessively cautious Torrio) usually preferred to employ underlings far down the organizational ladder for highly visible executions. At any rate, Police Commissioner Russell seemed willing to arrest anyone and everyone who might conceivably have been involved in the massacre. "It's a war to the finish," he sputtered in fury. "I've never known a challenge like this." And he vowed to make the St. Valentine's Day slayings "the knell of gangdom in Chicago."

A week after the massacre, the police recovered the getaway car in an abandoned garage; the car had been disfigured and partially dismantled with an acetylene torch and hacksaws. Then they received an even bigger break. The chauffeur of the president of the Chicago Board of Education had observed the Cadillac fleeing the scene of the crime, and he noticed that the driver—one of the men in police uniform—was missing a front tooth. An alert detective matched that tip with the description of Fred "Killer" Barnes, a former member of the "Egan's Rats" gang in St. Louis. Barnes, the detective knew, had a penchant for wearing a police uniform as a disguise during bank holdups; in fact, at that time he was already a fugitive under indictment for murder and bank robbery in Ohio.

Barnes was also a prime suspect in the unsolved murder of Frankie Yale. Police investigators had traced the guns used in the Yale slaying to Miami, where they obtained a confession from Paul Henderson, Jr., the son of a former mayor of the city, that he had purchased the weapons for Capone. (Scarface, of course, had been comfortably ensconced in his Florida hideaway when Yale was killed in Manhattan.) New York detectives also theorized that Capone had played an integral role in Arnold Rothstein's death, possibly as a result of a dispute over the rapidly expanding narcotics traffic; an informant tentatively placed Jake McGurn at the Park Central Hotel around the time Rothstein was murdered. So, at the end of February 1929, Brooklyn assistant district attorney Louis Goldstein journeyed to Miami to question Capone. "I invited Capone to come to New York," Goldstein revealed after meeting the gangster. "We would like to question him under oath about several cases." But Capone obstinately ignored all efforts—including a federal grand jury subpoena from Chicago—to dislodge him from his Palm Island hideaway. He was enjoying himself far too much hobnobbing with the social and financial elite of the nation in America's newest winter playground to answer any official inquiries about murder or his bootlegging operations.

The highlight of the Miami Beach social season that year was the heavyweight title fight between Jack Sharkey and Young Stribling, two of the leading pretenders to the throne vacated the previous summer by Gene Tunney. At ringside on the evening of February 27, Scarface Al mingled convivially with the likes of Flo Ziegfeld, Edsel Ford, Charlie Mitchell, Babe Ruth, John S. Pillsbury, Johnny Weissmuller, and Walter Chrysler. It was a terribly dull fight (Sharkey won a unanimous decision), but nobody really cared. Americans were relying on Wall Street to provide them with all the excitement they needed in the winter of 1929; and as spring approached, the action on the stock market was just beginning to heat up.

# PART TWO: GREED

---

# VIII

# The Perils of Prosperity

"President Hoover is expressing aptly the temper of a
vast majority of his countrymen. It is perhaps just as well
that they should have a leader who is capable of taking
them efficiently toward the direction in which they
want to go. If what they find along the way proves
disappointing to him and to them, it will be the
fault of the line of march, not of the captain."
——NEW REPUBLIC, *March 13, 1929*

Shortly before seven o'clock on the morning of March 4, inauguration
day, President Coolidge climbed quietly out of his four-poster mahogany
bed, dressed himself without disturbing his wife, and descended in a
private elevator to the first floor of the White House. For the last time,
Silent Cal prowled wordlessly through the empty offices of the Executive
Wing, poking into pigeonholes and searching through desk drawers and
under blotters for any last bits of memorabilia that had so far escaped his
thorough searches.

Coolidge was in a nasty mood. When he spied head usher Ike Hoover,
he growled, "What's the weather?"

"Rather uncertain," the majordomo replied. "Looks as if it might
rain."

"Well, I hope not," muttered Coolidge grimly. "But it always has
rained on my moving days." Then the President strolled through the
kitchen, barely nodding to the hired help, and walked out into the White
House grounds for his morning constitutional. Later, after breakfast, Coolidge stubbornly refused to change into formal attire for the forthcoming
ceremony; when the carriages of dignitaries began to pull into the driveway at ten o'clock, the President still was wearing his everyday suit of
clothes.

To the last days of his administration, Calvin Coolidge remained extraordinarily popular with the American people and the press. When he
bade farewell to the Washington press corps, some of the hard-bitten

reporters actually had tears in their eyes. In his final weeks in office, Coolidge was swamped with so many requests for autographed photos that he had to omit his usual midday nap for nearly a week to sign them all; at the end of February, an administration spokesman announced that the White House supply of pictures had been exhausted, and that admirers who wanted the President's autograph had to supply their own photos. And as Coolidge and his wife made their way to and from the First Congregational Church at Tenth and G streets on the Sunday before the inauguration, they were greeted with adoring applause and shouts of goodwill ("Good-bye and thank you, Mr. President") from an estimated 3,500 admirers who thronged the streets and sidewalks around the Executive Mansion.

While Coolidge puttered sourly about the White House on the morning of inauguration day, Herbert Hoover already was hard at work at his desk in the library of his home on S Street, dictating letters and sorting stacks of mail. As the clock chimed ten, his valet, Boris (a Serbian veteran of the Great War), helped the President-elect into his gray pinstriped trousers and morning coat, adjusted his silk hat (Hoover hated silk hats), and retreated respectfully into the background as Senator George Moses of New Hampshire arrived and greeted the boss with a hearty handshake and an encouraging word. "You've been tagged," Moses chortled. "You're it; come along." "All right, in a minute or two," said Hoover, pulling quickly away from Moses' grasp.

At 10:45, the Hoovers arrived at the White House. They were shown into the Blue Room to join the rest of the official guests. Coolidge—who finally had put on his good clothes—walked in precisely at 11:00, nodded to everyone and stood uncomfortably shifting his weight from one foot to the other for a moment, and then barked in his nasal twang, "Time to go!" The buglers played "Hail to the Chief" as the party emerged into the overcast day, and when the chauffeur opened the door to the presidential touring car, Coolidge climbed in first and took the seat nearest the door, forcing Hoover to climb over him. The two men did not exchange a single word during the procession to the Capitol.

At the inauguration ceremony at the east portico of the Capitol, Chief Justice and former President William Howard Taft—who had stood in Hoover's place twenty years earlier—administered the oath of office to the incoming Chief Executive. A cold, drenching rain cast a pall over the proceedings. Although Hoover stood beneath a sheltered canopy, gusts of wind sent the rain beating down upon his face as he leaned forward to deliver his inaugural address. He shook his head to clear the water from his eyes. He looked out on a sea of black as hundreds of upraised umbrellas sprouted among the audience, fifty thousand strong, stretching beyond the edges of the Capitol plaza; many women, caught unprepared, fashioned makeshift head coverings out of the inaugural editions of Washington's daily newspapers. To one side, unprotected by the covered pavilion, the wives of diplomats, senators, and congressmen endured the downpour with stoic resignation as protocol demanded, their costly hats and gowns ruined by the swirling wind and rain. A group of Indians (friends and relatives of Vice-President Curtis), dressed in full war paint for the upcoming parade, displayed better sense and retreated beneath the main portico of the Capitol.

Hoover spoke into a bank of radio microphones that carried the inaugural proceedings, for the first time in history, across the nation and around the world, to London, Paris, Berlin, Rome, Mexico City, Leningrad, and Tokyo. (Hoover's performance was also the first to be recorded by sound motion picture cameras.) Listeners thought his voice sounded more confident than it had during the campaign. He spoke slowly, deliberately, invoking Divine guidance as he announced his intent to advance the cause of world peace (he specifically suggested that the United States ought to join the World Court) and his determination to launch a sweeping assault upon the burgeoning problem of crime in America. "Crime is increasing. Confidence in rigid and speedy justice is decreasing," Hoover admitted grimly. "It is only in part due to the additional burdens imposed upon our judicial system by the 18th Amendment [i.e., prohibition]. The problem is much wider than that. Justice must not fail because the agencies of enforcement are either delinquent or inefficiently organized. To consider these evils, to find their remedy, is the most sore necessity of our times."

Hoover then announced that he would convene a special session of Congress within six weeks, to devise solutions to the vexing problems of farm relief and tariff reform. And he capped his message with a dedication of the nation's energies to a "larger purpose" under his leadership, a sacred mission to "establish more firmly stability and security of business and employment and thereby remove poverty still further from our borders." "We are steadily building a new race—a new civilization great in its own attainments," Hoover proclaimed. "We have reached a higher degree of comfort and security than ever existed before in the history of the world. . . . In no nation are the fruits of accomplishment more secure." And then: "I have no fears for the future of our country. It is bright with hope."

The sodden crowd listened without much enthusiasm. There were only three prolonged outbursts of cheers: once when the new President acknowledged that the nation owed a tremendous debt to Calvin Coolidge; again when Coolidge stood to shake Hoover's hand; and finally when

Hoover vowed to enforce prohibition stringently. When the ceremony was over, the Coolidges headed for Union Station and the train that would take them home to Northampton. ("I wish to get accustomed to being a private citizen," Coolidge told his former cabinet officers, "and I might as well start this afternoon.")

Several decades later, veteran *New York Times* journalist Arthur Krock wrote in his memoirs, "I remember listening to Hoover's inaugural [address] and reading the subsequent rosy predictions with total disbelief." A year earlier, in the carefree springtime of 1928, Krock had conceived the notion of publishing a morning daily tabloid in New York that would eschew the format's traditional emphasis on sex and violence in favor of an intelligent and succinct presentation of the news. His employer, *Times* publisher Adolph Ochs, encouraged the proposal, and Krock eventually managed to attract sufficient financial backing from a number of wealthy patrons, including Bernard Baruch, who had previously employed Krock as a publicist shortly after he (Krock) arrived in New York from Louisville in 1923. Krock even developed a "dummy" edition as a prototype. But one day a troubled Baruch, who was having second thoughts, asked him how much time and money it would take before the venture turned a profit; Krock replied that he would need several years and between $3 and $5 million. Baruch then tried to persuade his friend to delay the project and wait for more auspicious times. "I don't like the look of this crazy bull market," Baruch said. "There is a strong possibility of a break before you got really going that would dry up your sources of revenue—pledges, circulation, and advertising alike." "I heeded his counsel," wrote Krock, "threw away the dummy, [and] abandoned the project." And so, with Baruch's warning still ringing in his ears, Krock recalled that he listened incredulously "to Hoover's inaugural portrait of mounting prosperity 'just around the corner.' "

By the spring of 1929, Bernard Baruch's occasional pronouncements on the state of the American economy had assumed the cloak of omniscience and infallibility previously accorded only to the Pope and the ancient oracle at Delphi. The son of a Southern belle, whose family's fortune was destroyed in the Civil War, and a Jewish German physician who fled to America to escape the Prussian draft, Baruch was born in South Carolina in 1870 and spent the first ten years of his life in a small country town in the state's pine-belt region. He and his family moved to New York in 1880, and though Bernard—"Shorty" to his friends—briefly entertained notions of becoming a doctor or a prizefighter (he had a stinging right jab and an admirable ability to take a punch without flinching), he obtained a position as a clerk in a Wall Street investment banking house upon graduating from college in 1889. He learned the intricacies

of the stock market by watching the most prominent speculators navigate
their way through the rough-and-tumble financial world of the Gay Nine-
ties; by the end of the decade he had amassed a fortune of several million
dollars through his own seemingly reckless operations, buying on margin,
often running against the tide of conventional wisdom, trusting his own
intuition and willingly risking his profits to earn even more millions.
"When I first went down to the Street, I was taught to respect certain great
minds of those days," Baruch explained years later. "I found they were a
pretty shallow set; in fact, I found there were more overrated men in Wall
Street than in any other street in the world. So I borrowed a motto from
a prizefighter. Was it Sullivan or Fitzsimmons? 'The bigger they come the
harder they fall.' Thereafter I did very nicely."

He did so nicely that he sold his seat on the stock exchange and
relinquished his partnership in a profitable Wall Street brokerage firm at
the age of thirty-two to "retire" to his isolated thirteen-thousand-acre
barony of Hobcaw (an Indian name that means "between the waters") on
the coast of his native South Carolina. But the market was in Baruch's
blood, and he continued to speculate until his fortune surpassed $25 mil-
lion. Blue-eyed, square-jawed, and garrulous when discussing his favorite
topic—himself—Baruch became a folk hero in that simpler and more
trusting era, though he was not, as some gullible people believed, infallible
in his financial judgment; he readily admitted that he occasionally committed the sort of costly error that "would make an ordinary married man go
out and shoot himself." Even to those who knew him well, Baruch appeared to have an unusually disordered mind, for no one else could follow
the complicated twists and jumps of his mental processes. When asked
how he arrived at his decisions to buy and sell stocks at any given moment,
the baron of Hobcaw replied cryptically (and perhaps flippantly), "I follow
the Indian signs."

In February 1918, after the United States had been at war for a full
year, President Woodrow Wilson turned to Baruch, who had earlier made
substantial contributions to Wilson's presidential campaigns, to organize
the stumbling and mismanaged American industrial supply effort. Although the idea of a Jewish stock juggler as czar of the omnipotent War
Industries Board appalled some conservative souls, Baruch proved to be
an exceptionally able administrator and shrewd judge of talent; he became
a sort of benign dictator over the nation's industrial base, allocating raw
materials and setting production goals, extending the federal government's reach to the farthest reaches of the domestic economy for the first
time. After the war, Baruch accompanied the American delegation to the
Paris Peace Conference as an economic adviser. The experience left him
with the firm conviction that American prosperity was inextricably inter-

twined with European recovery, and nowhere was that connection more evident than in the parlous state of American agriculture in the 1920s.

Farm relief became Baruch's personal crusade in the decade following the war. He realized that government appeals and the lure of temporarily inflated prices had overstimulated agricultural production during the conflict; despite sharply reduced demand after 1920, U.S. farmers had kept production (in Baruch's words) "running at full speed, like a motor with its accelerator stuck, piling up surpluses, while prices, responding inexorably to the law of supply and demand, plummeted, and despair swept the farm land." Responding to a desperate plea from the Kansas State Farm Board for advice, Baruch advocated a program that would utilize government credits to curtail surplus agricultural production and provide cooperative marketing facilities to strengthen the farmers' bargaining power. The agricultural bloc in Congress, however, stubbornly refused to support any measures to scale down production, and suggested instead that the federal government (1) erect a tariff wall to protect American farmers from foreign competition, and (2) guarantee farmers a minimum price for their crops. (This latter proposal was the much-ballyhooed concept known as parity, which indexed agricultural profits to a ten-year average of prewar industrial prices through a complicated formula that has remained unfathomable to laymen throughout the ensuing decades.) Under the farm bloc's program, the government would purchase a substantial portion of the domestic crop and then dump the surplus abroad, while imposing an "equalization fee" on farmers to compensate the government for the produce it was unable to sell in the international market. Twice Congress passed legislation—known as the McNary-Haugen Bills—embodying these proposals, and twice Coolidge vetoed the measures. In the face of an already existing worldwide commodity glut, the McNary-Haugen remedy was manifestly unworkable, though Coolidge's vetoes were based more on his dogmatic opposition to government intervention in the economy than on any reasoned analysis of the plan's chances for success.

Baruch, however, insisted that some form of special government assistance to agriculture was imperative, and that the ultimate solution to the farm depression in the United States lay in the revival of world trade, unencumbered by protective tariffs. "If the Continent could regain economic stability," he later wrote, "it would again consume American grain. The key to that stability, I believed, lay in the settlement of such issues as reparations, and the abandonment of American isolationist policies as expressed in our tariffs."

The links between agricultural recovery, European stability, and American prosperity subsequently came to govern Baruch's views on the future well-being of the U.S. economy and the stock market. He was convinced that any long-term American economic renaissance was unlikely while such a large and significant segment of the national economy—i.e., the farmers—remained locked outside the charmed circle of prosperity. "A nation's economy," he declared unequivocally, "cannot be healthy when a basic element in it is sick." And since the successful disposition of America's agricultural and industrial production depended upon the reestablishment and maintenance of European prosperity, it behooved the United States to forsake its pigheaded isolationism and assist the Continental powers in settling the long-standing issues of war debts and reparations. Surveying the state of international affairs in the late 1920s, Baruch claimed, "I could see where a new surge of prosperity [in the United States] might be touched off if we could solve such problems as the farm collapse, reparations, and war debts. But while these problems remained unresolved, there seemed to be no justification for the prices people were willing to pay for securities. Stock prices may have been booming, but if one took the trouble to study the business situation carefully, he could find reasons for being uneasy." Specifically, Baruch was worried about the slumping automobile and construction industries. And, of course, the veteran speculator realized that sooner or later the bull market had to break.

Hence Baruch's cautionary advice to Alexander Woollcott, Heywood Broun, and several other members of the Algonquin Round Table during a weekend excursion to Atlantic City. "As we strolled along the boardwalk," Baruch recalled, "the conversation got around to the market, as it usually did. My opinion was asked. My advice was to pull out of speculative situations, get out of debt, and put one's funds into sound bonds. I don't think my advice was well-regarded," he added ruefully. And hence Baruch's prudent counsel to Will Rogers, who asked the financier for investment advice in the spring of 1929 after signing a contract that would bring the cowboy humorist nearly $1 million over the next three years. Baruch advised Rogers to pay off the mortgage on his Western property before he did anything else. When Rogers resisted the suggestion, Baruch reportedly told him, "What you want to do is gamble. But I want to tell you that you're sitting on a volcano. That's all right for professional volcano sitters, like myself, but an amateur like you ought to take to the tall timber and get as far away as you can. There may come a time when the man who holds your mortgage will want his money and you may not have it, and your friends won't have it either." Rogers sat slumped in his chair as he listened silently to Baruch's lecture, chewing his gum and scratching his head.

Although Baruch already had begun to liquidate his own stock portfolio by the time of Hoover's inauguration, putting part of his profits into bonds and piling up a healthy cash reserve, he had not forsaken the market entirely. Since 1924, Baruch had made millions of dollars in the Coolidge bull market, and he had lost hundreds of thousands of dollars in 1927 and 1928 by selling short at periodic intervals when he thought he recognized the signs of an imminent collapse. So Baruch retained a modest portion of his stock holdings, and even issued a series of optimistic public statements early in 1929 based on his conviction that the forthcoming European conference of financial experts, guided by the wisdom of Owen Young and J. P. Morgan, Jr., would succeed in finally liquidating the troublesome economic legacy of the Great War. According to the Baltimore *Sun*'s Frank Kent, who interviewed Baruch at his Hobcaw estate, Baruch believed that a viable solution of the reparations and war debts problems would produce "an industrial boom incomparably greater than any that have preceded it." In a similar vein, Baruch told an interviewer for *American* magazine that "the economic condition of the world seems on the verge of a great forward movement."

> For the first time in history, we have sound reason for hope for a long period of peace. For the first time, the business men of all nations are supplied with statistical information, together with some understanding of the laws of economics. For the first time, we have sound centralized banking systems in all the countries and close cooperation between those systems internationally. Because all these factors are favorable, and because of the universal stirring of desire and ambition . . . I believe in the "industrial renaissance." We are already seeing something of it in the United States.

So much for the vaunted prescience of Bernard Baruch—although in fairness it should be pointed out that Baruch did not necessarily believe that even the rosiest forecasts for the American economy as a whole justified the wildly inflated stock values of the spring of 1929.

Baruch also expressed full confidence in President Herbert Hoover, whose executive abilities he had come to admire at the Paris Peace Conference in 1919. Soon after inauguration day, Baruch acknowledged that he believed the new Republican in the White House to be entirely "sound." There is no evidence that any substantial segment of American public opinion disagreed with that assessment in the spring of 1929. If Hoover did not excite enthusiasm among a majority of Americans, he certainly commanded their respect as he embarked upon his first months as Chief Executive. The President's personal prestige was enormous. He had won more popular votes than any President in the history of American politics, rolling up majorities in every section of the country. His party controlled both houses of Congress. He inherited the leadership of a country that had become the richest nation in the world, and Hoover had only to maintain the economic momentum, or prevent it from being reversed, to retain public favor. Voters had been sold irrevocably on the twin notions that the Republican party was the special guardian of prosperity and that Hoover was one of the most talented men in the United States. "If Mr. Coolidge has done well," ran the popular refrain, "Mr. Hoover ought to do twice as well." Lulled by reassuring statements about expanding productivity and rising profits from Coolidge, Mellon, and Hoover himself, the American people simply could not believe that anything could be seriously wrong with the nation's economy in the spring of 1929. If anything should go amiss, surely the Great Engineer would know what remedies to employ. It was this conviction that kept stocks rising despite the gloomy warnings of Federal Reserve authorities and maverick economic experts.

And this was precisely why Hoover sat upon such a precarious perch. Never before, since the United States had become an industrial power, had the nation gone so long without a depression, and "the fact that so many people have become supremely confident that there is no danger on the horizon is itself, to the historically informed, one of the main signs of warning," wrote journalist and popular historian George Soule in a remarkably farsighted article in the *New Republic* shortly before inauguration day. A severe downturn already was long overdue, Soule warned, and he predicted that if the setback occurred during Hoover's administration, the unfortunate President would be visited by "a special nemesis." "This expert," he said, "this engineer, this statistician, will fall from a very high pedestal indeed if Coolidge prosperity does not continue. If he does something, the trouble will be blamed upon what he does. Ironically, the very measures he may undertake which are best calculated to avert or mitigate a depression would be blamed for the depression. Nor can he sit back and let his opposition be the scapegoat, for he has no opposition powerful enough to be blamed for anything."

Soule recognized the cracks that already existed in what he termed the "uncontrolled over-confidence of Coolidge prosperity": building construction had begun to slacken; banks and landlords had been grumbling for months about growing vacancies in apartments and commercial real estate; the domestic market for new automobiles had become satiated; real wages in manufacturing, railroads, and mining had remained stationary for the past several years, and employment in those vital sectors appeared to be shrinking. Farmers' net income had been falling steadily, and the rising tide of protectionist sentiment threatened to dislocate foreign trade. "Suppose building slacks up, instalment credit fails to grow as before, and there are fewer new purchasers and users of automobiles, radios, and so on," wondered Soule. "Where will be the purchasers' stimulus for industrial growth?"

Mr. Edgar D. Brown of Pottsville, Pennsylvania, was mad as hell when he arrived in New York City in the spring of 1929. The specific target of Brown's wrath was Charlie Mitchell's National City Company and its somewhat unorthodox methods of operation. Since November 1927, when he had answered a National City magazine advertisement that promised expert investment advice, Brown had watched Mitchell's smooth-talking salesmen fritter away his original nest egg of $100,000. Now, as he entered the company's offices at 55 Wall Street to complain of irregularities in a recent purchase of Andes Copper stock and to voice the gnawing concern that, in his words, "I was being a shorn lamb," Brown recalled how it all began.

In ill health at the end of 1927, Brown had decided to sell the chain of theaters he owned and managed in Pennsylvania, and retire to the more salubrious climate of California. Because National City Company promoted itself as a nationwide financial institution capable of managing the investments of people who found themselves transferred to an unfamiliar city, Brown contacted the corporation and soon thereafter received a visit from a National City salesman named Fred Rummel. Brown told Rummel that he owned $25,000 in U.S. and Italian government bonds and would soon realize another $75,000 from the sale of his theaters, and asked for Rummel's guidance in investing those funds. Brown's only restriction was that he wanted to confine his investments to fixed interest securities— under no circumstances did he wish to invest in common stocks.

Rummel conferred with his superiors and returned with a recommendation to sell all the bonds Brown currently held (they were all wrong for him, Rummel said), and purchase a different set of securities—including a block of the soon-to-be notorious Peruvian bonds—through the good offices of National City Company. Rummel also suggested that Brown take out a $75,000 loan with National City Bank to purchase still more bonds. "My attention was called by Mr. Rummel," Brown later testified, "that if I could buy bonds below par that were paying 7½, netting 7½ per cent, and borrow the money at 5 or 5½ per cent, that I could make the difference on the borrowed money and pay off those loans when the bonds came back, as he expected they would go to par."

Brown eventually borrowed approximately $125,000, which National City obligingly invested along with his original $100,000 savings. Throughout 1928, Brown watched as National City bought and sold and swapped securities on his account so furiously that he literally could not follow the convoluted path of paper transactions. The company bought Erie Railroad bonds and sold Greek government securities, purchased large blocks of bonds of such exotic concerns as Norwegian Hydro, State of Rio Grande de Sul, Saxon Public Works, and the Mortgage Bank of Chile, and sold Fiat S.F. 7's, Northern Ohio Power and Light's, and German General Electric's. (German bonds formed a third of National City's foreign business during the late 1920s.) The blizzard of trading continued until Brown finally figured out what was happening; at the end of 1928, he complained to Rummel that most of the bonds National City had bought for him appeared to have declined in value. "Well," Rummel replied, "that is your fault for insisting upon bonds. Why don't you let me sell you some stock?"

And poor Mr. Brown took the bait, hook, line, and sinker. Since he was neither blind, deaf, nor unusually stupid, Brown knew that the Coolidge-Hoover bull market had been rampaging upward while his listless bond portfolio sagged, and so he agreed to allow Rummel to buy stocks for him. Then the frenzied trading resumed at an even faster pace as hundreds of shares of Andes Copper and Cannon Mills were exchanged for Mohawk Carpet and Postal Telegraph and Cable. That was when Brown decided to take the bull by the horns, so to speak, and visit the National City officers in their Wall Street lair.

Upon arriving at number 55, Brown was introduced to a supervisor named H. W. Beebe, to whom he complained that his original sum of money, notwithstanding the rising market and a seemingly random series of rapid and violent transactions, had—so far as he could determine—declined even more in value. Moreover, the loans he had taken to purchase the additional bonds had left him more than $100,000 in debt. "I told him that I was fearful that a reaction in the market would wipe me out, and that I had no income," Brown recalled. Beebe assured the worried man that he would contact the manager of National City's Philadelphia office and see what arrangements could be made.

After Brown returned to Pottsville, Rummel reappeared and recommended that he trade all his remaining securities for shares of National City Bank itself, Anaconda Copper (the stock Charlie Mitchell's pool partners were trying to unload after artificially inflating the price for their own profit), and several other well-known corporations. Then, suggested Rummel, Brown should "sit still on that and see what would happen."

From March through May, the stock market bounced crazily up and down, buffeted by the continuing battle between the bulls and the Federal Reserve Board. It was an extremely nervous market that spring; every time the bogeyman of higher interest rates loomed menacingly on the horizon, speculators scurried to liquidate their holdings.

The first sharp decline in stock prices during the Hoover administration occurred on March 26. Although Coolidge, prior to leaving office, had assured the public that America's economy was "absolutely sound," and that securities were "cheap at current prices," the market had been spooked shortly after inauguration day by unusually blunt words of warning from Paul Warburg, a founder of the Federal Reserve Board and one of the most respected members of the international banking community. Delivering his annual report as chairman of the International Acceptance Bank, Warburg said that he believed the Federal Reserve system already had lost control of the American money market, a regrettable development that he feared eventually must end in tragedy. The banking system of the United States, Warburg charged, was "tossing about without its helm being under the control of its pilots. . . . When the savings of the masses are deposited as margins for Stock Exchange speculations, and when the extravagant use of funds for speculative purposes absorbs so much of the nation's credit supply that it threatens to cripple the country's regular business, then there does not seem to be any doubt as to the direction in which the Federal Reserve System ought to exercise its influence quickly and forcefully." If it did not do so, Warburg perceived little hope for the future: "History, which has a painful way of repeating itself, has taught mankind that speculative over-expansion invariably ends in over-contraction and distress. . . . If orgies of unrestrained speculation are permitted to spread too far, however, the ultimate collapse is certain not only to affect the speculators themselves, but also to bring about a general depression involving the entire country."

Warburg's pessimistic forecast was followed by an offhand and completely unexpected announcement from Secretary Mellon, whom Hoover had decided to retain at the Treasury (with some reluctance, since Mellon was so closely associated with the legacy of Calvin Coolidge). Following a series of clandestine (so as not to spook the market) meetings with the President and officials of the Federal Reserve Board, the venerable Mellon mentioned during a press briefing on March 14 that present market conditions offered investors an excellent opportunity to purchase bonds; it was far easier, he said, for investors to select a sound bond than a sound stock. Although he did not directly warn against purchasing stocks, Mellon did go so far as to say that some stocks "are too high in price to be good buys. For prudent investors I would say, if making a suggestion, that now is the time to buy good bonds."

Somehow, investors simply could not credit the spectacle of Paul Mellon, one of the patron saints of the New Era and the Coolidge boom, attempting to scare them away from further speculation. (Actually, Mellon made the statement under heavy pressure from Hoover, who was seeking to dampen speculation without interfering directly in the market mechanism.) Thus the bulls reacted perversely to Mellon's announcement by sending their favorite issues spurting upward even further in extremely heavy trading. "Investors in stocks may in the long run find that they have been bitterly deceived," observed the *Journal of Commerce*, "but while they hope, and while so many hopes are being fulfilled, the voice of official wisdom will not induce them to transfer their allegiance to safe and sound securities."

But the market as a whole did not surge ahead during March. On March 21, the *New York Times* reported that most common stocks seemed to be stuck in the doldrums, "getting nowhere at all. Each day a handful of issues is taken in hand and rushed violently upward under the impetus of good-sized and skillfully-placed professional orders. The body of stocks, however, do nothing at all, fluctuating only moderately and very irregularly. The gyrations of a few issues, however, give general trading an appearance of strength, but it is to be noted that it is usually a new set of stocks which move each day, and when analyzed the market as a whole shows neither consistent nor persistent strength."

It was the spectacular advances that earned the headlines, producing an illusion of generally rising prices. The common stock of General Motors, for instance, reached an all-time high of 91¾ on March 21, making G.M. the first "four billion dollar company" in Wall Street history. Gulf Oil stock appreciated by more than $210 million in the first few months of 1929; when one added the rise of $191 million in the value of the common stock of the Aluminum Company of America (Alcoa), one discovered that the Mellon family—which owned a majority of both corporations' securities—had increased its fortune by nearly $300 million since January 1. Stock of the First National Bank, an institution with close ties to J.P. Morgan and Company, surged from $5,450 per share to $7,100, a phenomenal jump that netted the bank's chairman and major shareholder, George F. Baker, approximately $31 million in easy profits. And RCA surged from $74 to $109 in less than ten days, propelled by a pool that included Durant, Raskob, Swope, Chrysler, the Fisher brothers, Charles M. Schwab, William Kenny, Percy A. Rockefeller (John D.'s nephew), and James Riordan. At that point, the pool began to sell its shares, netting the sixty-three participants a total profit of $5 million (Raskob's share came to $291,700, and Durant received a neat $145,800), and the price of RCA promptly dropped back down to the mid-eighties. It was the desire to participate in just this sort of frenzied advance before the bubble burst that led so many cash-poor people to seek loans from their brokers, and it was precisely this sort of insider trading operation that invariably left greedy small-time investors holding the bag.

When the members of the Federal Reserve Board gathered in Washington for their monthly meeting on Friday, March 22, they were dismayed to learn that brokers' loans had actually risen by $124 million since they had initiated their antispeculative campaign on February 6, despite—or perhaps because of—the fact that member banks had been calling in their loans to investors, thereby creating a credit squeeze that pushed interest rates on the call-money market all the way up to 12 percent. Even more distressing was the news that corporate "bootleg" loans to brokers now totaled more than $2.8 billion. What was happening, quite simply, was that corporations were rushing in where the banks now feared to tread. Although the board did not disclose any new antispeculative measure at the close of its meeting, such was the unsettled state of the stock market that nervous investors began to sell their holdings on Monday, March 25, simply on the assumption that the board *intended* to take more drastic action. "There are two things that can disrupt business in this country," observed Will Rogers wryly. "One is war and the other is a meeting of the Federal Reserve Bank."

The wave of liquidation became a flood on the morning of March 26. The night before, brokers had sent out hundreds of margin calls—demands for more collateral to replace the vanished value of stocks that had been used as collateral, but whose price had abruptly declined—and when many harried investors proved unable to provide additional security, their stocks were dumped on the market for whatever they would bring. Amateur speculators panicked, overwhelmed by the avalanche of falling prices. "The morning smash was one of the widest on record," reported one observer. "Stocks dropped like plummets, from 5 to 17 points and with no visible signs of support. Thousands of accounts were wiped out in this violent swing and many thousands of speculators, on their own volition and in a stage bordering panic, committed financial hari-kari. Every brokerage house in New York and throughout the country was jammed to the doors with excited customers."

Meanwhile the desperate demand for cash created a severe credit stringency; the interest rates for call money mounted hourly to 15 percent, and then 18 percent, before finally peaking at 20 percent—the highest rate in nine years—at 1:30 in the afternoon. At that prohibitive rate, potential buyers were severely discouraged from bolstering the falling market. The rush to turn stocks into cash became so hysterical that the ticker fell ninety minutes behind, leading some investors to think that they had sold at a higher price than they actually received. Although a portion of the market rallied late in the afternoon, the upswing came too late to save the pathetic victims of the panic. By the time it was all over, more than three hundred issues (about one-fourth of the total) on the New York Stock Exchange had descended to new lows for 1929.

Purely by chance, the sound of the closing bell on the floor of the stock exchange at three o'clock that afternoon coincided exactly with the liberation of George McManus—the accused slayer of Arnold Rothstein—from a ground floor room in the Tombs, the New York City prison whence he had been lodged for the past several months. Released by a state supreme court justice because prosecutors were dragging their feet in bringing him to trial, McManus was cheered by a thousand sympathetic onlookers as he emerged, grinning, into the sunlight, and passing motorists honked their horns in salute.

The five terrifying hours of panic established March 26, 1929, as easily the worst crash of the Coolidge-Hoover era and the heaviest day of trading in the history of the New York Stock Exchange—8,246,740 shares changed hands, surpassing the previous record by more than 1,200,000. The whole business scared the bejabbers out of Charlie Mitchell, not solely because his National City Company was stuck with 300,000 shares of Anaconda Copper, which he had intended to unload on an unsuspecting public at inflated prices in April. (The scheme was ruined, at least temporarily, by Anaconda's plunge from 174 to 142 on that one miserable day.) More important, Mitchell was fully aware that any recurrence of panic might cause the bull market to collapse entirely. That, of course, would be a very bad thing for National City, the country's recognized leader in the retail marketing of securities. It would also likely set off a chain reaction of corporate and bank failures that would send the nation spinning into a full-scale depression. So, he reasoned, if investors were selling because they feared that credit might dry up entirely, then Charlie Mitchell—as the head of the largest bank in the country—had a patriotic duty to reassure them. Accordingly, Mitchell hurriedly called a press conference for the morning of March 27 and announced that National City Bank was prepared to inject $5 million into the call-money market at an interest rate of 15 percent, and an additional $5 million for every 1 percent raise in the rate, until it reached 20 percent. Several other New York banks, Mitchell told reporters, also had expressed a willingness to supply additional funds to the market to ease the temporary credit stringency.

This maneuver appeared to be a slap in the face of the Federal Reserve Board, since Mitchell's action evidently was intended to revive the faltering speculative boom. Mitchell himself encouraged this impression by tactlessly stating that his bank would provide the necessary funds "whatever might be the attitude of the Federal Reserve Board." "So far as this institution is concerned," he said, "we feel we have an obligation which is paramount to any Federal Reserve warning, or anything else, to avert, so far as lies in our power, a dangerous crisis in the money market." In Washington, Senator Carter Glass violently denounced Mitchell for treating the board's policy "with contempt and contumely," and called for the banker's resignation as a director of the New York Reserve Bank. ("That's very interesting," Mitchell calmly replied, "but I have no comment to make.") Several other influential legislators, including the ranking Democrat on the Senate Banking and Currency Committee, joined Glass in demanding Mitchell's head on a platter, and Senator King of Utah announced that he planned to introduce a resolution calling for a congressional investigation of "speculative excesses" as soon as the special legislative session convened on April 15.

But Mitchell had not, in fact, thumbed his nose at the Federal Reserve Board. Privately, several members of Mitchell's rescue squad had requested and obtained approval from Governor Young of the Reserve Bank of New York (and, through him, from the Reserve Board in Washington) before offering their money to the call-money market. Since the Federal Reserve Board had no wish to preside over a wholesale, panic-stricken liquidation of security values, it had no quarrel with Mitchell's decision to avert an imminent crisis (though it did object to the intemperate tone of his language). The fact that National City's funds would be loaned only at the prohibitive rates of 15 percent or higher indicated clearly that Mitchell did not intend to perpetuate what he subsequently referred to as a "speculative debauch." As the *New York Times* pointed out, "Paying 15 per cent for money to speculate with ceases to be speculation and becomes insanity." Certainly Bernard Baruch believed that Mitchell, a business acquaintance and sometime bridge partner, had acted properly, and he told Mitchell so in a friendly note that also bitterly accused the Reserve Board of attempting to evade the responsibility for the speculative boom it had engendered by foolishly lowering interest rates in 1927.

Reassured by Mitchell's statement and the huge (albeit temporary) reduction in brokers' loans after the debacle of March 26, the market regained its equilibrium—for a few days. Then, on April 1, stocks dropped sharply again, though the retreat was far more orderly than before. Over two hundred stocks on the New York Exchange sank to new lows for the year, with many plummeting past the depressed levels reached in the sharp break of December 1928.

This was the last straw for Billy Durant. Having lost two fortunes in two decades to market crashes, he would not stand idly by while his third and presumably final fortune vanished in a prolonged panic. Now Durant made his oft-delayed journey to Washington, and at 9:30 on the evening of April 3, he appeared at the White House for a conference with President Hoover. The meeting was a closely guarded affair; Durant stealthily arrived in a taxicab instead of his customary limousine, to avoid attracting attention. Hoover listened noncommittally as Durant implored him to restrain the Federal Reserve Board. America's economic health was based on the unfettered extension of credit, Durant argued, and any concerted effort to restrict credit unduly—for whatever misguided purpose—would produce a "financial disaster of unprecedented proportions." He suggested that instead of threatening to raise interest rates, the board should actually lower the rediscount rate to 3 percent. But Hoover already had implemented a subtle campaign (imperceptible, in fact, to many contemporaries) through administration spokesmen and the press to warn the public against the "unduly high price of stocks," and so he gave no comfort to Durant.

Despondent, Durant returned to New York and promptly launched a public crusade to revive the bull market by ridiculing the Federal Reserve Board. For the rest of the spring, the nation was treated to the spectacle of Durant and his allies waging a propaganda offensive against the forces of financial moderation, which included, on this occasion at least, Charlie Mitchell, who startled the banking community by declaring his support for a one-point *increase* in the rediscount rate to 6 percent. On April 14, Durant purchased fifteen minutes on the Columbia Broadcasting System to broadcast a nationwide radio address that flayed the board's campaign to limit speculation. "Let the Federal Reserve Board keep its hands off business," snapped Durant, who charged that American businessmen were paying "an outrageous and unnecessary penalty" in higher interest rates as a result of the board's actions. In a typically flamboyant stunt, Durant informed his audience that he had sent questionnaires to prominent American industrialists in twenty cities, asking if they supported the board; 451 out of 463, he said, had replied in the negative.

Mitchell responded by endorsing wholeheartedly the board's efforts to restrain speculation, and called upon American investors to display "an attitude of sanity" by selecting securities more carefully and reducing their overextended credit margins. If investors were purchasing stocks with their own money, Mitchell explained, no one would be unduly concerned about the level of stock prices or the amount of capital tied up in the stock market: "But at the point when trading in stocks takes an undue proportion of the supply of credit through the banking system, as the evidence already cited clearly shows to be the case at the present time, it becomes properly a matter of concern to the banking authorities."

Indeed, the widespread diversion of credit to Wall Street already was producing dangerous cracks in the nation's economic foundation, confirming the Reserve Board's worst fears. Although steel and automobile production continued at near record levels through the spring, railroad shipments declined noticeably in March, and the output of coal mines dropped drastically. More important, building construction in the first quarter of 1929 fell 15 percent behind the same period in 1928; instead of rising in March, as it usually did, the level of new residential and commercial construction declined further as money became more scarce and much more expensive.

Farmers, too, were feeling the pinch. In an emotional speech on the floor of the Senate on April 11, Republican Arthur Capper of Kansas complained that "money needed at home is being drawn from western banks to continue this orgy of speculation at the expense of western agriculture and western business interests." Midwestern banks, Capper claimed, were sending funds to Wall Street in unprecedented amounts to take advantage of the exorbitant interest rates on the call-money market. "Under the circumstances, for western bankers to throw their millions into New York's call money market, that the stock gamblers may bet the entire country's available resources on their gigantic poker game as they have been doing the last weeks, seems almost criminal," Capper cried. "Any one can see what a strain this speculative craze must be on the credit of the country." Unless bankers reversed the trend and supplied farmers and legitimate businessmen with the loans they required, the senator concluded, "there can be only one end to the orgy of speculation which seems to have lost the power to cure itself except in a sudden crash that may involve the country."

And the dangers did not stop at the water's edge. A total of $400 million in gold flowed from foreign central banks to New York over the first four months of 1929, including $41 million from the German Reichsbank alone during a two-week period in late March and early April. (The sudden loss of gold forced the Reichsbank to raise its discount rates to the highest level in three years, introducing another element of uncertainty into the already difficult German economic situation.) Unless this trend was reversed by autumn, there was a very real danger that foreign trade would be severely disrupted; there simply would not be sufficient purchasing power abroad to sustain American industrial and agricultural exports at current levels.

If financiers in the capitals of Europe were not unduly concerned about the drain on their gold reserves, it was only because they believed that the Wall Street speculative boom had nearly run its course. Banking officials in France and Germany recalled that the European bull markets before the Great War had exhibited the same rapid up-and-down movements, with relatively little change in the average level of prices, as they expended their final, fitful bursts of energy. The financial editor of the prestigious *Berliner Tageblatt* characterized the chaotic events on Wall Street in March and April as "the handwriting on the wall," and pondered the ironic prospect that Hoover, whose election was supposed to be a guarantee of prosperity, might be called upon to guide the United States through the worst economic disaster in American history. Other European forecasters predicted that since the American boom had lasted for eight years, with only a few insignificant interruptions, the inevitable reaction might also be unusually prolonged.

Similar prophecies of financial catastrophe were being made with increasing frequency in the United States. Paul Clay, an executive of the United States Shares Corporation, told a gathering of financial analysts in New York that he expected a break of 15 to 25 percent in the stock market before Labor Day because the mania for speculation was "hampering the flow of surplus capital into such expansion of industry as was necessary for the country to remain prosperous." The editors of the *New Republic* agreed; in mid-April, the liberal journal warned that "if the speculators continue their stubborn course . . . prices of shares will go on up, and brokers' loans will go on increasing, until legitimate business, which depends on commercial loans, is seriously embarrassed, a credit shortage develops which nobody can ameliorate, and an irretrievable crash of values occurs."

On April 29, John Foster Dulles, a partner in the prominent Wall Street law firm of Sullivan and Cromwell, reminded the annual meeting of the Chamber of Commerce of the United States that the speculative boom was endangering American exports and the health of the international economy. The extraordinarily high interest rates on the call-money market, Dulles said, were "creating an abnormal demand upon the foreign central banks for dollar exchange which their citizens would use, not to pay for American goods, but to loan to brokers at 10 per cent"; he concluded with a warning that the drain of foreign gold to Wall Street "cannot long continue without a collapse which will mean the realization of the dangers which were forecast ten years ago, but which since then have been so successfully avoided."

Perhaps the clearest indication of which way the wind was blowing came when Kuhn, Loeb and Company, the second-largest investment banking firm on Wall Street, decided to withdraw a substantial portion of its capital from the call-money market—then offering 14 percent interest—and place it instead in a new offering of New York City bonds that paid only 5¼ percent. At a May meeting of the firm's principals at their elegantly paneled offices in downtown Manhattan, Mortimer Schiff—Kuhn, Loeb's senior partner—announced in precise, clipped tones that he sensed danger in the overheated condition of the stock market; he had therefore arrived at the conclusion, Schiff said, that he would "rather forgo the high interest and see more of the firm's capital in safe, fixed-interest-bearing obligations." Despite mild opposition from Otto Kahn, whose generous patronage of the arts (from George Gershwin to the New York Metropolitan Opera) had made him one of the most famous men on Wall Street, the rest of the partners concurred in Schiff's decision, and so they purchased the high-grade bonds for their own portfolios; since there were more than enough to go around, they subsequently sold part of the issue to John D. Rockefeller, Sr., as shelter against the coming storm.

The stock market drifted through the rest of the spring in a state of suspended animation. The pool operators stood on the sidelines and waited; Durant sailed for Paris and a vacation to calm his nerves; the Federal Reserve Board conferred but said nothing. Spring traditionally established the character of a market for the rest of the year, but it did not do so in 1929. One day the market marched up the hill in a halfhearted rally; the next day it marched back down. The volume of trading fell off by 60 percent from the furious pace of March. Even the news that U.S. Steel established a new domestic record for quarterly earnings in peacetime failed to generate much enthusiasm. "Wall Street, at the moment, reminds one much of the dwellers in a riverside town who gather on the wharf to watch the steamer come in, possibly to meet some traveler or get a little news," remarked Alexander Dana Noyes, veteran financial editor of the *New York Times*. "There is something listlessly attentive about the brokerage office hangers-on in these days. Without having anything particular to do, they appeared yesterday to be just standing around, watching the idle market and hoping that the whistle will sound soon and that they will be able to get a little excitement. Just where it was to come from no one seemed to know."

# IX

# The Inescapable Legacy of War

"Wall Street has become another world power, with more authority
than the League of Nations, and more subtlety than Bolshevism."
—LORD ROTHERMERE,
*owner of the London* Daily Mail, *July 1929*

From his vantage point at the reparations conference in Paris, more than
three thousand miles from the tempestuous atmosphere of Wall Street,
Owen Young saw the storm clouds gathering across the Atlantic. Between
September 1927 and February 1, 1929—the day he sailed for Europe—
Young had purchased approximately $2.2 million worth of stocks and
bonds, mostly on margin. Alarmed by the Federal Reserve Board's demonstrated inability to bring the speculative boom under control, Young suddenly decided to get out of the market altogether; by March 1, he had
liquidated his entire brokerage account and repaid nearly all his outstanding bank loans. His assistant in Paris, RCA vice-president David Sarnoff
(who had become close friends with Bernard Baruch over the past
decade), held on to his securities until June, and then he, too, sold every
share of stock he owned.

Young, Sarnoff, and Jack Morgan had arrived in Paris on February 8.
Most of the American delegation to the reparations conference took rooms
at the Ritz Hotel; Morgan, as usual, preferred to go his own way and rented
a modest suite overlooking the Arc de Triomphe in the small, conservative
Hotel Princess just off the avenue du Bois de Boulogne.

On February 11, the German, Allied, and American delegates—
known formally as the Experts' Conference, for they met as financial
experts and not as accredited representatives of their governments—
convened for the first time and, to no one's surprise, elected Young chairman. Negotiations began in earnest the following day when the delegates
gathered in a conference room at the new and luxurious Hotel George V.
There they heard Young address his opening remarks to the German
delegation, summarizing the European economic scene as he saw it. "We

are subject to no orders," Young announced in his laconic, matter-of-fact style. "We represent no Government. We have a plan to propose. You are free to accept it or reject it. To me as an outsider the facts are evident. These are the facts. You have had a great picnic here in Europe. The beach is covered with litter. How are you going to clean the beach and get ready to resume your occupations?" Ignoring the wisdom of Young's homespun homilies, the conferees soon made it evident that they preferred to pelt one another with the litter rather than clean it up. Although the atmosphere at the Hotel George V seemed markedly more congenial than the tension-filled Dawes conference five years earlier (this time, at least the Germans were permitted to sit at the same table with everyone else), the discussions got off on the wrong foot when the leader of the German delegation, Herr Hjalmar Horace Greeley Schacht, who also served as head of the Reichsbank, launched into a lengthy recitation of the reasons why Germany could not meet her scheduled payments under the Dawes Plan. (Schacht's middle names, incidentally, were the legacy of his parents' residence in New York State from 1871 to 1876, during which time his father came to idolize the liberal and marvelously idiosyncratic newspaper editor and Democratic presidential candidate Horace Greeley. Hjalmar himself was conceived in America and born shortly after his parents' return to Germany in 1877.)

In a four-hour lamentation, Schacht enumerated his country's economic woes: American loans had saddled the German Republic with $240 million in interest payments every year; nearly 20 percent of Germany's labor union membership was unemployed; workers were rioting in Berlin to protest the rising cost of food; and the Allies expected Germany somehow to pay $595 million in reparations before the end of 1929. Affairs had deteriorated to the point where an alchemist had duped German investors (including General Ludendorf) out of 7 million marks (about $1.75 million) with a fantastic scheme to discharge the Fatherland's reparations obligations and restore national prosperity by turning lead into gold. (Gullible authorities in Bavaria had even placed a fully equipped laboratory at the alchemist's disposal.)

It was not an auspicious start to the discussions. Since plenary sessions of the entire conference seemed doomed to degenerate into fruitless debating exercises, Young established a series of smaller subcommittees, each of which tackled a separate aspect of the tangled reparations and war debts quandary. But these bodies, too, failed to accomplish anything until the end of February, when Schacht paid a secret visit to Young and proposed the formation of an international bank that would, in Schacht's words, "demand financial cooperation between vanquished and victors that will lead to community of interests which in turn will give rise to mutual confidence and understanding and thus promote and ensure peace." According to Schacht, Young's long face broke into a broad grin as he replied, "Dr. Schacht, you gave me a wonderful idea and I am going to sell it to the world."

Young realized that an international bank such as Schacht proposed— the institution soon became known as the Bank for International Settlements—could provide the means to transfer the war debts and reparations issues from the volatile political arena to the more rational, calculated world of high finance. Specifically, the BIS would encourage the commercialization of Germany's war debts through the sale of bonds, while replacing the infrequent sessions of the Reparations Commission with regular meetings of the governors of the central banks of the member nations, all of whom presumably would willingly cooperate to make the bank a profitable venture. As an additional bonus, the BIS could serve as a clearing house to facilitate foreign exchange and international trade, mobilize reserves (in much the same fashion as each nation's central bank did), and reduce the disruptive short-term movement of gold between nations by substituting paper securities based upon the Bank's capital. The financiers fervently hoped that the complexity of the bank's transactions would allow them to obscure the precise total of German reparations payments in a maze of paper. As one perceptive observer pointed out, "The new bank does not change the underlying economic difficulty, but it makes possible the submergence of German transfer in the tangled skein of international credits and investments."

But at precisely the moment when Young had managed to sell the BIS to skeptical European delegates, who feared that Wall Street would control the new bank for the benefit of American interests, Hoover permitted Secretary Mellon to throw a monkey wrench into the delicate negotiations. On April 9, Young received a lengthy message from Washington denouncing the proposed bank (Mellon apparently was worried that Germany and the Allies would form a debtors' coalition against the United States) and declaring that under no circumstances would any official of the United States government (specifically including the directors of the Federal Reserve Banks) be permitted to "participate in the collection of German reparations through the agency of this bank or otherwise." And the administration reiterated in no uncertain terms its unalterable opposition to any settlement that explicitly linked Allied war debts to Germany's capacity to pay reparations.

When the substance of this message leaked to the press, Young strongly considered tendering his resignation. His own government had sandbagged his mission just as he was beginning to make headway. Morgan, who was equally outraged at Washington's interference, persuaded

Young to stay on. Privately, however, Young complained to Mellon that the Treasury message, which he characterized as "condemnatory at every point," had left him "humiliated and hurt by one whom I have held in the highest regard." Young hoped that Mellon would forward his cable to Hoover, from whom he had expected more wisdom and better treatment. Surely, Young thought, the President's wide and varied experience in the world of international business would enable him to take a more sympathetic view of Young's difficult position in Paris; surely Hoover would recognize the manifest advantages inherent in the proposed bank. But no encouraging word came from the White House.

Undeterred by Washington's official pigheadedness, Young kept the negotiations alive and finally cajoled the Allies into reducing their reparations demands to $28 billion over fifty-eight years. Then he confronted Schacht with that figure. (This was, incidentally, the first time since the war ended that Germany had ever been presented with a definitive bill for the damage.) Schacht nearly fainted. "Neither the figures nor the conditions are acceptable to Germany," he shouted. "We would far rather remain under the conditions of the Dawes Plan." When pressed, Schacht admitted that Germany could pay $15 billion over thirty-seven years; but even that sum, he said, was conditional upon the restoration of the German Reich's eastern provinces (which the Treaty of Versailles had awarded to Poland) and its colonies in Africa and Asia.

Now it was the Allies' turn to respond with apoplectic outrage, and as Schacht hastily retreated to Berlin for consultations with his government, it looked very much as if the conference would collapse in a shambles. "If our committee is not already dead," acknowledged a candid Japanese delegate, "it is certainly dying with dispatch." Only the untimely death of Lord Revelstoke, the chief British delegate, at that precise moment avoided an irrevocable rupture; out of respect for Revelstoke's memory, the conference adjourned for a brief holiday. In London, Winston Churchill took advantage of the recess to denounce Young's $28 billion compromise plan as far too lenient. "The kind of proposals which were foreshadowed in the newspapers yesterday," Churchill thundered in the House of Commons, "will in the opinion of the government be unacceptable, and the government will in no circumstance entertain them." French newspapers mercilessly flayed Uncle Shylock (i.e., the United States) for endeavoring to cheat them out of their legitimate claims for war damages.

Wall Street reacted with stunned surprise to the imminent break in Paris. In Berlin, the German mark fell to its lowest level since the chaotic days of 1924; alarmed by the crisis and the unceasing outflow of gold, the Reichsbank raised its discount rate by a full percentage point, further dampening German trade. At the end of April, Hoover's assistant secretary of commerce, Dr. Julius Klein, returned from a tour of Germany and reported gloomily that "throughout the German republic there is a feeling of unrest and dissatisfaction among the laboring classes. If this feeling brings about the expected strikes in many industries, 3,000,000 persons will be thrown out of work, adding a severe problem to a nation which, without the strikes, is endeavoring to absorb the 2,000,000 already unemployed."

If anything, Klein was understating the impending danger. Germany was seething with discontent and appeared to be perched on the edge of anarchy. In the bloodiest clashes since the deadly winter of 1919, heavily armed Communist revolutionaries rioted in the streets of Berlin and fired on police from rooftops and barricades of barrels, carts, and bricks; by the time the carnage ended, scores were dead and hundreds wounded. A powerful reactionary paramilitary organization known as the Stahlhelm (Steel Helmets) threatened to depose the republican regime and install a right-wing dictatorship; if the Weimar government refused to "recognize the signs of the times," barked the leader of the Stahlhelm, "if they dare to continue the fight against the parties of the right and against patriotic officials—then we shall answer them." And Alfred Hugenberg, the blustering newspaper and movie magnate who had captured the leadership of the German National party (only slightly to the left of the Nazis), dispatched a letter to three thousand American businessmen—many of whom had a financial stake in the maintenance of German stability—warning that if Germany was driven to despair "through unreasonable policies and unbearable burdens . . . she will also be driven into the arms of Bolshevism." "Would the future history of the world say that in 1929 America tried finally to introduce slavery in Europe?" screeched Hugenberg. "These were means of dealing with niggers and Indians, but a people like the Germans would ultimately prefer to be buried under a blazing heap of ruins, which would spread to the near and distant neighbourhood, rather than yield."

No wonder Jack Morgan retired to his yacht and sailed for the Mediterranean with his good friend the archbishop of Canterbury. "If Hell is anything like Paris and an International Conference combined," the weary financier wrote to a friend, "it has many terrors, and I shall try to avoid them."

But Young would not give up. Nor would Schacht, who had stared into the face of chaos once before, when he assumed the presidency of the Reichsbank during the runaway inflationary crisis of 1924. When Schacht dutifully returned to Paris, Young presented him with a new compromise: Germany would be required to pay an average of $487.6 million annually (approximately 2 billion marks) for thirty-seven years, compared with the Dawes Plan's schedule of at least $595 million. One-third of this reduced payment would be made unconditionally in cash and payments in kind; the rest would be financed by the sale of bonds on German railroads and privately owned industries through the Bank of International Settlements. Although Young's proposal ostensibly required the payment of reparations through 1988, there was an implicit assumption that the profits from the bank would be used to defray Germany's debt to the point where virtually the entire bill ($8.88 billion plus 5 percent interest per annum) would be paid by 1966. All foreign political controls over the German economy would be removed. After considerable deliberation, Schacht accepted Young's plan subject to two additional conditions: if Germany suffered a severe economic crisis, the Allies would grant a two-year moratorium on the conditional portion of the reparations bill; and the humiliating requirement that Germany help finance the Allied army of occupation in the Rhineland must be deleted. At last, after several more weeks of inter-Allied haggling over details, the conferees finally voted to adopt the modified Young Plan.

At home, Will Rogers greeted Young's accomplishment with glee. "Sunshine and prerogatives are mighty scarce in us Democrats' lives," he wrote in his daily column, "but just lest you forget, this Owen D. Young that is doing such splendid work in Paris trying to divide one bone with half a dozen dogs and not even having the bone to divide . . . well, this young man is a Democrat, strange as it may seem." Adolph Ochs, publisher of the *New York Times,* exuberantly informed Young in a telegram, "You have established yourself as the wisest and greatest peacemaker of our time stop Having an abiding confidence in the wisdom of the American people I predict that you will be in the White House if not in four years in eight years."

In Paris, nearly all the exhausted delegates praised Young for guiding the settlement through an exceedingly trying and turbulent course. On June 7, the conference convened for its final session at the Hotel George V. While the fourteen delegates wasted another hour wrangling over semicolons and commas, an overheated movie lamp set fire to several of the window curtains, and the acrimonious discussion had to pause while waiters and servants tore down the flaming tapestries and sprayed them with fire extinguishers. ("It did not augur well for the stability and permanence of our work," noted Schacht dryly.) Then each delegation affixed its signature to the two-inch-thick document that enshrined Owen Young's name in the history of twentieth-century Europe. Emile Moreau, governor of the Bank of France, provided the appropriate benediction. "The report is not entirely satisfactory to any one country," he observed.

"Therefore it is highly satisfactory to all." All unresolved issues—including an exact partition of the spoils among the Allied powers—were postponed until a subsequent conference at The Hague, scheduled for August.

Shortly after his return to the United States, Young accepted an invitation to lunch with Hoover and the cabinet at the White House at the end of June. Presumably the discussion was strained, for the nation's newspapers were filled with editorials boosting Young as a Democratic candidate for President in 1932, a possibility that went far toward explaining Hoover's unhelpful attitude toward Young's achievement in Paris. Certainly the White House chat was not terribly productive, for soon afterward Hoover announced that the United States would not sign the agreement Young had hammered out so painstakingly in Paris, and Secretary of State Stimson reiterated the administration's obstinate refusal to permit any Federal Reserve official to participate in the management of the Bank of International Settlements.

But Young at least had the satisfaction of winning a straw poll conducted by the Harvard Business School in the summer of 1929. When Harvard officials asked a graduate seminar class of two hundred businessmen from twenty-seven states and three foreign countries to name "the greatest businessman in America," Young finished in first place with 52 votes, followed by Henry Ford, Andrew Mellon, and, in fourth place, Herbert Clark Hoover.

To an impartial observer, the Young Plan appeared to be a rational response to the flaws that had marred the Dawes scheme. For the first time, the Allies and Germany had negotiated a definite sum of reparations payments, a total that could only be revised downward, and not increased—as the Dawes Plan had provided—if Germany prospered. All foreign political controls were removed from the German economy, and the Allies' right to impose military and economic sanctions (such as the occupation of the Ruhr Valley by French troops) was replaced by an agreement to settle disputes by arbitration. And at the Hague Conference later that summer, German foreign minister Gustav Stresemann succeeded in obtaining a French promise to evacuate the Rhineland by June 30, 1930, four and a half years ahead of schedule.

Yet Owen Young had unwittingly spun into motion a chain of events that ultimately sounded the death knell for the Weimar Republic and propelled Adolf Hitler into national prominence in Germany for the first time. Before a definitive reparations bill had been prepared, many Germans had hoped (perhaps foolishly, certainly naively) that the Allies eventually would come to their senses and abandon the whole tiresome, vengeful, and dangerous game of exacting an annual installment of retribution that kept the hatreds of wartime alive and the scars unhealed. Now, however, Schacht's signature on the document forged in Paris—and its subsequent confirmation by Stresemann at The Hague—shackled the Reich to the payment of tribute to the Allies for at least two generations to come; and the notion of condemning German children yet unborn to a lifetime of deprivation and financial servitude just because the Kaiser and his generals had lost a war in the dim, distant past struck all sectors of German public opinion as a particularly reprehensible injustice.

Schacht himself quickly disowned his own handiwork and claimed that "from an economic point of view the Young Plan was completely crazy." Moderate politicians such as Center party leader Heinrich Brüning, former chancellor Hans Luther, and Konrad Adenauer, the mayor of Cologne, likewise denounced the Paris proposal as a monstrous *Diktat.* Physicist Max Planck, too, expressed his opposition. Instead of strengthening the stability of the Weimar Republic, the Young Plan ultimately served as a unifying point for the republic's enemies. The political pressure groups of the radical right—including the Stahlhelm and the Pan-German Association—submerged their petty internecine squabbles in an alliance with Hugenberg's Nationalists and the ruffian National Socialists of Adolf Hitler, and all the frustration, hostility, and chauvinistic fury that had lain repressed through the long and humiliating postwar decade suddenly erupted in a volcano of violent protest. In July, this coalition of superpatriots, nominally under Hugenberg's leadership, founded the Reichscommittee for a German Plebiscite and urged the Reichstag to pass a document called "A Law Against the Enslavement of the German People," which would have effectively nullified the Versailles Treaty. When the Reichstag, as expected, showed no signs of yielding to their wishes, they launched a campaign to present the measure to the German electorate in an extraordinary plebiscite.

The Reich's industrial barons viewed the Young Plan with special hatred, for in their eyes it threatened to transform Germany into a vassal state ruled by foreign financial interests. Carl Duisberg of I.G. Farbenindustrie (the largest chemical and explosives manufacturer in the world), Emil Kirdorf, the Ruhr coal tycoon, and steel magnate Fritz Thyssen, leader of the Union of German Industry, provided substantial moral and financial support to the nationalist campaign of resistance. "I became convinced that the fight against the Young Plan was unavoidable if a complete collapse of Germany was to be prevented," wrote Thyssen a decade later. "In my judgment the financial debt thus created was bound to disrupt the entire economy of the Reich. . . . Anybody with the power of clear judgment saw that the Young Plan meant the pledging of Germany's entire wealth as a pawn for Germany's obligations. As a result, American capital was bound to flood Germany." And hence, in Thyssen's view, "the Young Plan was one of the principal causes of the upsurge of National Socialism in Germany."

Hugenberg, whose wealth was matched only by his Prussian vanity, invited Hitler into the anti–Young Plan coalition because he believed he could easily manipulate the brash, unsophisticated forty-year-old demagogue. Of course Hugenberg was wrong. Hitler never served as any man's pawn. The agitation against the Young Plan provided the Nazis with a heaven-sent opportunity to expand their base of support, and made Hitler himself respectable—*salonfahig,* capable of appearing in polite society— for the first time in his tumultuous political career (though some, like the wife of munitions manufacturer Alfred Krupp, persisted in regarding Hitler as "an ill-bred guttersnipe"). As the industrialists' cash flowed into the National Socialist coffers, the Fuehrer forsook his monastic quarters in a modest bourgeois boarding house in Munich for a luxuriously furnished nine-room apartment in one of the most exclusive sections of the city, where he soon began entertaining a seventeen-year-old shop girl named Eva Braun. For himself, Hitler bought a flashy new automobile (complete with chauffeur); for his party, he purchased a three-story brownstone building, the Barlow Palace, with Thyssen's money. Whatever cash remained was passed along to Dr. Goebbels to finance the inimitably venomous Nazi propaganda campaign against the Young Plan.

Germany had never witnessed anything like it. Nazi orators flayed the Young Plan as a "death penalty on the unborn" and the "Golgotha of the German people"; bloodthirsty foreign bankers, the Nazis said, were "nailing [Germany] to the cross with scornful laughter." At protest demonstrations in cities across the land, Hitler ranted against the perfidious agreement that would transform the Fatherland into a "Young colony" of slave laborers for three wretched generations or more. From Berlin, Goebbels repeatedly broadcast a radio speech in which he warned that Germans were being condemned to a humiliating existence as "a slave people." "From the standpoint of international law," Goebbels screamed, "they trail behind the last Negro colony in the Congo. All the rights of sovereignty have been taken from us, and now we're just good enough so that the stock exchange capitalists can fill their sacks of gold with interest, money, and percentages." The lame little propaganda chieftain plastered the city with posters adorned with swastikas and anti-Semitic slogans that raged against the Jewish international bankers who, Goebbels said, controlled Wall Street. (Even such an authority as Henry Ford admitted as much.)

Amid the cacophony of outrage and protest, ordinary German citizens attempted to squeeze every bit of pleasure that remained from the summer of what later became known as "the last good year." They flocked to movie theaters to see such classic films as *Women Are My Weakness, The Loves of the Rott Brothers,* and *Eroticism.* In the remarkable span of six weeks, Hugenberg's Ufa film production company completed the Weimar Republic's most impressive cinematic achievement, *The Blue Angel,* a sound film starring matinee idol Emil Jannings as a sadomasochistic bachelor professor enslaved by a long-legged dancer-whore named Lola Lola, played with provocative sensuality by newcomer Marlene Dietrich. Based loosely on a novel by Heinrich Mann and directed by Joseph von Sternberg, who had already achieved considerable fame in Hollywood with such films as *Underworld* and *The Last Command, The Blue Angel* immediately struck a responsive chord in European audiences with its themes of sexual obsession, degradation, and the ecstasy of surrender to man's basest instincts.

On another stage in Berlin, avant-garde dancer Harold Kreutzberg writhed in the agonized contortions of a madman whose movements reflected the shattered rhythms of his brain. "A maniac, sad and pitiable, danced with an imaginary partner," wrote one astonished critic who witnessed a Kreutzberg recital featuring a piece entitled "Three Mad Figures." "In the robe of red, he heard within his mind the relentless ticking of a monster clock. Succeeding him came a lunatic, frothing and murderous, listening to the distorted succession of screams and yells, of dance music, of weeping themes, to which he must dance. And a third poor fool, crashing himself against the walls, running from the figures which besiege him and into the open spaces which he imagines."

The best-selling novel in Germany—and Europe and the United States—in the summer of 1929 was Erich Maria Remarque's *All Quiet on the Western Front,* a chilling story of a generation of men "who, even though they may have escaped the shells, were destroyed by the war." As the narrator and his comrades in the German army slogged through the mud and the death in the trenches, murder—"that very crime on which formerly the world's condemnation and severest penalty fell"—became their highest aim. Their universe was reduced to an eternal hell of man-made destruction: "Bombardment, barrage, curtain-fire, mines, gas, tanks, machine-guns, hand-grenades—words, words, but they hold the horror of the world." And when the guns at last fell silent, the survivors went home, "burnt-out, rootless, without hope." The *Manchester Guardian* immediately crowned *All Quiet* "the greatest of all war books," though the hideous reality of Remarque's prose proved too much for the editorial board of the Book-of-the-Month Club, who deleted seven "offensive" phrases before offering the book to their members.

The phenomenal success of *All Quiet*—together with the publication of such war memoirs as Robert Graves' *Goodbye to All That* and Hugh

Quigley's *Passchendaele and the Somme,* and the immense popularity of the British theatrical production *Journey's End,* set in the mud and terror of the trenches on the western front—reflected the lingering, persistent obsession of Western society with the cataclysmic experience of the Great War. The images of war and its horrific violence had been burned with exceptional vividness into the minds of a generation, and ten years of peace and widespread prosperity had served to intensify rather than eradicate the ghastly memories. The demons would not be exorcised until the world was shaken by another catastrophe of comparable severity.

# X

# The Business of Politics

---

"He had that quality that political scientists call charism,
of being able to excite people merely by appearing before
them, which all the great mass leaders in history—for example,
Hitler, Gandhi, Lincoln, Franklin D. Roosevelt . . . have had."
—T. HARRY WILLIAMS, *on Huey Long*

**H**uey Long hated Standard Oil. Actually, Huey hated all big sonofabitch corporations. But he especially detested Standard Oil. In no uncertain terms, for Huey was never shy about expressing himself in colorful and occasionally crude metaphors, he accused the Rockefellers and their corporate henchmen of having raped and plundered his native state of Louisiana for decades. And now that he was governor, Huey surely intended to do something about it.

Huey had been elected to the governor's mansion in 1928, at the age of thirty-four, after a spectacular decade of service on the state Railroad and Public Service commissions, where he had challenged head-on the powerful and previously sacrosanct out-of-state corporations that had dominated Louisiana political and economic life since the late nineteenth century. An obstreperous upstart, Long had recognized very early in his career that he could only obtain power by posing as the champion of the state's neglected middle and lower classes, and that suited him just fine, because he was consumed by a burning desire to seek revenge on the wealthy bastards who had kept his family and thousands of others like them shackled to perpetual poverty. As a boy, Huey's favorite book was *The Count of Monte Cristo.* He later said that he used to read it every year when he was growing up. "That man in that book knew how to hate," he told a friend, "and until you learn how to hate you'll never get anywhere in this world." Although he liked to pretend that he had been dirt poor when he was growing up in Winn parish, in the northern part of the state, the Longs were, in reality, one of the richest families in the parish. But that was not saying much, because Winn was one of the poorest areas in the state, and the Longs were still nothing more than hog and cattle farmers who operated on a very slim margin of profit, and they certainly had no hopes of penetrating the inner circle of aristocratic plantation owners and wealthy businessmen who governed Louisiana from New Orleans and Baton Rouge.

At an early age, Huey decided that he wanted to be a politician more than anything else in the world, but he began his career as a traveling salesman, peddling ersatz lard, Faultless Starch, and patent medicines up and down the Gulf coast. Huey was a great salesman; people said he could even have sold secondhand coffins had he tried. Everywhere he went Huey watched how the local political leaders operated. He studied their style, the ways they worked the crowds and manipulated the hidden levers of power. Then, when he could wait no longer, Huey taught himself law in seven months and passed the state bar examination at the age of twenty-one. In 1918, he won election to the state Railroad Commission, which soon broadened its authority and renamed itself the Louisiana Public Service Commission, and that was when Huey launched his assault upon the entrenched privileges of the "foreign" corporations that had been siphoning off the state's wealth unmolested by conscience or Louisiana's elected officials. The most visible culprit, and hence Huey's favorite target, was John D. Rockefeller's Standard Oil, which Huey loved to portray as "the evil enemy of progress."

First, Huey succeeded in imposing a severance tax on resources extracted from the state, a measure that forced Standard Oil to contribute at least a pittance from its profits to improve Louisiana's public services. Then in 1927, when the ruling conservative clique in the state capital split into quarreling factions, Huey ran for governor on a populist platform that promised free schoolbooks, better roads and bridges, improved hospitals, and honest government. "Where are the schools that you have waited for your children to have, but have never come?" he asked the dirt-poor farmers. "Where are the roads and the highways that you send your money to build, that are no nearer now than ever before? Where are the institutions to care for the sick and the disabled?" And Huey won their votes and the election.

Despite the presence of an entrenched reactionary faction in the state legislature (known as the Dynamite Squad for their ability to blast reform legislation into oblivion), Huey blustered and bullied the assembly into passing bills to build better highways and provide free schoolbooks. For good measure, he raised the severance tax rates, too. In the meantime, Huey built up his own personal political machine through the adroit and frequently vindictive manipulation of the patronage system. Opponents began calling him the kaiser of Louisiana and "the despot of the delta," but Huey astutely realized that the only way he could maintain himself in power was to build an organization that was just as ruthless and merciless as his enemies.

Then in the spring of 1929, as he began his second year in office, Huey suddenly was threatened with political extinction. Responding to requests from civic groups in New Orleans, the governor had launched a series of raids on gambling houses in and around the city. Unfortunately, the national guardsmen whom he dispatched to clean up these dens of iniquity performed their duties a bit too zealously—women patrons allegedly were stripped and searched, albeit by policewomen—and some very powerful, traditional interests were grievously offended by this gross breach of decorum. Then, on March 16, Huey called a special session of the legislature to consider a 5-cents-a-barrel "occupational license tax" (i.e., a manufacturers' tax) on oil refineries.

This was too much for the conservatives. Standard Oil mobilized its considerable financial and political resources to fight the bill. Newspapers castigated Huey as a bumbling fool and predicted that the tax would drive industry out of the state. Naturally he fought back with every weapon he possessed, assailing Standard Oil for brazenly attempting to defeat the sovereign will of the people. "No sooner had this bill hit the Legislature," Huey cried, "than the Oil Trust woke up and shook this state from one end to the other like a toy. This nefarious criminal element and its newspapers began immediately to say that if I did not draw down this proposition that I should be impeached. Standard Oil money was turned loose in sluices in Baton Rouge." But Huey badly overplayed his hand when he tried to bully one recalcitrant newspaper publisher named Douglas Manship into supporting the bill by threatening to publicize the fact that Manship's brother, a shell-shocked veteran of the Great War, was a patient in a state mental hospital.

When the legislature gathered to consider Huey's tax proposal (which never really had a chance to pass anyway), a member of the Dynamite Squad introduced a motion to impeach the governor on the flimsy strength of a preposterous accusation that he had tried to hire an assassin to murder one of his political opponents. Within seconds the assembly chamber degenerated into an unseemly melee of angry, shouting baldheaded and potbellied men, as Huey's supporters and opponents punched and shoved one another and tried to grab the podium; paste pots and inkwells were flying everywhere. By the time order at last was restored to a session that became known to posterity as "Bloody Monday" (several legislators suffered minor cuts and bruises), Huey had been formally charged with bribery, misuse of state funds, intimidation of public officials and the aforementioned newspaper publisher, usurpation of the powers of the legislature, attempted murder, corruption, favoritism, incompetence, carrying a concealed weapon, using abusive language, and engaging in drunken debauches in cabarets where Huey allegedly had "played the role of a singing fool" and permitted girls clad only in hula skirts to sit on his lap.

In the ensuing battle for votes, both sides engaged in dirty tricks, bribery, intimidation, and coercion. Huey personally penned a call to arouse the people ("The Same Fight Again! The Standard Oil Company vs. Huey P. Long!") and published it in a circular that was distributed statewide by his lieutenants. "I had rather go down to a thousand impeachments than to admit that I am the governor of the State that does not dare to call the Standard Oil Company to account so that we can educate our children and care for [the] destitute, sick, and afflicted," he vowed. "If this State is still to be ruled by the power of the money of this corporation, I am too weak for its governor." He hired a staff of lawyers and clerks to prepare his defense, and toured the state to rally public support. In one of the most melodramatic and incoherent speeches in the history of Louisiana politics, one overwrought pro-Long legislator even compared Huey to Jesus Christ and accused his enemies of crucifying Huey on a cross of gold. Meanwhile, the impeachers subpoenaed practically everyone in the state who had anything bad to say about the governor, and brought them to Baton Rouge to testify against Long.

Despite the fact that the bill of accusations was nothing more than the trumped-up product of a political vendetta, designed to remove the troublesome Huey from Louisiana politics once and for all, the House voted to impeach Huey on the Manship "intimidation" charge on April 6 by a margin of 58–40. The vote marked the first time a governor of Louisiana had ever been impeached. Huey's case then proceeded for trial to the state senate, where the impeachers needed 26 out of 39 votes to convict. But the final confrontation never took place. Through a combination of cajolery, legal suasion, and blatant offers of future patronage plums, Huey obtained the signatures of fifteen senators on a round robin petition that asserted that the impeachment proceedings were illegal and unconstitutional. With more than one-third of the senators formally pledged to vote against impeachment, the anti-Long campaign collapsed. For the rest of his political career, Huey never forgot the men who had rescued him in the crisis; nor did he forgive his enemies. "What the impeachment did was impress on him the lengths to which the conservatives would go to destroy anyone who proposed change," remarked one observer. "It sharpened a determination that he probably already had to destroy the conservatives, or, more specifically, their bases of power. . . . He would try to see to it that his enemies could never again place him in danger."

But for the moment, Huey accepted defeat on the occupational tax bill, which had provoked the controversy in the first place. After receiving petitions from a coalition of Louisiana bankers and businessmen who feared that the tax would drive industry out of the state, Huey declared that he was withdrawing the measure from consideration. Almost immediately thereafter, Standard Oil of New Jersey announced plans for the construction of a $20 million chemical plant in Monroe, Louisiana, under the auspices of the American I.G. Chemical Corporation, a recently incorporated joint venture of Standard Oil, Ford Motors, and the giant German chemicals and explosives trust I.G. Farbenindustrie. In recent years, I.G. Farben researchers reportedly had made great strides toward the synthetic manufacture of gasoline from coal, and Ford and Standard Oil both sought to obtain American rights to the process. In return for an exchange of scientific data, I.G. Farben—which hoped to manufacture enough gasoline to meet the growing demands of the Reichswehr, the German army— received a badly needed infusion of American capital, namely, 2 percent of Standard Oil of New Jersey's common stock, which at that time represented a value of approximately $35 million. The board of directors of the new American I.G. Chemical Corporation included Walter Teagle of Standard Oil, bankers Paul Warburg and Charles Edward Mitchell, and Edsel Ford. It was the first time Ford had sat on the board of any outside company, and the sight of Henry's son and a prominent Jew (Warburg) on the same corporate letterhead struck many contemporaries as amusing if not bizarre. But business, after all, was business. In a related transaction, Henry Ford sold the entire minority share of stock (40 percent) of his new German subsidiary to I.G. Farben, instead of offering it to the German public as originally planned.

Not surprisingly, the bonds of the fledgling American I.G. Chemical Corporation were distributed through Charlie Mitchell's National City Bank of New York. The initial issue of securities sold out in less than an hour.

New York's Governor Franklin D. Roosevelt, too, spent the spring and summer of 1929 locked in combat with a hostile legislature and the forces of Big Business, although Roosevelt conducted his fight on a considerably more gentlemanly level than Huey Long. At the start of the legislative session, Roosevelt had introduced a comprehensive, though certainly not radical program of social welfare measures: an extension of workmen's compensation to cover all occupational injuries and diseases; the establishment and funding of a commission to study old-age pensions for the state; farm tax relief; labor reform; new state hospital construction; and a proposal to examine the feasibility of publicly owned development and transmission of hydroelectric power.

By the time the state assembly adjourned at the end of March, virtually every one of Roosevelt's measures had been gutted by the reactionary Republican majority. As they left Albany, the Republicans sniggered over their triumphs, but Roosevelt had barely begun to fight. In an address to the people of New York, the governor bitterly denounced the "slaughter" of his program by "the same old crowd" that had thwarted Al Smith's efforts to promote social justice, and then he boldly vetoed scores of pork-barrel and selfish special privilege bills the legislature had cynically passed. In a special shortwave radio message broadcast from the Hotel Astor to Commander Byrd in Antarctica, Roosevelt jocularly suggested to the intrepid explorer, "You might be glad to invite the Republican Legislature to spend the Winter at the South Pole with you. I wish you would do that; you would help me very much."

On July 4, Governor Roosevelt addressed the annual Tammany Hall Independence Day celebration at the brand-new Tammany "wigwam" (meeting hall) at Seventeenth Street and Union Square. Following his introduction as "our next President of the United States," Roosevelt launched into a forceful denunciation of the growing connection between Big Business and government. "No period in history has been so rich in social and economic changes as those that have taken place in the last twenty-five years," he asserted. "We may well ask: Are we in danger of a new caveman's club, of a new feudal system, of the creation in these United States of such a highly centralized industrial control that we may have to bring forth a new Declaration of Independence? It is not that these great industrial and economic mergers are necessarily bad from the economic point of view, but the fact is that independence in business is a thing of the past." As Al Smith and Jimmy Walker nodded their agreement on the platform behind him, Roosevelt vowed to continue "the fight against business controlled government" that Smith had begun ten years earlier. "It is pretty serious for any individual to go out against these big combinations," he concluded. "People hesitate to do so. The intention of the men working on these consolidations may be the best. . . . But they are becoming increasingly more powerful in the influence they are building in State and nation, an influence that some day will have to be met. . . . Their power will have to be combated."

The specific combination of financial power that worried Roosevelt in the summer of 1929 was the Niagara-Hudson Power Corporation, a $500 million utility system formed in June by J.P. Morgan and Company and associates through the merger of New York State's three largest electric power systems. (As one might have expected, the merger sent the stock of each of the individual systems soaring on Wall Street.) According to the *New York Times*, Niagara-Hudson represented "the greatest superpower system in point of assets" in the United States. The merger also gave Morgan and Company control over nearly a quarter of the nation's hydro-electric production through a chain of giant utility corporations that stretched in an almost unbroken ring from southern New England to Florida. Since holding companies were specifically exempt from public regulation, one might reasonably expect such a corporation as Niagara-Hudson to overvalue its services, and as Roosevelt toured the state that summer he discovered that utility rates indeed appeared to be unjustifiably high, especially compared with Canadian rates just across the border. Nevertheless, New York's attorney general (a Republican) ruled that the merger had violated no state laws, and so Roosevelt's fight to break up the monopoly would have to be waged in the political arena.

And that was fine with FDR, because his struggle for social welfare legislation and public power was bringing him an avalanche of favorable nationwide publicity. After the July 4 speech at Tammany headquarters, Will Rogers (who was always on the lookout for a viable Democratic presidential candidate) predicted that Roosevelt's address had "just about" assured him of being the next Democratic nominee for the White House. "Now there is a fine man," wrote Rogers. "You can start now trying to dig up something and in three years you won't have found anything wrong with Franklin Delano Roosevelt outside of being a Democrat." For the record, the governor denied any interest in the job and laughed at his friends in the press for inventing "Arabian night tales about Presidential possibilities and candidacies," although his chief lieutenant, Louis Howe, already was spending most of his time in New York City, surreptitiously gathering support for a Roosevelt run for the White House in 1932. "I am not a candidate for President," Roosevelt insisted to reporters at a press conference in Albany. "This is a man-sized job which takes all my time, and I have not devoted and shall not devote any time or thought to purely speculative matters which do not concern this state."

But insiders knew better. At the annual spring dinner of the Gridiron Club, the irreverent fraternity of Washington newspaper correspondents, Roosevelt (who was one of the club's three political guests that evening) heard a gleeful chorus of singing reporters wonder whether the governor would "wish for something higher, / When at Albany you're through? . . . Will the White House beckon you?"

Naturally, Hoover—the club's second honored guest—also came in for his share of ribbing at the hands of the journalists, who already had come to realize that his administration was "the most completely one-man affair since Woodrow Wilson left the White House." Hence, when the master of ceremonies introduced the members of the Hoover "cabinet," ten human "robots" appeared, each made up to look like the President; and to the tune of "The Isle of Our Dreams," the robots sang a ditty called "Who but Hoover":

> When you're serving in the Cabinet
> There is just one thing to do:
> Do not worry 'cause it's Herbert
> Who's reflected there in you.
> Be content to be just echoes
> If he plays a one-man game,
> Then when trouble comes a-knocking
> Just let Herbert take the blame.
>
> For the path is not all lined with roses,
> And the brickbats are part of the game.
> When a target they hunt he'll be there out in front—
> Who but Hoover will get all the blame.

From his first day in the White House, Hoover had indeed made it clear to reporters that all significant administration pronouncements would come directly from him. Abandoning Coolidge's pretense of making statements in the guise of an anonymous "spokesman," Hoover permitted newspapers to attribute quotes directly to him. That was merely the first change Hoover wrought in White House routine. Instead of using a telephone in an adjoining room, he installed a telephone directly on his desk in the Executive Office. (Malicious critics later joked that Hoover could call anyone but hear nothing.) He also reorganized the disorderly White House filing system and designed a series of buzzers to summon at his will any or all of his five secretaries—all of whom were male, because Herbert did not favor women in public service. Mrs. Hoover refurbished the White House (mostly with her husband's own money), turning one room into a tropical aviary, with exotic birds in swinging cages. Another room was transformed into a sort of shrine to the Great Engineer, featuring scores of honorary degrees, plaques, and photographs of Hoover with famous personalities from around the globe. The President's German shepherd, King Tut, and his wife's collie, Bellhaven Behoover, took up residence in the White House kennels, and their pet opossum, Billy, found a suitable home somewhere on the grounds. Hoover closed the White House stables, retired the *Mayflower* yacht, and exchanged Coolidge's fleet of cars for four new Pierce Arrows, a Packard, and a Lincoln. Unlike Silent Cal, who seldom missed his morning constitutional, Hoover hated to walk; for exercise, the President (usually dressed in a heavy black sweater and gray flannel trousers) and a few close friends gathered on a tennis court on the south grounds—in an area shielded from inquisitive reporters by high shrubbery—at seven o'clock every weekday morning to toss an eight-pound medicine ball back and forth over the net for half an hour before retiring for a shower, massage, and breakfast.

Gradually Hoover withdrew from public view. After two days in office, he decided to eliminate the traditional noontime receptions; and following a marathon session during which the President dutifully shook hands with 1,757 visitors, he advised congressmen that they could no longer send their constituents to the White House for a presidential handshake on a regular basis. Callers who appeared at the Executive Office without an appointment were deflected to his secretaries. Hoover sharply curtailed his speaking engagements so he could work unmolested at his desk. He did appear on opening day at Griffith Stadium, and sat through the entire lopsided contest as the Philadelphia Athletics destroyed the Senators, 13–4. (The less hardy Mellon departed shortly after the game began.) But at the end of April, Hoover began to slip secretly out of Washington on the weekends; usually he retreated to the secluded, 1,500-acre wooded estate in Maryland's Catoctin Mountains that one of his secretaries had recently acquired (and which later became known as Camp David). There he could fish in peace and complete privacy, undisturbed by cameramen or reporters. Later that spring, the President obtained a second vacation home in the Shenandoah National Park, along the trout-filled Rapidan River, about three hours' drive from Washington and nine miles from the nearest small (very small) town of Criglersville, Virginia. Until the Army Corps of Engineers built a road, the cabin was accessible only by horseback.

Generally, Hoover received favorable press notices during his brief honeymoon in office. "Hoover does not run away from his troubles," remarked the previously skeptical *New Republic* after the first ninety days. "He feels competent to solve them, and acts in most cases with a promptness and decision which have not been seen in the White House since Mr. Wilson's early days. He is, moreover, filled with a general attitude of good will, the temper which in some of his enthusiastic supporters has caused them to be called 'Boy Scouts.' While it is easy to make fun of this attitude, it is greatly preferable to its opposite, and there is good reason to believe that it will find reflection in some admirable social legislation before Mr. Hoover's term is ended."

Congress, however, proved less tractable than the fourth estate. Against Hoover's opposition, the special legislative session that convened in the middle of March passed a farm relief measure that included a version of the controversial McNary-Haugen export debenture plan. Hoover indignantly vetoed the measure as a direct subsidy to "special interests," and supported instead a less ambitious and not very effective substitute proposal, the Agricultural Marketing Act. Then when Hoover proposed a "limited" revision of the industrial tariff rates, Congress passed completely out of the President's control. Lobbyists from every American industry trampled down the doors in a flagrant rush to obtain greater, and often wholly unjustified, protection for their products from foreign competition. The traditional and venal legislative practice of logrolling was elevated to a fine art as deals were struck right and left and congressmen cynically agreed to safeguard the industries of one another's districts. Caught between the conservative (high tariff) and progressive (low tariff) factions of his party, Hoover seemed paralyzed, unable to provide direction as the debate dragged on through the summer and into the autumn.

Nor would the President act effectively and openly to dampen stock market speculation. He allegedly dispatched an old banking acquaintance from California to Wall Street to warn of the potential dangers looming on the horizon, and he did order the Justice Department to launch a drive against the illegal "bucket shops" that sold fictitious securities, but that was all.

And there was no doubt that Hoover recognized the possibility of an imminent crisis. As construction statistics sagged further in May and automobile sales began to fall off, the President tersely instructed his personal financial adviser to liquidate some of his (Hoover's) holdings "as possible hard times coming"; Hoover asked that his funds be placed instead in "gilt-edged bonds."

But in the President's mind, the most grievous danger facing the nation was not farm relief, nor the tariff, nor even the overheated boom on Wall Street. It was the reign of terror maintained by hoodlums, bootleggers, and racketeers against honest American citizens. At an Associated Press luncheon in New York City on April 22, Hoover asserted that "a surprising number of our people otherwise of responsibility in the community have drifted into the extraordinary notion that laws are made for those who choose to obey them. And in addition, our law-enforcement machinery is suffering from many infirmities arising out of its technicalities, its circumlocutions, its involved procedures, and too often, I regret, from inefficient and delinquent officials." Five weeks later, Hoover appointed a National Commission on Law Observance and Enforcement, headed by former attorney general George Wickersham, to investigate the "entire question of law enforcement and organized justice." And between tosses of the renowned medicine ball on the White House lawn, the President instructed Attorney General Mitchell to "get" Al Capone.

In the spring of 1929, Al Capone was perfectly willing to be "got" by the Feds if they would promise to protect him from his enraged rivals. Bugs Moran had vowed vengeance on Scarface after the St. Valentine's Day Massacre, and so Al decided that a furnished room in a state penitentiary might be the safest place for him to hide out until the storm blew over. First, though, he had to answer the insistent call of a grand jury investigating the bootlegging business in the Chicago area. Capone attempted to evade the subpoena by pleading illness (his doctor claimed that Capone had a bad case of "bronchial pneumonial pleurisy," even though he had been well enough to attend the Sharkey-Stribling fight), but an unsympathetic judge gave him just eight days to get better and then demanded his presence in Illinois. When Capone reluctantly returned to the Windy City from Florida, he assured reporters, "I don't know anything about the Chicago Heights liquor or gambling rackets. I've been in Florida for the last year and a half mostly. I am not in any racket now."

After testifying—to no particular end—Capone took care of another piece of unfinished business. One of his lieutenants had uncovered evidence that implicated three of Capone's Sicilian associates in a plot to take over his bootlegging and racketeering businesses. On May 7, Capone invited the three alleged traitors to a private banquet at the Hawthorne Inn in the Chicago suburb of Cicero, the seat of Capone's empire. They suspected nothing. Capone toasted their health and laid before them a feast of fine food and liquor that lasted until the early hours of the morning. Tradition satisfied, Capone stopped grinning as soon as the meal ended. His bodyguards stepped forward and tied the stunned guests to their chairs with wire and gagged them. Then Capone, snarling curses, grabbed a baseball bat and methodically proceeded to beat each man to death, one at a time, slamming the wood down upon their shoulders and chests again and again until nearly every bone in their bodies was broken. Then his bodyguards applied the traditional coup de grace, a bullet to the head. The bodies were placed in a car and abandoned in a ditch at the desolate outpost of Spooner's Nook, just across the Indiana state line. Police authorities naturally concluded that the three luckless Sicilians had been slain by Moran's gang as retribution for the St. Valentine's Day Massacre.

The following week, Capone, his wounded honor soothed by the bloodletting, betook himself to Atlantic City to attend a three-day conference of the nation's organized crime bosses. By his own account, he urged his colleagues to forgive and forget past grievances. "I told them there was business enough to make us all rich and it was time to stop all the killings and look on our business as other men look on theirs, as something to work at and forget when we go home at night," he later explained. "It wasn't an easy matter for men who had been fighting for years to agree on a peaceful business program. But we finally decided to forget the past and begin all over again and we drew up a written agreement and each man signed on the dotted line."

But Bugs Moran was not in Atlantic City, and he certainly had not been deluded by the sacrifice of the three Sicilians, and so a worried Capone contacted an old acquaintance on the Philadelphia police force, Jim "Shooey" Malone, who had visited briefly with Capone at the Stribling-Sharkey fight in Miami in February. After leaving Atlantic City, Capone and a bodyguard named Frank ("Slippery") Rio stopped in Philadelphia to see a movie. As they walked out of the theater, Malone and another cop stepped up to Scarface and, following the prearranged script, Malone said, "You're Al Capone, aren't you?"

To complete the charade, the detectives identified themselves and arrested Capone and Rio for carrying concealed weapons. After pleading guilty to the weapons charge, Capone confidently expected a light sentence—perhaps a few months at most—but Judge John E. Walsh socked him with the maximum penalty of a full year in jail. Screaming that he had been railroaded, a very unhappy Capone was sent to Holmesburg County Prison, where the guards were brutish and the cells were filthy and overcrowded. His friends tried to bribe the Philadelphia district attorney to secure his release or reduce his sentence, but the D.A. refused to budge. So Al spent the summer pitching for the prison baseball team (he had a nice slider) and improving his public image; when someone asked him for a $250 contribution to the Philadelphia Children's Hospital, Capone replied indignantly, "A mere $250 contribution to a hospital? Nothing doing. It'll be $1,000 or nothing. . . . I've got a kid myself." And he wrote out a check for $1,000.

# XI

# In the Twilight Palace

"I make them all pay and pay and pay."
—F. SCOTT FITZGERALD

The Marx Brothers spent the spring of 1929 commuting between the Paramount movie studio in Astoria, Queens, where they were filming *The Cocoanuts* every morning and afternoon, and the Forty-fourth Street Theater in Manhattan, where *Animal Crackers* was still playing to capacity audiences every evening. Between the two acting jobs and their extracurricular activities (women, the ponies, and the stock market), the boys were getting a bit frazzled. "Sometimes," Groucho admitted, "I'd get so punchy that I'd find myself spouting the dialogue from 'Animal Crackers' in a scene I was doing in 'Cocoanuts,' and vice versa." But script mix-ups were the least of their troubles.

Although Paramount wanted to finish the movie as quickly as possible, the shooting stretched out for five chaotic months. All four brothers were chronically late in arriving at the studio, and frequently vanished from the set for hours at a time: Groucho usually could be found discussing call options with his broker on the telephone; Harpo was either asleep in his dressing room or playing the harp in some private hideaway; and Chico—who figured that he could do whatever he wanted, since no one had paid a ticket to watch him—wandered off to play bridge or place a few bets with his bookie. The producer finally solved the problem by caging, literally, all four Marx Brothers. "He had the four cells used in the jail scene bolted to the studio floor," recalled Harpo. "He had four signs made, one for each cell—CHICO, HARPO, GROUCHO and ZEPPO—and he had a telephone installed in the one labeled CHICO. Now Chico could call his bookie any time he felt like it, without bringing production to a standstill. Between takes we were locked behind bars."

Friction soon developed between the director, a distinguished French filmmaker named Robert Florey, and the volatile Groucho, who was not used to having his freedom of movement curtailed by the technical requirements of cinematic production. Pacing frenetically back and forth while delivering his lines, Groucho constantly overstepped his mark and disappeared altogether from the camera shot, forcing Florey to re-shoot the scene. Then, said Florey, Groucho stubbornly "insisted on paint-ing his mustache with a shiny black varnish," a habit that left his close-ups looking pretty silly "with the light reflecting between his nose and his mouth." When a studio executive suggested that he use crepe on his mustache instead of paint, Groucho stormed off the set in a huff. (Or, as Groucho would say, in a minute and a huff.)

Production also suffered from the usual assortment of glitches that plagued virtually every "talkie" in those days. Since the first full-length sound movie, Al Jolson's *The Jazz Singer,* had appeared less than two years earlier, everyone in the film industry had been struggling to master the intricacies of the new technology. Equipment broke down with distressing regularity, and electrical connections routinely shorted out; extraneous noises on the set—the buzzing of insects, the crackling of paper, or the giggling of cameramen (who were eventually enclosed and practically suffocated in hermetically sealed soundproof booths)—drowned out the dialogue; and no one was quite sure how to cut the sound track to mesh with the final, edited copy of the film.

When Florey finally finished *The Cocoanuts,* the movie seemed static and oddly (for the Marx Brothers) stilted. Critics did not hesitate to point out the shortcomings of the screen version, which originally ran for two and a half hours. "The director," noted one caustic reviewer, "never made up his mind whether he was making a movie or photographing a musical show; for the most part the production might as well have been a moving picture of what took place on the stage. The movie added nothing." The brothers themselves reportedly were quite dissatisfied when they viewed the final product, fearing that it would wreck their budding movie careers. Even with its problems, however, the film enjoyed tremendous success with audiences right from the start; in its first six months of distribution, it earned nearly $2 million.

By the time *The Cocoanuts* was released, *Animal Crackers* had gone into storage for the summer—most theaters were not yet air-condi-tioned—before heading back onto the road in the fall, so to earn some extra money the Marx Brothers agreed to play a two-week engagement as headliners on a bill at the Palace Theater in Manhattan. According to *Variety,* the boys were paid handsomely for their first appearance on a vaudeville stage since 1921: $7,000 per week for a daily thirty-five-minute performance, a magnificent sum only bandleader Paul Whiteman and actress Sarah Bernhardt had ever commanded. Appearing on the same bill with the Marx Brothers was Duke Ellington and his band, on loan from the Cotton Club. Alas, *Variety*'s reviewer found Ellington's "hot" band something less than boffo. "This colored cafe band," the critic sniffed, "was not fully prepared for vaude. . . . Sax section, brass section, string section, etc., are superb alone. [But] when they join in crescendo, it's a battle of instruments, or it sounds that way. They finish by themselves and apparently when they want to."

No matter; vaudeville was nearly dead anyway. The legitimate theater, too, found itself in severe financial straits in 1929 as the tidal wave of talking motion pictures swept away everything in its path. One after another, the major film studios—led by Warner Brothers—announced plans to cease production of silent movies and concentrate solely on sound films. Distribution chains hastened to wire their theaters for sound, and Hollywood put out a desperate call for playwrights and songwriters. Sadly, Sam Goldwyn estimated that half the current crop of cinema actors would be out of a job within two years, partly because fewer movies would be produced (talking pictures cost approximately twice as much as silent films), and partly because the actors themselves were unfit for the unique demands of sound pictures. (Since audiences would be looking more closely at the face of a talking actress, casting directors suddenly began to pay close attention to the condition of starlets' teeth in screen tests.) Goldwyn also warned that the public would be less tolerant of bad talkies: "People will walk out on them. If a silent film is bad audiences sleep through it, but they won't be able to sleep through talkies. The theater used to be a fine place to sleep but it isn't any more."

Perhaps not, but for the women who made up nearly three-fourths of the movie-going public in 1929, a trip to the theater permitted an escape into a world of luxurious fantasy for a few blissful hours. This was the era of magnificent picture palaces, of deluxe four-thousand-seat theaters where uniformed ushers bowed patrons to their seats through lobbies and foyers that opened into one another like chambers in some Byzantine maze, with soft carpets that sank sensually beneath tired feet, with walls draped with crimson velvet and fine oil paintings, and nude marble statues in the recesses. "When she goes home that evening," remarked a writer who understood the magical appeal of the palaces to harried housewives, "she will perhaps clean spinach and peel onions, but for a few hours, attendants bow to her, doormen tip their hats, and a maid curtsies to her in the ladies' washroom."

> In the dim auditorium which seems to float in a world of dreams and where the people brushing her elbows on either side are safely remote, an American woman may spend her afternoon alone. Romantic music . . . gives her a pleasant sensation of tingling. Her husband is busy else-

where; and on this music, as on a mildly erotic bridge, she can let her fancies slip through the darkened atmosphere to the screen, where they drift in rhapsodic amours with handsome stars. In the isolation of this twilit palace, she abandons herself to these adventures with a freedom that is impossible in the legitimate theater, where the lights are brighter and the neighboring seat-holders always on the edge of her vision; the blue dusk of the "de luxe" house has dissolved the Puritan strictures she had absorbed as a child.

Perhaps the setting was erotic; but the material had better not be. The advent of sound movies presented the nation's guardians of public morality with a king-sized headache in 1929, but the censors rose manfully—or, more often, womanfully—to the challenge. Although the motion picture industry attempted to regulate itself through its own "morals" code, enforced by the office of movie production czar Will Hays, most states enforced their own restrictive judgment on the films distributed within their borders. Sometimes special agencies were established for the specific purpose of censoring movies, but more frequently the job was handed over to an existing organization. In New York, for example, the state Department of Education supervised the theaters, and when the department was overburdened, it turned some of the films over to state troopers for inspection. And since most censorship boards contained a disproportionate number of unmarried females, the regulations tended to reflect a rather restricted notion of permissive behavior.

For instance, the sound version of *Sal of Singapore* was banned in New York, even though the state board had approved the silent version. The mayor of Lynn, Massachusetts, ordered *Our Dancing Daughters* out of town, calling it "indecent, immoral and lascivious," despite the fact that he had never seen it; in less puritanical regions, it became one of the box office hits of early 1929. Robert Benchley's satirical short *The Sex Life of a Polyp* was mangled beyond recognition by humorless philistines. The chairman of the Pennsylvania Board of Censors proudly boasted that not even the President of the United States could deliver a speech through the talking movies without the prior approval of his board. And, in a fit of fundamentalist fervor, a censor in Memphis, Tennessee, ordered the deletion of certain allegedly sacrilegious scenes in the biblical epic *The King of Kings,* despite the film's enthusiastic endorsements from clergymen of all denominations across the America.

Undaunted by witless censors and technological stumbling blocks, a few astute businessmen realized that the advent of talking pictures had fired the imagination of the public and rendered Hollywood an exceptionally inviting target for financial exploitation. And for a man as well versed in the fine art of exploitation as Joseph P. Kennedy, the movie industry represented a particularly delightful opportunity for both profit and pleasure.

By the time Kennedy arrived in Hollywood in 1926, he already had amassed a fortune of nearly $2 million, along with a reputation as a shrewd, ruthless hustler who never let friendship or conscience stand in the way of his hard-edged ambition. Although he had attended one of the finest prep schools in Boston and held a degree from Harvard, Kennedy always felt self-consciously Irish, a parvenu outsider among the Yankee elite of New England and Wall Street, and this pervasive sense of insecurity governed his life and provided him with an obsessive determination to establish an unassailable financial empire for himself and his children. Joe Kennedy first learned the inner workings of the stock market as a customer's man for one of Boston's leading brokerage houses in the years immediately following the Great War. In 1922, at the age of thirty-four, fortified by steel nerves, a superlative sense of timing, and the invaluable knowledge that Wall Street was governed by human emotions and mass psychology as much as (and frequently more than) cold statistics and profit statements, Kennedy went into business for himself. As an associate pointed out, Kennedy also knew how to find and manipulate the loopholes in the Wall Street racket that "made Al Capone look like a piker."

Like his close friend Bernard Baruch, Joe Kennedy laughed at the way an upstart such as he had defeated the Brahmins at their own game. "Here I am, a boy from East Boston, and I took 'em," he bragged to his sons. But money alone did not satisfy the high-strung young Irishman's craving for respectability and fame. In 1926, backed by a syndicate of bankers, Kennedy purchased a small film-producing company named Film Booking Offices, and proceeded to churn out a stream of entirely undistinguished potboilers such as *A Poor Girl's Romance, Rose of the Tenements,* and *The Flame of the Argentine.* (Art meant nothing to Kennedy, but profits did.) Then he merged FBO with Pathé Pictures and the Keith-Albee-Orpheum chain of theaters, and subsequently convinced David Sarnoff—who was searching for a cinematic application for RCA's "Photophone" sound recording technology—to join him in establishing a huge holding company known as Radio-Keith-Orpheum, or RKO. With Sarnoff at its helm, RKO appeared to be a highly rational venture: Film Booking Offices and Pathé provided the studios to make the films, RCA supplied the broadcast facilities and technology, and KAO owned the theaters required for distribution.

Besides the salary (over $2,000 per week) Kennedy enjoyed as chairman of the board of his various enterprises, and the commissions he earned from promoting the series of mergers, and the millions of dollars' worth of stock he held in Pathé Pictures, there was another, more personal attraction that bound Joe to Hollywood. Her name was Gloria Swanson, and she was without question one of the most glamorous cinema starlets of the era. By the time she became Kennedy's mistress, Swanson already had gone through three husbands and several small fortunes; her profligate spending habits ("There is no star in Hollywood who lives in such gilded luxury as Gloria Swanson," gushed one columnist) had brought her to the edge of bankruptcy. At the request of a studio executive, Kennedy became Gloria's financial adviser; then he became much more. Certainly his wife, Rose Fitzgerald Kennedy, daughter of former Boston mayor John J. "Honey Fitz" Fitzgerald, knew about the affair, and surely Joe knew she knew. He simply didn't care.

But by the summer of 1929, the charms of both Gloria and Hollywood had begun to wear thin for Kennedy. He had invested, by his own admission, eight hundred thousand dollars (Swanson later claimed it was actually her money) in the production of a film entitled *Queen Kelly,* which was supposed to be the spectacular capstone to his lover's acting career; but incessant squabbling on the set, a fundamental indecision as to whether the movie should be silent or sound, and the increasingly eccentric behavior of the film's director, Erich von Stroheim, had forced the studio to shelve the project. Although Kennedy had extracted a considerable fortune from his Hollywood companies, he had also managed to run FBO and Pathé nearly into the ground in the process. He didn't particularly care about that, either, but he did still possess that large chunk of Pathé securities, and so his sometime friends from Wall Street, the Irish-Catholic contingent of John Jacob Raskob, William F. Kenny, and Mike Meehan, obligingly launched a well-publicized pool to inflate the value of Pathé stock by hinting broadly (and quite falsely) that they were seriously interested in purchasing the company.

Between 1926 and the spring of 1929, Kennedy had been far too emotionally and financially involved in his Hollywood escapades to give affairs on the stock market his undivided attention; in fact, he had reduced his holdings by more than 50 percent by the time Herbert Hoover was inaugurated. Now, as Joe returned from the seductive pleasures of southern California to the bosom of his family and his estate in Riverdale, New York, he began to pick up disquieting vibrations from Wall Street. According to his own account (which is not necessarily reliable, for Kennedy was a shameless fabricator of autobiographical myths), he went to see Jack Morgan to discuss the danger signals, but Morgan brusquely refused to meet with the upstart Irishman. An old business colleague named Guy Currier, however, confirmed Kennedy's suspicions. "It looks to me that there is about an even chance that we are in for some degree of business depression," Currier wrote in a letter of April 1, 1929. "Present money conditions are slowing up building and will restrict public works. How far it will affect the auto industry I don't dare to guess. On the whole it is not an attractive time to go into new matters."

So Kennedy, who knew that "only a fool holds out for top dollar," sold virtually every share of stock he owned, except for his Pathé securities, and kept the profits in cash or municipal bonds. Like David Sarnoff before him, and Bernard Baruch, and Paul Warburg, and the partners of Kuhn, Loeb, and Company, and Owen Young, and President Herbert Clark Hoover, Joseph Kennedy had decided that the bull market on Wall Street was headed for a disastrous crash.

Zelda and Scott Fitzgerald arrived in Paris in April, after spending a month at Cap d'Antibes on the Riviera, where the drunken Scott kept getting himself arrested for disorderly conduct. Zelda resumed her ballet lessons, torturing her body with diets and disciplines designed for much younger women. Her appearance deteriorated as she drove herself to exhaustion; her complexion turned pallid, almost ashen, and her eyes took on a haunted, frightened look. An old friend noticed the manic quality of her laughter: "The laughter was her own, not like a human voice. Something strange in it, like unhinged delight. It was ecstatic, but there was a suppressed quality about it, a low, intimate sound that took one completely off guard." By this time she was teetering on the edge of madness.

Scott sank further into his degraded submission to alcohol and the demons that refused to unlock his literary brilliance. "My latest tendency," he wrote to Hemingway, "is to collapse about 11:00 and, with tears flowing from my eyes or the gin rising to their level and leaking over, tell interested friends or acquaintances that I haven't a friend in the world and likewise care for nobody, generally including Zelda, and often implying current company—after which the current company tend to become less current and I wake up in strange rooms in strange places. The rest of the time I stay alone working or trying to work or brooding or reading detective stories—and realizing that anyone in my state of mind, who has in addition never been able to hold his tongue, is pretty poor company. But when drunk I make them all pay and pay and pay."

Hemingway returned to Paris in April, too, but he told his friends not to give his address to the Fitzgeralds, for he had no wish to be pestered by Scott's drunken binges or Zelda's sudden outbursts of paranoia. But he relented to the extent of giving Scott a copy of the completed manuscript of *A Farewell to Arms;* when Scott returned it with minor criticisms, Hemingway responded in his typically thin-skinned manner by writing on Scott's note, "Kiss my ass." Hemingway gave another copy of the manuscript to James Joyce, who was nearly blind and living in a solidly bourgeois apartment house near the Gare Montparnasse with his deep-bosomed wife, Nora. Like Joyce before him, Ernest was experiencing the shoddy depredations of censorship in America; the May issue of *Scribner's* magazine, which carried an excerpt from *Farewell,* had been banned in Boston, and Hemingway's editor, Maxwell Perkins, bombarded him throughout the spring and summer with requests for euphemisms to permit the book to be published with as few cuts as possible. "If you decide that [balls] is unprintable how about b——ls," Hemingway suggested wearily. "I suppose on galley 57 C——S——RS and C——ks——r will do for the other too. . . . Certainly those letters cannot corrupt anyone who has not heard or does not know the word."

Hemingway spent much of that summer boxing in the gymnasium at the American Club, sparring often with a young Canadian writer named Morley Callaghan. Though he was considerably smaller and lighter than Hemingway, Callaghan was a talented fighter who often left Ernest with a bloody nose. "He was a big rough tough clumsy unscientific man," observed Callaghan, more in admiration than criticism. Sometimes their timekeeper was Ernest's friend the Spanish surrealist painter Joan Miró. "He was about the size of Napoleon," Callaghan recalled. "He wore a neat dark business suit, and the kind of a shirt I hadn't seen for a long time; it had a stiffly starched front with stripes running crosswise. His hair was clipped close, and he had a quick warm smile and lively eager eyes. Unfortunately for me, he couldn't speak a word of English." Miró topped off his outfit with a hard black bowler hat.

When he wasn't admiring Hemingway's pugilistic prowess, Miró took time to escort his young compatriot Salvador Dali around Paris, showing him the sights, pointing out the host of renowned artists and writers who frequented Montparnasse (Picasso, Matisse, André Gide), and introducing him to wealthy patrons of the avant-garde. Dali needed all the help he could get. "He is thin to the point of anorexia," noted one observer, "with deep hollows in his cheeks, around his mouth, and under his eyes," and he was totally at sea in the bewildering Parisian metropolis. "He couldn't even cross the street," said French author André Thirion. "His only means of transport was a taxi. He fell down several times a day." Dali was afraid of insects, of malevolent demons, and of exposing his feet in public (which made it difficult for him to purchase a pair of shoes that fit properly). He refused to descend into the subway alone. "He was the absolute victim of rigorous habit," wrote biographer Meryle Secrest. "Each day he ate the same things in the same restaurants and took the same walks. His ability to lose his keys and his wallet, and leave his change behind was already legendary. Whenever he went out, he hung on to an elaborate cane and always carried a little piece of driftwood from the beaches around Cadaques to ward off evil spirits." And all the while, Dali was painting at breakneck speed, fashioning his terror-ridden, hallucinatory images of decay, death, animals' heads, disembodied limbs, and smiling faces that floated in the air.

Sergei Prokofiev dealt in far more conventional images. In May, the Ballet Russes staged the debut performance of the composer's latest work, *The Prodigal Son,* but only after lengthy arguments between Prokofiev, who preferred literal, realistic staging, and choreographer George Balanchine, whose abstract interpretation finally won out with the support of the ballet company's director, Sergei Diaghilev. The work was given a glittering premiere at the Theatre Sarah Bernhardt, with Coco Chanel and Sergei Rachmaninoff among the audience, and Stravinsky's *Renard* on the same program. This would be the final Paris season for the Ballet Russes; Diaghilev was dying of diabetes, his body tortured with open abscesses. His most famous protégé, Vaslav Nijinsky, had gone mad ten years earlier. In August, Diaghilev passed away and Prokofiev prepared to return to Moscow, where he would soon encounter Stalinist censorship in all its repressive vigor.

Americans swarmed through Paris that summer like ravenous insects, trading the money they had made on the stock market for a glimpse of a different, larger sort of life, seeking freedom and a spiritual sustenance that had escaped them at home. "There were Americans at night," remembered Zelda, "and day Americans, and we all had Americans in the bank to buy things with." Gloria Swanson was there, staying at the Hotel Paris-Athénée, and so was Joe Kennedy and his wife, Rose, who went shopping with Gloria at the salons of the city's leading couturiers. William Durant, too, was in Paris for a while that season. In Montmartre, the price of champagne kept rising as the tourists kept paying; the Ritz bar was crammed with businessmen from the Midwest; and the "in" show was the French version of an American Negro musical revue called *The Blackbirds.* Gigolos charmed and sometimes robbed wealthy American women, until the French government insisted that the city's gigolos be licensed just as prostitutes were. "That year," complained Morley Callaghan, "Paris was crawling with Americans wanting to see everything, and having the money to see it, not knowing that in a few months the stock market would crash and the year of Panic would begin." They kept reminding the French that the United States was the richest country in the world, that France should pay its war debts, that America had made the world safe for democracy, that the U. S. was the richest country in the world, that France should pay its debts, and that Americans were the most generous people in the world. At the Deux Magots Café the tourists might even view the remains of Scott Fitzgerald, the barely conscious symbol of "all that was reckless, prodigal and extravagant, all the women who were beautiful and damned and golden" in that glittering, irresponsible, tormented era that was dying, like Fitzgerald, before their eyes. They watched him slip into an alcoholic daze and they whispered to one another.

"Eternal youth," muttered Hemingway, "has sunk the Fitzes." Not to mention prosperity.

# XII

# Assault from the Left

"Everything to-day has been
    Heavy and Brown
Bring me a Unicorn
    To ride about town."
        —ANNE MORROW LINDBERGH, *"Unicorn,"* 1926

In the worldwide wave of reaction that followed the Great War, the forces of radical reform and revolution had suffered a series of discouraging defeats that drove the leftist movement underground in one country after another for most of the decade of the 1920s: in the United States, labor union membership declined dramatically after 1919, and most progressive reformers abjured their faith or went into hiding (some even became stockbrokers); in the Soviet Union, the heirs of Lenin appeared ready to abandon or at least drastically modify the goals of the revolution; and Britain seemed condemned to muddle through the indefinite future under the uninspired supervision of Baldwin and his unattractive Conservative colleagues. But far beneath the surface, discontent among the dispossessed had been growing throughout the decade, and in the spring and summer of 1929 the Left suddenly broke through with an unexpected and vigorous display of strength.

Baldwin and Churchill never saw it coming. The government had been coasting nonchalantly through nearly the whole electoral campaign; there was such a dearth of controversial issues and colorful personalities that contemporary newspapers called it the dullest general election in British history. Practically the only spark of excitement came from those two old war-horses and former wartime allies David Lloyd George and Winston Churchill. In March, Lloyd George promulgated a bold government program to alleviate the crushing unemployment problem; by then, the number of jobless British workers had reached nearly 1.5 million. In a sixpence Liberal manifesto entitled *We Can Conquer Unemployment* (the pamphlet was popularly known as the Orange Book), Lloyd George advocated an emergency program of public works, particularly road and bridge construction, to stimulate the economy at little or no cost to the British taxpayer. Theoretically, the initial cost of the Exchequer loan to fund the program would be reimbursed through users' fees and increased revenue once prosperity returned. Based on the "pump-priming" schemes of Liberal economists John Maynard Keynes and Hubert Henderson, the Orange Book eventually became one of the most significant intellectual influences on the New Deal in the United States.

But Churchill and his Conservative allies treated the scheme with undisguised ridicule. "How crude, barbarous, and ignorant is a policy which would gather hundreds of thousands of unemployed together in gangs and set them to make racing tracks for Liberal profiteers to run their cars upon," jeered Churchill in an election address of April 27. His criticisms sometimes were remarkably frivolous—"In many cases work on the roads would spoil men's hands for their own trades," he charged—and taken as a whole they revealed that the chancellor of the Exchequer had missed the Keynesian point completely. The Liberal program, Churchill predicted, "would interrupt the whole natural recovery of industry, and when the money for the relief work had been spent they might, it is true, have a good many more fine roads for motorists to go forty or fifty miles an hour upon, but the people who had made them would be thrown back upon the labour market, they would return to empty homes and the country would be saddled for several generations with the interest upon the money that had been borrowed and spent." Instead, Churchill advocated continued patience as he assured an unimpressed electorate that there was no shortcut to prosperity.

Until the election returns began to arrive at No. 10 Downing Street on the evening of May 30, Baldwin and Churchill truly believed that they were going to win the election. One eyewitness recalled a stunned Churchill adding up the figures in red ink,

> sipping whisky and soda, getting redder and redder, rising and going out often to glare at the machine himself, hunching his shoulders, bowing his head like a bull about to charge. . . . As Labour gain after Labour gain was announced, Winston became more and more flushed with anger, left his seat and confronted the machine in the passage; with his shoulders hunched he glared at the figures, tore the sheets and behaved as though if any more Labour gains came he would smash the whole apparatus. His ejaculations to the surrounding staff were quite unprintable.

Labour emerged with fewer popular votes than the Tories, but with a shaky plurality in the Commons: 287 seats, to the Conservatives' 261 and the fading Liberal party's 59 (though the Liberals received nearly one-fourth of the total popular vote). Baldwin resigned at once, and the King, who was on his way home at last after spending an extended period of recuperation at the resort of Bognor-on-Sea, called for Ramsay Mac-Donald.

Although Churchill had won reelection (narrowly) for his own constituency, and remained for a time one of the leading members of the Conservative "shadow cabinet," he would not hold cabinet office again until the dark days of May 1940, when the Nazi blitzkrieg was tearing its way across western Europe and Britain turned to the redoubtable Winston as its savior. Meanwhile, in the summer of 1929, at the age of fifty-four, Churchill wandered into a political wilderness largely of his own making. He had built no national constituency, he possessed no solid base of personal political support. His Conservative colleagues distrusted him for his flirtation with the Liberals before and during the Great War; the Liberals considered him a pompous renegade; and the Labour party never forgave his inflammatory activities during the General Strike of 1926.

Yet no British politician was more resilient than Churchill, and he had no intention of fading meekly into obscurity. On June 28, the former chancellor of the Exchequer wrote to his old friend Bernard Baruch to let him know that he would be touring Canada and the United States from August through October. Churchill told Baruch that he had received an invitation to address the New York Chamber of Commerce, and had earlier promised Henry Ford that he would stop by and visit him in Detroit. Besides, the last volume of Churchill's history of the Great War had just been published, and the free publicity of an American tour certainly would help boost sales. Churchill also expressed a wish (actually, he considered it a duty) to meet with his old wartime nemesis Herbert Hoover in Washington. "I want to see the country and to meet the leaders of its fortunes," he told Baruch. "I have no political mission and no axe to grind." He did, however, possess a substantial portfolio of American stocks.

On the morning of May 22, an extraordinary passenger train pulled out of Mexico City bound for Laredo, Texas. The train bristled with troops and guns; one hundred heavily armed soldiers of the Mexican army rode in two armored cars and a special guard coach. Ahead, an exploration train bearing twice as many troops scoured the tracks for saboteurs. This imposing display of military might, at least as great as the escort afforded the President of the Republic when he traveled, was designed to protect one man from the depredations of the insurgents who were threatening to plunge Mexico into yet another round in that nation's seemingly interminable chain of civil conflict. The object of the government's solicitude was probably the most valuable and certainly the most famous foreign dignitary in Mexico in the tumultuous summer of 1929: Ambassador Dwight Whitney Morrow, former partner in the House of Morgan.

Morrow was not fleeing Mexico to escape the bloody revolt; in fact, the leftist government of President Portes Gil was winning that battle, gradually clearing the rebels out of their strongholds in the more remote regions of the country. Morrow had a much more personal reason for returning to his home in Englewood, New Jersey. In four days, his daughter, Anne, was going to be married to Charles Augustus Lindbergh.

The Morrows had met Colonel Lindbergh for the first time in December 1927, when he flew *The Spirit of St. Louis* nonstop from Washington to Mexico City; Ambassador Morrow had suggested the trip as a gesture of U.S. goodwill toward the Latin American republics. Anne, who was on vacation from her senior year at Smith College in Coolidge's hometown of Northampton, Massachusetts, arrived in Mexico City several days after Lindbergh arrived. She had decided ahead of time that she "certainly was *not* going to worship 'Lindy,' " but was nonetheless captivated from the start by the Lindbergh mystique. Anne was introduced to America's most eligible bachelor at an embassy reception: "a tall, slim boy in evening dress—so much slimmer, so much taller, so much more poised than I expected," she confided to her diary. "A very refined face, not at all like those grinning 'Lindy' pictures—a firm mouth, clear, straight blue eyes, fair hair, and nice color." "He is very, very young," she decided after spending a few moments with the hero "and was terribly shy—looked straight ahead and talked in short direct sentences which came out abruptly and clipped. You could not meet his sentences: they were statements of fact, presented with such honest directness; not trying to please, just bare simple answers and statements, not trying to help a conversation along. It was amazing—breathtaking. I could not speak. What kind of boy was this?"

Anne, an especially sensitive and bashful young woman who loved to write poetry (her best was "Unicorn": "And I will kneel each morning / To polish bright his hoofs / That they may gleam each moonnight / We ride over roofs"), was amazed at the crowds' fanatical adoration of Lindbergh—sometimes they actually endangered his life by swarming onto an airstrip when he was trying to land, and occasionally someone nearly brained him by hurling a box of flowers at his head. She saw how they followed him around as though he were a god descended from the sky instead of a shy Minnesota farm boy who simply loved to fly more than anything else in the world. "Who has moved men like that before—not with a speech, not intentionally, not trying to move them by any means—

just standing there, just existing?" she wondered. "What *does* he think about it? What does he suppose he's doing?"

Well, what he was doing, besides exuding a sort of homespun good-will, was conducting preliminary research for a transamerican airline route. Seeking a contract from Washington as the primary airmail carrier between the United States and South America, Pan-American Airways retained Lindbergh as a technical adviser; when Pan Am won the contracts, Lindbergh helped open the route in February 1929 by making the first airmail flight (in a Sikorsky seaplane) between the Florida Keys and Panama, a three-day, 750-mile voyage that required stops in Cuba, Honduras, and Nicaragua. Lindbergh also served as a consultant to the Trans-Continental Air Transport company, which planned to provide coast-to-coast domestic passenger service by linking short air routes with existing train connections. (For instance, passengers took an overnight train from New York to Columbus, Ohio, then boarded a pair of Wasp-motored Ford air transports that took them to Wayonka, Oklahoma, whence they rode a sleeper to Winslow, Arizona, and then made their way by air to Los Angeles and San Francisco.) And in his spare time, Lindbergh worked as an adviser to the aeronautical branch of the U.S. Department of Commerce and as an unofficial mentor to the Mexican army, to whom he graciously demonstrated how to pilot an airplane the Gil government had purchased with the intent of bombing the hell out of the insurgents.

One might have wondered where, amid this hectic schedule, Lindbergh found time to court Miss Morrow, but presumably he managed somehow. Will Rogers waxed poetic when he heard the announcement of their engagement. "The world's mind is on romance," he gushed. "It's Annie and Lindy that our minds are on today. . . . It's our boy and that fine girl we are thinking of tonight—a great girl from a fine, wholesome family." The public devoured whatever details of the romance leaked to the press, turning the courtship into a game of hide-and-seek. Often the nation's obsession with the lovers crossed the line into absurdity; after Anne, doggedly pursued by a pack of newspapermen, purchased some neckties for her fiancé at a Madison Avenue haberdashery, the half-dozen patterns she selected were advertised far and wide as "the Lindbergh neckwear outfit."

Their wedding took place in complete secrecy at the thickly wooded Morrow estate in Englewood. Ever since the engagement had been made public, a contingent of policemen had kept reporters far away from the entrance to the estate; the main house, which was located at the end of a long driveway, and the surrounding gardens were sheltered by a tall fence and high shrubs. (Security was tightened even more after the Morrow family received letters threatening to kidnap Anne's younger sister,

Constance.) To deceive the press as his wedding day approached, Lindbergh asked a friend to fly his plane to Rochester, and he kept a motor launch carefully hidden off the Long Island shore. Not even the servants were told of the impending nuptials; the unsuspecting caterer who made the wedding cake was instructed to write only "L" and "M" on the top in rosebud icing. Few of the twenty invited guests, almost all of whom were immediate members or very close friends of the Morrow family (Lindbergh invited only his mother), realized what was going to happen—assuming that his phones were tapped, Dwight had casually invited them over for lunch and bridge—until Mrs. Morrow asked everyone to assemble in the living room and Anne shyly appeared in an informal wedding gown. The ceremony was stark in its simplicity. The Morrows' house was not decorated at all for the wedding, and there was no altar, nor a wedding march or music of any sort. Lindbergh himself picked his bride's bouquet of larkspur blossoms in the gardens. The couple drove away alone after the ceremony, and since the news of the marriage was not announced until several hours later, they succeeded in eluding reporters for five days until someone recognized them at New Harbor, Rhode Island. An enterprising journalist in a seaplane finally caught up with Lindy at Woods Hole on Cape Cod. When he asked the hero if he and his bride were heading up to the Morrows' summer home in North Haven, Lindbergh—who refused to talk to reporters about anything except aviation—said only, "Uh, glad to see you."

"Where do you expect to live?" the reporter asked.

"Nothing to say," replied Lindbergh.

"Are you going abroad this summer?"

"Glad to see you."

After half an hour of similarly unenlightening repartee, the reporter finally gave up.

In July, Morrow returned to Mexico City to resume his official duties (of which he was, by this time, heartily sick and tired). Soon General Augusto Sandino, too, arrived in Mexico, and with even more fanfare than Charles Lindbergh's father-in-law.

Lately the Sandinista cause had fallen upon hard times, despite the fact that the gringo soldiers were leaving Nicaragua en masse. President Hoover, who had never favored Coolidge's military adventures in Latin America, had wisely withdrawn nearly two-thirds of the 3,500 marines who were left in Nicaragua, and most of the remainder had been removed from combat duties and assigned as advisers to the National Guard (which presumably would do most of the actual fighting henceforth). But President Moncada continued to press the weary rebels, and the Sandinista movement began to languish for want of military supplies. So, in the spring of 1929, Sandino dispatched an emissary to Mexico's President Gil seeking arms and ammunition. Through a misunderstanding, Sandino apparently believed that Gil had promised him material aid; Gil steadfastly maintained that he had offered only political asylum. After conferring with Gil, Morrow consented to Sandino's presence in Mexico, on the conditions that the Mexican government would not provide Sandino with a "base of operations," and would keep the rebel out of Mexico City.

Armed with a pass that gave him safe conduct through Honduras, El Salvador, and Guatemala, Sandino crossed the border into Mexico on June 25. Gil provided him with a lavish reception and permitted him to indulge in some typically florid anti-imperialist oratory. Then the president shuttled Sandino and his contingent of traveling bodyguards off to a hotel in the village of Merida on the barren Yucatan Peninsula, suggesting that he wait there until the government cleared some preliminary matters out of the way. Six months later, Sandino was still waiting.

As the stock market slumped morosely into May, the Federal Reserve Board's indecision about whether or not to raise interest rates was starting to get on the nerves of American business. A survey of industrial executives by the New York *World* revealed widespread support for the board's goal of easing credit for legitimate business purposes by liquidating brokers' loans; but the board still obdurately refused to raise its rediscount rate, despite a pointed suggestion by the Federal Advisory Council and repeated entreaties from the directors of the Federal Reserve Banks of New York and Chicago. The prolonged monetary uncertainty among speculators manifested itself in a decline in eastbound bookings on express steamships in May; captains of transatlantic luxury liners complained that their ships were leaving New York with scores of empty first-class passenger berths.

Suddenly, in the last hour of trading on the afternoon of May 20, the market broke violently for no discernible reason; the *New York Times* called it "one of the most dramatic episodes in recent years on the Stock Exchange," and suggested that it was due to profit taking by professional traders. Two days later, another drastic wave of liquidation overwhelmed the market in the heaviest trading session since the debacle of March 28. Judged by the *New York Times'* average of fifty industrial and rail stocks, it was the sharpest decline in the history of the New York Stock Exchange. Brokerage houses were deluged with "sell" orders from all parts of the nation; distressed margin traders threw stocks overboard in a desperate attempt to cover. Pool favorites such as General Electric, Woolworth's, and General Motors, deprived of artificial support, led the decline. One veteran financial reporter claimed that "the pessimistic feeling in stock market circles was more pronounced probably than it has been at any time this year."

But the worst was yet to come. After drifting downward for the rest of the week, the stock exchange was wracked by another violent selling movement on May 27, shortly after the Chicago grain market reported an especially sharp drop in the price of wheat. Entertainment stocks were particularly hard hit; Fox Studios, for instance, dropped to its lowest point in a year and a half. Ominously, the giant investment trusts did not rush to buy up the bargains that littered the floor of the exchange. Although some Wall Street watchers attributed the break to renewed apprehension about the intentions of the Federal Reserve Board, others wondered aloud whether "the long bull market that started with Coolidge's election was about over."

Once more the Senate chamber resounded with enraged demands to curb the wayward speculators before the whole precarious structure crashed to the ground. South Dakota Republican senator William E. Borah, longtime champion of the nation's agrarian interests, warned that a worldwide money panic lay just around the corner unless the government succeeded in reducing the swollen volume of brokers' loans. "The call-money market in Wall Street," Borah charged, "has become a direct menace to legitimate business operations throughout the world. It has sucked $6,000,000,000 into the pot called brokers' loans, and that pot now completely dominates the credit situation in two hemispheres." After once again chastising National City Bank's Charlie Mitchell for abetting the "frightful orgy of speculation which has almost paralyzed the legitimate commercial and industrial credits of the nation," Virginia's acerbic Senator Glass took out after William Durant, who he claimed had "lured more innocent amateur gamblers into the market than any other forty individuals in the United States." In a cable from Paris, Durant replied by disdainfully dismissing the "sarcastic and inaccurate statements by a few noisy United States Senators" who threatened to disrupt the rising tide of American prosperity.

To rein in Mitchell, Durant, and their fast-trading cronies, Glass proposed a 5 percent tax on transfers of stock certificates held for fewer than sixty days. Not surprisingly, Glass' proposal met with universal hostility on Wall Street. "The proposition is so ridiculous," sputtered one leading broker, "that it's hard to believe that such a level-headed man as Senator Glass could have made it."

When the accountants tallied up the damage at the end of May, they discovered that the aggregate decline in stock values totaled slightly more than $3 billion for the month. At the time it seemed like a staggering sum; six months later it would be nothing more than a drop in the ocean.

Ella May Wiggins was a common laborer in the red-brick cotton mill of the Manville-Jenckes Company in Loray, just outside the pretty little city of Gastonia in the hills of North Carolina. Though she was only thirty-five years old, Ella May's face already bore lines of worry and fatigue. Her cheeks were hollow and sunken. She had given birth to nine children, but only five were still alive in the summer of 1929; the other four had caught whooping cough while Ella May was working eleven and a half hours, six days a week, earning less than $3 a day on the night shift at the Loray Cotton Mill. "I asked the super to put me on day shift so's I could tend them," she said, "but he wouldn't. I don't know why. So I had to quit my job and then there wasn't any money for medicine, so they just died. I never could do anything for my children, not even to keep 'em alive, it seems. That's why I'm for the union, so's I can do better for them."

Ella May could sing like an angel, and she could write rhymes, and so she wrote new words to the old mountain ballads, turning the melodies into laments of the harshness of life in the mill towns of the South, or hymns to the workers' hopes for better days. "The boss man wants our labor, and money to pack away," she sang in a clear, strong voice. "The workers wants a union and the eight-hour day. / The boss man sleeps in a big fine bed and dreams of his silver and gold. / The workers sleeps in a old straw bed and shivers from the cold."

In the early years of the twentieth century, the American textile industry had migrated en masse from New England to the South, driven out by rising costs and high demand, attracted by promises of cheap white Anglo-Saxon labor and plentiful power. Soon company towns sprouted among the ancient hills of North and South Carolina, Tennessee, and Kentucky. Workers—impoverished mountain people drawn by the lure of steady wages, however minimal—were sheltered in bleak mill houses, most of them three or four rooms each, gathered around the factory. The companies charged rent of 50¢ per week per room; usually there was no indoor plumbing, but for an extra two bits, workers could have a sink and toilet with running water installed on the back porch. Wages averaged between $12 and $15 dollars per week. Most of the families lived on bread, molasses, coffee, potatoes, and beans; after paying the company for rent and groceries at the company store, very few had any money left over for store-bought clothes or shoes. Usually the children, dull and emaciated from malnutrition, worked in the mills from the time they were nine or ten years old because there was no reason for them to go to school.

Shifts at the mill ran for eleven or twelve hours at a stretch. Day workers received a half-hour break for lunch, but those on the night shift worked straight through from six o'clock to five-thirty. Inside the mill, the air was hot and humid and saturated with dust from the fibers. Accidents were common and a risk the worker bore alone. "Once I mashed my thumb in the mill," reported one woman who worked in a mill at Greenville, South Carolina. "I was out for two months with it and I didn't get anythin'. I went to pull a loom and the handle on the lever slipped because the gear was too tight and it mashed my thumb. The company don't pay anythin' for a thing like that." No. "I ain't a-feared of Hell," another worker said. "I've spent 20 summers in the mills." It was a palpable measure of America's shame that these miserable conditions were still preferable to the brutal poverty of Southern farm laborers, most of whom were black and earned less than half the wages of the average mill worker.

In the late 1920s, many of the textile mill owners (a majority of whom were Northerners) callously attempted to increase profits by instituting "scientific management" systems—in this case, a euphemism for the speed-up and the stretch-out—which forced workers to tend more machines and produce more goods at the same time that their already disgracefully inadequate wages were cut. With their backs up against the wall, workers struck in one town after another throughout the hill country. Most of the strikes were spontaneous, and many lacked any union leadership, because the spineless men who ran the American Federation of Labor had largely ignored the plight of the Southern textile industry. Management responded to the walkouts with their usual sledgehammer tools of company police, strikebreakers, and sometimes the state militia; when union organizers did appear, frequently they were kidnapped or run out of town at the point of a gun. Mill owners blamed the strikes on "foreign" (i.e., Northern) radical agitators, but a committee of the South Carolina House of Representatives officially denied that accusation, declaring that "we find the whole trouble in the textile area has been brought about by putting more work on the employees than they can do."

But there were Communist sympathizers willing to take advantage of the discontent in Gastonia and dozens of other distressed mill towns. Stepping into the vacuum created by the fecklessness of the AFL, the National Textile Workers Union, a New York–based organization affiliated with the Communist Party of America, began recruiting members at the Loray mills at the end of 1928. If nothing else, they succeeded in awakening the workers to their shameful degradation at the hands of the company. In April, the NTWU called a strike after management summarily dismissed several workers for their union activities, and 1,700 determined men and women (about 80 percent of the mill's labor force) walked off their jobs. The union demanded a forty-hour, five-day week, recognition of the NTWU, and a $20 minimum weekly wage. Management considered the strikers' demands for three minutes and then rejected them out of hand, refusing even to negotiate; the term "collective bargaining" clearly was not in the company's lexicon. Fearful of civil disorder, although the strike had been fairly peaceful up to this point, the governor of North Carolina called out five companies of the state militia (including a howitzer company) to patrol the streets of Gastonia with bayonets. Manville-Jenckes imported strikebreakers from the hills to keep the mills running. After a few weeks, strikers were deemed "discharged employees"; guards evicted them from company housing, tossing their possessions out onto the sidewalks, and forcing the strikers to erect a village of makeshift tents on the edge of the city.

To arouse public opinion against the strike, the company took out advertisements in the Gastonia daily newspaper that read, "RED RUSSIAN-ISM LIFTS ITS GORY HANDS RIGHT HERE IN GASTONIA": "Do the people of Gastonia, Gaston County, and the South realize what the Communist Party is? . . . It is a party that seeks the overthrow of capital, business, and all of the established social order. World revolution is its ultimate goal. It has no religion, it has no color line, it believes in free love—it advocates the destruction of all those things which the people of the South and of the United States hold sacred."

As might be expected, this sort of inflammatory rhetoric provoked violence. In the dark hours shortly before dawn on April 18, a mob of about a hundred masked men attacked the headquarters of the NTWU in Gastonia and smashed the flimsy frame building to pieces with crowbars and sledgehammers. Union officials who had been sleeping at headquarters were awakened at gunpoint; union documents were destroyed or scattered in the streets, along with foodstuffs that had been donated to the strikers' relief funds. When the National Guard finally arrived, the beleaguered union representatives were arrested and charged with rioting.

Still the strike dragged on, though by now it was clear that the union was losing badly. Six weeks later, on the evening of June 7, the strikers set out to march to the Loray plant when the Gastonia police swooped down on them, broke up the demonstration, and beat the union's leaders. The strikers retreated to their tent village and reformed their lines in an attempt to resume the march. Again the police appeared, with no warrant, claiming that they were responding to reports of fighting among the strikers. This time the union's sullen armed guards—who by now were justifiably suspicious of the authorities—told them to stay off their property. In the confusion that followed, shots were fired from the union side and four police officers, including the chief of police, Orville F. Aderholt, were wounded, as was one union official. Chief Aderholt died from his wounds the following day.

"The blood of these men cries out to high heaven for vengeance," screamed the Gastonia *Gazette.* "This community has been too lenient with these despicable curs and snakes from the dives of Passaic, Hoboken, and New York. . . . This display of gang law must not go unavenged." So sixty-five strikers and union officials were arrested and charged with murder. When prosecutors came to their senses, they released forty-nine of the accused and prepared to try the remaining sixteen—three women and thirteen men, including union leader Fred Erwin Beal—for conspiracy to commit murder. Northern sympathizers organized a defense fund, the International Labor Defense, and retained New York attorney Arthur Garfield Hays as counsel. And Ella May Wiggins added a new song to her repertoire:

> Come all of you good people and listen to what I tell;
> The story of Chief Aderholt, the man you all knew well.
> It was on one Friday evening, the seventh day of June,
> He went down to the union ground and met his fatal doom.
>
> They locked up our leaders, they put them in jail,
> They shoved them in prison, refused to give them bail.
> The workers joined together and this was their reply:
> We'll never, no we'll never let our leaders die.
>
> We're going to have a union all over the South,
> Where we can wear good clothes and live in a better house.
> Now we must stand together and to the boss reply
> We'll never, no, we'll never let our leaders die.

The American business community might have had absolutely no use for a Communist labor union in North Carolina in the summer of 1929, but the prospect of selling boatloads of American goods to a Communist-governed nation of 150 million potential paying customers was another matter entirely. Since 1926, the volume of trade between the United States and the Union of Soviet Socialist Republics had nearly doubled. Two thousand American corporations were doing business with the Soviet Union. The value of American exports to Russia in fiscal year 1928 approached $100 million, despite Washington's persistent refusal to grant diplomatic recognition to the Soviet government (a short-sighted policy that left American businessmen in Russia bereft of commercial attachés and consular support). The Soviet Union had become the chief European market for American agricultural machinery, and the third largest purchaser of U.S. electrical machinery. From the standpoint of Soviet exports, the United States was Russia's second-best customer, behind only Germany.

In the first half of 1929, the pace of trade relations between the United States and the Soviet Union quickened. "It is with the greatest satisfaction," exulted Maxim Litvinov, Soviet commissar for foreign affairs, "that we observe the uninterrupted rapid growth of our economic relations with the United States." General Electric signed an agreement with Soviet representatives to provide between $21 million and $25 million worth of machinery and equipment over a six-year period. Detroit architect Albert Kahn, famous for his work for the Fords and other wealthy American and European industrialists, contracted to design a mammoth tractor factory in Stalingrad. Montana wheat tycoon T. D. Campbell journeyed to Russia to advise the Soviet government on large-scale agricultural production, and engineer Arthur Powell Davis, former director of the Bureau of Reclamation in Washington, agreed to supervise a $250 million irrigation project in Turkestan. Naturally, representatives of National City Bank turned up in Moscow and Leningrad for discussions with the president of the Soviet State Bank, and in July a party of about a hundred American bankers, manufacturers, engineers, and editors—the first United States trade delegation to Moscow—traveled to Russia at the invitation of the Russian-American Chamber of Commerce.

By that time, Henry Ford finally had concluded his negotiations with the Soviet government. On May 31, Ford and the vice-chairman of the Soviet Supreme Council of National Economy, acting on behalf of his government, signed an agreement at Dearborn calling for the purchase of $30 million worth of Ford cars by the Soviets within four years. In return, Ford promised to provide technical advice and assistance for the construction of an automobile factory with a production capacity of one hundred thousand cars per year at Nizhni Novgorod, on the banks of the Volga. To make the arrangement worthwhile, the Soviet government also pledged to invest approximately $150 million in a road improvement program. "No matter where industry prospers," chortled Ford, who allowed photographers to take his picture with the Soviet officials, "whether in India or China or Russia, all the world is bound to catch some good from it." Shortly thereafter, the USSR awarded a $50 million contract—the largest of its kind in Soviet history—to Cleveland's noted engineering firm, the Austin Company, to build an entire city (tentatively named Austingrad) in fifteen months for the twenty-five thousand workers who would staff the Ford plant.

It was not by chance that the Soviet Union chose this moment to throw open its doors to foreign development capital. At the end of 1928, the Soviet government had embarked upon an extraordinarily ambitious—impossibly ambitious, in fact—program of industrial expansion. Formally approved by the Sixteenth Party Congress in April 1929, this Five-Year Plan (the first such economic blueprint adopted by the Soviets) contemplated nothing less than the wholesale transformation of the Russian nation into a major industrial power virtually overnight. The plan called for total capital investments of $33 billion, almost three times the actual investments of the previous five years; most of these funds were earmarked for the construction of industrial plants and the purchase of foreign machinery and equipment. Imports were projected at $3.2 billion over five years, and steel production was targeted to increase from four million tons to more than ten million. The plan further proposed to boost the nation's output of electricity from five hundred million kilowatt-hours to twenty-two billion hours, while doubling the production of coal. "The purpose of the Five Year Plan," gushed an official Soviet economic journal, "is to lend such a tempo to Russia's economic development that, at first, it should catch up with the foremost capitalistic countries of the world and, later, should outspeed them. At the end of this five-year period the total production of Russia's agriculture must rise by 142 per cent, and that of Russia's industries by 135 per cent." There was no end to the grandiose schemes, and some outsiders even believed them. "The figures make one dizzy," concluded the editors of the *Nation.* "The Russian five-year plan would seem like a wild dream if it were not for the fact that the Soviet Government has previously announced plans to an incredulous world, and at times carried them out with astonishing fidelity."

But an anti-Soviet publication in Paris viewed the proposal with considerably less enthusiasm. "The Soviet Congress, by approving the Five Year Plan, indorsed the policy of the new destruction of Russia now in progress," charged the daily *Posliednia Novosti.* "The most important factor in the decisions of this Congress relates to agriculture. The Congress has passed a death sentence on the millions of individual peasant farmers."

And so it had. To feed the vastly expanded industrial labor force the Five-Year Plan required, the Soviet government desperately needed to increase agricultural output; and that meant the transformation of a land of twenty-five million individual peasant households—employing primitive, inefficient farming methods—into a more rational, mechanized, and centralized instrument capable of supplying food for the growing urban population. For the past six years, the bureaucrats in Moscow essentially had left the countryside alone, permitting the *kulaks,* the wealthy (by Russian standards) peasants, to dispose of their surplus crops for their own profit. But the exigencies of the Five-Year Plan required more stringent controls. To Joseph Stalin, the paranoid and cold-blooded secretary general of the Soviet Communist party, there was only one viable solution: the forced collectivization of the nation's agricultural base, and the wholesale liquidation of the kulaks, those incipient rural capitalists whom orthodox Communist doctrine condemned as petit bourgeois counterrevolutionaries, the most dangerous class enemies of the revolution.

Since the death of Vladimir Lenin five years earlier, Stalin had assiduously plotted and dealt his way to supreme power within the Soviet bureaucracy. Forty-nine years old, a native of the southern Russia province of Georgia, Comrade Stalin (née Dzhugashvili) was a survivor of what George Kennan has aptly termed "the seething, savage underworld of the Transcaucasus." Stalin joined the Communist party in 1904 as a hired thug and proceeded to make himself indispensable by robbing Czarist bank messengers to finance subversive Bolshevik activities. Although party intellectuals dismissed him as an uncouth, uneducated young tough, Stalin possessed the sort of native cunning and joy in deceit that carried him unscathed through the vicious internecine power struggles that continued to plague the Soviet Communist movement after the overthrow of the Czar's government in 1917. He gradually consolidated his hold on the party machinery by installing his own loyal subordinates—men who owed their careers solely to Stalin's favor—in critical posts. And when he finally grasped the reins of power firmly in his own hands, he began to eliminate his most prominent rivals.

First he turned against the threat from the Left, and Leon Trotsky in particular. Trotsky despised Stalin. He considered him a roughneck and a prototypical Asian despot who sought "to strengthen his position at the expense of the Soviet Republic"; in 1926, Trotsky openly predicted that Stalin would be the gravedigger of the party and the revolution. Within two years, Trotsky had been relieved of his official duties and exiled to Turkestan for allegedly fomenting anti-Soviet plots and scheming to provoke a new round of civil war. "There is actually no difference between Trotsky and any other counter-revolutionary," declared Stalin, "and his empty phrases about revolution and Leninism cannot deceive a child." In January 1929, Stalin deported his enemy to Constantinople and launched a widespread drive to root out all vestiges of deviationist Trotskyite sentiment in the Soviet bureaucracy.

Then Stalin turned against his rivals on the Right, notably the trio of *Pravda* editor and Central Committee member Nikolai Bukharin, Premier Alexis Rykov, and Michael Tomsky, head of the Soviet Labor Federation and the Council of National Economy. These were the men who had criticized most vehemently Stalin's obsessive drive toward forced collectivization; instead, they favored limited concessions to the kulaks to obtain their voluntary cooperation. To support his arguments, Bukharin pointed to the miserable failure of the government's heavy-handed effort at the beginning of 1928 to extract a larger surplus from the Russian peasantry while simultaneously slashing grain prices. The end result had been a disastrous decline in production as peasants devised a multitude of ingenious methods to restrict supply by withholding their crops from the market until prices rose again.

But the bitter disappointment of this coercive effort merely confirmed Stalin's suspicions of the treacherous kulaks. Before moving against the peasants, however, Stalin decided he first had to eliminate Bukharin and his political allies. So in February 1929, Stalin dutifully advised the Politburo that Bukharin, Rykov, and Tomsky had formed a dissident factional group that threatened the security of the party. In reality, Bukharin had been guilty only of poor judgment—he repeatedly said of Stalin that "he will slaughter us"—but the advent of food rationing in the cities (a result of the poor harvest in the fall of 1928) and shortages of consumer goods in the winter and spring of 1929 convinced the Politburo that the beleaguered nation could tolerate no dissent.

So Bukharin, Tomsky, and Rykov were unceremoniously stripped of power for "persisting in their mistakes"; they were replaced on the Politburo by pro-Stalin loyalists such as Vyacheslav Molotov and Anastas Mikoyan. With all political opposition effectively crushed, Stalin at last could hurl the full force of his tenacious and megalomaniacal personality into the ambitious and murderous crusade to drag the Soviet Union into the twentieth century. In August 1929, the party's Central Committee approved Stalin's plan for "mass and rapid collectivization of whole regions." The campaign would be carried out with brutal vigor; no misplaced concern for the welfare of individuals would be permitted to endanger the success of the grand experiment.

# XIII

# Everybody Ought to Be Rich

---

"Belief in the idea of progress and the good life was never stronger.
If the Arabs were slaughtering Jews in Palestine, if there was labor
trouble in Gastonia . . . if one had to flout the law by frequenting
speakeasies and patronizing bootleggers—well, these were minor
irritations in a world that was essentially on the right track. . . .
[The American's] materialism was benevolent and forward-looking,
previsioning a future that would engulf everyone in a tide
of lasting prosperity."
                    —LEO GURKO, *on "The American of 1929"*

For a few brief shining moments, it looked as if everything would be all
right.

There was no midsummer business slump in America in 1929. At the
end of June, the high-quality glamour stocks—public utilities, railroads,
and the industrial giants—resumed their rampage upward. With call
money hovering around the more reasonable level of 7 or 8 percent, Wall
Street once more was filled with talk of a "roaring bull market." On July
4, while the U.S. markets were closed for the holiday, American issues such
as United States Steel, Pennsylvania Railroad, and the Atcheson, Topeka,
and Santa Fe established record highs on the London Stock Exchange. By
the middle of the month, the stock of the First National Bank of New York,
"the aristocrat of all bank stocks," shot up $500 in a single day on the New
York Curb Exchange, fetching a price of $7,900 per share. (George F.
Baker, the bank's chairman, reportedly held twenty-two thousand shares
of its stock, which meant that he had received a windfall profit of $11
million in the space of five hours.) U.S. Steel, which had retired its entire
bonded debt by the simple expedient of issuing new shares of common
stock, jumped nearly seven points on July 19, thereby adding another
$51,152,184 to the value of its outstanding stock. Not to be outdone, AT&T
eclipsed that mark by increasing its stock value by more than $75,800,000
in one day.

As the good economic news continued to pour in, nobody worried very much about the Federal Reserve Board anymore. "This country is enjoying a surprizing midsummer industrial boom, rarely equaled," crowed Arthur Brisbane, leading editorial writer for the Hearst chain of newspapers. Moody's Investor's Service confidently predicted that "as the year progresses, the probabilities are that much of the uncertainty will disappear and results for the full year make a very excellent showing." The steel industry continued to operate at nearly 95 percent capacity . . . newspapers carried reports of excellent corporate earnings for the first half of 1929—for companies ranging from Congress Cigar to White Rock Mineral Springs—which surpassed even the swollen profits of the comparable period in 1928 . . . industrial output for July showed a marked gain over 1928, though there was a slight and seemingly unimportant decline from the previous month . . . and the nation's investors received a record monthly sum of $863,355,828 in interest and dividend payments in July.

Much of that money was plowed right back into the stock market, as was a growing percentage of corporate profits. Although the bulls on Wall Street were laughing at the impotence of the Federal Reserve Board in the summer of 1929, the fact was that the board had succeeded in pressuring its member banks to reduce their speculative loans. The slack had been taken up by corporations and wealthy individuals; it was they, and not the banks, who were responsible for elevating the total of brokers' loans to the record-shattering sum of $5,813,000,000 in July. Standard Oil of New Jersey had an average of $69 million out on the call-money market every day. Warner Brothers, which had previously advised its employees that it would dismiss anyone caught playing the market, did an about face and formed its own bank to take advantage of the boom in security values, and a former vice-president of the National City Bank founded a new corporation—the First Call Money Company of America—specifically for the purpose of supplying speculative funds to the market.

The *New York Times'* index of fifty industrials rose fifty-two points in June, and then roared upward another twenty-five points in July. By no means, however, were these gains uniformly reflected across the board. A substantial portion of the issues traded on the New York Stock Exchange actually drifted downward throughout the summer, giving the list as a whole an exceptionally ragged appearance. At the time, few amateur investors paid any attention.

On the Fourth of July, Calvin Coolidge quietly celebrated his fifty-seventh birthday at his home in Northampton. When three reporters discovered the former President sitting alone on his front porch, rocking contentedly and smoking a cigar, he invited them in for a big slice of one of the birthday cakes sent by his admirers. Later he went fishing, attired in a business suit, a wide-brimmed straw hat, and black hip boots.

Curiosity seekers still plagued Silent Cal. Sometimes he looked out of his living room window at night and saw strange faces peering at him through the window. Nearby hotels distributed maps marking the route to the Coolidge home. One reporter tried to sneak into his bathroom while the former president was taking a shower. Gradually, however, the novelty of Coolidge's presence wore off, and he was allowed to fall into a congenial small-town routine of fishing, sleeping, and loafing at his former law office. He seemed heartily glad to have escaped the spotlight at last. "On the whole," observed William Allen White, "he kept himself strictly to the character he had assumed at Cinderella's hearthstone, very much the drab step-sister in the cold ashes of private life."

Coolidge did, however, accept a place on the board of directors of the New York Life Insurance Company; according to company executives, Coolidge was given the task of maintaining "human contacts" between the home office and its agents. When asked why he had accepted this post after turning down a multitude of other, more remunerative offers, Coolidge explained that he viewed his presence on the board as a "public service" rather than a money-making venture. "Our insurance companies, rising above all other business and financial institutions, stand at the very summit of moral responsibility," he declared. "If ever our industries are depressed, if ever the credit of our banks becomes strained, the knowledge that the enormous investments in insurance are still sound, that their assets are still intact, will be an impregnable security for our economic redemption."

Coolidge himself invested no money in common stocks. Instead, the former Chief Executive, who had presided over one of the most prolonged bull markets in American history, placed virtually all his savings into real estate and gilt-edged bonds.

Al Smith, too, had become a director of an insurance company; in his case, it was Metropolitan Life Insurance, a much larger company than Coolidge's New York Life. Along with his buddy John Raskob, Smith also retained his seat on the board of Jim Riordan's County Trust Company, and on the side he wrote a weekly syndicated newspaper column. At the end of the summer, the Happy Warrior's autobiography, *Up from the Streets*, hit the bookstores, but sales were disappointing because nobody really cared to read about a failed presidential candidate who obviously had no future in politics.

In August, Smith announced that he had accepted an offer to serve as president of the Empire State Building Corporation, a company formed to erect an eighty-story office building on the site of the old Waldorf-Astoria Hotel in Manhattan. Beaming with pride, Smith reported that the $60 million Empire State Building was going to be the tallest and largest building in the world; it would soar nearly eleven hundred feet in the air (approximately the length of five city blocks stood on end) and would contain enough office space to house sixty thousand tenants—about half the population of the city of Syracuse. For "supervising" the construction and management of the building, Smith was going to receive an annual salary of $65,000, enough to permit the former fish market salesman and his wife to move into a brand-new, plush apartment suite at 51 Fifth Avenue.

Among the Empire State Building Corporation's board of directors were Pierre S. Du Pont and the project's guiding force, John J. Raskob. Raskob was spending the summer doing everything he could to perpetuate the illusion that stock prices could keep rising indefinitely. In May, he had revealed a scheme to introduce the installment buying plan to Wall Street; as Raskob explained it, he planned to form (sometime in the indefinite future) an investment trust company that would permit a factory mechanic in Detroit to purchase $500 worth of stock on margin by paying $200 down and negotiating a bank loan for the balance, putting up the stock as collateral and paying off the loan in installments of $25 per month. Raskob claimed that his motives were entirely altruistic—"I have all the money I want and now I want to help a lot of other people make some"—and he uttered soothing reassurances about the state of the stock market. "I have heard some opinions," he said, "that the present time is not opportune for investment because the general level of prices is too high and perhaps it's true that some stock may be selling at 20 per cent less in another year; but, in my judgment, many stocks are not too high even at their present level." Those who knew what Raskob was really doing behind the scenes probably laughed when they heard these reassuring words. When Raskob said that he already had "all the money" he wanted, what he meant was that he was quietly liquidating almost all his stock holdings and getting the hell out of the market. He certainly wasn't going to get caught in the storm when the bubble finally burst.

His personal financial dealings in the summer of 1929 made Raskob's famous magazine article "Everybody Ought to Be Rich" a remarkable inside joke. Published in August in the *Ladies' Home Journal,* the article was based on Raskob's calculation that "if a man saves fifteen dollars a week and invests it in good common stocks, and allows the dividends and rights to accumulate, at the end of twenty years he will have at least eighty thousand dollars and an income from investments of around four hundred dollars a month. He will be rich. And because income can do that I am firm in my belief that anyone not only can be rich but ought to be rich." Of course, Raskob ignored the fact that the average weekly wage for American workers in 1929 was between $25 and $30, which meant that they could not save anywhere near $15 a week; moreover, Raskob's scheme obviously assumed that laymen could discern a sound stock from a dud (which most could not); and, most important, it assumed that the stock market would continue to rise at its present rate, uninterrupted, for two entire decades.

On July 18, the spokesman for a committee of 682 prominent New York citizens presented Mayor Walker with a petition practically begging him to run for reelection in November. After listening to the committee recite his accomplishments and sing his praises for what seemed like an eternity, Walker stood up and replied guilelessly, "Who could say no?"

Actually, Walker had made up his mind to run several months earlier, when Al Smith, whose strongly conventional sense of sexual morality had been offended by Walker's open affair with actress Betty Compton, had clumsily attempted to persuade him to step aside. Enraged by Smith's interference in his private life, Walker decided to show the former governor who was *really* in control of the Tammany machine. Although his administration was peppered daily with accusations of corruption, favoritism, and incompetence, Gentleman Jimmy himself remained unassailable. The mayor had presided over an enormous public works program (including subway improvements and school construction), which boosted the city's annual budget from $100 million to $538 million. "I don't care what the budget amounts to in dollars and cents," he said, "if we're going to improve New York we've got to pay for it." And the people loved Jimmy for it because he spent their money in such a good-natured way. He had spent nearly a quarter of his days (and nights) outside the city limits since he became mayor, but the voters just laughed and said that was okay because a politician could do no harm while he was out of town. Even the stuffy *New York Times* admitted that "probably no man in New York better understands its public business. . . . Everybody who knows Mr. Walker well is confident that he has in him the makings of a remarkable chief magistrate of this city."

Since none of the usual silk-stocking Republican candidates were eager to run against Walker, the party turned instead to a rambunctious, six-term Italian-American congressman from Harlem, Fiorello La Guardia, the "Little Flower."

Another team of civic-minded reformers, headed by Albert Ottinger, the former New York attorney general who had lost to Roosevelt in the 1928 gubernatorial election, pressed John D. Rockefeller, Jr., to run against Walker as a fusion candidate. "With his genius for organization, his vision, his immortal contributions to hospitals, colleges, and schools," chirped Ottinger, "he could not be defeated. With practical working out of his ideals New York would have a government worthy of the greatest city."

Perhaps, but Johnny Rock was preoccupied with a host of real estate deals in the summer of 1929. The year before, he and his father had announced their plans to restore the faded and somnolent town of Williamsburg, Virginia, to its colonial splendor as the capital of the commonwealth. Then in February 1929, John D., Jr., magnanimously agreed to purchase and preserve George Washington's birthplace, a 287-acre estate in Wakefield, Virginia. The following month, Rockefeller bought (for $700,000) the entire town of East View, New York; he planned to raze every building in the community so he could divert the New York Central Railroad's tracks from the Rockefeller estate of Pocantico Hills (where the railroad held a right-of-way). In May, he met with Mayor Walker to discuss a model tenement project on the Lower East Side similar to the Paul Laurence Dunbar apartment development Rockefeller had sponsored for the city's black residents. (The Dunbar project opened in late 1929 with celebrities such as Bill "Bojangles" Robinson and W. E. B. Du Bois among the first tenants.)

By far the most ambitious Rockefeller development project, however, was the multimillion-dollar cultural-office-shopping complex he planned to build in midtown Manhattan, along the three blocks between Fifth and Sixth avenues and 48th and 51st streets, not far from Al Smith's Empire State Building. The original impetus for the project came from Otto Kahn, the financier-impresario who had approached John D., Jr., in 1928 about a new home for the Metropolitan Opera; Kahn suggested a site on a Columbia University–owned tract along Fifth Avenue. By the time Rockefeller negotiated a lease with Columbia, the blueprints had expanded to include skyscrapers, viaducts, apartments, esplanades, hotels, and enough fine shops to make it the most exclusive shopping district in the world. Although the project was formally known as Metropolitan Square at its inception, the public soon began referring to it by the more aptly descriptive name of Rockefeller Center.

Although all legal means to obtain his release met with failure, Al Capone did succeed in obtaining a transfer from filthy Holmesburg Prison to the more hospitable surroundings of Eastern Penitentiary in Philadelphia. They moved Scarface in the early morning, while the other inmates were at breakfast, to thwart any possible attempts upon his life. At Eastern, Capone became the new library file clerk, and received abundant special privileges, including a private room (the quarantine cell, actually) furnished with paintings, carpets, a $500 radio console, and comfortable furniture. Capone was permitted to receive visitors twenty-four hours a day, and anytime he wished he could use the telephone in the warden's office. Mostly he called his brother, Ralph, and Jake "Greasy Thumb" Guzik, who were managing his empire during his extended incarceration.

In Chicago, meanwhile, state and federal grand juries indicted ninety-six citizens of Cook County, including numerous prominent politicians and police officials, for a variety of offenses including graft, embezzlement of public funds, and the manufacture and sale of three million gallons of bootleg liquor. And a twenty-seven-year-old Justice Department agent named Eliot Ness assembled a squad of nine tough, incorruptible young raiders to launch a crusade against Capone and his murderous organization.

In Paris, Billy Durant tenaciously continued his fight against the Federal Reserve Board and the bearish prophets of doom. Striving mightily to maintain the mood of unrestrained optimism upon which the Hoover bull market depended, Durant fired another broadside at the board during a speech at the American Club at the end of May. "Say what you will," Durant insisted, "confidence—not half-way confidence, but 100 per cent confidence is the real basis for our prosperity. With all the wealth in the world, confidence lacking, we never could have reached the position we occupy today, and this great asset, confidence, should not be destroyed. That is the reason why the business men of America are almost a unit against the present policy of the Federal Reserve Board." Durant charged that the crashes in March and May, which he attributed directly to the perverse blundering of the board, already had led to the loss of hundreds of millions of dollars by "hundreds of thousands of people, who have contributed to the prosperity of America"; the result, he said, had been "fear, trembling and destruction of confidence, so essential to our prosperity." Upon his return to the United States at the end of June, Durant again assailed the Fed for "lining up with the destructive forces of Wall Street . . . fussing about brokers' loans, and interfering with business generally." "We can and will have a 'bull' market as soon as this question is settled," the Dream Maker predicted, "and when it is settled, seasoned securities of merit and those having possibilities will sell much higher than ever before."

Governor Franklin D. Roosevelt passed the summer months in a pleasant, peaceful 5,500-mile inspection tour of New York State's waterways. Roosevelt loved to travel by boat; he said that he would rather view the natural beauties of his native countryside "while being seated . . . on the deck of a boat going along at a speed of six or seven miles an hour than I would from the most luxurious automobile ever made travelling along at forty or fifty miles an hour." The weather was gorgeous, the waters placid for the governor. The acute agricultural distress he encountered along the tour, however, convinced him of the necessity for radical farm relief measures. And Roosevelt scoffed at the temerity of John J. Raskob (whom he wished to remove as national chairman of the Democratic party) for publicly suggesting that the United States might conceivably enjoy "a fifty per cent increase in prosperity and values for every year that goes by between now and the year 2000." "Do you still feel as I do," Roosevelt wrote to a friend on August 5, "that there may be a limit to the increase of security values?"

Charlie Mitchell's National City Bank opened its first office in Mexico at the beginning of August. The Mexico City branch was National City's one hundredth foreign office in a chain that stretched from China and India to South America, and the bank celebrated the occasion with a lavish reception, attended by Ambassador Dwight Morrow, at the famous Chapultepec Garden Restaurant. Naturally, National City's representatives invited the Mexican people to join with businessmen and -women all around the world in investing in American prosperity.

Mitchell himself was busy that summer consummating a merger between National City Bank and the Corn Exchange Bank Trust Company. The acquisition promised to vault National City to the very top rung of international finance; with more than $2,386,000,000 in resources, it would become the largest bank in the world.

In Charlotte, North Carolina, Fred Beal and his fifteen codefendants went on trial for their lives at the end of July for the murder of Gastonia police chief Orville Aderholt. For those who were willing to look beyond the Communist affiliation of the National Textile Workers Union, the courtroom drama provided a reminder of the desperate, grinding poverty that still oppressed millions of American families. The testimony from Charlotte validated the grim findings of sociologists Helen and Robert S. Lynd in their epochal study of "Middletown, U.S.A.," released several months earlier. In their investigation of a small manufacturing city in the Midwest (apparently Muncie, Indiana), the Lynds discovered that 27 percent of the working class in "Middletown" lived in houses valued at $2,500 or less, and that one-fourth of all the houses in the city lacked running water. According to the Lynds, "most of the working class still live in the base-burner and unheated-bedroom era." And the authors' unsweetened description of the typical working-class Middletown home was worthy of Theodore Dreiser in his bleakest moods:

> The poorer workingman coming home after his nine and a half hours on the job walks up the frequently unpaved street, turns in at a bare yard littered with a rusty velocipede or worn-out automobile tires, opens a sagging door, and enters the living-room of his house. From the room the whole house is visible—the kitchen with table and floor swarming with flies and often strewn with bread crusts, orange skins, torn papers, and lumps of coal and wood; the bedrooms with soiled, heavy quilts falling off the beds. . . . The whole interior is musty with stale odors of food, clothing, and tobacco. . . . A baby in wet, dirty clothes crawls about the bare floor among odd pieces of furniture.

"The United States ought to be happy," proclaimed noted Harvard Law School professor Zechariah Chafee, Jr., in his commencement address at Brown University that summer.

> We have long desired to be the richest nation on earth, and now we are. Like the Village Blacksmith, we can look the whole world in the face, for we owe not any man. Instead, most of the others owe us. We have most of the gold, most of the automobiles, most of the telephones; we buy most of the great pictures even if we do not paint them. We have so much on earth, that we can look forward to very little more in heaven except space enough to park two cars for every family, and a stock market and a tariff which will always be going up. The time seems rapidly approaching when everyone will make so much money in Wall Street that we can all retire and live on our dividends.
>
> And yet we are not particularly happy. Our fellow-countrymen, as described by Edith Wharton, Sinclair Lewis, and Eugene O'Neill, exhibit very disagreeable states of dissatisfaction. . . . Should we dismiss all this discontent as fiction, the sober facts painstakingly surveyed by the authors of "Middletown" are equally unalluring. . . .
>
> It is not enough to have prosperity. The vital question is: What are we going to do with it?

On Thursday, August 8, after the closing gong ended trading for the day on the New York Stock Exchange, the Federal Reserve Board announced that it was raising its rediscount rate from 5 to 6 percent. The news took Wall Street completely by surprise; after six months of indecision, no one expected the board to take such a bold step without warning. Apparently the action was precipitated by reports that brokers' loans had mounted to the staggering sum of $6,020,000,000, a perilous trend that could not be permitted to continue indefinitely without choking off credit to the rest of American industry. But once again the board had waited too long to act, and its decision to increase interest rates succeeded only in introducing another element of uncertainty into an already wildly disarranged market situation.

The following day, brokers began receiving "sell" orders well before the market opened at nine o'clock. As the *New York Times* reported, the Federal Reserve Board's announcement "put stockholders of the country into a frame of mind in which they wanted to get rid of their stocks to save such profits as existed, to prevent further losses or to 'get out of the market entirely,' as many did." As it turned out, they were the lucky ones.

Two billion dollars' worth of stock values vanished in five stormy hours of panic-stricken selling. It was the heaviest day of trading since the precipitous decline of May 28; on the floor of the exchange, brokers angrily pushed and shoved one another to execute their stacks of sell orders. As measured by the *Times'* index, it was the most severe decline the market had suffered since 1911, when the newspaper began keeping track of such things. As usual, thinly margined accounts received the worst battering; hundreds of small speculators found themselves completely wiped out as their stocks plunged downward. "Any business that can't survive a one per cent raise must be skating on mighty thin ice," remarked Will Rogers acidly. (Rogers, incidentally, had taken Baruch's advice and reduced his own stock holdings to a minimum.) "Why, even the poor farmers took a raise of from six to ten per cent, with another ten per cent bonus, to get the loan from the banks," he added. "It took all that to completely break them, and nobody connected with the government paid any attention. But let Wall Street have a nightmare and the whole country has to help them get back in bed again."

Surveying the wreckage, Durant denounced the board's move as "only another blunder." "The day of reckoning is approaching," warned the man they called the King of the Bulls. "The business interests of this country are determined and will demand Congressional investigation and proper control of this group of men." Indeed, by virtually any measure the Federal Reserve Board appeared to have committed an egregious blunder. After the momentary panic of August 9, the speculative favorites on Wall Street recouped their losses almost at once and resumed an even more dizzying ascent, while the rest of the market kept inching downward in a slow, sad fall. The board's decision to raise its rates affected only its member banks, of course, and did nothing to restrain the ever-increasing flow of bootleg corporate loans to Wall Street; but it did put a further pinch on the farmers and small businessmen who had no other source of credit. One percentage point meant nothing to the speculators, but it threatened to push many legitimate businesses, already perched precariously on the edge, into failure and bankruptcy. "This will mean not only here, but all over the country, a tremendous curtailment of commercial, agricultural and real estate loans and cause great hardship and business depression," predicted former New Jersey governor Edward C. Stokes, then chairman of the board of First Mechanics National Bank. "This action will aid Wall Street's activities by drawing money to that centre through the highest rates offered to the loaner. It punishes . . . every security holder and legitimate borrower."

"The end of the story is not yet," warned the *New Republic:*

> We may still see the pace of production and trade slackened on account of tight credit. If that happens, what will happen to the price of stocks, boosted far above any logical relation to their earnings even on the basis of present business activity? If the Federal Reserve authorities have no longer any power to moderate the overconfidence of the speculators, that may be after all the speculators' loss. We shall be lucky if many of the rest of us do not lose also.

For the rest of August the market presented a strikingly schizophrenic appearance. Stocks whose prices already far outstripped any rational measure of real value (some were now selling at thirty times annual earnings) kept rising ten, twenty, or even forty points per day—solely on the expectation that they could be passed on to someone else at a higher price in a day or two—while lower-priced stocks continued to decline. "It has been," observed the *New York Times* on August 22, "a confusing and perplexing performance."

The last three weeks of August represented the climax of America's long, exhilarating climb toward the evanescent pinnacle of prosperity. More than at any time since the bull market began five years earlier, the speculating public—at this point, slightly more than one million individuals carrying approximately three hundred million shares on margin—was blinded by the dazzling vision of a select group of stocks whose advance seemingly could not be checked by any force on earth. Even Owen Young got swept up in the madness in August, as he ventured back into the market to purchase nearly $2 million worth of stocks on margin. Brokerage firms in Manhattan reported a spectacular increase in business; the streets and subway stops around their uptown offices were thronged with customers, many of whom had given up their jobs as the value of their stock portfolios soared into hundreds of thousands of dollars. "By Stock Exchange opening time," observed John Brooks,

> all along Wall and Nassau, Broad and Broadway and Pine, the customers' rooms are jammed—there is standing room only and perhaps not even

that, there is a premium on positions from which the quote board can be seen. Still, they all are sure it is worthwhile being there, right on the scene; they feel themselves to be part of something tremendous, and perhaps, too, they feel their physical presence in Wall Street makes them insiders, gives them some slight advantage over those who are maintaining the same vigil elsewhere—the barber or chauffeur or cab driver whose ear is cocked for a tip his important client may let fall, even the important man himself who has given up his vacation not in substance but only in spirit, and, sacrificing a seat in the sun, is glued all day to one in an office in Bar Harbor or Newport or Southampton or in a Catskill Mountain hotel.

Ocean liners installed brokerage branch offices, complete with short-wave radios and ship-to-shore telephones for their first-class passengers traveling to or from Europe. ("We were crowded in the cabin / Watching figures on the Board / It was midnight on the ocean / And a tempest loudly roared," went one parody.) At the U.S. amateur golf championship at Pebble Beach, California, E.F. Hutton and Company pitched a tent near the eighteenth green, where they set up a temporary office for the convenience of the gallery (and more than a few of the players, too). In the staid capitals of Europe, events on Wall Street dominated the minds and souls of the wealthy and fashionable set. "Scores of thousands of American shares are bought everyday in London alone," reported Viscount Rothermere sourly, "and Paris, Berlin, Brussels, and Amsterdam are pouring money into New York as fast as the cable can carry it. Wall Street has become a colossal suction-pump, which is draining the world of capital, and the suction is fast producing a vacuum over here."

"The Big Bull Market had become a national mania," recalled Frederick Lewis Allen. "Across the dinner table one heard fantastic stories of sudden fortunes: a young banker had put every dollar of his small capital into Niles-Bement-Pond and now was fixed for life; a widow had been able to buy a large country house with her winnings in Kennecott. Thousands speculated—and won, too—without the slightest knowledge of the nature of the company upon whose fortunes they were relying, like the people who bought Seaboard Air Line under the impression that it was an aviation stock." (It was really a railroad.) The *New York Times* carried a front-page story of a poor young Southern girl who had earned $4 working in the tobacco fields and tried to invest it in Standard Oil of New Jersey. In a letter to Standard Oil's offices, she explained innocently that she wanted to purchase "as little an intrest or shear in your Oil Wells as $4.00 four dollars to start with and then take what it makes for me and add to the four dollars until it amounts to a fifty dollar share for me." She asked the company to let her know when she could "start drawing money off of it."

"I am a poor girl and I work on a farm with my home people," she said, "and I hired out to work in Tobacco to get this money which I want to put in the oil wells so I hope you will have a good heart and take this much to help me along a little and if you help me this much I hope the good Lord will bless you all in every way, so please answer real soon." Fortunately for her, the company sent the money back.

Some analysts believed that stock prices were being driven up primarily by the giant investment trusts, which had so much money at their command that they had to put it *somewhere*. And still people rushed to join every new trust that appeared; when the eminently reliable banking firm of Goldman, Sachs and Company formed the Blue Ridge Corporation investment trust with assets of $127.5 million in mid-August, shares sold at a premium, and the original issue was heavily oversubscribed within hours.

"Money is king," noted Brooks of those last frenzied weeks, "—but there is something else. It is a high, wild time, a time of riotous spirits and belief in magic rather than cold calculation, a time of Dionysius rather than Apollo. . . . It is almost as if they believed the market existed for taking chances not on money but on happiness."

"People sang louder, drank deeper, danced longer and squandered themselves in every direction," wrote playwright Ben Hecht. "They fornicated in cabanas, in rumble seats, under boardwalks. They built love nests like beavers and tripled their divorce rate. High, and many of the low, gave themselves hedonistically to the pleasures of the hour." The statistics supported Hecht's claim; America's divorce rate jumped to one out of every six marriages, the highest rate in the nation's history.

It may have been just a coincidence that the late summer of 1929 witnessed an outbreak of nudity on the beaches of America and Europe. The cult of sun worship had originated in Germany, where, according to Stephen Spender, it symbolized "the great wealth of nature within the poverty of man." "The sun healed their bodies of the years of war, and made them conscious of the quivering, fluttering life of blood and muscles covering their exhausted spirits like the pelt of an animal," wrote Spender of the thousands of German nudists who spent their summer basking contentedly on the shores of rivers and lakes, losing all sense of human identity as they dissolved into the magic circle of nature: "And their minds were filled with an abstraction of the sun, a huge circle of fire, an intense whiteness blotting out the sharp outlines of all other forms of consciousness, burning out even the sense of time."

The movement spread to Russia, where bathers soaked up the sun's rays on the quays of Odessa and the banks of the Moscow River ("Between the noonday whistles," wrote one American observer, "the whole city it seemed came down to the river to play and to worship the sun"), and to France, where nudists established a colony on an island in the Seine near Paris, and even to England, where elderly (but spry) George Lansbury, the Labour government's first commissioner of public works, declared himself wholeheartedly in favor of nude sunbathing in London's public parks, though some Britons wondered whether there would be enough sunny days to make the exposure worthwhile. In America, sun worshipers enjoyed themselves discreetly in the bathhouses of south Boston or in individual cabins on Florida beaches, on isolated Rocky Mountain slopes or Manhattan rooftops or sometimes in sheltered spots amid the driftwood on Fire Island. "If the republic wants to go native and can hold to it with any fidelity," remarked one dedicated cultist, "it will probably do more than any other conceivable action to balance the inhibitions and pathological cripplings induced by the machine age and the monstrous cities in which we live."

Other mass crazes swept across the United States at the end of that summer. People started drinking sauerkraut juice for no discernible reason, and broccoli made a comeback on America's dinner tables after a well-deserved absence of nearly a century. At Milton Crandall's Eternity Hop, the winning couple finally collapsed after dancing on blistered arches for 534 hours, 1 minute, and 3½ seconds. "Americans are crazy people," declared famed newspaper cartoonist Ralph Barton. "They drink too much, do everything too much. They like something for fifteen minutes, then turn about and like something else. They are faddists. They idolize some hero of the hour beyond all sensibility, then leave him flat for some one else."

"Amos 'n' Andy" made its debut on radio and attracted record-breaking audiences for its fifteen-minute shows every night (except Tuesday) at 11:00 P.M. Rural movie theaters reported that their most popular features were chorus girl revue pictures: "It matters not how long or how short the films are," observed *Variety*, "providing they have a good looking line, the less dressed the better, doing its stuff to canned music." Americans sang "Honey" ("I'm in love with you, Honey, / Say you love me too, Honey"), "Blue Hawaii," and "I'm thirsty for kisses, I'm hungry for love." French import Maurice Chevalier was the newest movie idol, and girls of all ages swooned over suave crooner Rudy Vallee. MGM's *Broadway Melody* became America's first "100 percent ALL Talking, ALL Singing and ALL Dancing movie," and *Gold Diggers of Broadway* introduced the first dance sequences in color. Arthur Fiedler and the Boston Symphony Orchestra inaugurated an experimental and extraordinarily popular series of free, outdoor concerts on the Charles River Basin Esplanade, and Clarence Mackay, father-in-law of Irving Berlin and chairman of the board of directors of the New York Philharmonic Society, brought the mercurial genius of Arturo Toscanini to the United States as the Philharmonic's new conductor.

Although Remarque's *All Quiet on the Western Front* was still the best-selling novel in the United States, a gangster epic entitled *Little Caesar* by W. R. Burnett was blasting its way up the fiction list. Outraged American citizens threatened to boycott the postal service if Congress approved the new 3¢ rate for first-class mail. At the midpoint of the baseball season, batting averages in both the American and National leagues were up nearly fifty points; despite official denials from the A.G. Spalding and Brothers Company, it seemed obvious that the ball had been juiced up. Connie Mack's Philadelphia Athletics, led by young slugger Jimmy Foxx, ran away from the rest of the American League, while Pittsburgh and Chicago vied for the lead in the senior circuit.

The Gershwin brothers, George and Ira, contributed their songwriting talents to Flo Ziegfeld's latest review, *Show Girl,* which featured dancer-actress Ruby Keeler (Mrs. Al Jolson) and the Duke Ellington band. But the lion's share of the accolades from *Show Girl* were stolen by nightclub and speakeasy veteran Jimmy "Schnozzola" Durante, a.k.a. "Jimmy, the Well-Dressed Man," in his first appearance on the legitimate stage. Critic Gilbert Seldes wrote of Durante that "no one now playing in New York approaches his warm humor, his enormous zest, and his talent." Instead of singing the Gershwins' original songs, Jimmy (accompanied by his longtime cronies and hoofing partners, Eddie Jackson and Lou Clayton) sang his own inimitably lunatic numbers: "I Can Do Without Broadway (but Can Broadway Do Without Me?)"; the interior decorator's theme song, "Shades, Yellow Shades for the Window"; "So I Ups to Him"; and the unforgettable "Who Will Be with You When I'm Far Away (Far Out in Far Rockaway)?" "Their entertainment is verbal slapstick and hokum, burlesque, parody, old jokes, and throwing hats," noted an immensely amused reviewer. "Almost all their speech is shouting or half-whispered asides; they are always moving things or throwing things; they kid the piece, themselves, and the audience unceasingly." Despite Durante's inspired antics, *Show Girl* folded after an unexpectedly brief run, partly because Ruby Keeler reportedly could not stand the nightly strain of doing the show, and partly because the rest of the show simply was not very good.

George Gershwin's reputation suffered not at all from the flop. At the end of 1928, he had introduced his brilliant jazz symphony *An American in Paris,* which elevated him to the top rank of American composers. At a private party in Gershwin's honor following the world premiere of the tone poem at Carnegie Hall, Otto Kahn delivered a fulsome tribute to the composer:

George Gershwin is a leader of young America in music in the same sense in which Lindbergh is the leader of young America in aviation, and in more than one respect has qualities similar to those of the young and attractive Colonel. . . . Without self-seeking or self-consciousness, he is in his art thoroughly and uncompromisingly American. In the rhythm, the melody, the humor, the grace, the rush, and sweep and dynamics of his compositions he expresses the genius of young America. But in that American genius there is one note lacking. It is the note that is a legacy of sorrow, a note that springs from the deepest stirrings of the soul. The American nation has not known the suffering, the tragedies, the sacrifices, the privations nor the mellow romance which are the age-old inheritance of the peoples of Europe.

Far be it from me to wish any tragedies to come into the life of this nation for the sake of chastening its soul, or into the life of George Gershwin for the sake of deepening his art, but "the long drip of human tears" has strange and beautiful powers. They fertilize the deepest roots of art, and from them flowers spring.

Like Jack Morgan, Bernard Baruch spent the better part of August rousting grouse on the moors of Scotland. Although he received a steady stream of optimistic reports from Swope and other friends at home extolling the strength of the American economy, Baruch hesitated to do anything more bold than purchase a few hundred shares of stock in a few obscure corporations he believed were undervalued. When he received an invitation to participate in Goldman, Sachs' new Blue Ridge investment trust (a company Baruch frankly described as "financial whoopee"), he requested advice from several trusted banking friends, including Charlie Mitchell, who were closer to the domestic scene. The first two replies were noncommittal, but on the sixteenth he received Mitchell's cabled response:

GENERAL SITUATION LOOKS EXCEPTIONALLY SOUND WITH VERY FEW BAD SPOTS. . . . BELIEVE CREDIT SITUATION PRACTICALLY UNAFFECTED BY DISCOUNT RATE ACTION. MONEY SEASONABLY WEAK. SHOULD STRENGTHEN AS MONTH CLOSES. STRENGTH IN STOCK MARKET CENTERS LARGELY IN SPECIALTIES, WHICH IN MANY CASES SEEM UNDULY HIGH, WHILE THERE ARE MANY STOCKS, SUCH AS COPPER AND MOTORS AND CERTAIN RAILS THAT LOOK UNJUSTIFIABLY LOW. I DOUBT IF ANYTHING THAT WILL NOT AFFECT BUSINESS CAN AFFECT THE MARKET, WHICH IS LIKE A WEATHER-VANE POINTING INTO A GALE OF PROSPERITY. BELIEVE THERE IS LESS PESSIMISM AROUND THAN WHEN YOU LEFT.

Yet Baruch was not so certain. "After I got this cable," he related some years later, "I went for a walk with General Pershing, who was my guest. We talked at length about the state of affairs in America, and I expressed my growing concern over the danger signs in the market. As we strolled along, I went over all the factors involved in the Shenandoah and Blue Ridge issues; even at a distance of three thousand miles, I could see that these and many other enterprises were foolhardy. My intuition, which after all is only the accumulated force of experience, was sending out warning signals." Baruch decided to cut short his vacation in Scotland, and while he waited in London for his ship to depart for New York, Mitchell's exuberant message kept running through his mind. Several times Baruch cabled purchase instructions to his office in New York, only to reconsider and countermand the orders each time. On the voyage home, Baruch used the ship's brokerage wire to begin selling the stocks that remained in his portfolio.

After receiving Baruch in Britain in July, Winston Churchill departed for Canada and the United States on August 3 on a liner named (appropriately for an old imperialist) the *Empress of India,* accompanied by his brother, his nephew, and his son Randolph. Winston recently had received £1,000 in royalties and £2,000 more from selling shares of utility stock, and he had a promise from the *Daily Telegraph* to pay him another £2,500 for a series of articles about his forthcoming voyage. Acting on the assumption that financial security would be "a wonderful thing" and quite attainable, Churchill invested "every shilling he could spare" in the New York stock market.

For the journey across Canada, Charlie Schwab loaned Winston his private railway car, complete with a radio over which Churchill listened closely to the latest stock quotations. The financial news during the early part of the voyage, he wrote to his wife Clementine, had been "entirely satisfactory."

On August 10, Herbert Hoover celebrated his fifty-fifth birthday at the presidential retreat on the Rapidan River in Virginia. There were no more than a dozen guests, including journalists William Allen White and Mark Sullivan, New York banker Jeremiah Milbank, and America's favorite newlywed couple, Charles and Anne Lindbergh. Anne and Herbert's wife, Lou, planned the birthday party, surprising the President after he and his male guests had spent a busy morning pitching horseshoes (Lindbergh won the title of camp champ; Hoover just stood and watched), horseback riding, and building a rock dam in a mountain stream—under the Great Engineer's direction—to form a sunning pool for trout. After the party returned to the White House at the close of the weekend (Lindbergh drove one car and reached Washington far ahead of everyone else), Anne wrote a letter to her mother, describing their visit: "We have had really a lovely weekend—'slow' riding (suited to my taste), walks down the stream, and around a fire at night. For opinions I must wait. President and Mrs. Hoover have been very kind. She is the most tireless, energetic hostess, every moment given to thinking of and planning for her large brood of guests. He has a nice dry wit."

But Hoover could not relax. He was oppressed with the continuing problems of crime and farm relief and tariff reform. The Senate refused to give him discretionary power to alter tariff rates because it feared he would set them too low; in fact, the prohibitive import duties being discussed in Congress already had brought a chorus of protest from twenty-five foreign nations. When Hoover appeared at an official welcoming ceremony at the fairgrounds in the nearby town of Madison the following week, he seemed pale and tired. "He spoke slowly," remarked one correspondent, "and his appearance was that of a man who had not enjoyed a good night's rest." Some measure of Hoover's frustration with the unremitting rigors of life in Washington could be discerned in an uncharacteristically wistful and revealing speech to the gathering at the Madison fairgrounds. "I have discovered why Presidents take to fishing, the silent sport," he said:

> Apparently the only opportunity for refreshment of one's soul and clarification of one's thoughts by solitude to Presidents lies through fishing. . . . Fishing seems to be the sole avenue left to Presidents through which they may escape to their own thoughts and may live in their own imaginings and find relief from the pneumatic hammer of constant personal contacts, and refreshments of mind in the babble of rippling brooks. Moreover, it is a constant reminder of the democracy of life, of humility and of human frailty—for all men are equal before fishes. And it is desirable that the President of the United States should be periodically reminded of this fundamental fact, that the forces of nature discriminate for no man.

Such was the state of the President's mind on the eve of the Great Crash.

# PART THREE: DESTRUCTION

# XIV

# From the Smart to the Dumb

---

"Fall came. The permanent party took the launch to the mainland, got
on board the Delaware & Hudson, and played hearts all the way back to
the city. Another new season began in New York, another grueling
nine months of all-night poker and all-day croquet, Round Table lunches
and Long Island weekends. It was back to the grind of cooking up puns
and practical jokes, needling Woollcott and embarrassing Kaufman,
and playing the newest party game—The Market."

—HARPO MARX

**W**hen people speak of the Great Crash of 1929, they usually have in
mind the appalling havoc wreaked upon stock prices during the two most
horrifyingly destructive days Wall Street has ever known: Black Thursday,
October 24, and Black Tuesday, October 29. But the dramatic events of
those terrifying days—a total of ten hours, in all—were in reality only the
most spectacular phase of a far more protracted and painfully drawn-out
affair that lasted for nearly two and a half months. A close examination of
the historical evidence reveals that the collapse of the fabled bull market
of the 1920s actually began in earnest during the first week of September,
when the stock market embarked upon a long, agonizing slide that accelerated with breathtaking speed in the second half of October, plunging
thousands of Americans into the depths of despair before it finally ground
to a halt in the middle of November, leaving the richest country in the
world exhausted, vulnerable, and very frightened, on the brink of the
Great Depression.

In the twilight of the exuberant, carefree summer of 1929, however,
the nation was paying scant heed to the warning signs of impending
disaster. Wall Street returned from the Labor Day holiday full of anticipation, eager to soar further into the stratosphere. August had been an
extraordinary month: 95,704,890 shares changed hands, a record volume
for August and one of the busiest months on the street in history. Despite
the severe break on August 9, the value of 240 representative stocks (as
selected by the *New York Times*) increased by a total of $4,465,381,600,

bringing the total value of all the issues on the New York Stock Exchange to nearly $90 billion. Yale economist Irving Fisher's index of the 215 "most important stocks on the market" reached a new pinnacle of 208.6, up nearly 15 points since the end of July, and a full 63 points—about 30 percent—higher than the average of August 1928. Brokers' loans were also at an all-time high, having risen by $407,825,132 during August (following similar $400 million increases in June and July), bringing the total to an astounding $7,881,619,426, according to the official figures released by the New York Stock Exchange. (The exchange's figures generally were higher than the Federal Reserve Board's, because the board only counted loans made by banks.) The startling rise in brokers' loans meant, of course, that a record number of shares were being purchased on margin by small speculators with call money supplied by corporations, wealthy individuals, and investment trusts looking for a profitable outlet for their surplus cash; but as long as the speculative favorites kept smashing upward through all previous ceilings, the spectacle of widespread public participation seemed an occasion for rejoicing rather than alarm.

The boom at last had become a full-fledged stampede. Several years later, Otto Kahn looked back toward the early days of September 1929 and concluded that the speculative movement had gained so much momentum by that time that nothing short of a crash could have brought it under control. The American public, Kahn testified, was "determined to speculate. They were determined that every piece of paper would be worth tomorrow twice what it was today. I do not believe the whole banking community could have prevented it. . . . When it had taken full sway of the people and there was an absolute runaway feeling throughout the country, I doubt whether anyone could have stopped it before calamity overtook us." To liberal journalist Gilbert Seldes, the final days *before* the crash were the true time of panic. "I call it panic to be afraid to sell at a profit, lest an additional profit be lost," Seldes wrote. "The panic which keeps people at roulette tables, the insidious propaganda against quitting a winner, the fear of being taunted by those who held on, all worked together. It became not only a point of pride, but a civic duty, not to sell, as if there were ever a buyer without a seller."

When the opening gong sounded on Tuesday, September 3, a rush of speculative enthusiasm drove the Dow Jones average to an all-time peak. One excited analyst remarked that the feverish market looked like it was "being pushed up as if propelled by a financial volcano." Some measure of the immense strength of the Coolidge-Hoover bull market may be gleaned from a comparison of the prices of certain popular issues on that blissful day with the levels of March 1928, eighteen months earlier. General Electric stood at 396, up from 129; RCA reached 505, a huge jump from 94½; United States Steel had more than doubled in value, from 138 to 279; and Montgomery Ward had risen to 466½ from 133. Although no one—*no one*—knew it at the time, those exalted levels would not be attained again for a quarter of a century.

Beneath the exhilaration and slightly hysterical enthusiasm, however, a vague and ill-defined sense of unease began to spread through the financial community. There is no doubt that contemporary observers—who were not blessed with the hindsight afforded historians—could discern the jittery, dangerously unsettled condition of the market six weeks before the crash. The signs were there for those who chose to see, and many did. "As the fall begins, there is a tenseness in Wall Street. Its presence is undeniable," observed *Business Week* in the journal's premiere issue, which appeared on the nation's newsstands in the first week of September. "There is a general feeling that something is going to happen during the present season." Brokers reported that an unusual number of "old, high-denomination" stock certificates were being redeemed by wealthy clients who were leaving the market in droves. Seldes cited a fortunate circle of his own acquaintances who had sufficient faith in their own convictions to challenge the prevailing propaganda of prosperity and sell out their holdings just in time. Even Billy Durant, it seems, expected some sort of break and decided to take at least part of his profits before the fall; reliable financial records indicate that Durant unloaded approximately $244 million worth of stock in 1929 (compared with only $204 in purchases), and Wall Street buzzed with rumors that the King of the Bulls had been selling throughout the summer under cover of John Raskob's optimistic public pronouncements, which skillfully inflated prices while he and his friends unloaded their securities. Although the *Wall Street Journal,* the chief journalistic promoter of the boom, maintained its traditionally optimistic front, the editors of *Business Week* charged unequivocally that "stock prices are generally out of line with safe earnings expectations, and the market is now almost wholly 'psychological'—irregular, unsteady and properly apprehensive of the inevitable readjustment that draws near."

In fact, only 388 of the nearly 1,200 issues listed on the New York Stock Exchange had advanced between January 2 and September 3, while more than 600 stocks already showed substantial declines from their highest point of the past few years. Pepsi-Cola was down from 19 to 10; Philip Morris had skidded from 41 to 12; Celanese had fallen all the way from 118 to 66; and Studebaker was down by 22 points. "This has been a highly selective market," observed the Cleveland Trust Company's resident market guru, Colonel Leonard P. Ayres. "It has made new high records for volume of trading, and most of the stock averages have moved up during considerable periods of time with a rapidity never before equaled. Nevertheless the majority of the issues had been drifting down for a long time. . . . In a real sense there has been under way during the most of this year a sort of creeping bear market."

Clearly no healthy market would have taken fright at the gloomy prophecy issued on the afternoon of September 5 by a frail, wispish gentleman named Roger Babson, a Massachusetts economist and soothsayer who was known, somewhat disparagingly, as "the Sage of Wellesley." Babson was a man whom Wall Street had cheerfully chosen to ignore on several previous occasions. Since he first ventured into the forecasting business in 1927, Babson had fallen into the habit of making annual predictions of an impending disaster on Wall Street, thereby earning himself a reputation as "the prophet of loss" and "a statistician who has been always wrong." Now, surveying the state of the stock market in September 1929, Babson reiterated his prophecy of doom. "I repeat what I said at this time last year and the year before; that sooner or later a crash is coming which will take in the leading stocks and cause a decline of from 60 to 80 points in the Dow-Jones Barometer," he confidently told a gathering of delegates to the sixteenth National Business Conference. While most of the market declined or stagnated, he explained, the host of advancing stocks was becoming narrower and smaller, drawing fewer and fewer issues along for the ride as the favorites continued their lonely surge upward. And, Babson asked rhetorically, what did the future have in store?

> Fair weather cannot always continue. The economic cycle is in progress today, as it was in the past. The Federal Reserve System has put the banks in a strong position, but it has not changed human nature. More people are borrowing and speculating today than ever in our history. Sooner or later a crash is coming and it may be terrific. Wise are those investors who now get out of debt and reef their sails. This does not mean selling all you have, but it does mean paying up your loans and avoiding margin speculation. . . .
>
> Sooner or later the stock market boom will collapse like the Florida boom.* Some day the time is coming when the market will begin to slide off, sellers will exceed buyers, and paper profits will begin to disappear. Then there will immediately be a stampede to save what paper profits then exist. . . . As soon as word gets abroad that the large American investment trusts are selling, the European houses will begin to sell out their customers who are now buying in the American market. The general public will then follow with a desire to cash in, then margin accounts

---

*Between 1925 and 1926, hundreds of thousands of Americans rushed to Florida, feverishly purchasing property to take advantage of rapidly rising land prices. The boom ended abruptly when prices crashed in 1926.

will be closed out, and then there may be a stampede for selling which will exceed anything that the Stock Exchange has ever witnessed.

Although Babson's prophecy seems extraordinarily accurate from the perspective of history, it was actually little different from the sort of gloomy predictions he had issued in the previous two years. This time, however, the market panicked when the text of Babson's speech came over the tickers at two o'clock. The effect of the statistician's words was magnified by the news that brokers' loans had risen by another $137 million during the preceding week. In the turbulent final hour of trading that afternoon, two million shares were dumped on the market in a torrent of liquidation; as stop-loss orders kicked in, the descent became even steeper, sending prices sharply downward in the widest decline since August 9.

The furor over Babson's prediction interrupted Billy Durant's plans to form an omnipotent bull pool of millionaire stock market operators to bid prices up even higher; in fact, Durant had been reaching for the phone to invite Joe Kennedy to join the venture when his secretary rushed into his office and told him that the United Press was calling "with terrible news. The bull market is over and will Mr. Durant comment?" He would not. And when Raskob read the bad news from Wall Street coming over the wire, he telephoned Jim Riordan and suggested that the market might need steadying in the very near future.

All hell had broken loose in Palestine. At the end of August, a series of relatively inconsequential disputes concerning the privileges of worship for Jews and Moslems at the Western Wall and the Mosque of the Dome of the Rock, respectively, erupted into an orgy of bloodletting as the Grand Mufti of Jerusalem, Hadj Amir el-Hussein, deliberately incited his Arab followers to launch a holy war to exterminate the Jewish settlers who, he said, were threatening to "annihilate the Arab nation in its own country in favor of reviving a non-existent nation." The Grand Mufti's incendiary accusations were given a certain perverse measure of legitimacy by the ill-advised boasts of certain Zionist champions, both in Palestine and at the recent Zionist Congress in Zurich, which seemed to indicate that the Jews had every intention of eventually seizing complete political and economic control of their ancient homeland from the Arab majority. Aroused to a fever pitch of religious frenzy, mobs of fanatical Arabs brandishing swords poured out of the Mosque of the Dome of the Rock and swept through Mea Shearim, the Jewish quarter of Jerusalem, killing thirty Jews and wounding more than a hundred in two days of rioting. Aged Jewish mourners at the Western Wall were stoned; a young boy playing ball was fatally stabbed; Jewish shops and homes were plundered; the ancient town of Safed, for centuries a center of scholarly Jewish mysticism, was sacked and burned by enraged Arabs, leaving piles of corpses in the streets.

Twenty miles south of Jerusalem, at the village of Hebron, an Arab mob attacked a rabbinical college and massacred sixty-four Jews, including eight American students. Scores of more fortunate Americans were evacuated to Haifa. At the small Jewish settlement of Motzah, in the mountains outside Jerusalem, one survivor recalled the terror:

> When the attack first started, on Saturday, August 24, I was seeking help near by. Hearing cries, I rushed back and saw Arab bands approaching our homestead, hurling huge stones. My brother Moshe came out, shouting, "What do you want?" and as if in reply they shot him dead, also firing at my sister, Rifka, who was standing on the veranda, killing her instantly. Then my father ran out and fell under a heavy fusillade. I managed to enter the house under a hail of bullets and stones, and the Arabs soon broke in, shooting my sister Mina. Before my eyes they seized my mother and stabbed her mercilessly, inflicting an endless number of wounds. Don't ask how I escaped. I don't know and I shall never understand how so great a miracle occurred. Five other persons in the house at that time also survived, but the poor 80-year-old village rabbi and one neighbor were murdered.

Belatedly, Britain rushed military reinforcements to the region to restore order. Eighteen British warships converged upon Palestine; low-flying airplanes armed with machine guns strafed Arab strongholds in the streets of Jerusalem; and armored cars fired warning shots into rebellious crowds. The high commissioner, Sir John Chancellor, who had been out of the country when the outbreak began, rushed back to Jerusalem and imposed a rigorous curfew and a virtual blackout on news within the area. In an official proclamation, Sir John left no doubt as to where the responsibility for the violence lay. "I have returned from the United Kingdom," he said, "to find to my distress the country in a state of disorder and a prey to unlawful violence. I learned with horror of the atrocious acts committed by bodies of ruthless and bloodthirsty evil-doers, of savage murders perpetrated upon defenseless members of the Jewish population, regardless of age or sex, accompanied, as at Hebron, by acts of unspeakable savagery, of the burning of farms and houses in town and country and of looting and destruction of property. These crimes have brought upon the authors the execration of all civilized peoples throughout the world."

Enraged by the high commissioner's protection of the Jews, Arab leaders turned their hostility toward the British. As the danger grew of a coordinated Arab incursion by tribesmen from Syria, Jordan, Iraq, and

Arabia (where Ibn Saʼud was making threatening noises), British reinforcements were rushed to the frontiers to repel the invaders. By the middle of September, an uneasy peace had been restored, but at least 109 Jews and 83 Moslems lay dead, and many hundreds more had been seriously wounded. In the United States, Jewish organizations held rallies to raise funds for the relief of the survivors, and philanthropists such as Felix Warburg (Paul's brother and a partner in Kuhn, Loeb and Company) donated hundreds of thousands of dollars. At a gathering of 2,000 Jews in Brooklyn, Mayor Jimmy Walker donned a skullcap and shouted, "Lead on! Whether to Palestine or elsewhere, we will follow and see that never again shall the hand of the persecutor be laid on you in any other land!"

Although the market recovered quickly from its sudden attack of "Babson-mindedness," recouping in two days most of the losses suffered on September 5, the rally foundered in the following week. Even optimistic pronouncements by Secretary of Commerce Robert Lamont—"Practically all the indicators of business activities . . . have stood at higher levels during June, July and August of the present year than in 1928, or, indeed, than in any other year of our history"—and a chorus of Republican party chieftains praising the blessings of Hoover prosperity could not rouse the market from its lethargy.

On September 10 and 12, prices plunged again, leaving even such favorites as U.S. Steel and General Motors 10 to 20 percent below their previous highs. "Business optimism is becoming slightly, but more distinctly, overcast with anxiety about speculation and the credit situation," reported *Business Week*. "The stock market feels it and is acting a bit jaded and nervous."

Disturbing nuggets of economic news heightened the mounting sense of anxiety. Steel production, for so long a barometer of the boom, fell off slowly but steadily until it stood about 9 percent below the peak attained in May. As automobile purchases slackened, so did the output of nearly every car manufacturer except Ford. Building construction, restricted by high interest rates, continued to decline. Nor was the news from abroad more encouraging. Unemployment in Germany jumped another notch at the end of August, and the drain on Britain's gold reserve reached alarming proportions.

In the face of these ominous tidings and the obvious nervousness of the market, however, brokers' loans perversely soared by another $120 million in the space of a single week. And when the investment firm of Lehman Brothers issued stock in a holding company called, simply, Lehman Corporation, which was totally devoid of assets save for its stock certificates, eager speculators snapped up the securities so fast that the price jumped from 100 to 135 within the space of a few hours. Veteran Wall Street analysts confessed that they were thoroughly befuddled at the public's remarkable behavior. "The situation is in many ways so peculiar as to make generalization or prediction exceptionally difficult," remarked a financial columnist in the *New York Times.* "Nobody fully understands the scope of the novel economic influences at work on the present market, or is sure of their ultimate result. The economists are floundering along with professional Wall Street."

On September 14, a truckload of striking mill workers left Bessemer City, North Carolina, bound for a union rally in nearby Gastonia. Ella May Wiggins was sitting in back of the truck. As they approached Gastonia, the strikers were turned back by an angry crowd of mill officials and loyal employees. The mob started cursing the strikers. "You fellers are going to get shot up," someone shouted. The truck headed back toward Bessemer City, but after it had gone about two miles it was overtaken by an automobile that suddenly swerved in front, forcing the driver to pull over and stop. Fifteen more cars pulled up in back. Men with shotguns emerged, and someone started firing into the back of the truck.

A bullet struck Ella May Wiggins in the left breast. "Lord," she cried, "they done shot and killed me." Minutes later she was dead.

Terrified, some of the strikers jumped from the truck and started running across the cotton fields. The men from the cars chased after them, firing their shotguns as if they were hunting rabbits. One of the strikers said he must have heard forty or fifty shots fired.

At the dead woman's home, they hung a sign: "ELLA MAY, SLAUGH-TERED BY THE BOSSES' BLACK HUNDRED, MARTYR TO THE CAUSE OF ORGANIZED LABOR."

The first trial of the men and women accused of murdering Chief Aderholt ended in a mistrial when one of the jurors suddenly went insane. He lost his mind when the prosecution wheeled in a ghastly life-size plaster dummy of Aderholt, dressed in a bloody uniform and covered with a shroud. That night the unhinged juryman begged a deputy sheriff for a gun to kill himself, and the next day the sheriff found him crawling under a bed, asking to be buried face down. Afterward, several talkative jurors acknowledged that they probably would have voted to acquit the defendants, since the state's case was so weak.

That revelation was too much for a furious mob of rabid anticommunist townspeople, who proceeded to kidnap a British labor leader named Ben Wells who had come to North Carolina to help organize the mill workers. They blackjacked Wells, took him to a woods, forced him to strip, and then brutally flogged him. The brave boys fled when they heard someone approaching; they thought it was the law, but it was only a possum hunter. Another bunch of about three hundred vigilantes surrounded the courthouse in Charlotte and demanded that the authorities release "that red-headed bastard Fred Beal" and his fellow defendants so they could lynch them.

"Irrespective of its source or the occasion, there is no place in North Carolina for terrorism in any form," declared Governor O. Max Gardner, who went on to suggest that higher wages, shorter hours, and abolition of the mill village system would be the best cure for most of the state's labor troubles. (The governor was a cotton-mill owner himself who treated his employees very well and enjoyed excellent relations with them.) "You cannot drive out Communism with Anarchy," said the Raleigh *News and Observer,* and even the ultraconservative Charleston *News and Courier* agreed that "no Communist is worse than a flogger or lyncher. When an agitator arrives in Gaston county and is subjected to assault by a mob, it is the best of evidence that he is making Communist converts—for if the only answer to Communistic doctrine in North Carolina is the doctrine of lawless violence, North Carolina would as well be Communistic, for its end in either case will be anarchy."

Fourteen men were arrested for kidnapping Wells; they were held on bond of only $1,000 each. Then police raided a union rooming house in Charlotte and seized eight labor organizers who had accumulated (rather understandably, considering the circumstances) a small arsenal of shotguns, riot guns, and revolvers, and charged them with "conspiracy to overthrow by force the existing government in the State of North Carolina." On September 18, another union leader was kidnapped, taken across the state line into South Carolina, and flogged.

But the bloodiest confrontation came in the mill town of Marion, about forty miles northwest of Gastonia, where members of a moderate union affiliated with the eminently respectable AFL gathered in front of a Marion Manufacturing Company plant to persuade the rest of the company's workers to join a strike. Sheriff Oscar F. Adkins, who had been summoned to the mill by the company president, discharged a tear gas gun to disperse the crowd. A lame sixty-seven-year-old worker retaliated by swinging his cane at Sheriff Adkins; in the confusion, Adkins' deputies started shooting. People screamed in pain and horror as the deputies kept firing and the bodies fell to the ground. Three men were killed instantly, three were fatally injured, and two dozen more (including one woman) suffered serious gunshot wounds. Almost all of them had been shot in the back as they tried to flee. The sheriff, thirteen of his deputies, and two mill foremen were arrested and charged with murder.

Ella May Wiggins was buried on a day gray with rain. The funeral cortege traveled to the graveyard in battered old cars over muddy red roads; other workers arrived on foot through miles of cotton fields. As they lowered her pine casket into the ground, the mourners sang one of Ella May's songs:

> How it grieves the heart of a mother,
> You every one must know,
> But we can't buy for our children,
> Our wages are too low.
> . . . . . . . . . . . . . . . . . .
> But understand, all workers,
> Our union they do fear.
> Let's stand together, workers,
> And have a union here.

"Things have never been better," Charlie Mitchell told reporters on the evening of Friday, September 20, as he and his wife stepped aboard the White Star liner *Olympic* for a month's vacation in Europe. Flanked by Secretary Mellon, whose son was traveling on the *Olympic*, too, Mitchell cheerfully advised investors to "be a bull on America." "Money is all right," he assured everyone. "There is nothing to worry about in the financial situation in the United States." Secretary Mellon had absolutely nothing to say. Bernard Baruch, who had landed in New York a week earlier, on Friday the thirteenth, wired bon voyage to Mitchell.

Earlier that day, stock prices on the New York Exchange had plunged again, spooked by the news that brokers' loans had risen by $95 million over the past week, and by reports that a major British corporation was in danger of collapse. The British concern in question was, in fact, a diverse group of companies that had been assembled into a glittering but dangerously precarious empire by a balding, flamboyant financier-promoter named Clarence Charles Hatry. Since the turn of the century, Hatry had made and lost a succession of fortunes in silk, insurance, war materiel, and, most recently, coin-operated photograph machines. By the fall of 1929, when he was on the verge of putting together the largest steel-producing consortium Britain had ever seen, Hatry had managed to build up a tremendous pyramid of paper profits by the simple expedient of floating additional securities whenever he required cash. But Hatry went to the well once too often; in an attempt to obtain a desperately needed loan from a trust company, he and his associates put up as collateral nearly a million dollars' worth of forged municipal stock certificates. When the fraud was discovered, Hatry was arrested and placed in Brixton Prison, and the shares of his companies plummeted £2.5 million in forty-eight hours. And when investigators realized that Hatry's "empire" had incurred liabilities of £19 million, against only £4 million in assets, the governing committee of the London Stock Exchange took the unprecedented step of suspending trading in seven of his companies.

The Hatry revelations were followed by an even heavier blow from the City. On September 26, the hard-pressed Bank of England raised its discount rate a full point, to 6½ percent, the highest level in eight years. Clearly the measure seemed to be the only viable means of stemming the outflow of gold from Britain to Wall Street—the bank had lost £30 million in the last three months alone—and just as clearly it was bound to depress British trade by rendering money more scarce and more dear. Stock prices sagged badly on the London Exchange as nervous investors, fearing a full-scale smashup, dumped their securities on the market. The Federation of British Industries issued a dark warning that manufacturers and merchants "must be prepared to face an actual contraction in the aggregate total [of credit] available for all purposes. This means that funds for developments in new directions can only be obtained by reducing activity in other directions. Abroad, the rise is bound to produce serious international unsettlement."

"There are plenty of clouds on the horizon," noted the *Manchester Guardian* with growing apprehension at the end of September. (It was an odd metaphor, considering the weather; at the time, Britain was enduring its longest drought—thirty-two days without rain—since 1859.) "The Hatry affair is a big and black one," warned the *Guardian.* "Dear money is another, and it is not at all certain that we have seen this one as yet in its full proportions. In this thundery atmosphere nerves are none too good, and people are looking round for hints of trouble in all conceivable quarters. . . . At such a moment the vitality of institutions and of the men who lead them is put severely to the test."

In the United States, *Business Week* recognized a similar chill in the air. "There is a premature feeling of fall in the falling percentages of steel operation, a touch of yellow in the leaves, as buyers leave larger stocks of autos on the hands of dealers. Chilly little drafts drift through the stock market." Wall Street swirled with rumors that a prominent American investment banking firm was indirectly involved in the Hatry fiasco and would suffer heavy losses in the next few days. Brokers debated whether the irregular decline of the past three weeks meant that stocks were entering "the bargain zone," or if the reaction was just beginning.

A clue appeared on Tuesday, September 24. In the widest day of trading on record, when shares of 863 different issues were dealt, prices on the New York Stock Exchange tumbled downward again. "By the middle of the last hour," reported the *Times,* "the market was in full flight, with the good, bad and indifferent shares sagging raggedly, and without any indication of the presence of organized or intelligent support."

Undaunted, the irrepressible John J. Raskob convened a gathering of prominent stock market operators at his suite in the Carlton House in downtown Manhattan. Billy Durant was there, and Jim Riordan, along with Arthur Cutten from Chicago, Percy Rockefeller, and two pairs of brothers—the Du Ponts and the van Sweringens. Dressed in a natty, color-splashed shirt to establish an upbeat tone from the outset, the gnomish Raskob implored his millionaire guests to maintain "a positive belief" in the market, insisting that the masses of small investors—like docile, compliant sheep—required the leadership of big speculators if the bull market was to surmount the recent avalanche of bad economic news. "In a healthy market we prosper," Raskob pointedly advised the men in the room. "In a sick market we suffer."

When the opening gong sounded on the morning of September 25, the New York Stock Exchange was buffeted by wild whispers of impending disaster; prices again started to slide downward, "melting away," someone said, "like a summer snow flurry." By mid-morning the twenty-five leading industrials were off by nearly fourteen points. Then all at once there was a rush of organized buying to support the usual speculative favorites: General Electric, Standard Oil of New Jersey, RCA, United States Steel, and Anaconda Copper. As word spread by ticker and telephone that these stocks were leading a rally, the rest of the market snapped back to life and closed the day with only minor losses. One financial analyst claimed that it had been "about the most nervewracking day that Wall Street has experienced in many a month," but matters were just beginning to get interesting.

Convinced that the market was on the brink of a spectacular rebound, Durant went to Bernard Baruch and tried to persuade him to join his proposed multimillion-dollar bull pool. Baruch adamantly refused, despite the Dream Maker's insistent entreaties; in fact, he earnestly tried to dissuade Durant from throwing his money away. "I'm sorry you can't see it my way, Willie," Baruch said as he walked away.

In his memoirs, Baruch contends, "Immediately after arriving in New York [on the thirteenth], I began to sell everything I could, in anticipation of the break I now felt to be imminent. This was near the end of September. The condition of the market could be measured by its wild fluctuations, followed by assurances from every direction that all was well. But I had heard this lullaby before. I knew that the continuity of confidence was beginning to break." And yet it was not that simple; Baruch's somewhat disingenuous account omits certain details that indicate that even he was not entirely certain the bull market had finally run its full course.

Shortly after his return to America, Baruch had unwisely purchased five thousand shares of the new Lehman Corporation issues that Otto Kahn viewed with well-deserved disdain. At the same time, however, Baruch and Herbert Bayard Swope sold short nearly $2 million worth of RCA stock, with the expectation that it would soon decline—which, of course, it promptly did. (Swope generously tipped off Irving Berlin before he and Baruch launched their bear raid on RCA.)

The rally that began on September 25 lasted precisely one day. It was stopped dead in its tracks twenty-four hours later by the startling announcement that brokers' loans had risen yet again, by the astounding sum of $192 million in the past week. The entire increase in the loan total came from corporations or investment trusts that were liquidating their holdings and hence had surplus cash at their disposal. This meant that the banking community, including such giants as National City Bank that might otherwise have enforced at least some measure of restraint, had lost all control over the speculative boom.

Wall Street, quite frankly, was stunned at the almost incomprehensible leap in brokers' loans. Ever since September 3, prices of virtually every issue had been sliding downward; sales had been brisk as thousands of investors rushed to reduce their portfolios. Ed Barrow, president of the New York Yankees, advised his players to get out of the market as soon as possible. (Barrow did not have to worry about Babe Ruth; the high-living Yankee slugger went through money so fast that he usually had nothing left to invest.) By the end of September, Owen Young had largely withdrawn from the market after his late summer spree, selling everything except his seven hundred shares of General Electric and a relatively insignificant block of utility and aluminum securities. But Young's stocks, and millions of shares sold by other prudent investors who decided to take their profits while they could, had been snapped up by eager and unwary buyers—by people who had little cash and therefore were purchasing on margin with little collateral, by greedy speculators who apparently assumed that they were getting a bargain by buying at such depressed prices. As Colonel Ayres succinctly put it, "It seems probable that stocks have been passing not so much from the strong to the weak, as from the smart to the dumb."

This bizarre spectacle scared the professionals on Wall Street to death. The selling pressure intensified as more experienced investors continued to dump their holdings and take their profits. On September 27, hundreds of millions of dollars vanished as the market suffered a full-scale rout. General Electric lost over twelve points, Westinghouse tumbled by eleven, U.S. Steel was off nine, and AT&T fell by eight points, as did Simmons Company (the furniture and bedding manufacturer in which

Winston Churchill had invested heavily, primarily because he liked their advertisement: "You can't go wrong on a Simmons mattress"). It was the worst break since August 9. Most of the gains of that last magnificent month of the last summer of the boom already had been wiped out. As September came to a close, the number of stocks setting new lows for the year vastly outnumbered those reaching new highs.

"The question which now confronts the financial district," wrote Alexander Dana Noyes, "is just how much of a recession will be necessary to once more put the market in a healthy condition."

Few American tourists remained in Paris by the time Hemingway returned to the city, on September 20. Many of those who had departed would soon lose everything they had in the crash; they would never again enjoy the hedonistic pleasures of bohemian life in Montmartre or the Quartier de l'Europe. At the end of the month, Hemingway's second novel, *A Farewell to Arms,* was published in America. Like Remarque's *All Quiet on the Western Front, A Farewell to Arms* was an attempt to illuminate and perhaps lay to rest the searing experiences of the Great War; and it was one more reminder of the hold the war still exercised upon the creative imagination of a generation.

With few exceptions, critics lavished unstinting praise on Hemingway's accomplishment. "Mr. Hemingway is a writer for whom I have considerable respect," said T. S. Eliot. "He seems to me to tell the truth about his own feelings at the moment when they exist." Writing in the *New Republic,* T. S. Mathews summarized Hemingway's faith—a very masculine faith—in the words of the book's hero, Frederick Henry: "Nothing ever happens to the brave."

Such was Hemingway's counsel to Scott Fitzgerald at the end of the summer of 1929. "You just have to *go on* when it is worst and most helpless," Hemingway wrote to the swiftly fading Fitzgerald in September. "There is only one thing to do with a novel and that is go straight on through to the end of the damn thing." But Scott could not do it. "No Real Progress in ANY way," he wrote disgustedly in his journal, "+ *wrecked myself with dozens of people."* Leaving the Riviera, Scott and Zelda headed back to Paris, too. As they sped along a mountain road in the south of France, Zelda suddenly grabbed the steering wheel and tried to drive both herself and her husband over a cliff. She later claimed that the automobile seemed to have a will of its own. "It was going into oblivion beyond and I had to hold the sides of the car," she said.

In Nicaragua, President Moncada's duly elected government launched a brutal campaign of political repression, arresting and deporting scores of political enemies on charges of conspiracy. And throughout the countryside, the killing went on remorselessly as the National Guard and the marines pursued the Sandinista rebels. Finally a coalition of newspaper editors could stomach no more violence, and they addressed an appeal to Moncada: "We have reached the limit. On the one side the Marines and on the other the National Guard . . . are committing disgraceful acts left and right. . . . We are complying with our inalienable duty as editors and patriotic Nicaraguans in pointing out the danger and calling the attention of the Nicaraguan Government . . . to the need of enforcing order and decency in the troops who command us." Unmoved, Moncada blandly replied that the "outrages of which the press complains in connection with the Marines and the National Guard are transitory, as are all human institutions."

Between Labor Day and the end of September, the 240 leading issues on the New York Stock Exchange lost $2,814,255,346 in value. U.S. Steel was off by 13 percent, Montgomery Ward by 14 percent, and Westinghouse by a full 20 percent. The *New York Times* average had slid 12.99 points from its post–Labor Day high. More shares had been traded during that month than in any September in history, more even than in the heady days of August. The combination of heavy volume and declining prices was an ominous sign. "The thin ice of overbuying cracked badly under the market," remarked *Business Week,* "and the Street began to learn again how the cold waters of despair feel."

On the commodities market, wheat prices fell in reaction to the losses on the stock exchange. Wall Street was buffeted by bad news as the government released its latest economic statistics at the end of September: coal production was running about 10 percent below normal; exports showed a sharp decline for the first time since 1920; business failures were on the rise; building contracts dropped sharply; steel and pig iron production fell another notch; railway car loadings of merchandise and freight declined slightly. Reports from retailers indicated that consumers were mortgaging the future by purchasing an ever greater percentage of nonessential goods on installment plans. A survey of automobile dealers' stocks revealed a sharp increase in the number of unsold models, and car manufacturers already had begun to curtail production; Henry Ford, whose plants had been operating at or near capacity for most of the year, gave up his ambitious six-days-a-week experiment and cut back to five days for machines and men. Despite Charlie Mitchell's professed optimism, National City Bank reminded its customers in its monthly news bulletin that a dearth of credit at reasonable rates continued to thwart business expansion: "Tightness of money continues the principal handicap which business must surmount." In San Francisco, Craig Hazlewood, the president of the American Bankers Association, agreed wholeheartedly with National City's assessment. "It may be fairly said that many conservative bankers in this country are gravely alarmed over the mounting volume of credit that is being employed in the carrying of security loans, both by brokers and by individuals," he informed the annual convention of the ABA. "It is definitely known that many of our banks, and especially some institutions in our larger cities, have increased their loans on collateral securities to peaks never before attained. Some of them are overloaned—in some cases they are borrowers and in some cases, even if they are not borrowers, they have exhausted their secondary reserves."

"There has possibly not been a time this year when Wall Street has been so overcome by melancholy as it is now," observed the *New York Times* after prices plunged another five to ten points on October 1, the same day that Al Smith and John J. Raskob formally initiated demolition proceedings at the venerable Waldorf-Astoria Hotel, the site of the future Empire State Building. ("This historic building, known all over the world, must come down in the northward march of progress," beamed Smith brightly.) A few dozen blocks southward, the news that brokers' loans had risen by another $43 million—during a falling market in the last week of September—fell like a bombshell on the stock exchange.

Now the market was flat out scared. "Fear is in the saddle," remarked one veteran financial writer. On October 3, the New York Stock Exchange suffered its widest break of the year. U.S. Steel alone lost $80 million in value. Investment trust stocks went begging. When the smoke cleared, General Motors showed a paper loss of over $1.25 billion since its high point of 1929. Chrysler, which earlier had sold at 135, fell all the way down to 52. "The midnight blackness of the year's worst wide-open break in the market," mourned *Business Week,* "was enough to lead the strongest to despair."

And the weakest to suicide or violence. After suffering a loss of $124,-000 in the market over the past six months, a vice-president of the Earl Radio Corporation leaped to his death from the window of his room on the eleventh floor of the Hotel Shelton on Lexington Avenue in Manhattan. "We are broke," read the suicide note. "Last April I was worth $100,000. Today I am $24,000 in the red." In Chicago, gangsters who received margin calls from their brokers responded with threats of physical retaliation. One brokerage credit manager's office was dynamited into smithereens; stink bombs were tossed into several others. "A new form of wolf has invaded La Salle Street," snapped the city's deputy police commissioner:

"the racketeer who responds with a bomb when he is called for more margin."

In Germany, Foreign Minister Gustav Stresemann was dead at the age of fifty-one, felled by a massive stroke, his body and spirit worn out by his Herculean efforts at the recent reparations conference at The Hague, where the problems left unresolved by the springtime gathering of financial experts in Paris finally had been settled. When Stresemann's death was announced, the Berlin Stock Exchange—which had been recovering well—promptly fell to its lowest level since 1926. Hugenberg, Hitler, and the rest of the belligerent anti-Young forces took heart at the departure of their most dedicated foe. "While the Nationalist threat to invoke a national referendum for the purpose of rejecting the Young Plan agreement is not yet dangerous," decided an American observer, "it is undeniable that the man who could best have knocked that foolish proposal on the head is no longer here."

As the outstanding statesman of the Weimar Republic, Stresemann had been the one politician with sufficient influence, craft, and personal force to stem the drift toward anarchy and the reaction toward totalitarianism within Germany; he was also the most powerful spokesman for European reconciliation and reconstruction. "He was a man of great courage frankly facing the difficulties of his country and steadfastly meeting them," said Young in tribute. "He longed for a world at peace which meant to him something more than freedom from war and he was ambitious for his country to play its part in that accomplishment." Stresemann's death, mourned German diplomat and author Count Harry Kessler, was "an irreparable loss whose consequences cannot be foreseen. . . . This frightful year 1929 continues to garner its harvest. Hofmannsthal, Diaghilev, Stresemann. One landmark after another of the world, as I and my contemporaries knew it, disappears. Truly an *'Annee terrible.'* . . . What I fear, as a result of Stresemann's death, are very grave political consequences at home, with a move to the right by the People's Party, a breakup of the Coalition, and the facilitation of efforts to establish a dictatorship."

On October 4, the New York Stock Exchange was staggered again by the overwhelming force of a flood of involuntary liquidation. It was the heaviest day of trading since the debacle of March 26. Many small traders—"the little fellows," Wall Street condescendingly called them—found themselves unable to answer their brokers' frantic overnight calls for more margin; they watched their precious paper profits melt away as their

shares were dumped on the market for whatever they would bring. European investors, too, withdrew millions of dollars from the railroad and
blue-chip stocks that had enticed them into the market. Worried by the
bad news from London, the death of Stresemann, and the shocking decline on Wall Street, the Paris Bourse broke badly.

By this time, Mr. Edgar D. Brown of Pottsville, Pennsylvania, had
taken up residence in Los Angeles. As the market staggered through
September, he noticed that the price of the stocks National City's enterprising salesmen had sold him were, of course, declining in value. So
Brown decided to "clean out the whole business" at the first opportunity.

On October 4, while stock values were plummeting right and left,
Brown walked into the Los Angeles branch office of National City Bank
and asked them "to sell out everything." To his surprise, he was (by his
own account) "placed in the category of the man who seeks to put his own
mother out of his house. I was surrounded at once by all of the salesmen
in the place," Brown recalled, "and made to know that that was a very,
very foolish thing to do." Above all, the salesmen said, he would be especially shortsighted to sell his National City stock. So Brown reluctantly
agreed to maintain his portfolio intact for a little while longer.

"There is a more or less general feeling in the London market at the
week-end," reported a British correspondent of the *New York Times,*
"that the long continued Wall Street boom has at last passed its peak."

Winston Churchill and Bernard Baruch departed Chicago on the
evening of Saturday, October 5, in Baruch's private railway car. On the
way to New York, Churchill regaled his old friend with tales of his recent
tour through southern California; to Winston, it had seemed "a carnival
in fairyland." He and his family entourage had spent four days at newspaper publisher William Randolph Hearst's fabled castle and opulent pleasure dome, San Simeon, amid medieval tapestries, tennis courts, priceless
paintings, and wild game in the woods. Winston liked Hearst; he thought
him "a grave simple child—with no doubt a nasty temper—playing with
the most costly toys" (including actress Marion Davies, Hearst's mistress).

Before they left California, Hearst escorted the Churchills around
Hollywood, introducing them to film mogul Louis B. Mayer and a score
of actors including Wallace Beery, Pola Negri, Bebe Daniels, and Charlie
Chaplin. At the time, Chaplin—a temperamental perfectionist who stubbornly refused to join the stampede toward talking movies—was struggling to complete *City Lights,* the melodramatic story of a blind flower
girl befriended by the Little Tramp. Churchill found Chaplin, a native of

London's East End, a most agreeable companion ("He is a marvelous comedian—bolshy in politics & delightful in conversation"), and in ensuing years the two men spent many pleasant holidays at Churchill's estate at Chartwell.

During his sojourn on the West Coast, Churchill had noticed that every large hotel in Los Angeles possessed a stock market ticker: "You go & watch the figures being marked up on slates every few minutes," he explained in a note to his wife, Clementine. Although the figures had not been very good lately, especially for Winston's beloved Simmons stock, Churchill remained pleased with his broker—an agent with E. F. Hutton's investment firm—who was manipulating a £3,000 portfolio (about $15,-000) for the former chancellor of the Exchequer. "There is money enough to make us comfortable & well-mounted in London this autumn," Winston told Clemmie, "& you shd be able to do the nursery wing all right. Go on with yr plans & have it all ready for us to settle when I get back."

Doubtless Baruch provided his guest with a less encouraging outlook. As he weeded out his own portfolio, Baruch continued to sell RCA short and decided to dump his shares of Anaconda Copper for a nice profit.

Upon their arrival in New York on October 6, the Churchills took a suite of rooms at the Savoy-Plaza at Fifth Avenue and Fifth-ninth Street, where Winston waited, rather impatiently, for Prime Minister James Ramsay MacDonald to return to the city. MacDonald had arrived in New York on October 4 for an official three-week visit to North America. The first British Prime Minister to set foot in the United States while in office, MacDonald had come primarily to obtain a naval arms reduction agreement, or at least a tacit understanding, with President Hoover and Secretary of State Stimson. The Prime Minister fervently wished to cut Britain's already strained defense budget, and he believed that second-rate naval powers such as France, Italy, and Japan would be compelled to follow Britain's lead if he could confront them with a definite Anglo-American understanding. (Churchill, incidentally, fully supported MacDonald's crusade to quash the nagging and potentially troublesome naval rivalry between Britain and the United States. "We do not want to be perpetually talking and arguing about warships and cannon and all the instrumentalities of war," Winston had told an audience during his brief stay in Chicago. "We want these matters gradually but steadily to recede in importance in the public mind.") So, on the morning of October 4, tugboats in New York harbor tooted a salute, and a punctilious Grover Whalen welcomed MacDonald as he stepped off the liner *Berengaria;* following a ticker-tape parade up Broadway, Mayor Walker greeted the dour Scotsman at City Hall and generously presented him with the freedom of the city. Being a man who preferred to waste no time, MacDonald promptly departed for Washington.

After one night in the White House, MacDonald accompanied Hoover to the presidential fishing camp on the Rapidan River for the weekend. There the two men, dressed in casual hiking attire, spent Sunday morning strolling along the river bank, where the President pointed out the various rock dams he and his previous guests had fashioned. For three-quarters of an hour they sat on an old fallen log, discussing ships and peace as the clear mountain water swirled and burbled and swept around the smooth red and gray stones in its path. It was precisely the sort of quiet, contemplative encounter Hoover cherished so dearly.

The next day all the dignitaries, their spirits presumably refreshed, returned to Washington. While MacDonald indulged his penchant for sightseeing for several days, Hoover plunged back into the pounding routine of political life, resuming his interminable battle with the Senate over the provisions of the tariff readjustment bill, discussing the latest European economic conditions with S. Parker Gilbert, and reviewing—on the White House lawn—the officers and midshipmen of a Japanese naval training squadron. In a futile attempt to bolster the slumping stock market, Hoover publicly denied a rumor that Secretary Mellon—the speculators' best friend in the administration—was preparing to resign from the cabinet. For his part, Mellon gave out the cheerful news that the administration was considering a further tax cut of $200 million, providing further (and wholly unnecessary) relief for wealthy Americans in the higher income brackets.

Wall Street had celebrated a brief but sharp two-hour rally on October 5, the day MacDonald and Hoover journeyed to Virginia and Churchill and Baruch left Chicago for New York. The rebound continued on October 7, albeit with a relatively light trading volume, as the market demonstrated its much-ballyhooed ability to "forget its troubles overnight" and search "for the silver lining of every cloud." While Charlie Mitchell continued his annual round of discussions with bankers in Europe, his National City Bank stock soared to a new peak of $522 per share amid speculation that additional profitable mergers were on the horizon.

But on the eighth, the market turned irregular, and on the following day the retreat resumed. Unlike the recoveries of previous months, prices this time failed to surpass their earlier peaks. European speculators continued to withdraw immense quantities of funds from Wall Street. An increasing number of brokers suddenly realized that stock prices, despite the recent reaction, still remained out of touch with reality, and they freely advised their clients to liquidate all but the best securities. "We would go through portfolios with a fine-tooth comb," suggested one agency spokesman quoted in the *New York Times,*

> and weed out all issues which were not of first rank merit, which did not have unusually good prospects immediately ahead of them, which were not of the character that we would be willing, if necessary, to carry through a further reaction in average prices. . . . We believe that the unbridled enthusiasm for so-called "equities" is not a thing which can endure indefinitely, and that ultimately prices of even the best common stocks must return to a level where they can either be justified by current income or by probable income at some reasonably near future time.

Despite the wave of forced selling of impaired margin accounts in the first days of October, brokers' loans declined by only $91 million for the week ending October 9; in fact, the amount of corporate bootleg loans actually increased to a new high of nearly $4 billion. As Wall Street drifted apprehensively toward the ides of October, the nation's financial press repeated the familiar litany of dreary economic news. Production of steel and automobiles had badly outrun consumption; auto dealers were saddled with nearly twice as many unsold cars in stock as they had had a year earlier, forcing automakers to reduce production for the third consecutive month; steel mills were compelled to cut back sharply to 79 percent of capacity, well below the levels of the autumn of 1928. Money remained dangerously tight; wheat and cotton prices were weaker; building contracts in September 1929 ran 24 percent below the previous year; and the quantity of "undigested" securities on the stock market continued to rise in a most ominous fashion. "Business has really passed its high point and is about to start downward for a period of unknown duration," predicted the New York *Journal of Commerce:* "The truth is that in spite of all that has been said on the subject the country is in a very extended and badly protected position from the credit standpoint." The Chicago *Journal of Commerce* noted that "the present level of business activity is sufficiently below that established during the first seven and a half months of the year to indicate that something more than seasonal adjustments is influencing business," and the *New York Times* chimed in with the observation that "there is less snap in the general industrial situation."

As if it needed more bad news, Wall Street learned on October 11 that the commissioners of the Massachusetts Department of Public Utilities had disapproved a stock-splitting plan proposed by the Boston Edison Electric Illuminating Company. The company had wanted to exchange each $100 share of its common stock for four shares worth $25 apiece, presumably to cash in on the public's demonstrated affinity for low-priced securities. (One felt so much more like a capitalist if one owned four hundred shares of stock rather than a mere one hundred.) The Massachu-setts commissioners, however, determined that the utility company was in a dangerously vulnerable position, having made a regular practice of distributing virtually all its earnings in dividends "with little provision for depreciation or surplus"; besides, its stock already had risen "to such a point that no one, in our judgment, viewing it from the standpoint of an investment on the basis of its earnings, would find it to his advantage to buy it." In the heyday of the Hoover bull market, such a statement would have been considered the rankest heresy. "No public interest will be served by the reduction of the par value of the stock at this time," con-cluded the commissioners. "On the other hand, it is likely to encourage the belief in the minds of many innocent people that it is the forerunner of substantial increases in dividends, with the consequent result of their investing in stock at a very high price without their hopes being realized."

For the next few days the market appeared confused and disorgan-ized. The fall in public utility stocks, a direct result of the Massachusetts decision, represented almost the only noticeable trend. Trading volume was light. Brokers who noticed that it had become far easier to buy than sell stocks advised their customers to sit tight. There was no need to rush into a buying spree just yet, one well-known house said: "The market is going to be here for a long while. There is no particular incentive to buy stocks at this level."

Sunday, October 13, was a sparkling, crisp autumn day in Washington. President and Mrs. Hoover took advantage of the weather to stroll through the business district of the city, window-shopping along F Street and Pennsylvania Avenue, accompanied by only one Secret Service agent instead of the usual team of four. Hardly anyone paid any attention to the President.

Early the following morning, the Hoovers boarded a train for Phila-delphia, where they watched the fifth and final game of the World Series between the Athletics and the underdog Chicago Cubs. Philadelphia's longtime owner-manager, Connie Mack, had practically stolen the first game by unexpectedly starting veteran right-handed pitcher Howard Ehmke, who had won only seven games during the regular season. The canny Mack realized that the blinding background in the extra grand-stands installed above the ivy-covered walls of Chicago's Wrigley Field suited Ehmke's unorthodox side-armed delivery perfectly; the lanky thirty-five-year-old's tantalizing off-speed (and occasionally damp) pitches simply disappeared in the ocean of white shirts in the bleachers. Ehmke established a World Series record by striking out thirteen frustrated Cub batters, and the A's scored two runs in the top of the ninth to take the initial game, 3–1. (Ehmke, explained Mack, "has one good day a year, and he knows when it's coming.") In the second game, young Philadelphia slugger Jimmy Foxx stroked his second home run in as many games as the A's romped by a 9–3 score. But the Cubs—armed with the potent bats of Rogers Hornsby, Hack Wilson, and Kiki Cuyler—were not yet dead. The National League champions easily captured the third game, and led the fourth game, 8–0, until the roof caved in during the seventh inning. As Wilson (never a graceful fielder at the best of times) lost two routine fly balls in the sun, the Athletics stormed back to score ten runs, win the game, and take a 3–1 lead in the series.

So back the clubs went to Philadelphia for game five. Hoover, who knew his baseball, watched appreciatively as the Cubs' twenty-two-game winner Pat Malone nursed a 2–0 lead into the bottom of the ninth inning. Then lightning struck again. First, George William "Mule" Haas, the Athletics' veteran center fielder, stroked a two-run blast over the right-field fence to tie the score. Obviously shaken, Malone retired catcher Mickey Cochrane, but gave up a double to Al Simmons. Chicago manager Joe McCarthy ordered Malone to walk Jimmy Foxx intentionally. Then another oldster, thirty-five-year-old right fielder Ed "Bing" Miller, slapped a shot into the gap that rolled to the scoreboard, scoring Simmons from second, and the game and the series were over. Philadelphia mayor Harry A. Mackey—who temporarily forgot that he was sitting next to the President of the United States—whooped and shouted and ran out onto the field to slap Miller on the back as Hoover stood and applauded as enthusiastically as presidential neutrality and propriety allowed.

Accompanied by his former friend Al Smith, Mayor Jimmy Walker officially launched his reelection campaign on October 15 with a brief address at the recently dedicated headquarters of Tammany Hall. For the past few weeks, Fiorello La Guardia and the Socialist candidate, Norman Thomas, both had been hammering at the alleged incompetence of Walker and Grover Whalen and the aura of corruption that seemed to envelop City Hall. Thomas charged the Walker administration with "rule by racketeering": "Run a legal poolroom and you pay the police," the Socialist charged. "Run an illegal speakeasy and you pay the police. Get a permit from the Building Bureau or somewhere else and, directly or indirectly, pay for it. If you go to court, hire a fixer. If you don't want trouble, pay the racketeers and their politician friends. That is the rule in New York as in almost every other American city." Both challengers quickly discovered that their most potent issue was the unsolved murder of Arnold Rothstein. La Guardia, who revealed himself as an extraordinarily talented and versatile campaigner who could travel through the city's ethnic neighborhoods denouncing his honorable opponent in Italian, Yiddish, German, or English as circumstances demanded, insisted that "there must be a searching investigation into the activity or lack of it of the police and the District Attorney's office in connection with the Rothstein case," and he went on to boldly promise, "I will solve the Rothstein murder case within a very few days after I arrive at the City Hall."

The ceaseless charges of corruption were blessed with a considerable measure of validity when La Guardia revealed that a city magistrate named Albert Vitale had received a loan of nearly $20,000 from a Rothstein-owned mortgage company in 1928 to cover the judge's stock market losses. Vitale denied any wrongdoing or any personal connection with Rothstein, but after a flurry of spectacular revelations, reformers demanded that Governor Roosevelt appoint a special investigator to conduct an independent inquiry. Roosevelt, vacationing in Warm Springs, realized that such an action would place him in a no-win situation, and so he astutely refused to intervene in what was obviously a matter for the local authorities. The governor was hunting bigger game; during a visit to the Southeastern Fair and the Georgia Tech–North Carolina football game in Atlanta on October 11, Roosevelt again was introduced as "the next President of the United States." "I have learned not to get a swelled head when I am welcomed so," he replied modestly. "This past summer when I was traveling in rural New York, I was greeted by a similar gathering at one of the towns. Three or four hundred people were around the car. An old man turned the corner. 'What's all the fuss about,' he asked. 'It's Governor Roosevelt,' someone told him. 'Pshaw, I thought it was Lindbergh.' Only to tell you the truth," added Roosevelt, laughing, "he did not say 'pshaw.' "

Some political analysts were less certain that Roosevelt would receive the Democratic nomination in 1932. There was still considerable sentiment among party professionals for liberal businessman Owen Young, whom many envisioned as the candidate who could best rebuild the fences shattered by the divisive campaign of Al Smith in 1928. While Smith and Mayor Walker were busy preparing for their appearance at Tammany on the evening of October 15, Young—who had just enjoyed a marvelously entertaining dinner with Winston Churchill—journeyed down to the French Line pier at West Fifteenth Street to welcome the legendary scientist Marie Curie upon her arrival in the United States. Young had invited Madame Curie to attend the dedication of a new laboratory (graced by a statue of herself) at his alma mater, St. Lawrence University; while she was in America, Madame Curie also planned to tour the General Electric plant, attend the ceremony celebrating the fiftieth anniversary of Edison's invention of the incandescent lamp, and spend some time reminiscing with her old friends President and Mrs. Herbert Hoover.

As Owen Young whisked Madame Curie away in a waiting limousine, economist Irving Fisher of Yale University informed a gathering of businessmen at a Park Avenue club that stock prices had reached "what looks like a permanently high plateau"; Fisher said he expected "to see the stock market a good deal higher than it is today, within a few months." At almost exactly the same moment, Charlie Mitchell met with reporters in London before embarking upon his return voyage to America. Admittedly Mitchell was a little out of touch with the situation after spending the last four weeks conferring with bankers in the financial centers of Europe, but he felt fully justified in dismissing the concerns of apprehensive investors about recent events on Wall Street. "Although in some cases speculation has gone too far in the United States," Mitchell said, "the markets generally are now in a healthy condition. The last six weeks have done an immense good in shaking down prices. Many leading industrial securities are now at levels which would have been considered perfectly sound and conservative even by the standards of ten years ago. The market values have a sound basis in the general prosperity of our country." And Mitchell concluded that "all the basic industries are doing satisfactorily and unless something unforeseen occurs, should continue to do so. I cannot see anything, such as some people are warning us of, to check that continued expansion."

The following day, the federal government released its latest set of statistics, in which several leading economic indicators (steel, autos, freight loadings) continued their disturbing—but by no means precipitous—downhill slide. Wall Street reacted violently. The former speculative favorites took another nosedive, losing between $5 and $30 per share, as more than $2 billion in values were washed away by a deluge of selling orders. Thousands of small traders who had somehow managed to scrape together enough cash to cover their brokers' previous calls for additional margin finally found themselves busted. Not surprisingly, brokers reported that an increasing percentage of professional traders were now buying on the short side, betting that the market would continue its descent. By contrast, the "small fry" who could still raise a loan seemed to be banking on a sharp rebound; on October 17, the Federal Reserve Bank of New York reported that brokers' loans had risen over the past seven days by $88 million.

That evening, as Winston Churchill dined with Otto Kahn at the financier's resplendent mansion, a chilling northwest wind swept across New York City, uprooting trees with gusts of nearly sixty miles an hour, driving temperatures down to a frigid record low for the date, bringing the first snow flurries and a hint of the approaching winter to Wall Street.

# XV

# The Storm Breaks

"Lately it hasn't been the same old market."
—*Wall Street Journal, October 25, 1929*

Late on the afternoon of Sunday, October 20, Herbert Hoover left Washington on an overnight train bound for Detroit. Save for his weekend excursions to the Rapidan fishing camp, the journey marked the first time the President had been out of Washington since his inauguration. Frustrated by his inability to dominate the hidebound, obstreperous old men in the Senate, where the now grotesquely warped tariff reform measure was still being held hostage by powerful special interest lobbies, Hoover had determined that he needed to forge an equally potent body of public opinion that would make it politically inexpedient for senators to thwart his will. To do that, however, he needed to break out of his cherished isolation in the White House and reestablish whatever personal rapport he had previously enjoyed with American voters, and so the President embarked on a four-day public relations swing through the Midwest. Meanwhile, Winston Churchill, who had journeyed down to Washington to pay a perfunctory courtesy call on Hoover the previous day, remained in Washington long enough to lunch with Baruch and an assortment of legislators at the Capitol before setting off on a tour of Virginia's Civil War battlefields.

As the President's special train sped through Maryland, West Virginia, and Ohio, Wall Street tried to pick up the pieces after the latest disaster. In just two devastating hours on the previous morning (Saturday), more than 3,480,000 shares had changed hands, the second-heaviest trading volume for a Saturday in the history of the New York Stock Exchange. Once again the investment trusts and the large traders had stood on the sidelines and watched unflinchingly as prices plunged, triggering hundreds of stop-loss orders, which in turn sent nearly every issue further downward. From the opening gong, brokers flooded the phone lines with calls for more margin. "The rule," reported the financial columnist of the

*New York Times,* "was to attempt to reach the customer by telegraph or telephone and, if he did not immediately respond, sell him out at the market. The trading pace was so fast and furious that procrastination could not be permitted under the circumstances."

Over the next ten days, the dreams of an entire generation of Americans were shattered.

While Wall Street and the nation's investors awaited the advent of the coming week with mounting apprehension, a glittering array of political and business leaders—including the President—were calmly gathering in Michigan for one of the most elaborate spectacles ever staged in America. The affair began rather dismally for Hoover, who arrived in Detroit shortly after nine o'clock on the morning of Monday, October 21. The weather there was gray and miserable and thoroughly depressing, reminiscent of inauguration day in Washington. A cold, driving rain stung the President as he and his wife rode in an open car (at Hoover's request) from the railway station to Detroit Plaza. Despite the downpour, Hoover graciously waved his hat in response to the thousands of spectators who saluted him as he passed. After a brief visit and change of presidential overcoats at City Hall, the cavalcade proceeded—in the same open car, through more stinging rain—to Dearborn, where Henry Ford greeted the Hoovers with a warm lunch and dry clothes.

In honor of the fiftieth anniversary of Edison's invention of electric light, Ford had painstakingly resurrected the Menlo Park, New Jersey, laboratory in which his longtime friend had conducted his momentous experiments. Ford had transported every available weathered plank, brick, stone, and time-worn gadget from Menlo Park to Dearborn to reconstruct the laboratory, along with seven carloads of Jersey soil. "Why, Henry's even got that damn New Jersey clay here," Edison chuckled as he kicked a chunk out of the familiar dirt floor.

Around the centerpiece of Edison's lab, Ford had reassembled a nineteenth-century replica of Greenfield Village, the automaker's beloved boyhood home. Somewhat incongruously, he also had imported Longfellow's blacksmith shop and an Illinois courthouse where Abraham Lincoln had practiced law. There was even an antique (1860) three-car train with a wood-puffing locomotive, the Sam Hill, which carried Ford, Edison, and the President over the three miles from the modern railway tracks to the reassembled station of Smith's Creek. When they arrived at Greenfield, the world-famous trio spied a few of the other celebrities—the titans of American business—who had come to Dearborn to pay tribute to Edison. They all seemed to be enjoying themselves immensely among the nostalgic relics of the past, the past they had destroyed so thoroughly through their own contributions to American progress: John D. Rockefeller, Jr., raindrops dripping off the brim of his hat, stood chatting amiably with friends outside the cobbler's shop; Otto Kahn was slipping (but not quite falling) in the muddy clay as he sought to navigate himself into a one-horse shay; Charles Schwab absentmindedly stole a green apple from the picturesque general store; and lanky Owen Young descended nimbly from a polished horse-drawn cab and strode easily across the street toward the Clinton Inn (circa 1832).

A reporter asked the President for his opinion of the day's tumultuous events on the stock market. Hoover had no comment.

Chaos reigned on the floor of the New York Stock Exchange. By 10:15 Monday morning, the avalanche of sell orders overwhelmed the beleaguered ticker; by noon the system was running an hour late in reporting the shocking price declines. "Not since March," wrote John Kenneth Galbraith, "had the ticker fallen seriously behind on declining values. Many now learned for the first time that they could be ruined, totally and forever, and not even know it. And if they were not ruined there was a strong tendency to imagine it." Margin clerks strove frantically to contact their customers, often to no avail. It seemed as though a fresh wave of liquidation, each more powerful than the last, washed over the market every hour. Apprehensive investors who still possessed some measure of profits dumped their securities, too, as did professional bear raiders, adding to the downward pressure.

One of the stocks that suffered the worst beating that day was Auburn Auto—it had dropped over 10 percent of its value by 3:00 P.M., but the fall was much steeper in the early hours of trading—and one of Auburn Auto's major shareholders happened to be Groucho Marx. Groucho was awakened that morning by a call from his frantic broker.

"There's been a slight break in the market, Mr. Marx," the broker explained apologetically. "You'd better get down here with some cash to cover your margin."

"I thought I was covered," Groucho mumbled sleepily.

"Not enough for the way things are going. We'll need more. And you'd better hurry."

When Groucho arrived at the Long Island branch office of Newman Brothers and Worms, he was met with a scene that might have been farcical had it not been so tragic: "Ticker tape was knee-deep on the floor, people were shouting orders to sell, and others were frantically scribbling checks in vain efforts to save their original investments." Groucho managed to scrape together enough cash to cover his margin in Auburn Auto for the moment, but he had almost nothing left in reserve.

By the time the frantic shouting was over, 920 issues had been involved in the trading—the broadest market on record—and an aggregate volume of 6,091,870 shares had changed hands, the second busiest day of the year (behind only the debacle of March 26) and the third busiest in the history of the exchange. Trading was equally heavy on local exchanges in Chicago, Boston, San Francisco, and Philadelphia. The London Stock Exchange also closed weak and sharply down in sympathy with Wall Street. "Taken as a whole," reported the *New York Times,* "the character of the market left Wall Street both bewildered and frightened," and so the Hoover administration felt compelled to issue soothing statements from Washington, assuring the public that its economic experts were monitoring the situation carefully, and that there was "no evidence of a serious business or financial situation which could be held responsible for the decline in Stock Exchange values." Yale's Irving Fisher, too, attempted to bolster sagging investor confidence by proclaiming that "in my opinion, current predictions of heavy reaction affecting the general level of securities find little if any foundation in fact." Fisher contemptuously dismissed the day's break as a "shaking out of the lunatic fringe that attempts to speculate on margin"; the market, he implied, was well rid of such amateur speculators.

In Charlotte, North Carolina, the jury in the trial of the Gastonia Seven returned to the courtroom after deliberating for only fifty-seven minutes. They declared Fred Beal and his codefendants guilty of murder in the second degree for the killing of police chief Orville F. Aderholt on June 7.

Despite the scrupulously evenhanded conduct of the presiding judge, the trial really had not been about murder at all. The grotesquely emotional closing arguments of the state's prosecutor, Solicitor John G. Carpenter, revealed the deep-seated prejudices and hatreds that lay buried only slightly beneath the surface in the courtroom. "Do you believe in the flag of your country, floating in the breeze, kissing the sunlight, singing the song of freedom? Do you believe in North Carolina?" Carpenter asked the jury. The union organizers, he bellowed, his arms flailing wildly, had come into Gastonia as "fiends incarnate, stript of their hoofs and horns, bearing guns instead of pitchforks . . . sweeping like a cyclone and tornado to sink damnable fangs into the heart and lifeblood of my community." Carpenter claimed that the good citizens of Gastonia had withstood the menace patiently and peacefully "till the great God looked down from the very battlements of heaven and broke the chains and traces of their patience, and caused them to call the officers to the lot and stop the infernal scenes that came sweeping down from the wild plains of Soviet Russia into the peaceful community of Gastonia, bringing bloodshed and death, creeping like the hellish serpent into the Garden of Eden." Carpenter completed his summation by lying prone on the floor, in the image of the slain police chief; then he rose and grasped the hand of Aderholt's widow as he pledged the vengeance of the state upon the murderers. "It was a grotesque piece of viciousness that should never have had a place in a courtroom," decided the Raleigh *News and Observer.* But it worked.

The judge sentenced Fred Beal and the three other Northern defendants to serve between seventeen and twenty years in the state prison at Raleigh; the four Southerners (who were deemed somehow less culpable) received slightly lighter sentences of five to fifteen years. Defense attorneys, who condemned the jury for delivering a "class verdict," at once gave notice of appeal.

In nearby Asheville, Thomas Wolfe returned to his native city to celebrate the publication of his first novel, *Look Homeward, Angel,* which had appeared on October 18. (It was the second literary masterpiece to emerge from the South that month; William Faulkner's *The Sound and the Fury* had been published on October 7.) Wolfe's neighbors took considerable umbrage at Tom's flamboyant, unsparing, and often unflattering portrayal of life in rural Carolina, though Wolfe swore he had written a book filled with *"great* people who ought to be told about." At any rate, Wolfe cherished the long-sought opportunity to escape from New York and wander through the scenes of his youth, especially as the land basked in the glorious golden glow of autumn, when "the bee bores to the belly of the yellowed grape, the fly gets old and fat and blue, he buzzes loud, crawls slow, creeps heavily to death on sill and ceiling, the sun goes down in blood and pollen across the bronzed and mown fields of old October."

On Monday evening, October 21, Owen Young served as toastmaster at the formal dinner honoring Thomas Edison. The festivities were held in Dearborn, in a Ford-built duplicate of Philadelphia's Independence Hall. Hoover was present, as was John D. Rockefeller, Jr., Madame Curie, Henry and Edsel Ford, Gerard Swope, Will Rogers, George Eastman, and Adolph Ochs. Edison almost missed the ceremony; exhausted by the day's activities, the eighty-two-year-old inventor had to be coaxed by his wife and fortified with an invigorating glass of milk before he consented to enter the banquet room. The guests ate their dinner by flickering candlelight, to remind everyone of what life had been like before Edison's epochal invention. The proceedings at Dearborn were carried live, nationwide, over the CBS radio network; in their homes, millions of Americans turned off their lights, too, and listened in darkness or candlelight. Young presented a gracious personal tribute to Edison's "unconquerable will and unquenchable fire," and read aloud telegrams of congratulations from the Prince of Wales and Germany's President von Hindenburg, and then the gathering heard Albert Einstein's voice coming over a radio hookup from Berlin. Alas, the bashful Einstein read his tribute to Edison in a soft, halting, almost inaudible voice (it was only his second radio broadcast), and in German besides, and so hardly anyone knew what he was saying until the very end, when he closed with a benediction in English: "Good night, my American friend." After signing off, Einstein went straight home to bed.

Following dinner, all the Dearborn guests trooped down to the reconstructed laboratory, where Edison recreated his famous experiment. ("Light 'er up, Francis, light 'er up," Edison called to his assistant, and the incandescent lamp dutifully shone.) Then, at the conclusion of the ceremonies, President Hoover returned to the twentieth century and the modern train that took him to Cincinnati, where he boarded a steamboat and traveled down the Ohio River through a cold, drenching rain to Louisville. The exhausted Edison collapsed shortly after the celebration ended and had to spend the next twenty-four hours recuperating at Ford's home.

From Paris, General Pershing cabled Baruch: "CONFIDENTIAL. WHAT DO YOU THINK OF THE GENERAL SITUATION. WOULD YOU HOLD SELL OR BUY ANACONDA. IF SELL WHAT WOULD YOU BUY. PLEASE REPLY." Back came the reply from Baruch: "I WOULD STAND PAT. BARUCH." Bernard graphically displayed his confidence by purchasing 1,400 shares of Warner Brothers stock and another 1,800 shares of one of his favorite issues, American Smelting. Unfortunately, no record exists of what he sold that day.

Although Manhattan was buffeted by fifty-mile-an-hour winds on Tuesday, October 22—several women were literally picked up by the gale and thrown against shop windows or into the street—the stock exchange observed a rare and blessedly peaceful day. Prices bounced amiably back and forth in moderate trading, gaining early in the day and then sliding back down toward the close. Financial analysts attributed the mild recovery in large part to the forcefully optimistic statement issued that morning by Charlie Mitchell upon his return from Europe on the *Majestic*. Pressed by reporters for his comments about the recent turbulence on the stock exchange, Mitchell emphatically declared that people were paying far too much attention to the so-called glut of "undigested securities" and the level of brokers' loans; the public, Mitchell joked, seemed to be suffering from "brokers' loanitis." The shake-out had actually been an encouraging sign, the banker insisted: "The present market decline is a healthy reaction which has probably overrun itself and there is nothing alarming about it. In a market like this, fundamentals are the thing to look for and if you could show me anything wrong with the situation generally, then I would be concerned. Brokers' loans if better understood would cease to be a factor. There should be nothing alarming about their present rise."

From his perch in Wellesley, the owlish Roger Babson refused to budge from his gloomy forecast. "This rebound will probably be only temporary," Babson hooted, "and the next downward movement will reach new lows in many instances."

In Los Angeles, Mr. Edgar D. Brown (formerly of Pottsville, Pennsylvania) kept trying to unload his stock portfolio. Alas, he was not successful. "I realize that this testimony sounds rather foolish," Brown later told a congressional investigating committee, "to think that a man can not go in and say, 'Sell that stock' and walk out. But it was not as easy as it sounds, because each time I would go to sell it they [meaning the salesmen at the National City branch in L.A.] would call my attention to the fact that it had gone up a couple of points." The salesmen told Brown that it was far more likely that his National City stock—then selling at slightly more than $500 per share—would reach 1,500 than dive below 300.

On the morning of Wednesday, October 23, while Hoover was still steaming downriver through a fog toward Louisville, the sun was shining brightly in New York; but Wall Street opened the day in a haze of uncertainty. Those who confidently expected Tuesday's halfhearted rally to continue were disappointed as the much-touted "organized buying support" failed to appear. By noon it was obvious that the market was heading for another sharp fall. And this time even the strongest nerves cracked.

Terror struck the stock exchange that afternoon. Selling orders deluged the market; prices plunged violently. It seemed as if everybody wanted to get out. In the last hour of trading, between two and three o'clock, more than 2.6 million shares changed hands. Investors watched, stunned, as their fortunes melted away. "In brokerage offices in Wall Street as well as throughout the land, the chairs were full of customers," reported one observer, "but they were nervous, excited and tense crowds of men and women who watched their stocks whirled about in the market maelstrom, and the chatter and brightness of the usual brokerage office scene was entirely missing."

In the upper Midwest, the unseasonable rainstorm that had plagued President Hoover's tour suddenly changed to snow and sleet, knocking down telephone and telegraph wires, making communication with Wall Street impossible and rendering speculators wholly ignorant of events in the East. Rumors ran rampant through the region, frightening demoralized customers into selling everything to salvage whatever they could. One brokerage house reported that its out-of-town customers were selling five times as many stocks as they were buying.

It was the second heaviest trading day in Wall Street history: 6,374,-960 shares changed hands. Reliable estimates placed the total losses for the day at more than $4 billion on the New York Stock Exchange alone—nearly 5 percent of the value of all listed securities. More than 170 stocks hit new lows for the year, including RCA, General Motors, Montgomery Ward, Chrysler, and Sinclair Oil. According to the widely venerated Dow Theory, formulated by the late financial analyst Charles H. Dow, this latest decline meant that Wall Street was now officially in the grasp of a major bear market.

Thousands of margin traders who had successfully weathered the earlier storms were wiped out in the flood. "At the largest commission houses," reported the *New York Times,* "it was admitted that yesterday was the saddest day margin speculators have passed through in recent years." Brokers were now demanding collateral worth as much as 75 percent of the market value of certain stocks; those who couldn't raise it were sold out. To raise enough cash to stave off complete disaster—Auburn Auto had dropped another seventy-seven points that day—Groucho Marx had been forced to borrow money from the bank and on his insurance. Then he mortgaged his house, the precious home for which he had saved for so many years.

One banker endeavored to find a silver lining in the black cloud that hovered threateningly over Wall Street. "It will send back to work many people who have been sitting around brokerage offices for a year or so on the trail of easy money," he claimed, not joking at all. "I have heard thousands of reports of merchants, farmers, and men and women in all walks of life literally giving up their businesses to watch the stock market. Most of them will, by necessity, have to go back to earning their living in normal ways."

Perhaps. But everything had changed over the past few months. Now all the support underlying the inflated bull market price structure had been washed away. All that was left were the rotten beams. That evening, as Herbert Hoover's presidential special left Louisville on the return trip to Washington, an "avalanche" of margin calls went out from Wall Street through the country.

Thursday, October 24.

At 9:45 A.M., John J. Raskob was sitting and fidgeting in his private office at 230 Park Avenue, glaring at the ticker for a full fifteen minutes before the market opened. Raskob reportedly had donned a wristwatch that morning for the first time in years. "I need to know the time," he explained lamely to his puzzled valet.

Anticipating disorder, Grover Whalen dispatched a squadron of police wagons to the financial district and instructed them to block the narrow entrance from Broadway to Wall Street.

On the floor of the exchange, nervous and exhausted brokers and clerks—many of whom had worked in their offices through the night to clear away the backlog of business that remained from Wednesday afternoon—took up their posts early. Nearly all the 1,100 members of the exchange were present, about 300 more than on a normal business day.

Matthew Josephson, who had forsaken a brief and not terribly successful career as a stockbroker to pursue writing as a full-time profession (and who had obtained the requisite financial independence by doubling his modest inheritance in the market), rode the subway to his broker's downtown boardroom that morning. "It was a minute or two before 10:00 A.M. as I reached the Wall Street station," Josephson recalled more than forty years later. "I heard—and I can still hear it—the sound of running feet, the sound of fear, as people hastened to reach posts of observation before the gong rang for the opening of trading."

In the words of one Wall Street old-timer, the market opened "like a bolt out of hell." Trading was extraordinarily heavy, involving more than 1,600,000 shares in the first thirty minutes alone. Until 10:30 the market seemed uncertain, directionless. Then it plunged straight down, and no power on earth could stop it.

A furious wave of selling engulfed the exchange. Good stocks, bad stocks, all were tossed indiscriminately into the maelstrom. Blocks of ten to thirty thousand shares of stock were unloaded wholesale upon the sinking market by frantic brokers who watched helplessly as prices dropped five or ten points *between each sale* of high-priced issues such as RCA, AT&T, and U.S. Steel. Mob psychology reigned unchecked. Minute by minute, the violence of the selling movement kept increasing until the market broke under the strain and became completely demoralized.

At ten minutes before eleven o'clock, a Wall Street shoeshine boy named Pat Bologna—who had managed to accumulate several thousand dollars from his wealthy and generous customers, and had invested it all in the market—stepped apprehensively into a brokerage customers' room near his station. The turbulent scene he witnessed remained burned into his memory for decades thereafter:

> In the crowd there's a Chinaman wearing a hat which rests on his ears. He's got a dead cigar in a mouth of dead teeth. He's standing on tip-toe to see over the shoulders of a woman wearing a big fancy hat. She's holding out her wedding ring and shouting "you want more margin—you can't have more margin." He's drunk as a lord. Everybody is shouting. They're all trying to reach the glass booths where the clerks are. Every-

body wants to sell out. The boy at the quotation board is running scared. He can't keep up with the speed of the way stocks are dropping. The board's painted green. The guy who runs it is Irish. He's standing at the back of the booth, on the telephone. I can't hear what he's saying. But a guy near me shouts, "the sonofabitch has sold me out!"

Doubtless the broker in question had little choice. Prices were collapsing so rapidly that many stocks were virtually worthless as collateral. Frighteningly, the ticker system was completely overwhelmed by the deluge—by 11:30, it was running forty-eight minutes late, which meant that the quotations it displayed were completely worthless, since stocks might have lost twenty or thirty points in the interval—and so most customers and brokers literally had no idea of where they stood. The market had gone blind. Panic ensued. Speculators sought to unload their stocks even more frantically than they had tried to buy them at the height of the boom; terror-stricken shouts of "Sell! Sell at the market!" echoed through boardrooms across the nation.

At the scene of the crash, however, the victims remained strangely subdued. When an inquisitive British journalist who was visiting an acquaintance in Manhattan wandered down to Wall Street to witness the human aspects of the unfolding catastrophe, he soon found himself swept up in "a sort of silent army streaming in the same direction." By the time the Englishman reached the financial district, a crowd had already gathered around the exchange: "Its sound was subdued, a kind of murmur, hardly more than a whisper, broken occasionally by the distinct, surrealistic cackle of an isolated hysterical laugh." The people—secretaries, businessmen, middle-class managers—drifting purposelessly back and forth through the narrow canyons of Wall Street, from the Trinity Church clock to the docks of the Cuba mail steamers, seemed to be dazed, overcome, wandering in a state of shock, unable to accept the reality of the cataclysm that was swallowing them up. A dozen movie cameras recorded the scene for posterity. "Photographs taken around noon that day of the front of the Sub-Treasury," remarked John Brooks, "show people standing on all its steps, lined up and looking blandly straight ahead as if posed to record the membership of some sort of organization. Their faces show no excitement or hysteria or chagrin. They stare in the way a caught fish stares as it lies on the beach or in the creel." Sometimes they could hear a vague, weird roar emanating from the thousand shouting men inside the exchange building.

The most horrifying hour came between 11:15 and 12:15 when numerous stocks could find no buyers *at any price.* These were the dreaded "air pockets," when prices shot straight down in a devastating free fall into an abyss that seemingly had no bottom. The *Wall Street Journal* deemed it "probably the most demoralized condition in stock market history," and even that was an understatement. The dizzying slide triggered the thousands of stop-loss orders that honeycombed the trading structure, continually releasing more waves of a seemingly never-ending flood of securities onto the beleaguered market. "By eleven-thirty, the market had surrendered to blind, relentless fear," wrote Galbraith. On the floor of the exchange, hysterical members began to resort to physical violence, pushing and shoving their colleagues out of the way to execute handfuls of selling orders among the mounting chaos. At Post Four, where Anaconda Copper and General Motors were traded, there was a sudden cry as a trader's frayed nerves suddenly snapped; a witness recalled seeing "a fat, perspiring man [who] became almost hysterical, yelling orders that made no sense until some friends seized him by the arm and led him away."

"Fear, running through the jungle like a flame, strong as ever," wrote one spectator. "Doom still makes a crackling sound, like summer thunder. Thousands of minor clerks and small trades-people, hearing faint noises of railroads they had never seen, mines they had never worked, steel they had never tempered, fled before the terror of dark."

Western Union's cable division shattered its old volume record as selling orders poured in from around the globe. Telephone lines throughout Manhattan were jammed as thousands of frantic customers tried to contact their brokers. At the Corner, where J.P. Morgan and Company's offices stood, the secretary of senior partner Thomas Lamont finally managed to contact Charlie Mitchell to request his presence at an emergency meeting of the heads of the four largest banks in the city.

John J. Raskob ate lunch alone in his office. He refused to leave the ticker by the side of his desk.

The Gastonia County grand jury—the same body that had indicted Fred Beal and his associates for the murder of police chief Aderholt—refused to indict the nine men whom the state had charged with the murder of Ella May Wiggins. All nine were released immediately. Neither did the grand jury bring indictments against the men accused of kidnapping Ben Wells. In both cases, the foreman cited "insufficient evidence" as the reason for the refusal to indict. The presiding judge instructed the grand jury to continue its investigation of the Wiggins case, and Governor Gardner posted a $400 reward—the maximum permissible under law—for the arrest and conviction of the guilty persons, but everyone knew the case was really closed. "It will not be safe for any so-called labor agitator to be caught nosing around here any time soon," snarled the Gastonia

*Gazette.* "The folks here are simply not going to put up with it any longer."

In Washington, the Federal Reserve Board—which was in direct contact with officials in Wall Street—met in continuous session from 10:45 to 1:00. Not surprisingly, the board concluded that the panic then in progress was the result of "undue speculation" and an insanely inflated securities market. For the time being, the board decided to do nothing, to simply wait and see if the market would right itself.

Following an early lunch with Bernard Baruch uptown, Winston Churchill went for a stroll along Wall Street. Around noon, a stranger recognized the former chancellor of the Exchequer and invited him into the visitors' gallery of the stock exchange to witness the carnage. By that time, some measure of order had been restored in the trading arena; Churchill—who perhaps expected to see blood on the floor—later reported, "The spectacle that met my eyes was one of surprising calm," and doubtless it appeared far less violent than, say, a full-scale engagement on the western front. "There they were," Churchill went on, "walking to and fro like a slow-motion picture of a disturbed ant heap, offering each other enormous blocks of securities at a third of their old prices and half their present value, and for many minutes together finding no one strong enough to pick up the sure fortunes they were compelled to offer."

Churchill may have viewed the scene with equanimity, but the exchange authorities did not; at 12:30 they ordered the visitors' gallery closed. This action only exacerbated the rumors of disaster that already swirled around the street. Someone said that eleven speculators had killed themselves that morning; someone else said that the exchange was going to suspend trading for the first time since the outbreak of the Great War in August 1914. (In fact, that option had been considered but was summarily rejected.) In an incident that has since passed into Wall Street folklore, a curious crowd gathered around a construction project where a workman sat perched on a steel girder, high above the ground; though the man was only taking a lunch break, peacefully smoking his pipe, everyone assumed he was a ruined investor preparing to commit suicide.

Between noon and one o'clock, as the ticker brought the heartbreaking price quotations of the previous hour into hundreds of brokers' offices across the country, "one saw men looking defeat in the face," according to Frederick Lewis Allen's memorable account of the tragedy. One ruined investor "was slowly walking up and down, mechanically tearing a piece of paper into tiny and still tinier fragments. Another was grinning shamefacedly, as a small boy giggles at a funeral. Another was abjectly beseeching a clerk for the latest news of American & Foreign Power. And still another was sitting motionless, as if stunned, his eyes fixed blindly upon the moving figures on the screen, those innocent-looking figures that meant the smash-up of the hopes of years."

By one o'clock, the staggering sum of $11.25 billion in market values had simply disappeared.

On the Cunard liner *Berengaria,* one day out of New York on the return trip from England, passengers watched in stunned silence as the board boy posted the latest figures in the ship's brokerage office. The office was crammed to capacity; those who were forced to remain outside simply sat silently, helplessly, gazing at the deck and the ocean as their fortunes evaporated. Uneaten meals grew cold in the dining rooms; no one was playing shuffleboard or making idle conversation. One passenger likened the dismal scene to a "death watch."

Back on Broadway, a few bold souls were trying to turn the disaster to their advantage; one enterprising speculator called his broker and asked for the latest quotation on National Casket. (It, too, was down.)

Charlie Mitchell was the first to arrive at the Corner for his midday meeting with the other financial titans of the city. The sight of the rugged chairman of National City Bank in his shirtsleeves, with a grave expression on his face, striding purposefully into the temple of J.P. Morgan and Company, provoked an intense feeling of apprehension among the crowd that had gathered outside. Was Mitchell there to stop the panic, or to save his own skin? (The mob already had been staggered by a rumor that John D. Rockefeller, Jr., had been quietly liquidating his non–Standard Oil stocks for the past few weeks.) Mitchell was followed closely by Albert H. Wiggin, chairman of Chase National Bank, William C. Potter, president of the Guaranty Trust Company, and Seward Prosser, chairman of the Bankers Trust Company. Together these men represented banks with approximately $6 billion of capital. George Harrison, governor of the Federal Reserve Bank of New York, also attended the meeting. For twenty minutes the bankers conferred with Lamont in private. Newspaper reporters crowded around the entrance to 23 Wall Street in eager anticipation. Then Mitchell emerged into the sunlight, looking serious but confident and certainly not downcast, and an audible sigh of relief ran through the throng assembled in the street.

As spokesman for the bankers' consortium, Lamont held a brief press conference. "There seems to be some distress selling on the Stock Exchange so far as we can see," Lamont announced calmly. (Frederick Lewis Allen later characterized this utterance as "one of the most remarkable understatements of all time.") "So far as we can find there are no houses that are in difficulty and reports from brokerage houses indicate margin position is satisfactory. . . . We consider the situation which arose on the

floor late Wednesday afternoon and today more in the nature of a technical situation rather than a fundamental one."

Then the bankers put their money—or rather, their customers'
money—on the line. They formed a pool—estimates of the total value
ranged from $20 million to $240 million—to purchase certain pivotal
stocks. The bankers' objective was to restore investor confidence by plug-
ging the most visible holes in the dike. Obviously they could not support
the price of every stock, nor did they necessarily believe they could avert
a substantial decline in the long run. What was most important at that
moment was an ostentatious display of faith in the market, to rally investors and prevent the sort of paralyzing holocaust that could jeopardize the
entire banking and financial structure of the nation.

So Richard Whitney, vice-president of the New York Stock Exchange
and the brother of Morgan partner George Whitney, walked smoothly
across the floor of the exchange at 1:30 that afternoon. Trading came to
an abrupt halt as the handsome and athletic Whitney, a magnificent figure
of a man, headed straight for the post where U.S. Steel was traded. In a
loud voice that seemed to reverberate throughout the building, Whitney
asked the price of the last bid for U.S. Steel; "195," they told him. Whitney
then placed an order for ten thousand shares at *205*, 10 points above the
previous asking price. As the members of the exchange watched in wonder and joy, cheering him on, Whitney made his way around the floor,
placing other equally strong orders.

From his estate in Hertfordshire, England, Jack Morgan cabled his
approval of Lamont's handling of the crisis: "Very glad indeed you were
able to get a strong party to work to act quickly and with judgement in
the matter." Morgan later told reporters that he felt "very proud" at the
way his subordinates had maintained their composure during the panic;
he said he felt rather like "the successful schoolmaster who finds his pupils
doing better than he ever could himself."

When Raskob heard the news of Whitney's exploits, he knew the
worst had passed. The bankers' strategy worked; the market steadied. In
the final hour of trading, a rally brought prices of some issues back toward
(but generally still below) their opening levels. Baruch joined the advance
by purchasing two thousand shares of Anaconda (at 104½), one thousand
shares of his favorite American Smelting, and four hundred shares of
Warner Brothers. Since the ticker did not catch up with the day's final
prices until 7:08 that evening, no one knew what these were when the
closing gong ended Thursday's tumultuous session at 3:00 P.M. (The sound
of the gong was accompanied by a disgusted chorus of "boos, hoots, and
Bronx cheers" from the exhausted brokers—many of whom still held
unexecuted orders in their hands—on the floor of the exchange.) When the

masses of paper were finally sorted out, the Dow Jones average ended the day off only about 6 points, which meant that speculators who possessed vast resources, like Billy Durant, managed to weather the storm only slightly worse for the wear. But for the "little people" who had sold out, or had been sold out by their brokers during the panic, even this partial recovery made absolutely no difference at all. Estimates of margined accounts that had failed during the height of the panic ranged between 20 and 70 percent; whatever the precise numbers, it was indisputable that the casualties had been far worse than in any previous break. And when it was all over, the market had lost $3 billion in stock values. Nevertheless, the late afternoon rally convinced Secretary Mellon and the Federal Reserve Board that they need take no drastic action for the time being.

The ripple effect of Black Thursday's stock market crash spread quickly throughout the nation and the international financial community. In Chicago, wheat prices broke sharply in frenzied trading, descending to a new seasonal low. The London Stock Exchange slumped badly, and trading on a subsidiary London exchange continued until long after dark as speculators sought to unload their American securities at almost any price. Smug British newspapers could scarcely conceal their glee at Wall Street's discomfort because they thought that sanity would now return to the world of commerce. "Now that the long pent-up storm has broken, we may reasonably expect sunnier days," chortled the *Evening Standard.* "The crash of the New York Exchange has come, as it was bound to come," crowed the *Daily Express* with considerable self-satisfaction. "The awakening of the diverse elements smitten by the gambling fever is rude and convulsive, and probably it will not in the least console them to know that until they did awaken—that is, until America's speculative fever was reduced to normal—there could be no financial stability anywhere." "For its own sake," added the *Star,* "London is glad of what has happened, although it sympathizes with the thousands of small investors who have lost heavily. London has suffered for the last two years from the wave of American speculation which broke yesterday. Not only were investors drawn away from England but the incessant borrowing of New York drew British money across the Atlantic in a glittering stream."

Herbert Hoover returned to Washington at 3:30 that afternoon and went immediately to the White House. He spent the rest of the day dictating replies to the pile of mail that had accumulated during his four-day Midwestern tour. The President made no public comment about the events on Wall Street.

The Senate, though, had plenty to say, as usual. The day's destruction of several billions of dollars' worth of stock values strengthened the anti-speculative forces in the capital and spawned a spate of I-told-you-so statements from various senators. "A year ago I said whatever went up must come down," huffed South Dakota's Senator Norbeck, chairman of the Banking and Currency Committee. "It is unfortunate that it did not come earlier. There would have been less damage." Senator Fletcher of Florida, the ranking minority member on the committee, agreed that "it was a gambler's market and had to topple. We can check it only by curbing the flow of money to Wall Street." Carter Glass, of course, blamed the debacle on his personal bête noire, Charlie Mitchell. "I am not surprised at what has occurred on the stock market," Glass snapped. "The present trouble is due largely to Charles E. Mitchell's activities. That man more than forty others is responsible for the present situation."

But Mitchell resolutely stuck to his guns. At about six o'clock, following a second meeting with his banking colleagues and Thomas Lamont, Mitchell obdurately insisted, "I am still of the opinion that this reaction has badly overrun itself." That unequivocal sentiment was seconded by most of the city's large brokerage houses, who sent out encouraging letters to their clients after the close of business. While recommending that its customers keep their margin accounts sufficiently supported with ready capital, Merrill Lynch and Company recommended that investors "with available funds should take advantage of this break to buy good securities," and the giant investment firm of Hornblower and Weeks republished in more than eighty major metropolitan newspapers an advertisement it had originally run in 1926: "We believe that present conditions are favorable for advantageous investment in standard American securities."

Reactions to the harrowing events of the day varied widely among investors who had been caught in the smashup. One financial journalist who made a tour of brokerage offices at the end of the day swore that he found a surprising lack of despair among customers, some of whom had lost huge fortunes in paper profits. A typical easy-come, easy-go comment came from a young widow who had watched a nest egg of $1 million disappear during the morning's plunge. "I had a perfectly stunning time while it lasted," she explained. "I never knew before what fun it was to make money. No wonder you men want to monopolize the business."

Others were less flippant about the destruction of their dreams. A finance company secretary in Seattle shot himself. A Manhattan realtor named Abraham Germansky disapeared; he was last seen walking up Broadway, hysterically tearing ticker tape to shreds. The crash wiped out Groucho Marx. At the low point of the day, his Auburn Auto stock had been down by seventy points; it finished the afternoon with a twenty-five-point loss. Groucho's cherished financial security had vanished. Not only had he lost his investment of a quarter of a million dollars, he was deeply in debt. When everything he had worked and saved for had been irretrievably sacrificed, Groucho paid a final call to the Long Island branch office of Newman Brothers and Worms. The only other person in the room was his broker, a man named Green. "He was a pathetic sight," recalled Groucho's son, Arthur. "He [Green] was sitting in front of the now-stilled ticker-tape machine, with his head buried in his hands. Ticker tape was strewn around him on the floor, and the place smelled of stale cigars and looked as if it hadn't been swept out in a week."

Groucho tapped Green on the shoulder and said, "Aren't you the fellow who said nothing could go wrong—that we were in a world market?"

"I guess I made a mistake," the broker wearily replied.

"No, I'm the one who made a mistake," snapped Groucho. "I listened to you."

"I lost all my money, too," said Green.

"Well, buck up," Groucho said with false gaiety. "Don't let it get you down. Just remember—twenty years from now you'll be looking back on these as the good old days."

In a curious twist of fate, a singer named George Olsen, who was headlining the nightly bill of entertainment at the Hotel Pennsylvania just off Broadway, was scheduled to introduce that evening a new song that originally had been written for a movie called *Chasing Rainbows.* Fearing a hostile reception to the tune after the market's crash, Jack Yellen, the lyricist, peered anxiously into the hotel's dining room and saw, to his dismay, "a handful of gloom-stricken diners . . . feasting on gall and wormwood." When Olsen looked at the title on the sheet music, he gave a hollow laugh, but passed out the parts anyway. The song was entitled "Happy Days Are Here Again." "Sing it for the corpses," Olsen said to the band. "After a couple of choruses," Yellen recalled, "the corpses joined in sardonically, hysterically, like doomed prisoners on their way to the firing squad. Before the night was over, the hotel lobby resounded with what had become the theme song of ruined stock-market speculators as they leaped from hotel windows."

1. The Marx Brothers—Groucho, Harpo, and Chico—cavorting in the carefree days before the crash.

2. "Scarface" Al Capone.

3. The St. Valentine's
Day Massacre, Chicago,
February 14, 1929.

4. Henry Ford meets with President Herbert Hoover at the White House.

5. Owen D. Young. His role in the European war debt negotiations earned him *Time* magazine's Man of the Year Award.

6. Governor Al Smith, "The Happy Warrior," with his trademark brown derby.

7. Edward, Prince of Wales, learning firsthand of the appalling poverty in Britain's coal-mining villages.

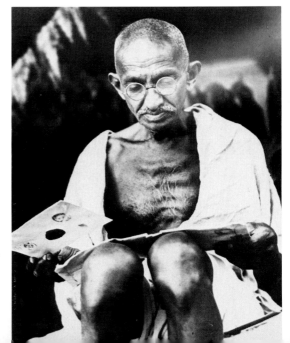

8. Mohandas K. Gandhi, shortly after his celebrated march to the sea.

9. F. Scott Fitzgerald accompanying wife, Zelda, and daughter, Scottie, on one of their frequent trips across the Atlantic.

10. Will Rogers, one of the survivors of the Great Crash.

11. Adolf Hitler vehemently denounced Germany's capitalist and communist enemies; the German economic collapse in the wake of the Great Crash helped bring Hitler and the Nazis to power.

12. Winston Churchill and Charlie Chaplin outside Chaplin's studio in Los Angeles.

13.  Black Thursday: anxious investors across from the New York Stock Exchange watched helplessly as their fortunes vanish.

14. Wall Street on Black Tuesday: the worst financial disaster
in American history.

# XVI

# In the Eye of the Hurricane

"If you've been in the game 30 minutes and you don't know
who the patsy is, *you're* the patsy."
—*Anonymous poker player*

On Friday morning, October 25, the market opened in a wholly unspectacular manner. Sheer physical and emotional exhaustion accounted for a large measure of order; bleary-eyed brokers and their clerks were so worn out from the previous day's frenzied activity and the strain of working through a second straight night (some investment firms had rented whole floors of midtown hotels for their employees) that, absent a bolt of lightning from the outside, the exchange simply lacked the energy to endure another five hours of chaos. Sightseers who took special excursion buses to witness firsthand the excitement in the financial district were greatly disappointed, though they did get to see some of the additional four hundred patrolmen and one hundred detectives Grover Whalen had dispatched to Wall Street early that morning.

Although there appeared to be a general, if unspoken, agreement that the long, glorious prosperity party was finally over (one farsighted Broadway brokerage firm even went so far as to prepare a special list of "depression-proof" stocks for its clients), the mood of the financial community on the Day After the Crash was unquestionably upbeat. Optimistic statements abounded in Washington and Wall Street as the nation's political and business leaders sought to rally public confidence. From the White House, President Hoover issued the statement that later became so famous and so maligned: "The fundamental business of the country, that is, the production and the distribution of commodities, is on a sound and prosperous basis." Although Hoover admitted that "the construction and building industries have been to some extent affected by the high interest rates induced by stock speculation" and that "there has been some seasonal decrease in one or two other industries," he steadfastly maintained that "these movements are of secondary character when considered in the whole situation." (Despite alleged pressure from the Morgan-led bankers' consortium, however, Hoover refused to go so far as to say that common stocks represented a bargain after the previous day's price decline.) Assistant Secretary of Commerce Klein followed Hoover's reassurances with a radio address to the nation in which he emphasized "the fundamental soundness of that great mass of economic activities on which the well-being of the vast majority of us all depends." Though the fearsome panic of Black Thursday had made a spectacular psychological impression, Dr. Klein deprecated its long-term importance to the American economy: "The number of citizens whose buying ability has been affected by the decline in the value of speculative securities is not very large; their purchases do not make up a very significant fraction of the demand for goods."

On Wall Street, the Morgan-led bankers' consortium genially informed reporters that it still possessed a substantial reserve of funds should the market require further support. "We have by no means used our big ammunition yet," a spokesman said. Other financial statesmen were equally confident. Charlie Mitchell, of course, insisted that "fundamentals remain unimpaired." "There's no question that the market yesterday got completely out of hand and prices were carried to levels beyond reason," stated F. Abbot Goodhue, president of the International Acceptance Bank. "Conditions do not warrant such a decline as we have witnessed. . . . The banking situation is distinctly good and fundamental conditions are sound." Walter Teagle of Standard Oil claimed that there had been no "fundamental change" for the worse in the petroleum business. Steel baron Charles Schwab grandly proclaimed, "In my long association with the steel industry I have never known it to enjoy a greater stability or more promising outlook than it does today," and the president of the Atcheson, Topeka, and Santa Fe Railroad System confidently agreed: "The business outlook in our territory is all right. I don't know why it should be affected by the break in stocks."

Nor did most of the press discern cause for serious concern. The editors of *Business Week* deplored the fact that the recent national obsession with Wall Street had grossly distorted the public's perception of business conditions. "At this time it is especially deplorable that such exaggerated emphasis should be placed upon what is going on in Wall Street," they argued. "There is no reason why business or the government should act at any time as though security trading or security values are of paramount importance in our economic life." All that had happened, suggested the *New York Times,* was that the eternal verities of economic life had been confirmed once again; the so-called New Era had been exposed as a complete sham. "No Iowa farmer will tear up his mail-order blank because Sears-Roebuck stock slumped," remarked the New York

*Sun* confidently. "No Manhattan housewife took the kettle off the kitchen stove because Consolidated Gas went down to 100. Nobody put his car up for the winter because General Motors sold 40 points below the year's high. So long as American industry is on a sound basis we shall have prosperity."

Yet there were a few disturbing, dissenting voices. B. C. Forbes, writing in the New York *American,* argued that the financial ruin of at least several hundred thousand speculators was bound to have a substantial economic impact: "Just as the stock-market profits stimulated the buying of all kinds of comforts and luxuries, so will stock-market losses inevitably have an opposite effect." More important, as the Washington *Post* astutely pointed out, "a collapse of the stock market has wider effects than the checking of unwarranted speculation. It gives rise to doubt and fear as to the future of business, and . . . will probably bring about at least a temporary shrinkage of both production and consumption. This shrinkage will reduce incomes and cause unemployment to an extent that can not be estimated."

And in a speech to a church gathering in Poughkeepsie on the evening after the crash, Governor Franklin D. Roosevelt reminded his audience that "it is not good to go too far on the theory of getting something for nothing. Much of the activity of the stock market is legitimate and proper, but in some cases improper schemes and questionable methods have been used in stock promotion, and many investors have lost sight of the real purpose of the Exchange."

Nevertheless, the market staged an impressive rally on Friday. Although the continuing outflow of margin calls indicated that the public, on balance, necessarily sold more stocks than it bought, the huge investment trusts, banks, and brokerage houses took up the slack. Professional traders (some called them scavengers) swooped back into the market, picking among the bones for bargains. Baruch thought he recognized at least one, as he bought another 5,500 shares of American Smelting, bringing his investment in that one stock alone to approximately $835,000. All in all, nearly 6 billion shares changed hands as scores of issues recouped nearly all their losses from Black Thursday.

On Saturday, October 26, Hitler, Hugenberg, and the other leaders of the Nationalist anti–Young Plan coalition staged massive rallies throughout Germany to arouse public opinion in favor of their so-called Liberty Law. According to the constitution of the Weimar Republic, any group could force the Reichstag to consider a specific measure by obtaining the signatures of 10 percent of the German electorate; in the autumn of 1929, that requirement translated into about four million signatures. The

Reichstag then was free to accept or reject the proposal, but if it voted no, the bill automatically went back to the electorate for yet another referendum. If 50 percent of German voters ratified it at that time, the measure automatically became law despite the legislature's disapproval.

Hugenberg's Liberty Law, which had been formally submitted to the German electorate for consideration on October 16 (the first step in the referendum process), provided for the unilateral repeal of the war guilt and Rhineland occupation clauses of the Versailles Treaty, and prohibited the Weimar government from adopting the Young Plan; any German official who signed any new reparations pledge was liable to imprisonment. To arouse public sentiment in favor of the proposal, Nazi and Nationalist disciples paraded through the streets of Berlin and Nuremberg (where the Nazis had held a spectacular and violent party rally in August), and orators harangued passersby from street corners in innumerable cities and towns. As the government launched a countermovement to reinforce support for its pro–Young Plan policy, clashes between the two groups grew ever more vicious, and President Hindenburg was forced to rebuke both sides for their intemperate behavior.

Meanwhile, the prolonged slide of Wall Street from September through October—and the subsequent evaporation of surplus American investment capital—already had heightened Germany's economic distress. At the end of October, a government spokesman in Berlin acknowledged that "all German commercial transactions have been affected by the reduced ration of foreign capital received this year. The German economy has become accustomed to large investments of foreign capital each year, and cannot forego their continuance without some disturbance to business conditions." Uncertainty over the Young Plan, a distressing rise in business failures, increasing unemployment, and a domestic stock market that had fallen to its lowest point in three years (largely because of the dearth of available credit) presented the Weimar Republic with one of the most difficult economic challenges of its brief life. And the effects of the crash of Black Thursday in the United States had not yet descended upon the European continent.

In Saturday's brief trading session, the agitated movement of blue-chip stocks on the New York Stock Exchange betrayed a slight but unmistakable weakness. Not surprisingly, brokers reported a shift in investor preference from stocks to fixed-interest bonds. The liquidation of impaired margin accounts continued, albeit at a more orderly pace.

At the end of trading on Saturday, the Fisher Index—based on the 215 "most important" stocks on the New York Stock Exchange—stood at 182.9, down nearly 10 percent from the previous week's average of 200.

"The stock market is just like a sieve," wrote a sarcastic Will Rogers. "Everything and everybody is put into it, and it is shaken, and through the holes go all the small stuff. Then they load it up again and maby hold it still for awhile and they start shaking again and through the little investors go. They pick themselves up, turn bootlegger or do something to get some more money, and then they crawl back into the hopper and away they go again."

Over the weekend, Charlie Mitchell pondered his personal financial difficulties. It seems that the most famous banker in America was facing a serious federal income tax liability problem, because his income for 1929 (including bonuses) was going to be well over $1 million. The crash-induced decline of his National City stock from its high of 522 to around 400, however, gave Mitchell a bright idea. Carefully he formulated a complicated scheme to sell a substantial portion of his own National City holdings to his wife, thereby creating a capital gains loss of $2.8 million that would wipe out his entire tax liability. But Mitchell also needed to reinflate the price of National City's stock because the proposed merger with the Corn Exchange Bank had fallen through as a result of the crash. (According to the terms of agreement, the Corn Exchange stockholders had the option of taking either cash or National City stock in return for their holdings; as the price of National City stock sank, it became obvious that they would opt for cash, a development that in turn made the transaction far too expensive for the National City stockholders, who threatened to veto the deal.) So, while Wall Street caught its breath after the most eventful week in its history, Mitchell decided to acquire another $12 million worth of National City stock, a move he hoped would act as a stimulus to attract other investors and raise the price of the issue; then he would turn around and sell most of the new purchase (which he would have bought at the depressed price) to his wife, thereby creating the desired tax loss. There was only one hitch: where could he borrow the $12 million he needed to buy the stock?

Nearly every brokerage office on Wall Street buzzed with activity on Sunday, October 27. For the first time in its history, the exchange instructed its members to have staff available on a Sunday to process the blizzard of paperwork that still remained from the record-breaking volume of transactions of the three previous stormy days. Sightseers on special excursion buses that toured the financial district gawked at the rows of limousines double-parked along the curbs (police suspended parking regulations for the day); those on foot picked up pieces of shredded ticker tape as souvenirs. In nearby churches, preachers cited the tragedy of the stock market crash as an object lesson in the deadly rewards of greed and temptation. Generally, the clerics agreed that speculators (i.e., gamblers) had gotten their just deserts, though they did express some measure of regret over the extraordinary degree of human suffering and humiliation. "But I shall not be sorry it has come if it has administered a severe blow to that gambling spirit which attempts to get something for nothing, to obtain larger profits at the ruin of others," thundered the Right Reverend Frank Theodore Woods, guest preacher at the Grace Protestant Episcopal Church at the corner of Broadway and Tenth. "The gambling craze practically means an attempt to get something for nothing, to secure a far higher reward for an investment than it really deserves, to obtain large profits at the expense of others. That is not the mind of Christ."

Meanwhile, at his office in the *New York Times* building, financial editor Alexander Dana Noyes penned a farewell to the fabled and now thoroughly defunct New Era philosophy fostered by stock promoters and Republican propagandists. "Whatever may be the sequel on the present occasion, last week's crash in stocks will certainly bring a change in some not unimportant directions," decided Noyes. "The philosophy which based its reasoning on the presumption that a rise in prices can go on forever, that the speculative 'outside public' is the best judge of intrinsic values, that buying of stocks on margin is really nothing but investment on the instalment plan, that 'bull leaders' buy stocks always and at all times and never sell, that stocks may just as well be valued at 'thirty times earnings' as at ten—this carefully cultivated philosophy of the past two years has been visibly and for the time irreparably damaged."

On Sunday evening, the Jewish Theatrical Guild held its annual celebration at the Commodore Hotel. Eddie Cantor, who had just dropped several hundred thousand dollars in the market by speculating in the stock of the Manufacturers Trust Company, served as master of ceremonies; George Jessel was the guest of honor. Grover Whalen was there in the audience, and so was Jimmy Walker, though the mayor arrived late as usual after hopping back from Boston where his girlfriend, Betty Compton, was preparing to open in the new Irving Berlin–Cole Porter show *Fifty Million Frenchmen.* (For the past few days, Walker also had been busy denying La Guardia's accusations that he was "a tango mayor" who spent all his time in night clubs. "Since Jan. 1, 1926," Walker replied archly, "I have been in a night club just three times. Upon each occasion it was our wedding anniversary. . . . As for being a tango mayor, I tried the tango once several years ago and sprained my ankle.")

Appropriately, Cantor opened the guild celebration with a comic monologue about recent events on Wall Street. "If the stock market goes any lower," Cantor predicted, "I know thousands of married men who are going to leave their sweethearts and go back to their wives. As for myself, I am not worried. My broker is going to carry me; he and three other pall bearers." In reply, Jessel raised a toast to the gathering: "Ladies, gentlemen, and the permanent mayor of New York. I started with $1.35, but am happy to say I now owe Cantor $83,000. I want to ask Eddie, what's going on with that Manufacturers Trust?"

Shortly after dawn on Monday morning, October 28, the sky north of Wall Street was blotted out by an eerie apparition of darkness as thousands of migrating blackbirds descended en masse upon Mount Vernon. For more than thirty minutes the swarm of starving birds foraged through the streets of the business district, searching desperately for food. Then they flew off as abruptly as they had arrived, leaving nearly a hundred of their flock behind, dead of hunger or exhaustion.

Monday witnessed the worst losses in the history of the stock exchange. To the obvious surprise of stunned brokers, prices plummeted right from the start and kept falling through the day. Once again, some blue-chip stocks plunged ten points between sales, and many smashed through the floor to levels no one had witnessed for years. The weekend respite had afforded investors a chance to step back, take a deep breath, and review the situation objectively, and they did not care a bit for what they saw. Shaken by the events of the previous week, the public simply refused to buy, and those who still held stocks refused to keep them any longer. Quite simply, all but a few hardy souls possessed far too much fear of the future to do anything but sell. For once, Bernard Baruch went along with the crowd, quickly disposing of 2,500 shares of American Smelting and 3,000 shares of Standard Brands.

Nor did the vaunted bankers' consortium intervene to stop the excruciating decline. Although Wall Street took heart at the sight of Charlie Mitchell entering J.P. Morgan and Company's offices again at one o'clock that afternoon, the expected wave of "organized support" never materialized. Though no outsiders knew it at the time, Mitchell had gone to Morgan's temple not to pledge funds to bolster the market, but to borrow $12 million to launch his personal stock-buying scheme. (The company generously gave him a $10 million loan.) There were no words of encouragement or consolation from Thomas Lamont; and when Richard Whitney—who had earned the nickname "White Knight" for his gallant actions on the terrible afternoon of Black Thursday—stepped onto the floor of the exchange, hardly anyone paid any attention as Whitney quietly went about his normal business routine. As the bankers acknowledged to the press after their conference late that afternoon, they had decided to permit the market to fall and seek its own level, though they remained determined to ensure that every stock had a buyer at some price, however low.

So this time there was no panic—even though nine and a quarter million shares were traded—and the dreaded "air pockets" failed to appear. But the retreat, although more orderly, was far more destructive in terms of total losses. Nor was the debacle limited to Wall Street; on local exchanges around the nation, in Chicago, Boston, Baltimore, Cleveland, and Philadelphia, stock prices set new record lows for the year. In all, approximately $14 billion worth of security values—almost three times the value of all the currency in circulation in the United States—vanished into thin air. Virtually all the gains recorded since January had been wiped out. The Dow Jones average fell nearly 13 percent. Sixteen former speculative favorites led the shattering decline on the New York Stock Exchange: AT&T dropped 34 points and more than $448 million; General Electric lost 47½ points and $342.5 million; General Motors, lower-priced to begin with, fell nearly 7 points but suffered a loss of $293,625,000; and U.S. Steel slid over 17 points and lost more than $142 million. The most ominous sign for the morrow was the extraordinarily heavy volume of trading during the last hour, when nearly three million shares changed hands and almost every issue sank to its low point of the day. There was little doubt that prices would have kept falling if trading had been permitted to continue.

Like mystics chanting their mantra, the high priests of the brotherhood of financiers kept reciting the same shopworn assurances in a vain effort to convince themselves and the public that the crash had bottomed out, that the turning point was near and the "fundamental soundness" of the nation's economy would soon send stock prices soaring again. Professional analysts complained that the public had simply become hysterical, that investors had collectively lost their heads and surrendered to unreasoning, abject fear. But that was precisely the point. Mob psychology had borne the bull market to irrational heights, and now mob psychology would drag it down far below any theoretical barriers erected by experts.

Administration spokesmen in Washington insisted that the storm had spent the worst of its fury. "So many shares have been thrown into the market at one time that I rather think the worst is over," remarked one official. "I do not believe this is going to last very long."

Because so many small speculators had been wiped out by the previous crashes (brokers' boardrooms across the country were far less crowded on Monday than they had been for months), this latest disaster struck primarily the professionals, the banks—including many small-town and rural banks—and the investment trusts who had mistakenly believed the slide had ended after Black Thursday. Observers called it "a rich man's crash." George F. Baker, chairman of the First National Bank, reportedly lost $14,737,000 in three stocks alone. That evening, Bernard Baruch hosted a dinner party at his Fifth Avenue home for Winston Churchill; the guests included Charlie Mitchell, Herbert Bayard Swope, Albert Wiggin, Charles Schwab, and John D. Ryan, president of Anaconda Copper. During the dinner, Mitchell rose and proposed a convivial toast to "my fellow former millionaires." Yet the captains of finance assembled to honor Churchill somehow managed to convince themselves, too, that the worst was over. "CONSENSUS OF OPINION OF MEETING AT BARUCH'S," reported Swope to a business associate, "WAS THAT THOSE WHO STAND PRESSURE WOULD NOT ALONE BE DISCHARGING PUBLIC DUTY BUT WOULD BE CONFERRING BIG FAVOR UPON THEMSELVES WITH CERTAINTY OF RECOVERY OF STOCKS WHOSE VALUES UNDOUBTEDLY FAR GREATER THAN TODAY'S MARKET."

Nor did the stock market debacle succeed in dampening the gay and opulent celebration along Thirty-ninth Street that evening as the Metropolitan Opera opened its forty-fifth season with Puccini's *Manon Lescaut,* featuring the formidably endowed Lucrezia Bori in the title role she had played in her American debut seventeen years earlier. As usual, Otto Kahn (whose nomination several days earlier as treasurer of the Republican Senatorial Campaign Committee had provoked a storm of controversy among the progressive wing of the party) was present at the glittering premiere, as were Thomas Lamont, Edward F. Hutton, Brigadier General Cornelius Vanderbilt, and the count and countess of Carlisle.

But Governor Franklin D. Roosevelt was not. Roosevelt was in Springfield, Massachusetts, that evening as the guest of honor at a gathering of the Western Massachusetts Democratic Club. (Regretfully, the invitation had forced the governor to turn down a request from Churchill for a meeting that day.) Reviewing the afternoon's events on Wall Street, FDR suggested, not really in jest, that if such a disaster had occurred with a Democrat in the White House, it would have been immediately attributed to amateurish bungling and mismanagement by the party in power.

Few people as yet blamed Hoover for the crash.

The Marx Brothers were opening a one-week run of *Animal Crackers* at the Maryland Theatre in Baltimore on Monday night. Shortly before the curtain went up, Harpo received a wire from his broker in New York: "FORCED TO SELL ALL HOLDINGS UNLESS RECEIVE CHECK FOR $15,000 TO COVER MARGINS." "I hustled the fifteen G's together," Harpo recalled, "and got it to the broker. Now, I figured, I had survived the crisis." But the tragedy had just begun.

Still shattered from the previous week's debacle, Groucho adamantly refused to go onstage. No amount of coaxing or cajoling from his brothers or the producer could entice the deeply depressed comedian from his dressing room. The Baltimore *Sun* reported that a stand-in took his place for the next two performances; the disappointed audiences were told that Groucho was "down on his back with a misery."

Monday evening, an officer of the Los Angeles branch of the National City Bank telephoned Mr. Edgar D. Brown, formerly of Pottsville, Pennsylvania, and told him, "Brown, things are looking terrible. I think the market might bust wide open tomorrow morning and let you out. You'd better come down and watch it. If they move off you get out from under."

# XVII

# Smashup

Tuesday, October 29. The nation's stock markets already had suffered two days of unparalleled devastation. Thursday's panic had wiped out thousands of small speculators, wreaking such psychological damage that an entire generation of Americans were permanently scarred by the experience. Monday's staggering losses had left wealthier investors battered and stunned and ready to get out of the market completely at the first sign of further deterioration in stock prices. And so the stage was set for the most destructive day in the history of American finance.

Mr. Edgar D. Brown arose at 6:00 A.M.—9:00 Eastern time—and hustled down to the National City branch office before seven. The first quotation that came over the ticker was a sale of forty-five thousand shares of Anaconda (of which he still owned a sizable chunk) at 80, down from Monday's closing price of 96. "Now if this thing strengthens up the first hour everything will be all right," his broker told him, "but if it does not, look out."

In the first thirty minutes of trading on the New York Stock Exchange, 3,259,800 shares changed hands, a full five hours' worth of business on any ordinary day. Immense blocks of stock were dumped on the market, at prices well below their Monday levels, by wealthy individuals and institutions: 50,000 shares at a time of Chrysler, General Electric, IT&T, the Rockefellers' Standard Oil of New Jersey, and the Morgan-sponsored United Corporation Trust. Under the relentless pressure created by steadily increasing sales of huge holdings, the market collapsed completely. U.S. Steel skidded past 190 . . . 180 . . . 170 . . . and kept going down. General

Electric opened at 245 and immediately plunged to 211. AT&T, which had reached a peak of 310 earlier in the year, smashed all the way down to 204, wiping out Clarence Mackay (who, one Wall Street journalist averred, suffered the greatest reversal of fortune of any individual speculator in America). RCA, a former favorite at 110, went begging at 26. Johns Manville plummeted from 240 to 110. Blue Ridge Corporation, the investment trust that had made its August debut at 100 with such spectacular fanfare, was sold at $3 per share when it could find a buyer.

A stock exchange official watched in shock and horror as one wild-eyed broker stormed out of the frenzied mob on the floor and lunged out the front door, "screaming like a lunatic." Eyewitnesses to the cataclysm on the exchange that day later testified that they felt as if they were surrounded by "hunted things."

At Little America, in the bleak white fastness of Commander Byrd's camp on the edge of the Bay of Whales, airplane pilot Dean Smith—who had purchased a substantial quantity of Chrysler stock—attempted to raise his broker by radio as he watched his investment "go down with the thermometer," tumbling ninety points. "It ruined me," he admitted to a friend. "And I thought I was going to have such a good time with that money when I got home." "Well," his buddy replied, "this is a grand place to be ruined. You don't have to keep up appearances."

Mr. Edgar D. Brown refused to be swept up in the prevailing hysteria. Unfortunately, his broker's nerves proved far less stable. After an hour or two of watching prices smash through every barrier that stood in their path, Brown and his wife left the terror-stricken customers' room for a breath of reality: "Everybody was groaning and my godding until I said 'Come on, let's go out into the air. This stuff will be all right. These folks are just getting panicky.'" In fact, at that moment Brown was perfectly prepared to purchase more Anaconda at what appeared to be a very attractive bargain rate. (It wasn't. Anaconda did not stop tumbling until it finally landed below $10 per share.) As he walked out of the room, Brown was accosted by his broker, who sputtered out the news that "City Bank is crashing. The banks are in on this thing and the market is actually way under what it is quoted out here. My advice to you is to get out. Bank stock is well down under 350." The broker also informed Brown that the local Los Angeles bank that held his margin loan was calling the note— which, Brown later discovered, was entirely untrue. "Well," Brown replied, "I don't have to sell, but if you think it is the right thing to do I suppose I'll have to ride along—I presume that even somewhat below the prices quoted on the board I'll have at least $25,000 left."

So National City sold out Brown's portfolio; at least, the broker sold his Anaconda and Eastman Kodak stock. But the company actually repurchased Brown's National City Bank stock at $320. Perhaps it was only coincidence that this transaction was carried out at the stock's low point for the day—and perhaps not. The day before, National City had stood at $450. "The next morning when I woke up," Brown recalled, "I discovered that . . . my calculated $25,000 was in reality $6,000."

By noon, 8,350,000 shares had been sold and bought on the New York Stock Exchange. In direct violation of trading custom, if not explicit exchange regulations, brokers deliberately delayed many transactions until a more reasonable bid appeared. The bankers' consortium, which now included Owen Young (who was still a director of the Federal Reserve Bank of New York), maintained its efforts to provide bids—albeit slightly below the market in virtually every instance—for certain key stocks, but every attempt to stem the descent proved as useless, someone said, as "trying to stem the falls of Niagara." (And that was why Baruch refused Lamont's invitation to join the group. "The day was past when the House of Morgan could rally Wall Street in such a crisis," was Baruch's comment.) Contemporary observers knew they were making history. "It was such a situation as probably never will develop again in this country," wrote a dazed *New York Times* correspondent, "and those who stood on the side lines and witnessed it were literally awe-struck by the violence of the shrinkage in values and the tremendous losses established by individuals and institutions."

Across the news tickers came the terse, urgent messages presaging—no one knew what: "Federal Reserve Board is in session in Washington with Secretary Mellon . . . Cabinet is meeting . . . Owen Young joins bankers conference at Morgan office . . . Hoover meeting with Secretary of Commerce Lamont . . . Telegraph, telephone, and cable systems carrying record volume of communications to Wall Street from around the globe . . . Leading wire houses say worst over." And there was a rumor that nearly every investment trust had gone bust.

So it went all day long.

Mayor Jimmy Walker spent his lunchtime exhorting a convention of motion picture exhibitors at the Hotel Astor to refrain from showing pessimistic films while the stock market crash continued. "Show pictures that will reinstate courage and hope in the hearts of the people," urged Walker. "Give them a chance to forget their financial losses on the stock market and look with hope to the future. . . . The morale of the people must be maintained, and you can do it."

Shortly after noon, the governing committee of the stock exchange assembled surreptitiously in a cramped room beneath the trading floor. They were there to decide whether the exchange should be completely shut down and trading terminated until the panic subsided. "The office they met in was never designed for large meetings of this sort, with the result that most of the Governors were compelled to stand, or to sit on tables," wrote Richard Whitney afterward. "As the meeting proceeded, panic was raging overhead on the floor. Every few minutes the latest prices were announced, with quotations moving swiftly and irresistibly downwards. The feeling of those present was revealed by their habit of continually lighting cigarettes, taking a puff or two, putting them out and lighting new ones—a practice which soon made the narrow room blue with smoke and extremely stuffy." After considerable discussion, the governors decided to keep the market open, at least for the moment.

An estimated ten thousand forlorn men, women, and children crammed into the canyons of Wall Street and the surrounding avenues. Once again Commissioner Whalen dispatched scores of additional detectives and patrolmen to keep order in the financial district, but they were really not necessary. One eyewitness described the scene as "a street of tarnished hopes, of curiously silent apprehension and of a sort of paralyzed hypnosis. . . . Men and women crowded the brokerage offices, even those who have been long since wiped out, and followed the figures on the tape." (Misery loves company.) "Little groups gathered here and there to discuss the fall in prices in hushed and awed tones. They were participating in the making of financial history. It was the consensus of bankers and brokers alike that no such scenes ever again will be witnessed by this generation."

Four wealthy women rode from one uptown brokerage office to another in a chauffeured limousine. They wore gold rings and jewels and smoked cigarettes in gold-tipped holders. They seemed to regard their staggering losses as a frivolous lark. At the last office, one of the dowagers sniffed, "This place is depressing," and they all went home.

An elderly vaudeville producer who had lost his entire fortune, some $75,000, was discovered by his son weeping like a child in his office. Men who had been washed up spent the rest of the afternoon wandering aimlessly, dazed, through hotel lobbies.

The sickening descent continued. It would not cease until the selling stopped. But the selling went remorselessly on because far too many people believed the end was not yet in sight. Every other consideration was brushed aside.

In Providence, Rhode Island, a businessman dropped dead in his broker's office as he stood watching the ticker. A Kansas City man shot himself twice in the chest. "Tell the boys I can't pay them what I owe them," he told a friend before he died.

"I have been in Washington on Inauguration Day, Claremore on Fourth of July, Dearborn on Edison Day," remarked Will Rogers. "But to have been in New York on 'wailing day'! When Wall Street took that tail spin, you had to stand in line to get a window to jump out of, and speculators were selling space for bodies in the East River. If England is supposed by international treaty to protect the Wailing Wall, they will have to come here to do it. The wall runs from the Battery to the Bronx. You know there is nothing that hollers as quick and as loud as a gambler. . . . Now they know what the farmer has been up against for eight years." Rogers himself had followed Baruch's advice and had withdrawn from the market shortly before the bubble burst. "I did what you told me," he told Baruch when they met after the crash, "and you saved my life."

As the losses mounted, London newspapers ceased their smug, self-righteous sermonizing. "We are not watching the inexorable operation of economic laws which American investors have defied," observed the financial editor of the *Daily Mirror.* "We are watching the complete disorganization of a complex market by an assault upon it of a leaderless and panic-stricken mob." Not only had the ranks of British investors in American securities been decimated, but the resulting decline in the confidence and purchasing power of American consumers and investors threatened to disarrange the entire precarious postwar economic structure. "The Wall Street slump will cause a recession in American business as surely as the present share slump was inevitably to follow the share boom," warned the *Evening Star.* "If the depression is so widespread that the average American citizen can no longer afford for the time being to buy imported goods, there will obviously be a serious reaction on European trade. The tariff wall will become temporarily almost insurmountable."

In Paris, the combination of events on Wall Street, the continuing lethargy of the London Exchange, and the resignation of the cabinet of Premier Aristide Briand sent the Bourse spinning sharply downward.

As usual, Ernest Hemingway had his own unique interpretation of the financial cataclysm; he viewed it as a cunning Republican conspiracy to artificially induce the inevitable deflation far in advance of the next presidential election. "They're liquidating now," he wrote to Maxwell Perkins from Paris, "so Hoover can have brought us out of this slump by 1932."

In Baltimore, Harpo Marx received another frantic telegram from his broker: "ADDITIONAL FIFTEEN THOUSAND DOLLARS TO COVER MARGINS." Somehow Harpo managed to scrape the cash together. His friend playwright George S. Kaufman had bought one stock on a tip from Harpo and Groucho and lost his entire $10,000 investment. But Kaufman's royalties from *The Cocoanuts* and his other plays more than made up the difference, and so the writer simply shrugged his shoulders and said, "Anyone who buys a stock because the Marx Brothers recommend it *deserves* to lose $10,000."

Between two-thirty and three o'clock, a weak but highly visible surge of buying braced the market. It seemed to be a marvelous opportunity to pick up bargains. Baruch, for instance, purchased five thousand shares of U.S. Steel, which finally had stopped falling at 167; even with the battering his portfolio had already taken, Billy Durant, too, began picking up steel and other blue-chip issues.

Despite this last-minute (literally) demonstration of support, more than $9 billion worth of securities values had disappeared on the New York Stock Exchange alone in the space of five hours. Estimates of the nation's total losses ranged as high as $15 billion. An astounding total of 16,410,000 shares had been traded on Wall Street. Because so many shares had been traded in huge blocks, the ticker did not run quite as late as it had on Black Thursday, when so many smaller investors had been wiped out; this time the final quotations (accompanied by an ironic "GOOD NIGHT") came across at 5:32 P.M. The Dow Jones average tumbled 31 points to 260.64, a new low for 1929, and 120 points below its September 3 high. The thirty leading industrials had fallen even further, losing nearly 40 percent of their value since Labor Day.

When all the declines had been totaled, it became clear that October 1929 had been the worst month in the history of the New York Stock Exchange. Virtually every listed stock stood well below its price level of October 1928, in the days just prior to Hoover's election. The horrifying sequence of disasters, declared the *Wall Street Journal* sadly, "dwarfs in extent any reaction since that of 1920." But in that immediate postwar year it had taken stocks a full twelve months to accumulate the volume of losses that had struck the market so violently in 1929; the terrifying Panic of 1907, too, had required eleven months to drive stock prices down by 45 percent. Nor did those crashes involve nearly as many investors as the fearsome Crash of 1929. "This slump cannot be compared with previous ones," the *Journal* warned. "It differs in that more individuals are being ruined probably than in all others combined. . . . With the public in its present mood, no one can guess whether liquidation will be completed in a matter of hours or days."

"Read 'em and weep," yelled the newsboys around Grand Central Station as dazed commuters scanned the afternoon's final market report. "BANK AND TRUST STOCK PRICES CRUMBLE IN RECORD TRADING; CROWDS AT TICKERS SEE FORTUNES WANE," lamented the *New York Times,* which devoted all of its first five pages to the day's events on Wall Street. Despite (or perhaps because of) its nervousness about the future, the *Wall Street Journal* sought to allay any fears of full-fledged panic by putting a more encouraging face on the news with its calm headline: "STOCKS STEADY AFTER DECLINE." *Variety,* the entertainment weekly, weighed in with its famous flippant comment "WALL ST. LAYS AN EGG," while the ultrasophisticated *New Yorker* observed with cruel humor that "the collapse of the market, over and above the pain, couldn't help but be amusing. It is amusing to see a fat land quivering in paunchy fright."

Herbert Bayard Swope had been wiped out. In September, he had possessed a paper fortune of $14 million; after the crash, Swope was more than $2 million in debt. "THANK GOD WE'RE STILL ALIVE," he cabled to Harpo Marx. Eddie Cantor was left with $60 in his pocket. "Sixty bucks," he muttered, ". . . and what I didn't even know—I owed $285,000 to the Manufacturers Trust Company, where the President had covered some of my calls for margin." The fabled Fisher brothers reportedly had lost several hundred million dollars. There were rumors that the Vatican, allegedly a heavy investor in American securities, had dropped millions of dollars. Clarence Mackay had lost nearly every penny; though he still possessed his fabulous estate, it was said that he did not even have enough cash to pay his servants. Mackay's son-in-law, Irving Berlin, was virtually broke, too. "I was scared," Berlin confessed. "I had had all the money I wanted for the rest of my life. Then all of a sudden I didn't. I had taken it easy and gone soft and wasn't too certain I could get going again."

Harpo Marx received yet another insistent telegram from his broker: "SEND $10,000 IN 24 HOURS OR FACE FINANCIAL RUIN AND DAMAGING SUITS. MUST HAVE $10,000 REGARDLESS WHETHER I CAN SELL YOUR HOLDINGS." But Harpo was tapped out. "In raising the dough for the three checks I had already sent," he said,

I had scraped the bottom of the barrel. I had liquidated every asset I owned except my harp and my croquet set. I had borrowed as far in advance as I could against my salary. My market holdings had shriveled to an average worth of one dollar a share. . . . As assets they were probably worth a medium-sized bag of jelly beans. I was flatter broke than the day the Shubert unit died in Indianapolis. Then I at least had seven cents in my pocket, and I didn't owe anybody any of it. This was a lot worse. I had much more to lose. I had much farther to fall. . . .

Life would never be, ever again, all fun and games. The bam-bang-sock-and-pow part was over, and so was the permanent, floating New Year's Eve party. Our million-dollar playground had been condemned.

# XVIII

# Aftermath

"Well, that's that—and it's pretty well all over,
except for an occasional bird who has lost everything
but his ego, and who hurls himself from a high window
with complete disregard for the busy people who are
really going somewhere on the sidewalks below."
—*Advertising company statement, November 5, 1929*

**W**inston Churchill awoke on Wednesday to the shouts of an excited crowd on the sidewalk outside the Savoy-Plaza Hotel. When he looked out to see what had happened, Churchill discovered that "under my very window a gentleman cast himself down fifteen storeys and was dashed to pieces, causing a wild commotion and the arrival of the fire brigade. Quite a number of persons," he added dryly, "seem to have overbalanced themselves by accident in the same sort of way."

On the morning after the smashup, the nation's newspapers were filled with reassuring pronouncements about the immediate and long-range prospects for American business. Since the crash clearly had been caused by a sudden, nationwide attack of doubt and despair, the most urgent task appeared to be the restoration of confidence before the shock waves from Wall Street brought the entire domestic economy tumbling to the ground.

Hence the Hoover administration's designated oracle of good cheer, Assistant Secretary of Commerce Klein, took to the radio airwaves once again and voiced his firm conviction that the stock market debacle was not a meaningful barometer of American business after all, nor would it adversely affect the existing patterns of production and consumption. "The [vital] factors have not been changed by the drop in stock prices," Klein declared soothingly. "The national income of the United States at this moment is hardly a fraction less than it was a month ago. Established indexes, such as the quality of output of our farms, our mines and our factories, and the volume of our railroad transportation, support this view." Klein's optimistic prognosis was seconded by a barrage of upbeat newspaper editorials. "What can be said, and what very much needs to be said, is that, however sour things may look to individuals at the moment, the country has not suffered a catastrophe," offered the New York *World*. "The stock market crash," agreed the Baltimore *Sun*, "obviously is the result of many forces, most of them transitory and all of them combined incapable of upsetting the firm base of prosperity." "LET'S GO!" urged *Business Week*, whose editors had the audacity to claim that "the collapse of 'the greatest bull market of all time' is the best thing that has happened to American business in the past fifteen years. It marks the end, we hope, of a period of war disturbance, speculative enthusiasm and economic instability; the beginning, we are certain, of a period of steady, substantial development."

Business leaders—especially those whose companies' stocks had been badly shaken by the crash—chimed in with their own encouraging, almost euphoric predictions. "Our October sales are the largest on record," chirped General Robert E. Wood, president of Sears, Roebuck and Company. "While the shaking of public confidence may impair buying power somewhat in the next few months, I see no grounds for any real depression in business." Walter Gifford, president of the severely battered AT&T, claimed that "the business prospects of the Bell Telephone System are as good as they ever have been." "The present hysterical selling of stocks is very unfortunate," sniffed Walter Chrysler, "and entirely uncalled for in the face of generally favorable conditions and prospects." General Motors' Alfred P. Sloan, Jr., returned from Europe with the pronouncement "I cannot see any logical reason for any such action as has occurred with present market values. Business is sound." "Let's not forget that millions upon millions of regular folks throughout this *grand, greatly-desiring, gorgeously-spending America,* need power, heat, light, food, transportation, recreation and adornment, same as always," shouted the advertising firm of Erwin, Wasey and Company. "They'll go on dreaming, and earning, and *buying*—in that lavish fashion that has always characterized the shortest-memoried and longest-confidenced people that ever lived."

Wrong.

Partly to restore public confidence, and partly to turn a profit on what appeared to be greatly depressed price levels, a number of well-known financiers made ostentatious returns to the troubled stock market. On October 30, Owen Young purchased 1,700 shares of General Electric at 228. (Eight weeks earlier, it had sold for 396.) John J. Raskob informed reporters that "the pendulum has swung too far. The list is filled with bargains and my friends and I are all buying stocks." Aided by the $10 million loan from his friends at J.P. Morgan and Company, and a $2 million pool National City Bank generously (and secretly) established to allow its officers to make interest-free loans to themselves during the crisis, Charlie Mitchell continued his efforts to accumulate thousands of shares of his bank's securities, all the while proclaiming loudly that "never before in the history of our country have our industries been better fortified as to cash, condition of inventory or soundness of corporate structure.... There has been no crisis in the banking system to aggravate the situation."

The biggest splash, however, was made by John D. Rockefeller, Sr., who issued a rare public statement from his home in Pocantico Hills in upstate New York: "Believing that fundamental conditions of the country are sound and that there is nothing in the business situation to warrant the destruction of values that has taken place on the exchanges during the past week, my son and I have for some days been purchasing sound common stocks. We are continuing and will continue our purchases in substantial amounts at levels which we believe represent sound investment values." (Eddie Cantor laughed when he heard that the Rockefellers, père et fils, were buying stocks. "Sure," he quipped, "who else had any money left?")

Although Henry Ford naturally avoided the stock market as if it were a den of particularly iniquitous vipers—a suspicion that was only strengthened by the crash—the nation's largest automaker did his part to stimulate business and restore confidence by slashing the price of his new cars and trucks by $15 to $200 per model. Actually, Ford cut his prices because he realized that the automobile industry was in deep trouble already, suffering from overproduction and a satiated consumer market, but he cleverly presented the move to the public as a patriotic gesture. "It is our belief that basically the industry and business of the country are sound," declared Edsel from Ford's Detroit headquarters. "Every indication is that general conditions will remain prosperous. We are reducing prices now because we feel that such a step is the best contribution that can be made to assure a continuation of good business throughout the country." In similar moves, the directors of U.S. Steel and American Can voted to declare an extra $1 dividend on each share of their common stock as an expression of their faith in the nation's economic stability.

As he sailed away from the United States on Thursday, October 31, Winston Churchill—ever the romantic—cast a wistful backward glance over the Manhattan skyline and waxed ecstatic over the future of his mother's native land. "No one who has gazed on such a scene could doubt that this financial disaster, huge as it is, cruel as it is to thousands, is only a passing episode in the march of a valiant and serviceable people who by fierce experiment are hewing new paths for man, and showing to all nations much that they should attempt and much that they should avoid," he decided. Apparently Winston was unaware as yet that he was one of the thousands to whom the crash had been so cruel; until he returned to office in the spring of 1940, Churchill would have to earn his living with his pen, churning out books and newspaper articles at a frantic pace.

And Churchill's erstwhile host, Bernard Baruch, shared Winston's buoyant predictions of imminent recovery. "We have gotten our minds and also prices of stocks down to a level where we can do business with real confidence," Baruch wrote to a friend in California at the end of that terrible month of October. "Business will probably be bad enough for the next sixty days, but it won't last long in this country. Just long enough for us to get a good investment market and a strong situation."

All the roseate expectations and glibly confident rhetoric—which, though not insincere, strongly resembled whistling one's way through the graveyard—succeeded in stabilizing the market for exactly a day and a half. On October 30, stock prices rallied moderately. The panic appeared to have subsided. The governors of the New York Stock Exchange decided that tranquillity had been sufficiently restored to permit them to reduce the active trading period from five to three hours on Thursday, October 31, and to declare Friday and Saturday official holidays, to give brokers and their staffs time to complete all the paperwork left over from Tuesday's avalanche of selling.

Wall Street's spirits were braced further by the welcome news that the Bank of England was reducing its discount rate to 6 percent; almost immediately thereafter, the Federal Reserve Bank of New York shaved a full point off its own rate, restoring it to the early-summer level of 5 percent. In the Senate, the seemingly interminable tariff debate—which allegedly was creating considerable uncertainty among American manufacturers—at last seemed to be moving toward a conclusion. And the New York Stock Exchange announced that the volume of brokers' loans, for so long a source of continuing concern, had dipped precipitously, by more than $1 billion, in the week of the crash. In fact, the corporations and smaller banks that had irresponsibly flooded the market with surplus capital during the boom had panicked during the crash, overreacted, and just as irresponsibly recalled more than $2 billion worth of loans. This, of course, made the flood of forced liquidation far more devastating than it might otherwise have been; had not the major New York banks stepped in to *increase* their loans to brokers by more than $990 million, the results might have been even more destructive.

Nevertheless, banks across the country were left with a tremendous quantity of securities in their vaults after taking over their customers' impaired accounts. Conservative by nature, and made much more so by the nerve-racking events of the past ten days, these bankers were exceedingly loath to jeopardize their institutions' solvency by holding on to these stocks for any length of time. So, as soon as prices began to turn upward even slightly, as they did on October 30 and 31, bankers and brokers at once began to unload their holdings.

That was why the market promptly took a wholly unexpected nose-dive when trading resumed at 10:00 A.M. on Monday, November 4. The brief rally at the close of the previous week had created optimistic expectations of a strong revival, but prices plunged right from the start in extraordinarily heavy trading—over two million shares changed hands in the first thirty minutes—as large blocks of so-called "support stock" (stock purchased to support clients) were dumped onto the market. The selling movement gathered momentum as the highly leveraged and badly distressed investment trusts, whose common stocks had lost nearly all of their collateral value, cleaned out their portfolios. Astonished by the explosive decline—the financial equivalent of a vote of "no confidence" in the short-term future of the market—individual investors scurried to reduce their holdings, too, sending prices spiraling downward even further and faster. By the time the closing gong sounded, the *New York Times'* industrial index had fallen another twenty-two points.

This was a most depressing development. All the fine words of hope and encouragement had accomplished nothing. If stocks had not yet reached the bottom even after the horrifying crash of the last days of October, then when, the nation wondered, would the plunge ever end?

In Germany, Hitler and Hugenberg watched with grim satisfaction as the anti-Young Liberty Law gained sufficient votes in the nationwide referendum to send the measure to the Reichstag for formal consideration. The campaign had grown increasingly frenzied during the final weeks, as both the Nazi-Nationalist coalition and their rivals sought to sway voters with impassioned rhetoric and ominous predictions of doom and, occasionally, physical violence. When the dust had settled, 7.7 percent of the German electorate had voted against the Young Plan. The majority of the support for the referendum appeared to come from the nation's major cities, including Berlin, where the anti-Young measure received 10.9 percent of the votes cast.

On Tuesday, November 5, the New York Stock Exchange took the day off for the city elections. For once, there was far less excitement on Wall Street than in the teeming back streets of the boroughs. Amid Republican charges of Tammany tampering, electoral fraud, and outright physical intimidation of voters, Mayor Jimmy Walker won reelection by a landslide, burying his closest challenger, Fiorello La Guardia, by an unprecedented margin—865,549 votes to 368,334. "I am licked, but there is no rancour, and I hope the election is all for the best," said La Guardia in his concession statement. In a surprisingly strong finish, Norman Thomas received nearly 175,000 votes, the best showing ever made by a Socialist candidate in a New York mayoral election.

After scanning the incoming returns with Grover Whalen at police headquarters, Walker described his victory as a vindication of Tammany Hall's administration of the city. "It surely looks as though a vast majority of the people approve and look kindly on this type and standard of leadership," he declared with a straight face. "After all, it looks to me as if New York City wants sober, sensible, modest, thinking and forward-looking public servants."

The market decline resumed with renewed violence the following day. Although (or perhaps because) the exchange decided to maintain its abbreviated three-hour daily trading schedule for the foreseeable future, there was a furious rush of selling, and prices dropped even more swiftly and precipitously than in Monday's break. Du Pont common stock lost over 19 points—nearly 20 percent of its value; General Electric tumbled 29 points, landing finally at 206; AT&T dropped another 22 points; and U.S. Steel—which Richard Whitney had steadied at 205 less than two weeks earlier—skidded down to 165. Reporters pressed Thomas Lamont for word of the bankers' consortium's plans; Lamont replied that the pool intended to permit the reaction to run its course as long as the retreat remained "orderly."

Cheered by the revelation that brokers' loans had been reduced by an additional $656,000 during the previous week, bringing the total down to the level of October 24, 1928 (in the days just before the postelection "Hoover boom"), the market bounced back up strongly in heavy trading on November 7. "LOOKS LIKE ALL TECHNICAL AND FORCED LIQUIDATION ABOUT COMPLETED," reported Baruch hopefully to a friend; but the end was not yet in sight. Trading was extremely light the following day, but on Monday, November 11, the inevitable wave of liquidation resumed as bankers and brokerage houses sought to cash in on the abortive rally.

As the sickening and, by now, seemingly inexorable slide continued, the search for scapegoats began in earnest. Carter Glass, of course, attributed the debacle to the plague he called "Mitchellism"; when someone asked Glass what could be done to stabilize the market, the Virginian suggested sarcastically, "Let Mitchell fix it." On the floor of the Senate, minority leader Joseph T. Robinson of Arkansas, the Democratic party's vice-presidential nominee in 1924, laid the blame squarely on the shoulders of the executive triumvirate of Hoover, Coolidge, and Mellon, and all the high priests of Republican prosperity who had misled an innocent and gullible public through their "unduly and repeated optimistic statements to the creation of enthusiastic, if not frenzied ventures in stocks." "Whatever causes may have contributed to the trouble," continued Robinson, "it must be admitted that neither the President, the Secretary of the Treasury (the greatest since Alexander Hamilton, we are told), nor any other leader or agent of the administration took adequate steps to prevent the collapse which they should have known must follow the orgy of speculation stimulated by their utterances; nor were any appropriate steps promptly taken to stay or check the recession."

Republican Senate leader Jim Robinson of Indiana, an old-line party hack who usually enjoyed baiting the straitlaced Hoover, found himself forced to defend the President. Neither Hoover nor Coolidge nor Mellon, he said, "has encouraged speculation of this kind." (As far as Coolidge and Mellon were concerned, of course, this was patently untrue.) "Neither has suggested in any way, directly or indirectly, that people should gamble in the market. . . . They had no more to do with the stock market crash than the man in the moon." On the other hand, the veteran GOP leader accused John J. Raskob, whom he characterized as a "lucky plunger" (and who, conveniently for the Republicans, was still Democratic National Committee chairman), of having deliberately enticed an unwary public— "every one, even people with small means"—into the speculative arena.

Stung, Raskob angrily denounced the Republican Robinson's charges as a "false, vicious, wholly unwarranted and manifestly political attack." "I do not gamble in the stock market," Raskob snapped. "I have always purchased stocks outright, investing in the securities of those companies that I thought had an attractive future, and have held the stocks until such time as I felt they were selling for all they were worth." Raskob flatly refused, however, to publicly discuss persistent reports that he had sold most of his stocks well before the market crashed.

The President, too, considered Raskob guilty, but of a different crime. Hoover was convinced that the diminutive financier was spearheading a Democratic bear market pool designed to embarrass the administration by driving the market back down every time it showed the slightest signs of recovery. (Hoover later added Baruch's name, quite unfairly, to the alleged conspiracy.) Actually, there was a certain amount of short-selling going on in the first weeks following the crash, but it was being perpetrated for personal, not political, reasons, and by people even less highminded than John J. Raskob. One of the leading shorts during this period reportedly was Joe Kennedy, who seemed entirely unconcerned—almost joyful, in fact—that his unsavory maneuvers were deepening the misery and despair of his fellow Americans. According to the former film magnate's lover, Gloria Swanson, Kennedy "was whacking his thigh with glee in the opening weeks of November. He told me he had sold all his Wall Street holdings well before the bottom dropped out of everything. Now he and his horsemen were playing a waiting game with the people who hadn't been so smart—waiting to pick up the pieces, for pennies."

Raskob could easily slough off whispers and innuendo from his partisan political enemies; but he was shattered by the death of one of his oldest and dearest friends. On the afternoon of Friday, November 8, Jim Riordan, president of the County Trust Company, shot himself in the head at his home at 21 West Twelfth Street in downtown Manhattan. He was forty-seven years old when he died. For the past two weeks, Riordan allegedly had been under medical treatment for "extreme nervous exhaustion." "He seemed depressed for days," the family doctor said afterward, "and I couldn't understand it." Although Riordan's friends issued vehement denials, there were persistent rumors that the banker had lost hundreds of thousands of dollars in the crash.

Al Smith heard the news that evening while he was at the Biltmore Hotel, preparing for a dinner in honor of Governor Roosevelt, who was getting ready to launch his bid for reelection to the executive mansion. Dazed, Smith rushed to Riordan's home, where he met Raskob and William Kenny. Together, the dead man's friends decided to try to keep the matter hushed up until Monday; with the public already close to panic, they feared that word of Riordan's suicide would cause a disastrous run on the County Trust Bank. Although Smith and Raskob later denied it, the chief medical examiner told reporters that they "urged me to withhold the news of the suicide until after the trust company had closed its doors on Saturday. I thought it a good thing to do, although I broke all of the rules and regulations."

Hurriedly, Smith convened the rest of the directors of County Trust to formally appoint Raskob temporary chairman. By the time the medical examiner officially informed Grover Whalen of Riordan's death on Sunday morning, Raskob had in hand a statement from the superintendent of banks affirming that "the County Trust Company is wholly liquid and in satisfactory condition and worthy of the fullest confidence." The bank weathered the storm, but Raskob took the occasion of Riordan's death to collect on the infamous $1.5 million note that Smith's closest backers had signed to cover the campaign loan from County Trust just prior to election day 1928—and that Raskob had sworn would never be called. Not everyone complied with the request. When Raskob visited sports magnate Tim Mara to collect his share of the loan, Mara practically threw him out of his office. "You can go to hell to get that $50,000 out of me," Mara screamed.

Riordan was not the only prominent suicide in the aftermath of the crash. Although it has been statistically proved that, contrary to popular legend, there was no sudden leap in the suicide rate in America in the autumn of 1929, there is no question that a number of men and women did kill themselves because they had lost heavily in the stock market. Churchill's experience notwithstanding, few people actually jumped out of windows; asphyxiation by gas appeared to be the most popular means of self-destruction. And the press inevitably wrung every drop of melo-drama from these bitter tragedies: the wife of a Long Island broker shot herself in the heart; a utilities executive in Rochester, New York, shut himself in his bathroom and opened a wall jet of illuminating gas; a St. Louis broker swallowed poison; a Philadelphia financier shot himself in his athletic club; a divorcée in Allentown, Pennsylvania, closed the doors and windows of her home and turned on the gas oven. In Milwaukee, one gentleman who took his own life left a note that read, "My body should go to science, my soul to Andrew W. Mellon, and sympathy to my credi-tors." (On a more cheerful note, the *New York Times* informed its readers that Abraham Germansky, the real estate broker who had been last seen frantically tearing up ticker tape as he walked through Manhattan's fi-nancial district, had been discovered safe and sound in a sanitarium.) Metropolitan hospitals reported a large increase in the number of women patients who had lost their savings and were displaying definite physical symptoms of acute depression; unfortunately, hospital administrators also acknowledged that a growing number of patients were unable to pay for their own medical care.

Newspapers also carried a steady stream of disclosures of embezzle-ment by bookkeepers, clerks, and businessmen who had stolen funds to speculate in the stock market; absent the crash, their crimes might have gone undetected for years. The most spectacular revelation involved the theft of over $3.5 million—an all-time United States record—from the Union Industrial Bank of Flint, Michigan, by a syndicate of the bank's officers. At the other end of the criminal spectrum was the armed robber who took $1,000 from an apartment house rent collector with the explana-tion, "I need your money to cover myself in the stock market." Some judges were not unsympathetic; in Camden, New Jersey, a magistrate handed out a lenient sentence to a businessman convicted of embezzling $75,000, on the grounds that the temptation to gamble in stocks had been "so strong that otherwise law-abiding men [were] conquered by it as this man apparently has been."

Every day brought new evidence of the havoc wrought by the crash upon businesses and individuals. By mid-November, several well-known investment firms had been declared insolvent; others were sued by clients who had been sold without their consent. The $20 million Minneapolis-based Foshay utilities empire went bankrupt. Proposed mergers fell through right and left as financing became impossible to obtain (hardly anyone had any money left to lend for nonessential purposes); Charlie Mitchell's National City Bank officially terminated its quest to take over the rival Corn Exchange Bank. Senator Brookhart of Indiana warned that if the stock market plunge continued for much longer, "banks all over the country" would inevitably fail. The drumbeat of depressing tidings reached such proportions that the membership of the New York Stock Exchange issued written orders forbidding their employees—on pain of dismissal—to spread rumors of impending failures, and newspaper publisher James M. Cox, former governor of Ohio and the unsuccessful Democratic presidential nominee in 1920, instructed the editors of his chain of journals to take all stock market news off the front page. "The purpose is obvious," Cox explained. "The inevitable reaction came. It is nearly if not quite over and yet all of our newspapers are filling the public mind with the idea of disaster. . . . The impression will grow that we are on the verge of a serious industrial depression. What is not in any sense justified by fundamental conditions now can be created by widespread timidity or fear."

But the business community already was deeply shaken. From Wellesley, Massachusetts, there came another disquieting prophecy from Roger Babson, whom many angry speculators blamed for casting the first fateful shadow of doubt upon the bull market. "It is practically inconceivable that the utter demoralization which the market suffered will not have complex and important reactions upon the mechanism of manufacturing and merchandising," Babson noted. "It is true that the crash in Wall Street found business conditions fairly sound, but it may not leave them so." The worst thing businesses could do, he suggested, would be to choke off credit recklessly and unnecessarily, to "clumsily jam on the brakes and yank the emergency, locking the wheels and overturning the car."

There was abundant evidence that this was precisely what was happening. The economy was spinning into a deep recession, at the very least, and the impending decline was being hastened by the psychological climate of doubt and fear engendered by the crash. Beset by what one financial editor called "unrestrained and unintelligent business gloom," executives in a wide range of industries deemed it prudent to postpone all plans for expansion. Hence *Bradstreet's State of Trade* noticed "a rather decided feeling of caution in the making of new commitments for the future," as one-third of the businesses surveyed by the periodical reported that they were doing less business than in 1928. Even as *Business Week* predicted that "retrenchments will have to be made by many companies and individuals affected by the decline," production and trade figures for the month of November revealed the sharpest monthly slump since 1924.

Industrial production fell by 7 percent in November, a decline that left it 11 percent below the levels of November 1928. Primary distribution statistics displayed an 8 percent drop. Steel and iron production continued to fall off, and so did their prices; as the trade journal *Iron Age* reported, "New business has been light and the placing of some prospective tonnage has been delayed, indicating that purchasers wish to obtain a better appraisal of the influence of the securities debacle on their own businesses before making further commitments in their raw materials. . . . As consumers grow more conservative, producers are taking off capacity commensurately." Overseas, the European Steel Cartel immediately recommended a 10 percent reduction in production quotas because of the expected decline in American demand.

"The remainder of this year offers extremely slim pickings for automotive sales," observed an auto industry analyst. "The outlook for next year is anything but bright. Sales have not kept pace with increasing production. . . . Some industry leaders believe the only solution is a production slash next year." Farm income declined markedly, falling more than 50 percent over the comparable total of October 1928. Commodity prices continued to tumble, as they had done since July. Residential construction slackened further as new mortgage funds dried up. For the past year and a half, savings and loan associations had watched helplessly as their depositors withdrew funds to speculate in the stock market; now they saw those same depositors remove even more money to meet their daily living expenses after losing their savings in the crash. On November 10, the American Banking Association reported that domestic savings accounts showed a nationwide decrease for the first time in twenty years.

By the second week of November, retailers noticed a marked drop in the purchase of luxury goods. One prominent Fifth Avenue jeweler received 260 cancellations on holiday orders in a single week. Gold-digging mistresses were unceremoniously dumped by their married boyfriends. Thirteen major diamond-cutting works in Amsterdam were forced to shut down. Pawnshops were flooded with new business. Sales of radio sets reportedly declined by nearly 50 percent in New York City. Transatlantic steamship companies acknowledged that scores of prospective travelers were canceling their vacation plans. Broadway theaters suffered a sharp slump in business: "People were in no mood for high priced amusement," mourned *Variety*. The elegant, ornate speakeasies in and around Wall Street that had flourished with the boom market, where expensive automobiles had once clogged the curbs, remained eerily silent and deserted. "The investing public may be nursing its sorrows," noted one observer, "but there is plenty of evidence that it is not drowning them."

It may have been true that most Americans weathered the crash with only a minor drop in income through the first two weeks of November. It was equally true that the illusion of wealth that had fueled the boom and a decade of Republican prosperity and—not coincidentally—the reckless speakeasy subculture, had vanished. People were not necessarily poor; but they no longer felt rich. Worn out by the strain of campaigning and his efforts to lift the city's drooping spirits, Mayor Jimmy Walker departed New York and disappeared on an extended vacation, refusing to tell anyone where he was going.

And on Wall Street, the stock market continued to fall. In the end, everything came back to the question of confidence. Haunted by the vision of the holocaust through which the nation had just passed, the public simply refused to reenter the market. On November 12, prices on the New York Stock Exchange plummeted sharply again as more than 6,400,000 shares were traded in an abbreviated three-hour session. The *New York Times'* industrial index dropped to a new low for 1929; at 113.79, it was within 50¢ of being halfway down the exalted peak it had reached in the halcyon, Indian summer days of September. From his sumptuous palace at San Simeon, William Randolph Hearst arrogantly instructed President Hoover to exert the sort of forceful leadership the nation expected of the Great Engineer, to make "some reassuring utterances . . . accompanied by vigorous action."

For this, Hoover needed no prodding from Hearst. Already the administration had launched a vigorous campaign—or at least what passed for vigorous in those days—to demonstrate its faith in the fundamental stability of American business. On Wednesday, November 13, Secretary Mellon announced that the administration would seek congressional approval of an immediate 1 percent cut in corporate and individual taxes, a move business leaders hailed as an invaluable show of confidence, and which, as Galbraith points out, was precisely the sort of action John Maynard Keynes would have recommended, though Mellon already had cut taxes so much that the effect was far more psychological than fiscal. (On the other hand, Hoover adamantly refused to increase federal spending; in fact, he planned to cut the budget if possible.)

To loosen the credit strings further, the Federal Reserve Bank of New York sliced its rediscount rate to 4½ percent, the lowest point since July 1928. President Hoover then issued a ringing declaration that he had invited the nation's industrial and financial leaders—including Owen Young, Thomas Lamont, Henry Ford, Pierre Du Pont, and Alfred Sloan— to a series of conferences at the White House to give the economic situation serious scrutiny and discuss steps that each branch of industry could take to dispel "foolish pessimism," stimulate activity, and assure "the orderly march of business and employment." "Any lack of confidence in the economic future or the basic strength of business in the United States is foolish," Hoover argued. "Our national capacity for hard work and intelligent cooperation is ample guaranty of the future."

The crisis should have evoked the peerless talents of the Great Engineer. Voters evidently had entrusted the nation's affairs to Herbert Hoover because of his wide experience in the business world, his presumed ability to solve the most complex and difficult economic problems, and his willingness to take bold, positive, progressive action. It should have been his finest hour.

Stock prices finally stopped falling on November 13. Since September 3, the stocks listed on the New York Stock Exchange had lost $30 billion out of a total of $80 billion; the losses on all of the nation's exchanges probably approached $50 billion. Nearly half the decline had been registered since the debacle of Black Tuesday, October 29. Aviation, automobile, electrical equipment, and investment trust stocks had suffered most grievously. Owen Young's General Electric stood at 168, less than half its 1929 high of 396. U.S. Steel sold for 151, down from 261. National City Bank securities, which had peaked at over 500, could be purchased for 200; Charlie Mitchell had lost his desperate battle to keep his stock afloat. RCA, the pool favorite that had reached 101 in September, bottomed out at 28.

It was the death of an era.

# PART FOUR: DESPAIR

# XIX

# Into the Abyss

"The general sentiment seems to be that this must never
and can never happen again. And yet I have seen no practical
suggestion as to how it is to be prevented. The eyes of
Optimism are always bigger than its stomach. Sooner or later
there will be another period of inflation and a subsequent crash and
headache. That is as sure as death and taxes."
                    —HEYWOOD BROUN, *November 1929*

Through the last six weeks of the year, there seemed to be a revolving door on the East Wing of the White House as a ceaseless procession of financiers and industrialists passed through the Executive Office to confer with one another and with President Hoover. The names and faces changed, but the results were always the same. After every meeting, the business leaders announced that they had pledged their cooperation to the President's program to ensure that the crash did not lead to a full-fledged depression. Employers agreed to maintain wage levels and refrain from laying off workers; workers promised not to disrupt the orderly flow of production with strikes or demands for higher wages. Henry Ford, in fact, went one step further and announced—much to Hoover's evident surprise and apparent displeasure—that his company was going to *raise* its workers' wages to protect their purchasing power and encourage increased consumption. To prevent further deterioration in stock prices, John D. Rockefeller gave his broker a standing order to purchase one million shares of Standard Oil of New Jersey if it ever sank to $50 per share. (It was going for 50½ at the time.) Owen Young, who already had invested a substantial sum in General Electric securities, announced that "those who voluntarily sell stocks at current prices are extremely foolish. Our banking position is extraordinarily strong. Our general financial conditions never were sounder." Patriotic advertisers launched a nationwide "Buy It Now" campaign. Most of the nation's business and popular press dutifully reiterated the administration's unshaken contention that "American business is fundamentally sound." "I anticipate a gradual but marked improvement throughout the country," predicted the editor of the *Manufacturer's Record* in a typical comment, and from Kansas, William Allen White's Emporia *Gazette* cheerfully reported that "unless all the economic experts are off their trolleys, the spring of 1930 will see a tremendous flood-tide of prosperity."

In response to a direct request from the President urging an "energetic, yet prudent, pursuit of public works," most of the nation's mayors and governors agreed to speed up the construction programs they had already scheduled. Skeptical observers noted that these pledges involved no additional outlay of expenditures; local and state governments merely consented to pump money into the economy a bit more quickly, or at least to refrain from curtailing normal expenditures. One of the few governors who responded with less than wholehearted enthusiasm to the President's crusade was New York's Franklin Delano Roosevelt, who tartly informed Hoover that he would not recommend any state spending in excess of tax revenues, nor would he ask the legislature for a tax increase to fund additional construction. More typical, though, was Jimmy Walker's promise to spend $1 billion on municipal improvements over the next four years, accompanied by a threat to fire any city employee who could not keep up with the quickened tempo of business. "I am going to work for this city," Walker told reporters after meeting with his chief bureaucratic subordinates, "and I told them that I expect every man and woman, down to the poorest paid employe, to do the same. The man who cannot keep the pace has got to fall out of line; he can't stay."

For his part, Hoover announced that the federal government would seek congressional authorization to spend the grand total of an additional $175 million for public works projects over a ten-year period. Embracing the same strategies he had employed as secretary of commerce, the President prescribed voluntary cooperation under the leadership of Big Business as the most promising path out of the crisis; he encouraged businessmen to coordinate their expansion plans, to pool information and statistics, to form trade associations that might streamline and rationalize industrial production and distribution. (This sort of "activism" irritated the hell out of traditionalists such as cantankerous old Secretary Mellon; Mellon's callous advice for purging the rottenness out of the economic system and restoring prosperity—and, not coincidentally, moral rectitude—was positively brutal in its simplicity: "Liquidate labor, liquidate stocks, liquidate the farmers, liquidate real estate.") The administration, Hoover promised, would facilitate such cooperative industrial activities as much as possible; for instance, the President established a Division of Construction within the Commerce Department to keep a close watch on local public construction projects. But that was all the government would do. "The people will take care of progress," Hoover solemnly assured the nation, "if the Government can put the signs on the road."

But this was no longer enough after the crash. "Prosperity cannot be commanded by proclamation," warned the *Nation*, "and we shall not be aided by cherishing unwarranted hopes and refusing to view realistically the difficulties that are in store for us." The initial burst of enthusiasm following the White House conferences ebbed away as quickly as it had come. Will Rogers irreverently dismissed "the rich man's game of Restoring Confidence": "Confidence hasent left this country," he scoffed. "Confidence has just got wise, and the guys that it got wise to are wondering where it has gone." Bernard Baruch stubbornly refused an invitation to join the seemingly interminable parade of financiers to Washington. "You can no more stop this liquidation with words than Al Smith could stop the cataract at Niagara with his brown derby," he said stiffly.

The stock market remained dull. Prices slowly drifted lower and volume declined; brokers' loans were down to $3.3 billion, their lowest level in a year and a half. Banks and brokers continued to liquidate their stock holdings, gradually feeding more and more securities into a listless market. Almost all the buying was being done by professionals who soon grew weary of trading back and forth among themselves. Soon the press was filled with epitaphs for the New Era that had promised perpetually soaring stock profits: "The golden bull has been melted down into a donkey," wrote one disillusioned critic.

Virtually every measure of economic activity showed a dispiriting slump. Unemployment rose inexorably nearly every week. "Every section of the United States reports a decrease in volume of business during November," stated a *Business Week* survey. In fact, statistics released by the Federal Reserve Bank of New York revealed that the November recession in trade and production was the sharpest drop since 1924.

"No one knew how to get the wheels going," wrote Lewis Mumford. "Those who knew least about it as a class were the bankers, the businessmen, the industrialists, whose rapacity and inordinate ambitions had largely brought on the catastrophe."

In the shadow of the crash, the business titans who had been the prophets of the New Era tumbled from their pedestals. Some prominent speculators, like Jesse Livermore, received anonymous threats against their lives and hired armed bodyguards for protection. Wall Street became a synonym for shysters and crooks. A popular music-hall song pleaded in mock desperation, "Don't tell my mother I'm a banker, she thinks I play the piano in a brothel." Paramount Studios rereleased a movie called *The Wolf of Wall Street,* a former flop that now did huge

business. "I dident have anything particular against Wall Street," remarked Will Rogers, "but knowing the geographical and physical attri-
butes of it, I knew that it was crooked. . . . You can stand at the head of
it, and you can only see the bend. . . . It just won't let you see all of it at
once as short as it is."

Charlie Mitchell was one of the first to go. Ministers in their pulpits
flayed him for irresponsibly leading unwary parishioners astray, down the
path to financial ruin. Persistent rumors that the directors of National City
Bank were preparing to fire him (and replace him with Owen Young)
swept through Wall Street, forcing Mitchell's ally Percy Rockefeller to
publicly deny such gossip as "too absurd to be considered by any sensible
person." But the Federal Reserve Board was sufficiently alarmed over
Mitchell's stewardship of National City Bank's resources to order a special
examination of the bank. The board's governor, Roy Young, later acknowledged that "Mitchell had his back up against the wall" in the weeks after
the crash; Sunshine Charlie was, claimed Young, "the most discredited
man in New York." It was during these dark days that Mitchell sold nearly
twenty thousand shares of National City stock—most of which he had
already pledged to J.P. Morgan and Company as collateral for the $10
million loan—to his wife to establish the desired tax loss of $2.8 million.
The transaction subsequently earned him a federal indictment for income
tax evasion.

Because he had foolishly relied upon the wisdom of Charlie Mitchell's
National City salesmen, Mr. Edgar D. Brown had lost all that he had. "I
am 40 years of age—tubercular—almost totally deaf—my wife and family
are depending on me solely and alone," he wrote to National City in a
bitter postcrash missive, "and because of my abiding faith in the advice
of your company I am to-day a pauper."

Groucho Marx had sunk into a deep black funk. Even though he was
making $2,000 a week in *Animal Crackers* as it toured theaters around the
country, and even though he and his brothers were under contract to
make four more movies for Paramount Studios at a joint salary of $200,000
per film, Groucho was inconsolable. "There's no justice," he muttered to
his family one night at dinner. "Chico's got the right idea. He has no
money either, but meanwhile he's had a hell of a time for himself—
gambling, the best hotel suites, private schools for his daughter. Well, from
now on, I'm going to live by his philosophy—eat, drink and make merry.
Ruth," he said to his wife, "run out and find me a girl named Mary!"

In the weeks after the crash, recalled Arthur Marx, "Father was worrying himself to the brink of a nervous breakdown. He never actually had
a breakdown, but he was in a state of severe depression for many months

afterwards." With all his savings gone, Groucho worried about the future, when he would be too old to make people laugh; he worried that Paramount might not survive the deepening economic crisis; he worried that the public might not find the Marx Brothers funny when the nation was passing through a depression. At night he could not sleep. For the rest of his life he suffered from severe insomnia.

Harpo accepted the loss of his fortune far more stoically. More than the money, he mourned the disappearance of the world he had loved since Alexander Woollcott first made him a show business celebrity. The economic catastrophe that slowly, inexorably enveloped the United States brought down the final curtain on the irreverent and ultimately inconsequential wit of the Algonquin Round Table. There simply was no place for the group in the postcrash order. "Martial law had been declared against us, against Croquemaniacs and Thanatopsians and Sitters of the Round Table, and all the other over-aged children of our world," wrote Harpo years later. "We were under house arrest. The sentence was the abolition of the 1920's."

In Paris, Morley Callaghan wondered whether he and his friends Ernest Hemingway and Scott Fitzgerald did not truly realize "in our hearts we would soon have to go home." Perhaps, Callaghan decided, Hemingway did not. "For him, committed as he was to the romantic enlargement of himself, did there have to be one adventure after another, until finally there was no home? And what could be left for Scott when the glorious wandering was over? When 'a primrose by a river's brim, a yellow primrose was to him, and it was nothing more.' My old theme. Nothing more; the wonder of the thing in itself. Right for me. But not for Scott." They all had been tormented spirits in exile, flying in desperation from the pain and anguish of life and death. "Ernest would never again write about his own country," Callaghan predicted. "And Scott, as long as possible, would go on drinking and rushing to the Riviera."

Haunted by the ghosts of prosperity, Scott and Zelda fled to North Africa, to Algiers, "to forget bad times," they said. Shortly thereafter, Scott wrote his own celebrated obituary for the late, lamented Jazz Age. "Somebody had blundered and the most expensive orgy in history was over," he said. Its death knell had been the sound of the crash, "because the utter confidence which was its essential prop received an enormous jolt, and it didn't take long for the flimsy structure to settle earthward."

Six weeks after the crash, the end of the decade of the Roaring Twenties was punctuated with grisly emphasis by the two gunshots that killed Harry Grew Crosby and a young society woman named Mrs. Josephine Bigelow. Police found the couple fully clothed, lying together on a bed in a friend's apartment in the Hotel des Artistes in midtown Manhattan, the victims of a suicide pact; apparently they had indulged in an opium orgy before Crosby shot his companion in the head with a .25 Belgian automatic pistol and then fired a single bullet through his own temple. Thirty-one years old, Crosby was the son of a partner in J.P. Morgan and Company; his mother was Mrs. Morgan's sister. Although his parents had bought him a seat on the New York Stock Exchange after his graduation from Harvard, Harry had volunteered for service as an ambulance driver in the war and then opted for a decidedly unconventional life as a writer and editor in the bohemian quarters of Paris, where he became a close friend of the alcoholic expatriate poet Hart Crane. Wealthy, handsome, and rather shy, Harry was a man of easy charm who smiled a lot and pursued pleasure in whatever form he could find it.

Like many of his fellow countrymen, Crosby had returned to the United States in the autumn of 1929. He had suffered some losses in the crash but had not been wiped out. Neither Harry nor his companion left a suicide note, but to his colleague Malcolm Cowley his death symbolized "the decay from within and the suicide of a whole order with which he had been identified": "Things had changed everywhere. The lost generation had ceased to deserve its name; the members of it had either gone under, like Crosby and Crane after him, or else had found their places in the world. The postwar era had definitely ended and people were saying that it had given way to another prewar era. . . . A financially bankrupt world had entered the age of putsches and purges, of revolutions and counterrevolutions."

On the eve of the twelfth anniversary of the Russian Revolution, Joseph Stalin suddenly emerged from weeks of self-imposed isolation and issued a ringing defense of the Politburo's industrial Five-Year Plan and his own savage, obsessive drive toward agricultural collectivization. With the reverberations from the crash on Wall Street still ringing through the Western World, the Soviet dictator could afford to gloat. "The American crisis shakes the whole structure of world Capitalism," jeered a government-inspired article in the Moscow press. "It explodes the legend about American 'perpetual prosperity' and the alleged permanence of capitalist stabilization." Already American credits were being replaced by German loans and British trade. "We are attacking capitalism all along the line and defeating it," Stalin shouted exultantly.

We have won the peasant masses—the "middle" peasants—to collective farming, and in two or three years we shall be one of the greatest, if not the greatest, grain-producing country in the world. With giant strides we

move toward Lenin's aims—industrialization, electrification, and mecha-
nization. . . . And then, when we have industrialized the Union of Soviet
Socialist Republics and set the mujiks [peasants] to driving tractors, let the
honorable capitalists with their "civilization" try to outstrip us. Then we
shall see which country can be called backward and which the vanguard
of human progress.

Stalin claimed to have converted thirty-seven million acres of Russian
agricultural land from private use to collective farms within the past
twelve months; the number of peasants working—not entirely of their
own free will—on the state lands had risen from four million to thirteen
million. "Villages do not follow towns to Communism," Stalin grimly reminded the people. "Towns must drag villages to Communism." In November, the Central Committee in Moscow voted to step up the pace of
the program even further. One American witness characterized the brutal
forced collectivization program as "a veritable earthquake which is standing the whole country on its head." While the party congratulated itself
on having exceeded the previous year's grain collections by 50 percent,
the accumulation of human suffering and heartbreak incurred during the
conversion was incalculable. "The kulak must be completely liquidated,"
Stalin ordered, and every week scores of kulaks were executed for crimes
against the state: the murder of government inspectors; failure to sow all
their grain fields; willful destruction of livestock to sabotage the government program; arson; refusal to sell all their grain to government collectors at the fixed price; incitement of their comrades to rebellion. In January 1930, the Central Committee issued another directive doubling the
tempo of collectivization. The government seized the kulaks' land and
then denied them permission to join the collective farms.

Oswald Garrison Villard, the former muckraking American journalist,
journeyed to the Soviet Union for a firsthand glimpse of the brutal experiment and heard other foreign visitors dismiss the Five-Year Plan as an
impossible dream. But Villard knew better; he understood that in the long
run at least, "the chances are on the side of the Kremlin." "The Bolsheviks
know their people and their limitless capacity for suffering and starving,
and they are banking on it," Villard wrote. "They believe they know how
far they can go; how long they can keep up their present rationing of
bread, and soap, and textiles, and how long they can deprive the people.
. . . What can the worker do about it? Life he knows is bitter hard; he can
only hope that it will not last forever. A prisoner in his own land—for he
cannot get a passport to leave—what alternative is there? He must bear
it. . . . Meanwhile the eyes of Stalin and his associates are fastened on their
goal, and toward its realization their whole drama progresses—at a speed,

they are certain, that no highly capitalized and individualized nation could possibly approach."

In the town of Durban, South Africa, native black workers who objected to the prevailing rigid apartheid restrictions broke out in a riot against the white establishment and then launched a tax strike against the government. Police responded by raiding the native compounds with tear gas and nightsticks, arresting and jailing six hundred blacks. The radical Afrikaners blamed the disorders on Communist agitators and whipped up hysterical fears among the white population, seeking to gather support for their legislative initiative to deprive natives of their voting rights.

At 3:29 P.M. on November 28, 1929, Commander Richard Byrd and three companions—a pilot, a radio operator, and a cameraman—took off from their Antarctic base of Little America in the Ford trimotor plane Byrd had named in honor of a late friend and fellow explorer, *Floyd Bennett.* For more than a week the flight had been postponed by poor weather; Byrd had grown increasingly nervous over the possibility that Sir Hubert Wilkins, who had returned to Antarctica after spending the summer gathering supplies from Europe and Australia, would be the first to fly over the polar cap. But at last the sky along the route had cleared, and so the lumbering plane headed toward the distant and imaginary point that, according to Byrd's calculations, represented the South Pole. The pilot and passengers were wrapped in thick furs against the bitter cold, which reached fifteen degrees below zero; ahead lay glistening, pure white glaciers, and mountain peaks aglow with the brilliant crimson reflection of the sun. "Everywhere we looked was some formation no living thing had ever before seen," thought an awestruck Byrd.

As they approached the last glacier that hid the polar plain, the pilot shouted that the plane was too heavy to make it over the peak; they would have to toss at least two hundred pounds of cargo overboard. If they dumped that much gasoline, they would not have enough fuel to make it all the way to the Pole and back. So Byrd decided to throw two sacks of food—enough to keep the expedition alive for six weeks—out of the plane; if the men subsequently had to make a forced landing in the uncharted wilderness without those supplies, they might well starve to death before anyone reached them.

But the *Floyd Bennett* soared over the final peak at eleven thousand feet, and a spectacular sight greeted Byrd's eye: "Now, with the full panorama before us, in all its appalling ruggedness and gothic massiveness, we had a conception of the ice age in its flood tide. Here was the core, the center point of the Antarctic ice sheet. . . . The parade of the mountains, the contrast of black and white, the upreaching peaks and the trisulcated troughs of the glaciers, the plateau spreading to an illusory horizon—it was something never to be forgotten."

At 1:14 A.M., the plane passed over "the center of a limitless plain": the South Pole. There time meant nothing, for this was the place where all meridians met, and the sun traversed the sky at virtually the same constant height every hour. There every direction was north. Byrd and his men continued past the Pole for a few miles, then circled back, and on the return trip the commander dropped an American flag, weighted with a stone from Bennett's grave, over the last place God made; then he released a package containing the flags of Great Britain, France, and Norway to celebrate the accomplishments of pioneers such as Amundsen and Scott, who had reached the Pole eighteen years earlier. "There was nothing now to mark that scene," wrote Byrd in his journal; "only a white desolation and solitude disturbed by the sound of our engines." The expedition arrived back at Little America at 10:38 that morning.

On December 3, President Herbert Clark Hoover delivered his first annual Report on the State of the Union to Congress. The crash, Hoover assured the legislators, had been the inevitable but essentially insignificant result of the "over-optimism" that had been stimulated by "the long upward trend of fundamental progress." It was true, the President acknowledged, that there had been "a reduction in the consumption of luxuries and semi-necessities by those who have met with losses, and a number of persons thrown temporarily out of employment." But there was no cause for alarm, Hoover promised: "We have reestablished confidence."

That month the Federal Reserve Bank of New York's index of general productive activity (including employment and building construction) fell to 15 percent below normal, the lowest figure on record since November 1921. Private construction was off 43 percent, and public construction was down 11 percent from the previous December. Distribution statistics slumped to their lowest point since September 1921. The rate of business failures suffered another jump. "The recession at the end of 1929," declared *Business Week,* "was in most respects more severe than any since the post-war depression of 1920–21. It was more marked than that in 1927 in every respect, more severe than in 1924 in most respects, and in some respects it was almost as severe as the 1921 decline." Employment agencies reported unusual difficulties in finding places for their clients during the normally hectic preholiday rush; organized charities received an increasing volume of pleas for assistance; crimes attributable to poverty kept rising steadily.

Disturbingly, sales of low-priced consumer goods were dropping faster than the high-ticket items; contrary to predictions, it was not primarily the luxury trades that were suffering six weeks after the crash, but the mass market items. Woolworth's December sales, for instance, fell more than $1,250,000 from the last month of 1928.

"If you are interested in the market you will notice that stocks are coming back," joked Eddie Cantor. "Yes, sir, they're coming back—but not to their original owners." Wall Street plunged deeper and deeper into its fatal lethargy as the market stubbornly refused to respond to the prescribed treatments. Bernard Baruch recalled his son, "a young broker who had shrewdly avoided the crowd madness, coming home exhausted and depressed by the scenes of despair and desperation at the stock exchange. Many of my friends, who had ridden the waves of the boom, now found themselves swamped, and needed help to keep from being sold out. Many people I had known for years, professionals in Wall Street as well as amateurs, were wiped out."

"By December a mood of permanent crisis and settled gloom had descended upon the Street," observed John Brooks. "Workers there who opened their office windows on mild days heard a steady, low murmur coming from the crowd that gathered daily outside the Stock Exchange." It was, of course, a far cry from the boisterous, excited noise of the bull market boom. "The sound went on all through trading hours," recalled one contemporary witness, "and reached its peak around noon. It wasn't an angry or hysterical sound. That was the most ominous thing about it. It was a kind of hopeless drone, a Greek dirge kind of thing. It was damned distracting, I must say."

The New York City district attorney's office finally brought George McManus to trial for the murder of Arnold Rothstein. But the state's witnesses hedged on the precise sequence of events during the fateful poker game that preceded Rothstein's death, and prosecutors failed to connect McManus with the murder weapon, nor could they establish a reasonable motive for the slaying. The defense never had to call a single rebuttal witness. As soon as the prosecution had concluded its sketchy case, Judge Charles C. Nott, Jr., directed the jury to acquit McManus.

McManus celebrated his release by attending a football game in Manhattan; while he was gone, burglars entered his Riverside Drive apartment and absconded with $8,000 worth of clothes and jewelry.

In mid-December, the most savage storm in nearly a century struck the European continent in full force. Two hundred lives were lost. On the Atlantic, sixteen ships were sunk and eight more abandoned at sea. Spanish cargo boats were pounded to splinters on the rocky shores of Cape Finisterre. The hurricane smashed a fifty-foot wave against the breakwater at Cherbourg; a huge hangar was flattened and the occupants crushed at the airport at Villacoublay. Dikes and windmills were wrecked and thousands of acres of farmland flooded in Holland. Houses and dams collapsed in Britain and angry flood waters swelled the Thames; the playing fields of Eton were submerged under eight feet of water. Along the coast, the barometer sank to the lowest point ever recorded in British history.

In Germany, the Reichstag threw out the anti-Young Liberty Law by a decisive margin of 318–82. On December 22, the third and final stage of the referendum process ended in an overwhelming defeat for the Hitler-Hugenberg coalition; in the nationwide plebiscite, only 14 percent of the German electorate voted for the Nationalist measure, far below the 50 percent required for adoption.

But the strenuous, violently emotional campaign had lured new converts to the National Socialist cause. In the Berlin municipal elections at the end of the year, the Nazis garnered three times as many votes as before, and placed their first representatives in the city administration. In Koblenz, they captured 38.5 percent of the vote in communal elections; in Thuringia, they tripled their share of the popular vote and elected the first Nazi minister in any provincial government.

As 1929 came to a close, Hitler scornfully denounced Hugenberg as a weak, tired old man, and defiantly severed relations with his erstwhile Nationalist ally. With renewed virulence, unfettered by any considerations of diplomacy or decency, Hitler resumed his vicious attack on the faltering Weimar Republic. The Nazi party staged recruiting nights, featuring black banners and the feared Brownshirt brigades, in towns and cities across Germany; it infiltrated respectable trade unions and professional organizations and twisted their legitimate objectives to meet the Nazis' own perverted ends.

By January 1930, Germany already had advanced far along the path toward economic chaos. No longer could the nation support itself by foreign borrowing; in the wake of the crash and the subsequent worldwide credit stringency, hard-pressed foreign investors anxiously withdrew the short-term loans that had kept the German economy afloat for the past six years. German businesses could not obtain the funds they needed for survival. The Berlin stock market crashed; exports dried up; agricultural prices dropped sharply and farm foreclosures rose; businesses went bankrupt, factories shut down and unemployment mounted to dangerous heights. Germany's short-term debt increased to 1.6 billion marks. The government deficit, swollen by rapidly growing unemployment subsidies, was even worse, totaling 1.7 billion marks, and only extensive emergency bank loans kept the nation from financial chaos.

By the beginning of the new year, wrote historian Joachim Fest, "it was obvious that nobody was going to be spared. The most prominent characteristic of the Depression in Germany was its totality." The economic crisis was transformed into an acute psychological trauma that destroyed "all political, moral, and intellectual standards and was felt to be something far greater than its specific causes: a shattering of faith in the existing order of the world. . . . It was more than an economic slump; it was a psychological shock. Weary of everlasting troubles, their psychic resistance worn thin by war, defeat, and inflation, sick of democratic rhetoric with its constant appeals to reason and sobriety, people let their emotions run rampant."

"A sense of total discouragement and meaninglessness pervaded everything," remarked another German observer, and Hitler manipulated the chilling despair like the consummate demagogue that he was. Displaying a supreme confidence that he and he alone held the key to the nation's salvation, Hitler offered the German people sacrificial scapegoats for their misery (the Jews and foreign capitalists) and fulfilled their unspoken spiritual longing for an ideology of hope, communal pride, sacrifice, and heroic grandeur.

On December 14, a Michigan highway patrolman stopped a sedan that had fled the scene of a hit-and-run accident. The driver, a man named Frederick Dane, promptly pulled out an automatic pistol and fired three bullets into the policeman, fatally wounding him. Dane then sped away, but police later found his wrecked car wrapped around a telephone pole on Highway 12. The registration papers in the glove compartment showed that Dane lived at an address on Lake Shore Drive in the nearby city of St. Joseph. When authorities searched the innocent-looking house, where Dane had been posing as a retired businessman, they discovered a vast arsenal of firearms including two machine guns, numerous revolvers, rifles, bottles of nitroglycerin, and tear gas bombs. They also found a cache of stolen bonds worth $319,850, identified as part of the booty from a recent Wisconsin bank robbery.

Inquiries revealed that "Frederick Dane" was in fact Fred Burke, whom police warnings identified as "one of the most infamous ex-convicts in the U. S. . . . the most dangerous man alive." Authorities guessed that Burke was the mysterious man with the missing front tooth who had been seen driving away from the scene of the St. Valentine's Day Massacre, and soon concrete evidence obtained from ballistics tests proved them right. A microscopic examination of bullets fired from two of the guns found in Burke's home matched several of the slugs removed from two of the massacre victims; and when New York police forwarded bullets extracted from the body of slain gangster Frankie Yale, Capone's former mentor, they found that these, too, had been fired from a machine gun in Burke's arsenal.

Rewards totaling $60,000 were offered for Burke's arrest.

Following a halfhearted prosecution by the state, a North Carolina jury acquitted the eight deputies accused of killing six striking workers outside the gates of a textile mill in Marion. After delivering the verdict, some members of the jury climbed out of the box to shake hands with the defendants. "The jury's verdict is in keeping with the performances in North Carolina in recent months," declared a spokesman for the American Civil Liberties Union. "Every officer or mill agent guilty of violence has been either not held for trial or acquitted. . . . At the end of seven months' struggle to organize, the strikers' toll is six men and one woman killed, twenty-four wounded, seven sentenced to prison for five to twenty years, seven kidnapped and five flogged by mobs. Not a single one of those responsible for the violence against the strikers has been brought to justice."

Herbert Hoover celebrated a sober Christmas Day 1929 in the White House with his family and the families of his cabinet members. From admirers across the land he received scores of presents, mostly wristwatches and neckties. J. P. Morgan, Jr., spent the holiday at his family estate on Long Island. "We had a very good Christmas," he told a longtime friend. "For the first time we had all fifteen grandchildren seated at the same table and being fed. It really resembled nothing so much as some of the families of pigs I have seen on the farm; but it was a cheerful sight all the same."

Others passed the day in considerably less satisfactory circumstances. "We have again arrived at a winter of unemployment and suffering," observed the *New Republic.* "Indices of employment show losses everywhere. . . . No sign comes from the White House that Mr. Hoover is any more alive to the problem than were his predecessors." In New York City, where a survey revealed that a full 17 percent of working class families were unemployed, a number of men deliberately broke windows in police station houses so they could spend the holiday in the warmth of a jail cell with something to eat. An alarmed Senator Robert F. Wagner of New York introduced legislation in Congress to prepare a comprehensive federal public works plan to alleviate unemployment if the crisis grew much worse.

From southern California, Will Rogers sent the nation some unusually bitter holiday greetings: "Passed the Potter's Field yesterday and they were burying two stanch old Republicans, both of whom died of starvation, and the man in charge told me their last words were, 'I still think America is fundamentally sound.'" And on December 30, Rogers warned that America once again would be subjected to "the usual New Years prosperity applesauce by our same men who are always rich enough to see a great year coming up." Sure enough, from the wizened secretary of the Treasury there came a prediction on January 1 that "the Nation will make steady progress in 1930." "I see nothing in the present situation," Mellon declared, "that is either menacing or warrants pessimism." Naturally, Sunshine Charlie Mitchell agreed. "A general feeling of confidence exists throughout the country," Mitchell told the National City stockholders at the start of the new year. "[It] does not appear probable that business will remain below the normal stage of activity for any protracted period."

But America was singing sad, wistful songs that winter: "When You're Counting the Stars Alone" (Paul Whiteman and his orchestra), "What Wouldn't I Do for That Man" (the tearful Helen Morgan), and "Lonely Troubadour" (Rudy Vallee crooning to the sound of a mournful saxophone). On the other hand, comedians reported that they had never had an easier time making people laugh; but the laughter, they said, had a certain desperate, almost demented quality. Miniature golf (also known as midget, tiny, or pee-wee golf) became the latest national obsession. Broadway was suffering a horrible slump, but attendance at the movies was still quite good. Audiences could enjoy Joan Bennett and James Gleason performing Irving Berlin's songs in *Puttin' on the Ritz;* William Powell as a doomed gambler in *Street of Chance,* based upon the life and death of Arnold Rothstein; *Untamed,* starring a very young and very lovely Joan Crawford; the desert melodrama of *The Lost Patrol;* an uninspired story of love and loss on *Wall Street;* and jazzman Ted Lewis' madcap and ironically titled vehicle *Is Everybody Happy?*

At the Palace Theater in New York, Jimmy Durante and his partners introduced a new song to their stage act: "Money to Burn"—"Money to burn, money to earn, money to throw away, money for you, and money for her, and money for him. Hurray!"—complete with hundreds of thousands of dollars of counterfeit money that the boys threw from the stage to the audience. At first Lou Clayton thought that Durante was crazy to suggest such a thing in the dolorous postcrash atmosphere. "Everybody's busted," explained Jimmy in his own defense. "What the hell! Let's cheer 'em up! Get all this stage-money printed, and we'll put bills in every pocket, and we'll have this money stickin' out of every pocket, our inside pockets, our little lapel on top, in our pants pocket, in our back pocket, and we'll have a great big canvas bag in the middle of the theater over the dome in the orchestra. And at a certain cue, when we holler, when we come to the lyrics that we've got money to burn, money to throw away, one of the prop men will pull a string . . . and this bag will open up and all this money will fly down and around." And the audiences loved every minute of it.

Meanwhile, the nation spun further into the misery of a major depression. The number of business failures in the United States during January was the highest for the first month of any year on record. In spite of (or perhaps because of) the Federal Farm Board's interference in the nation's agricultural markets, farm prices continued to slide downward. Bank deposits showed a decline of more than $1.7 billion from January 1929. The average price of issues on the New York Stock Exchange stood almost exactly at the level of 1926. "Business conditions, as yet, offer nothing to stimulate stock prices," complained *Business Week*. In fact, those who had hung on grimly through the crash were still patiently feeding their holdings back into the market whenever prices rose a few points. The category of sellers included the famous Morgan-sponsored bankers' consortium, too; in a brief statement to the press, George Whitney announced that the pool, which had actually stopped purchasing stocks on November 13, had finally completed the liquidation of its holdings. (Not surprisingly, the bankers apparently managed to make a small profit on the sum of their transactions.) Call money fell all the way down to 4 percent, but there was no rush to buy; brokers' loans continued to decline toward the $3 billion level.

In February, commodity prices—which had been falling steadily since July 1929—declined by another 2 percent. Cotton prices were down 29 percent from their 1929 high, wool was down 30 percent, wheat 14 percent, and rubber 36 percent. The business mortality rate was the highest for any February since 1922. Reluctantly, remembering what had happened the last time it slashed its rates, in 1927, the Federal Reserve Bank of New York cut its rediscount rate all the way to 4 percent (leading the Bank of England, in turn, to reduce its rate to 4½ percent), but business stubbornly failed to respond to the stimulus.

Despite the Federal Reserve's example, bankers clearly remained apprehensive about extending credit to anyone; one disgusted observer described it as "an orgy of conservatism." Just as they had loaned too freely during the speculative boom, the bankers were crawling too far into their shell, pulling in their resources behind them, traumatized by the shock of the crash. "There are clear signs that in the present situation our banking authorities are being guided in their policies not so much by the actual necessities of the situation as by a paralyzing conservatism and a superstitious fear of raising another bottle-genie of speculation which they could not control," complained *Business Week.* "The nightmare of the Great Bull market still haunts their sleep." Nor, for that matter, were many businesses willing to borrow money in the prevailing atmosphere of "widespread and disquieting uncertainty" even if funds became available.

Irving Fisher, the economist who had defended the speculative boom so staunchly on the eve of the crash, finally conceded that "the U.S. is headed toward a period of business depression, probably beginning within the next two years, which may exceed that which preceded the War." And now even Billy Durant, the Dream Maker, the King of the Bulls, joined the growing legion of doomsayers. "With keen regret I make the prediction that we will see next winter business conditions unimproved," said an unhappy Durant, "longer breadlines, more soup kitchens, continued uneasiness and distress and a more pronounced tendency to Socialism and Communism—this regardless of assurance from Washington that everything is all right." Durant himself had lost huge sums since the crash; reportedly he had reentered the market too soon, gambling on a quick rebound, and had lost millions of dollars. He was reduced to borrowing 187,000 shares of General Motors stock from his wife, but that, too, eventually vanished into the abyss. In February, Durant sued the New York *Telegram* and eight other newspapers for libel—for $45 million, the largest action ever based on one article—after they published a story linking him with shady stock market deals that had resulted in heavy losses for innocent investors. Then several brokerage houses sued Durant for unpaid commissions, leading Durant to file countersuits claiming that they had sold him out without his knowledge or approval. One disgusted observer dismissed this whole unedifying spectacle as nothing more than a disgraceful case of "a gambler squabbling with a tout."

Calvin Coolidge, who had recently bought a stately $40,000 home in Northampton, attempted to escape from the deepening gloom all around him by spending his winter vacation in sunny southern California. "We're just a couple of plain tourists seeking modest accommodations and a chance to look around Southern California quietly," the former President told reporters as he and his wife stepped off the train in Los Angeles, but tremendous crowds of adoring admirers dogged their steps wherever they went. Once when Coolidge tossed a cigar butt into the gutter, a dozen people scrambled for the trophy. In Hollywood, the Coolidges met Mary Pickford Fairbanks, Will Rogers, Marion Davies, and Jack Warner. "I have been in the movies for some time but never professionally," Coolidge joked. "I suppose everyone who comes here has a motion picture complex. I haven't." Will Rogers invented a fanciful interview with Silent Cal:

"Mr. Coolidge, what is your impression of the general condition of our country?"

"Yes."

"Who is the logical candidate in case Mr. Hoover don't care for another term?"

"Uh huh."

"Will you have another biscuit, Mr. Coolidge?"

"Probably."

Not a single communication had passed between Coolidge and President Hoover since inauguration day. Reporters speculated that Coolidge harbored a secret ambition to return to the White House if Hoover proved unable to surmount the growing crisis; one enterprising journalist even slipped into Coolidge's hotel suite and asked the former President (who was just emerging from the shower) whether it was true that he was planning to run again. Coolidge just waved a towel at the offending young man and shouted, "Depart!"

As the economy sank further into the depression, Coolidge spent hours sitting and looking out of the windows of his Northampton home, pondering the five years he had spent as Chief Executive, contemplating his share of the responsibility for the crash. Certainly he viewed the future as extraordinarily bleak. "In other periods of depression it has always been possible to see some things which were solid and upon which you could base hope," he told a longtime friend, "but as I look back I can see nothing to give ground for hope, nothing of man."

At last he could stand it no longer and so he wrote a scathing letter to Owen Young, complaining that the captains of American industry were not cooperating sufficiently with the administration's efforts to restore prosperity. Young, who knew where the blame truly lay (and who had recently been named *Time* magazine's "Man of the Year" for 1929), politely denied the accusation.

Hoover again spent his winter vacation in the Florida Keys, sailing on Jeremiah Milbank's yacht, but in 1930 the fishing was poor and the onerous burdens of office were great, and so the President cut short his holiday and returned to Washington after only six days.

Al Smith—who by this time probably blessed the fates that had kept him out of the White House—and John J. Raskob spent most of their winter in Palm Beach. Smith amused onlookers on the beach by the luxurious Breakers Hotel by floating on his back in the ocean while squirting a three-foot-high stream of water through his front teeth into the air. In the afternoon, he and Raskob usually played golf at the exclusive Everglades Country Club. Meanwhile, construction on the Empire State Building proceeded apace, unhindered by their absence.

Exhausted by a persistent cold, a chronic stomach ailment that resulted in a dangerous loss of weight, the strain of his illicit affair with Betty Compton (which had brought down upon the lovers a stern admonition from Cardinal Hayes, head of the New York archdiocese), and the crushing responsibilities of public office in a time of despair, forty-eight-year-old Mayor Jimmy Walker came to the edge of a nervous breakdown. His doctor, who was also the city health commissioner, insisted that Walker spend an extended period of rest and recuperation in Florida. Meanwhile, Republican legislators in Albany continued to press for a full-scale investigation of corruption in the Walker administration. Governor Roosevelt managed to delay official inquiries for the moment, but he cautioned the Tammany sachems that he might not be able to withstand the pressures indefinitely.

Surveying the collapse of the industrialized economies of the Western world, a sober Owen Young told an audience at the University of California's sixty-second anniversary celebration that "America is too rich to be loved." "Let no man think," Young warned, "that the living standards of America can be permanently maintained at a measurably higher level than those of other civilized countries. Either we shall lift theirs to ours or they will drag ours down to theirs."

# XX

# The Death of Dreams

"It was an easy, quick, adventurous age, good to be young in;
and yet on coming out of it one felt a sense of relief,
as on coming out of a room too full of talk and people into
the sunlight of the winter streets."
—MALCOLM COWLEY, *Exile's Return*

On March 7, 1930, Hjalmar Schacht resigned as president of the Reichs-bank in protest against the changes made in the Young Plan by the Allies at the Second Hague Conference in January; primarily he objected to the amendments providing for military sanctions against Germany in the event it defaulted on its reparations payments. "After the second Hague Conference," Schacht explained, "nothing remained of mutual co-opera-tion, nothing of confidence in Germany, nothing of helping Germany to carry out the difficult task prescribed in the Young Plan." Despite Schacht's reservations, the Reichstag ratified the amended Young Plan on March 12 by a vote of 270–192. President Hindenburg reluctantly signed the measure ("with a heavy but firm heart") the following day. The leading Nazi newspaper, the *Deutsche Allgemeine Zeitung*, commemorated the occasion with a front page bordered heavily in black: "As the chief of state, Marshal von Hindenburg has proved an ignominious failure, and his Presi-dency has been one of increasing martyrdom for all his faithful followers and admirers."

Less than two weeks later, the government of Chancellor Hermann Mueller resigned over a dispute on the funding and distribution of unem-ployment benefits. Hindenburg invited the Catholic Center Party's leader, Heinrich Brüning, an intelligent but uninspiring former political scientist, to form a new cabinet. Although Brüning succeeded in forging a narrow majority, his middle-of-the-road coalition was too unstable to last for long. German politics were becoming increasingly polarized as the extremists on both ends of the spectrum gathered force. Brüning soon found himself in a deadlock with the Reichstag over a controversial tax revenue measure; rather than compromise, the chancellor foolishly accepted the challenge of new elections.

Hitler poured all his resources into the ensuing campaign. "Working Germany, awake!" screamed Goebbels, playing on the rage and fury of the embattled German nation. "Break your chains in two!" The lame little propagandist knew the German people were sick and tired of the vacillating, ineffectual politicians of the republic. "Throw the scum out!" screeched the Nazi orators at party rallies and mass demonstrations and street corner gatherings. "Tear the masks off their mugs! Take them by the scruff of the neck and kick them in their fat bellies on September 14 [election day], and sweep them out of the temple with trumpets and drums!" "Strike down the political bankruptcies of the old parties!" raged Hitler. "Destroy the corrupters of our national unity! Down with those responsible for our decay! Volks-comrades! Join up with the Brown Front of awakening Germany!"

"Never in my life," Hitler later recalled, "have I been so well disposed and inwardly contented as in these days."

And his inspired blend of mysticism and grand promises for national regeneration worked far more effectively than even the Nazi leaders themselves had dared to hope. "What we felt, what our hearts compelled us to think, was this—Hitler, you're our man," explained a young convert to Nazism. "You talk like a human being who's been at the front, who's been through the same mess we were, and not in some soft berth, but like us an unknown soldier."

Hitler also played adroitly on the German bourgeoisie's fear of the Communist party, which, like the Nazis, was rapidly gaining converts as the economy deteriorated. Street fights between Reds and Nazi toughs were a common occurrence, and Goebbels prayed for casualties he could enshrine as victims of the antisocial leftists. Extremists of the right and left coexisted in an odd sort of symbiotic relationship in those days: both parties were battling for the votes of the disenchanted workers and farmers who had nothing but contempt for the political establishment; orators from both ends of the political spectrum couched their appeals in populist terms of solidarity against the bloodsucking financiers and Big Businessmen who allegedly were responsible for the nation's misery. So the same factors that propelled the Nazi cause to prominence also fueled the rise of the Communists, a development that scared the German middle class— which remembered with horror the bloody Spartacist revolts of 1919— and provided additional impetus to Hitler's crusade.

When the final ballots were tallied, the Nazis had won 6,371,000 votes—more than 18 percent of the total—and captured 107 seats in the Reichstag. A year and a half earlier, they had gathered only 810,000 popular votes and elected only 12 deputies. The Communist party, to Hitler's good fortune, also registered startling gains in the elections, increasing their share of the vote by more than 1,300,000 ballots.

The Nazis were now the second largest political party in Germany, and certainly the most dangerous.

"There are times when one spends perhaps a whole day, vaguely conscious that one has been through all its details before," thought Lewis Mumford. "Was it in a dream? Was it in the imagination? Or was in it actuality?"

On March 7, President Herbert Hoover announced that "all the evidences indicate that the worst effects of the crash upon unemployment will have been passed within the next sixty days."

By that time it was obvious to all but the most obtuse contemporary observers that unemployment had become a severe national problem for the first time since the postwar recession. The American Federation of Labor revealed that 43 percent of the nation's construction workers were jobless, and conditions were getting worse, not better, with the advent of springtime. In sharp contradiction to Hoover's optimistic forecast, New York State industrial commissioner Frances Perkins stated—and had the statistical evidence to back up her claim—that unemployment in New York was at the highest level in fifteen years. In Chicago, where 20 percent of industrial workers were idle, employment officials acknowledged that the crisis already had passed the depths reached in 1921; in San Francisco, 15 percent of union members were jobless. In Los Angeles, it was the worst year since 1907, with at least 100,000 men out of work. Even the Labor Department admitted that employment was at its lowest level since it began to compile reports in 1923, and the figures would have been far worse if hundreds of employers had not instituted a policy of reducing hours and retaining workers as part-time employees.

Bland statements of reassurance and confidence could no longer hide the truth. "The situation is serious," asserted Governor Roosevelt in a public statement at the end of March, "and the time has come for us to face this unpleasant fact as dispassionately and constructively as a scientist faces a test tube of deadly germs, intending first to understand the nature, the cause and effect, and finally the method of overcoming and the technique of preventing its ravages."

In New York City, breadlines stretched out for blocks; the YMCA in the Bowery fed 12,000 unemployed workers every day; the Church of the Transfiguration ("The Little Church Around the Corner") in Manhattan gave free meals daily to 1,000 more. Heywood Broun begged employers

to "Give a Job till June." Senator Wagner pressed his unemployment relief
bill through Congress, aided by photographs that juxtaposed the New York
breadlines with a picture of Calvin Coolidge being honored at a "prosperity dinner." AFL president William Green told Congress that at least 3.7
million workers were unemployed in America, and he warned that the
situation was approaching a flash point: "We shall face either Federal
unemployment insurance for the jobless or have a revolution on our
hands. The country cannot stand these continual shocks."

Already the jobless were turning to violence. In Washington, police
employed tear gas and blackjacks to disperse a demonstration of unemployed workers in front of the White House. Cleveland police charged a
jeering crowd of nearly ten thousand demonstrators and left one hundred
people injured. Mounted police confronted an unemployment rally in
Detroit, sending thirty-one people to jail and fourteen more to the hospital. Four hundred idle workers gathered outside a union hall in Newark,
New Jersey, to hear orators denounce Hoover as "the lackey of Wall
Street" and "J. P. Morgan's office boy"; police ordered the crowd to disperse and arrested those who refused. A mob of several thousand unemployed men and women battled police in Los Angeles, trapping hundreds
of innocent spectators in the melee.

New York City suffered its worst riot in years. Thirty-five thousand
protesters jammed into Union Square on a chilly March morning to hear
Communist speakers denounce the capitalists who had taken away their
jobs. The leaders of the rally informed Commissioner Whalen that they
intended to march to City Hall to present their grievances directly to
Mayor Walker. "You won't accomplish anything by numbers," Whalen
replied. "I am telling you now if you attempt to proceed we will break up
the parade." Undaunted, several thousand demonstrators headed down
Broadway. There they were met by hundreds of policemen who fell on the
parade with nightsticks and blackjacks and bare fists, swinging indiscriminately at anyone or anything within reach. "From all parts of the scene
of battle came the screams of women and cries of men, with bloody heads
and faces," reported the *Times*. "A score of men were sprawled over the
square, with policemen pummeling them. The pounding continued as the
men, and some women, sought refuge in flight."

Whalen defended his actions, and received a commendation from the
New York Chamber of Commerce for his anti-Red stand, but other observers expressed their bitter outrage at the incident. "A few lawless policemen did more in fifteen minutes to make Red Thursday in New York a
Communist success than all the Communists put together," scolded the
New York *World*. "There was absolutely no occasion and no excuse for the
bloody mess in Union Square."

In the first three months of 1930, the Communist Party of America increased its membership rolls by nearly 50 percent. Most of those who signed up were native-born, well-educated Americans. The disintegration of the nation's economy "recalled to some men of letters that they had been all too ignorant of political economy," observed Matthew Josephson. "They now began to inquire into the subject and to scrutinize the financial and political news in the morning newspaper. There seemed to be a good deal of truth . . . in what John Dos Passos, a fervent Marxist throughout the twenties, had long been saying about 'the inevitable decline' of the capitalistic regime in the United States."

The weather remained unseasonably cold in April in America; it seemed as if the springtime refused to appear. Across the land the tempo of bank failures increased. Exports in the first quarter of 1930 were down 25 percent from the same period in 1929. Hundreds of corporations, including AT&T, Du Pont, Western Union, and S.S. Kresge, reported declines in their quarterly earnings, leading even the venerable *Commercial and Financial Chronicle* to admit at last that "verily, trade and business in this country have undergone great shrinkage." A Federal Reserve survey of business found nearly every district reporting a discouraging downturn; ominously, commercial loans continued their downward spiral. Sparked by the Federal Reserve Bank of New York's decision to drop its discount rate to 3 percent—call money fell all the way to 2 percent—Wall Street witnessed a halfhearted rally in March and April, and some stock market favorites recouped nearly half the losses they had suffered in the crash, but once again the rising averages hid a sluggish and dispiriting performance by the rest of the issues on the board.

The nation waited and prayed for Hoover to propose some bold new initiative to stop the agonizing slide, but it waited and prayed in vain. "We are out of training, grown soft and confused. We need plans, leaders," argued the editors of *Business Week* at the end of April. "Except for a few brave efforts to apply the old emergency formulas in the storm which overtook business last year, we and most of the world have been drifting somewhat indolently down an ebb tide for several months, our moorings lost, our bearings a bit confused, without direction, ideas or leadership." "America needs leadership," echoed the Chicago *Tribune.* "The public looks to Business for it. The politicians in Washington are only a crowd of ranting actors." President Hoover, charged the Providence *News-Tribune,* "has not had either the Coolidge luck or the particular kind of ability needed to take its place."

In Congress, House minority leader John Nance Garner of Texas flayed Hoover for what he termed a "breakdown in Administration leadership." "The titular party leader in the White House is either lacking in courage or capacity to lead," snapped Garner, "and the consequent bewilderment of Congressional leadership is a reflection of the deepening disappointment of the American people in the promised and expected major part the President was to play in shaping national affairs to the better ends of national needs. There is not a Republican leader in either House who has the faintest glimmer of what the President wants and, worse still, they haven't the slightest idea that he wants anything particularly constructive or progressive." In his capacity as Democratic National Committee chairman, John J. Raskob hired a former New York *World* journalist named Charles Michelson to coordinate a partisan campaign of anti-Hoover rhetoric in the nation's press, but the job was really not necessary. The President's lack of experience in dealing with the perversities of human behavior under stress left him totally bereft of ideas to jolt the country out of its sickening descent into depression. He seldom ventured out of the Executive Office during that spring, and it was not a coincidence that the White House security force was increased from thirty-nine to forty-seven men.

With two months shaved off his sentence as a reward for good behavior, Al Capone was released from prison on March 16. They smuggled him out of Eastern Penitentiary in the warden's car to a nondescript suburb twenty-five miles outside of Philadelphia, where several of his henchmen picked him up in a blue Buick sedan and bore him away to safety.

During his incarceration, however, Capone's income tax returns had come under the scrutiny of a dedicated federal bureaucrat named Elmer L. Irey, chief of the Internal Revenue Service Enforcement Branch. Already the Feds had nailed Capone's brother, Ralph, for defrauding the government out of $300,000 in income tax, and sentenced him to twenty-two years in prison.

To make matters worse for the beleaguered gangster, Florida officials launched a strenuous campaign to evict Capone from his Miami Beach hideaway, which a local authority condemned as "a public nuisance and a source of annoyance to the community as a harbor for all classes of criminals and desperate characters." "It's no crime to let a rattlesnake live but if you allow one to roam loose in your backyard where it may bite children, any court in the world will declare it a nuisance and authorize its abatement," declared the state's attorney. "We endorse, commend and urge all legitimate efforts to exterminate from this community . . . a cancerous growth," concluded a Dade County grand jury. "We urge all law-abiding citizens to give their unstinted cooperation to the end that 'Scarface Al' Capone, his accomplices and their sinister influences shall not continue to be inflicted upon Florida." Finally a pair of detectives arrested Capone while he was driving along Biscayne Boulevard and locked him up for "investigation."

"I'm here for the rest which I think I deserve," replied the harassed gangster after his lawyer sprung him on a writ of habeas corpus. "All I want is a fair break. I've done nothing in violation of the law in Miami and will not. All I wish is to be left alone to enjoy my home here."

In April, Michigan law enforcement authorities tracked down and captured Fred Burke. They refused requests to extradite him to Illinois, choosing instead to try him for the murder of the state highway patrolman outside of St. Joseph in December. Burke was convicted and condemned to life imprisonment in the Michigan State Penitentiary, where he died.

Joe Kennedy finally managed to rid himself of his Pathé responsibilities by arranging a deal whereby RKO purchased all of Pathé's somewhat tarnished assets. Although the transaction netted Joe the cash he desired, it was a rotten deal for the Pathé stockholders. Some of them filed suit against Kennedy for fraud; others sent anonymous threatening letters to him. "We are going to put you on the spot," read one angry handwritten note.

> You have fair warning. We are not going to be like you, sell Pathé inc. out on the stockholders and then push them out with nothing. We are not going to plug you or we are not going to stick you in the back, but we are going to cut your throat from ear to ear as a warning to others what pulls the same deal. Now you may go to Florida, Europe or any other place but we will get you anyway when you least expect it, you know Kennedy the stockholders of pathe are all poor people and nothing else and you ruined them to make yourself more richer than what you are. . . . Well so long til we see you the sooner the better. You will have a note pinned on your cloth to tell why you passed out.

On April 23, Zelda Fitzgerald voluntarily entered the Malmaison Hospital just outside Paris. She was highly agitated, unable to relax, teetering on the edge of a nervous breakdown. "It's dreadful, it's horrible, what's to become of me," she moaned as she paced restlessly back and forth. "I must work and I won't be able to, I should die, but I must work. I'll never be cured." Against her physician's advice, she left the hospital the following week, but in June her husband and a friend convinced her to enter the asylum of Les Rives de Prangins on the shore of Lake Geneva in Switzerland for treatment. "Our ride to Switzerland was very sad," she wrote when her sanity returned. "It seemed to me that we did not have each other or anything else and it half killed me to give up all the work I had done. I was completely insane. . . . I had come to the end of my physical resources. . . . I loved my work to the point of obsession. It was all I had in the world at the time."

Late in April, General Sandino and three of his aides went for an automobile ride in the countryside around Mérida. They never returned. Instead, Sandino retraced his steps of the previous spring and journeyed incognito through Mexico, Guatemala, El Salvador, and Honduras, returning to Nicaragua in May. During his isolation in Mérida, Sandino had broken angrily with the Mexican Communist movement, refusing to subordinate his Nationalist struggle to the dictates of party ideology, and so the Communist press denounced him upon his return to his native land as a "traitor to the cause of world anti-imperialism."

Inspired by the reappearance of their chieftain, the Sandinista guerrillas stepped up the intensity of their subversive assaults against the Moncada government. But by June, they were fighting almost exclusively against the National Guard, for Hoover had withdrawn another 650 marines from Nicaragua, leaving only a token force of 950 Americans in that strife-torn land.

Since Britain bestowed neither self-government nor dominion status upon India in 1929, the Indian National Congress met at the end of that year and approved a declaration of independence by a virtually unanimous vote. To persuade the British to withdraw from India, the congress subsequently adopted a plan formulated by Mohandas Gandhi that called for escalating mass protests, nonpayment of taxes, desertion from the army, noncooperation by native officials with the raj, and a boycott of the government's monopoly on the manufacture and distribution of salt.

Gandhi himself led the campaign against the salt tax, which cost Indians hundreds of thousands of dollars every year. "The salt tax is one of the most immoral acts this Government has ever been responsible for," Gandhi explained, "especially because it is collected stealthily." In the middle of March, the mahatma, wrapped only in a light cotton cloth, set out from his ashram in Ahmadabad on a 165-mile march to the sea, where he planned to openly defy the British prohibition against distilling salt from the sea. He made no secret of his intentions, but the government dared not stop him. Seventy-nine disciples marched with him when he left Ahmadabad, and twenty thousand cheering sympathizers saw him off; one woman offered Gandhi a pony to use if any of his marchers fell ill.

Some days the frail little man walked for six hours along the dusty roads, but soon the blistering sun took its toll and he found it necessary to rest for an extra night in a friendly town. Sometimes the villagers were still asleep when he walked through the silent, empty streets in the hours just before dawn. "If you do now awake," Gandhi called to the blank windows of the houses, "you will be looted by other people, if not by Englishmen." One day each week he remained totally silent.

After he had traveled eighty miles, the mahatma began to display signs of fatigue. Eighteen of his followers, most of them younger men, already had collapsed from exhaustion. At night, his head was wrapped in cold compresses, his legs rubbed with ointment and swathed in cloth. Still he kept marching, and at every village he summoned the people to civil disobedience. "Money alone will not win self-government," Gandhi told them. "If money could win, I should have obtained it long ago. What is required, therefore, is your blood." In one town after another, scores of local officials resigned in protest against the salt tax; thousands of men and women of all castes pledged to join the movement for independence.

By the time Gandhi reached the impoverished little town of Dandi on the Gulf of Cambray on Sunday, April 6—twenty-five days after his departure from Ahmadabad—nearly 320,000 Indians were walking with him. As the people watched from shore, the mahatma and his original band of disciples prayed an ancient Hindu prayer of blessing and then waded into the warm waters of the sea and scooped up several gallons of salt water, which they set on the beach to be evaporated by the sun. The few tiny grains of salt that remained were promptly sold to eager bidders. Simultaneously, this symbolic procedure was repeated at numerous villages across India, prompting the British to arrest dozens of Nationalist demonstrators, including Jawaharlal Nehru and Ram Das Gandhi, one of the mahatma's sons. "Do not surrender salt," Gandhi advised his followers, "even if the police break your hands."

Although Gandhi expected the government to arrest him, too, it patiently refused to do so until the campaign of civil disobedience erupted in a wave of savage violence. When unarmed demonstrators marched on the salt works at Dharasna, police beat them brutally; an appalled American newspaper correspondent reported that "the spectacle of their beating the unresisting volunteers was so painful I frequently was forced to turn away. . . . I saw them kick volunteers already lying on the ground . . . fractured arms and wrists . . . bleeding." At the largest British salt reserve, at Wadala (near Bombay), the same reporter saw police break their staves on the bodies of the demonstrators. In response, Nationalist agitators staged mass protests in cities across the land, inaugurated a taxpayers' strike, and rioted in the streets of Bombay, Calcutta, and Delhi, burning banks, offices, and several British soldiers who were trapped by a furious mob.

By June, two million British workers were on the dole. Not only had the Labour government failed to alleviate the unemployment crisis, but an additional five hundred thousand men and women had lost their jobs since MacDonald had taken over. The London Stock Exchange stubbornly refused to budge from its lethargy. As world trade fell into a tailspin from the withdrawal of credit and the erection of national tariff walls, the value of British exports dropped from £839 million in 1929 to £666 million in 1930. It finally dawned on Winston Churchill that the Wall Street crash, which he came to refer to as an "economical blizzard," was turning Britain into "one vast soup kitchen."

Yet MacDonald's cabinet declined to initiate any bold new programs to stimulate the economy; indeed, it soundly rejected a dramatic program of centralized government control of industry proposed by Oswald Mosley. Aside from increasing unemployment benefits, the government simply "retreated into a cloud of impressive-sounding Commissions and Committees"—including a Committee of Enquiry into Finance and Industry, an Economic Advisory Council, and a Committee on National Expenditure—much like its counterpart in Washington. By December 1930, the number of unemployed in Britain was approaching two and a half million.

Grover Aloysius Whalen resigned as police commissioner of New York City in May and returned to Wanamaker's, whence he had come. He was replaced by Assistant Chief Inspector of Detectives Edward Pierce Mulrooney, a tough, career police officer who at least knew what he was doing. The murder of Arnold Rothstein remained unsolved.

At the Morrow home in Englewood, New Jersey, Charles and Anne Lindbergh celebrated the birth of their first child, a happy, smiling boy.

On May 1, Herbert Hoover stood before the annual meeting of the Chamber of Commerce of the United States and declared, "I am convinced we have now passed the worst and with continued unity of effort we shall rapidly recover. . . . We have succeeded in maintaining confidence and courage."

Over the next two days, stock prices broke badly in a whirlwind of selling—the heaviest trading of the year. It was the most precipitous decline since the crash. Prices did not stop falling until, at the end of June, all the gains that had been made so painstakingly since November 1929 had been wiped out completely, and many issues sank beneath their 1929 lows. The avalanche of selling on the market was nothing more than an accurate, if belated, reflection of the terribly depressed condition of American business, despite the Federal Reserve Board's desperate decision to lower its rediscount rate to 2½ percent, the lowest in the history of the Reserve System. "The market has never had the benefit of a business revival," lamented *Barron's Weekly,* "and now it finds that it can not prosper indefinitely on cheap money alone."

All the easy predictions of quick recovery had turned to ashes. "American business is giving a pretty poor exhibition of its proverbial spunk and shrewdness," complained *Business Week.* Instead of articles suggesting that "Everybody Ought to Be Rich," magazines began to publish pieces that gave readers "One Way to Beat Hard Times." Corporate earnings continued to tumble alarmingly; by May, they were running nearly 20 percent below the comparable period of 1929. Retail stores cut prices in a vain effort to boost sales. In violation of their pledges to Hoover, industrialists began slashing wages. A new wave of bank failures shook the nation. Nearly every basic commodity (copper, wheat, cotton, silver, sugar, rubber, etc.) was selling at a lower price than in any year since the war, and many had fallen below the lowest point since the turn of the century. In the face of this calamity, the Farm Board took absolutely no action whatsoever.

The slump intensified during June. Production of steel, automobiles, and agricultural equipment dropped again; railroad traffic declined as well. "It is becoming clear that it will take longer than expected for all the king's horses and all the king's men to put Humpty-Dumpty together again after his great fall from the midsummer boom of 1929," remarked *Business Week* discouragingly. Hoover responded by proposing the establishment of a National Business Survey Commission "to diagnose and suggest, but not to dictate, the future course of business." Alarmed at the shrinkage in income tax receipts as a result of the economic slowdown— the Treasury reported that the projected $122 million federal surplus for fiscal year 1931 was likely to turn into a $30 million shortfall—Hoover frantically warned Congress to cut spending at once, making a mockery of his previous exhortations to speed the pace of public works projects.

And then the President foolishly signed the extraordinarily protectionist Smoot-Hawley Tariff Bill, which Congress finally had succeeded in passing after nearly eighteen months of acrimonious wrangling and logrolling. It was an extremely selfish and shortsighted measure that promised to inflict great damage on international commerce, which already was in wild disarray from the gathering worldwide depression. Overall, the bill established the highest tariff rates in American history: an average of 41 percent ad valorem on all dutiable commodities, and a full 20 percent above the previous tariff passed in 1922. Instead of making the sort of minor adjustments Hoover had originally requested, Congress had revised the rates on 1,122 different items, from anvils, beans, and beef to lemons, pig iron, and sugar cane. Of course, almost all the changes (about 85 percent) were increases, many to prohibitive levels, in a misguided effort to keep out foreign competition and increase tariff revenues.

The bill met with vociferous protests from a wide array of industrial and financial leaders, including the chairman of the American Importers and Exporters Association, who predicted—quite rightly—that the tariff would "cause ill will and reprisals which will make it impossible for us to develop the export trade necessary to the continued prosperity of the U.S." A prominent labor union official denounced the Smoot-Hawley Bill as "the most atrocious and indefensible tariff revision ever considered by Congress." Auto executives, whose companies relied heavily on sales abroad, were particularly outraged. Henry Ford personally informed Hoover that the measure was "an economic stupidity," and General Motors' Alfred Sloan, Jr., pointed out with a bit more tact that "the economic position of the U.S. has completely changed during the past two decades. We cannot sell unless we buy. Additional restrictions in the way of raising the height of the tariff wall are bound to have an adverse influence on our domestic prosperity through reducing our ability to produce." Indeed, several European nations, including Italy and France, already had launched boycotts of American goods and promised retaliation in the form of their own protectionist tariff walls.

Never was Hoover's lack of leadership so evident. The President had completely lost control of the tariff battle in Congress, allowing greedy lobbyists and special-interest protectionists to run roughshod over the forces of moderation, and now he supinely consented to sign the grotesque resolution, despite his private characterization of the Smoot-Hawley measure as "vicious, extortionate and obnoxious." As he affixed his signature to the bill with six gold pens, Hoover lamely explained that while "no tariff bill has ever been perfect . . . [it] is urgent that the uncertainties in the business world which have been added to by the long extended debate on this measure should be ended. They can be ended only by completion of this bill. Nothing would contribute to retard business recovery more than this continued agitation."

On the New York Stock Exchange, prices at once plunged sharply in the year's most disastrous trading day thus far.

Already the national mood had shifted from exuberance to a sort of fatalistic desperation. The year 1930 "was one of nervous breakdowns," recalled Malcolm Cowley. "The psychiatrists were busy when every other profession except that of social service was losing its clients. One friend who was being psychoanalyzed told me that the doctor's office was crowded with people he knew; it was like a publisher's tea."

It was a year of suicides, not only among stockbrokers but also among wealthy dilettantes. It was a year when faces looked white and nervous; a year of insomnia and sleeping tablets. It was a year when classmates and former friends became involved in speakeasy brawls, divorces, defalcations and even murders; the underworld and the upper world were close to each other. Most of all it was a year when a new mood became perceptible, a mood of doubt and even defeat. People began to wonder whether it wasn't possible that not only their ideas but their whole lives had been set in the wrong direction.

America was beset by inertia; all motion appeared to be aimless, as if the nation was going dazedly around in circles, "trying to figure out the lost quality in equations that yesterday seemed so simple." "The lull is suspense," wrote columnist Anne McCormick. "Un-American as it sounds, we are all waiting, waiting for something to turn up. . . . If any nation was ever justified in a panic of the spirit, it is this country facing the problems pressing for solution today."

"Today fear, the most corroding of influences, is the moving cause," wrote Bernard Baruch in despair.

# Epilogue

"I heard you lost a lot in the crash."
"I did," and he added grimly, "but I lost everything
    I wanted in the boom."
"Selling short."
"Something like that."
                    —F. SCOTT FITZGERALD,
                         *Babylon Revisited*

In the summer of 1930, President Herbert Hoover greeted a delegation of American clergymen who had come to the White House to urge him to initiate an expanded federal public works program. "You have come sixty days too late," Hoover told them. "The depression is over."

If Hoover truly believed what he said, he was either a fool or a blind man. Between the summer of 1930 and the spring of 1933, the economies of the United States and the nations of western Europe spun ever more swiftly downward into the numbing misery of the Great Depression. The national income of the United States plummeted from $88 billion in 1929 to $40 billion in 1932–33. The output of American factories declined by 50 percent; automobile production fell to 20 percent of its 1929 high. In the depths of the depression, American steel mills were operating at 12 percent of capacity, and the production of pig iron stood at its lowest point since 1896. Banks failed with increasing and horrifying frequency across the nation: 659 banks went under in 1929; 1,352 in 1930; and 2,294 in 1931. Stronger banks refused to help their weaker brethren, and when the federal government finally provided relief (in the form of loans from the Reconstruction Finance Corporation) to the troubled financial community, bankers kept nearly all the proffered funds tucked away safely in their vaults—to stave off bankruptcy after fearful depositors withdrew their savings—instead of lending them out to get the economy moving again. But still the panic-stricken run on the banks continued.

Prices on the New York Stock Exchange struck rock bottom on July

8, 1932, a day when a mere 720,278 shares were bought and sold. When the dust finally settled, the Dow Jones industrial average, which had peaked at 452 in September 1929, had slid all the way down to 58. U.S. Steel fell from 262 to 22, General Motors from 73 to 8, and Montgomery Ward from 138 to 4. Anaconda Copper, too, landed in the basement at 4, and a share of the ill-starred Blue Ridge investment trust could be had for 63¢. Investment in stocks and bonds tumbled from $10 million in 1929 to $1 million in 1932.

Following a severe drought in the summer of 1930, the misery and despair of the American farmer reached previously unimagined depths. Farm income fell from $12 billion to $5 billion. Wheat prices declined from $1.05 a bushel in 1929 to a paltry 39¢ three years later; cotton went from 17¢ a pound to 6¢; and corn from 81¢ to 33¢ a bushel. Sheriffs endeavoring to foreclose on farms with unpaid mortgages were greeted by hostile armed mobs of farmers. "They are just ready to do anything to get even with the situation," a Farmers' Union spokesman told a Senate investigating committee. "I almost hate to express it, but I honestly believe that if some of them could buy airplanes they would come down here to Washington to blow you fellows all up. . . . The farmer is naturally a conservative individual, but you cannot find a conservative farmer today."

Between 1929 and 1932, employers slashed factory wages from $12 billion to $7 billion; the average weekly wage dropped from $25.03 to $16.73. Unemployment reached 6 million by the end of 1930, and kept climbing until a staggering 12.8 million workers—25 percent of the total labor force—were jobless in the spring of 1933. Someone compared the heartbreaking unemployment figures in the industrial cities of the north with the British casualty lists at the Somme, "so awesome as to become in the end meaningless, for the sheer statistics numbed the mind": 1 million people out of work in New York City; 50 percent of the Cleveland labor force idle; 80 percent out of work in Toledo; 660,000 unemployed in Chicago, where Al Capone financed a soup kitchen that provided 120,000 free meals to the jobless in the space of just six weeks. Henry Ford, on the other hand, pompously proclaimed that the depression was a "wholesome thing in general"—"It's a good thing the recovery is prolonged," Ford said, "otherwise the people wouldn't profit by the illness"—and suggested that since half the people in Detroit were looking for work, they should go back to the farm and live off the land. F. Scott Fitzgerald, who was appalled by the human tragedy he encountered on his return to New York, began reading the works of Karl Marx. "To bring on the revolution," Fitzgerald wrote, "it may be necessary to work inside the communist party."

As tax revenues declined, state and local governments slashed spending and reduced their already inadequate public works programs. Hoover stubbornly refused to engage in large-scale deficit spending to pump more money into the economy (indeed, when it appeared that the federal budget would post a deficit in 1932, Hoover actually asked Congress to increase taxes), nor would he permit the federal government to provide direct relief for the unemployed. "He made what was probably the last stand for a type of society and government that is gone," wrote journalist Tom Stokes a decade later, "the sort, as he had pointed out, that had given him the opportunity to battle his way to the top." To Herbert Hoover, a poor boy and orphan who had struggled and fought for everything he had gained, it was unthinkable to condone any sort of government initiative that might erode the individual's freedom of action or sap the initiative and vitality of the American spirit. He insisted that self-help and voluntary assistance on the part of the local community—what he liked to refer to as "the American way"—were sufficient to alleviate the worst elements of the economic catastrophe. Indeed, it is not certain that Hoover ever truly understood just how far and how deeply the appalling misery extended throughout America. "This is not an issue as to whether people shall go hungry or cold in the United States," Hoover explained to a nation shivering in fright.

> It is solely a question of the best method by which hunger and cold shall be prevented. It is a question as to whether the American people on the one hand will maintain the spirit of charity and mutual self-help through voluntary giving and the responsibility of local government as distinguished on the other hand from the appropriations out of the Federal Treasury for such purposes. My own conviction is strongly that if we break down this sense of responsibility of individual generosity to individual and mutual self-help in the country in times of national difficulty and if we start appropriations of this character we have not only impaired something infinitely valuable in the life of the American people but have struck at the roots of self-government.

But people were starving to death in America, and even such a staunch conservative as Winston Churchill was astounded by the sort of intransigence Hoover displayed on the issue of government-sponsored unemployment insurance. "I do not sympathize with those who think that this process of compulsory mass saving will sap the virility and self-reliance of our race," thundered Churchill. "There will be quite enough grindstone in human life to keep us keen."

Nor could the stolid Hoover project even the image of decisive action that might have inspired the American public to break through the vicious cycle of fear, despair, and deflation that carried the nation ever deeper into a seemingly bottomless abyss. "I have no Wilsonian qualities," he admitted dolefully to a friend. By the autumn of 1932, the Great Engineer had become a forsaken object of ridicule and derision, an austere, uncaring, cold-hearted shell of a man hidden away behind the iron gates of the White House. On one of the rare occasions near the end of his term when he consented to make a public appearance, Hoover journeyed to Charleston, West Virginia, to dedicate a memorial. As usual, the President received the traditional twenty-one-gun salute. As the sound of the shots died away, an old man standing nearby shaded his eyes from the sun and stared for a moment at Hoover, and then muttered under his breath, "By gum, they missed him."

By the end of 1930, Billy Durant, the King of the Bulls, had lost his entire fortune in the long, seemingly interminable decline of the same market that had brought him millions of dollars of profits in the past. "I'm wiped out," he confided to an old and dear friend on one cold December evening. Six years later, Durant formally declared bankruptcy, though he like to remind persistent reporters that he was still "the richest man in America—in friends." In 1939, Durant opened an eighteen-lane bowling alley in Flint, Michigan. "I haven't a dollar," he announced brightly, "but I'm happy and I'm carrying on because I find I can't stop." He subsequently suffered a series of strokes between 1942 and 1946 that left him progressively weaker and less able to function, until he died in March 1947 at the age of eighty-five.

On May 1, 1931, the Empire State Building—the world's tallest structure—was formally opened (slightly ahead of schedule) when Herbert Hoover pressed a button in the White House that switched on all the lights in the skyscraper. Two of Al Smith's grandchildren cut the ribbons to the front entrance. At a dedication ceremony and luncheon on the eighty-sixth floor, Governor Franklin Delano Roosevelt, who had won reelection to the executive mansion in Albany by the unprecedented margin of 735,000 votes in the fall of 1930, looked out over the vista and admitted, "I am still a little awestruck. . . . As a simple countryman who has only been down here in New York for twenty-five years, I still think in terms of fields and creeks." The entire project had been funded by four directors: John J. Raskob, Pierre Du Pont, a banker, and a mine company owner, aided by a $27.5 million loan from the Metropolitan Life Insurance Company. "It is but a short time ago that I wondered even with all the resourcefulness of Al Smith, how a building could get up quite this high and wide," added Mayor Walker in his tribute to the builders. "But recent developments have convinced me that after all he had not only an interest in official New York, he had a little sympathy for it, and he thought perhaps there might be a place higher, further removed than any other in the world, where some public official might like to come and hide, so he built this."

But the building might as well have remained dark. In the midst of the depression, there were so few tenants that elevators stopped running between the forty-second and sixty-seventh floors. The famous dirigible mooring mast proved entirely useless. During the Second World War, a military plane crashed against the tower, killing everyone aboard.

On October 23, 1931, Alphone ("Scarface") Capone was convicted of income tax evasion for the years 1925, 1926, and 1927 and for failure to file any return at all for 1928 and 1929. The judge sentenced him to eleven years in a federal penitentiary and ordered him to pay fines totaling $50,000, the harshest penalty ever meted out to a tax offender at that time. "It was a blow below the belt, but what can you expect when the whole community is prejudiced against you?" Capone whined on his way to jail. Even during his incarceration, Capone remained an object of fascination to the American public, inspiring numerous more or less factual books about his syndicate activities (bearing titles such as *The Inside Story of Chicago's Master Criminal*), as well as the movie *Scarface,* starring Paul Muni with a screenplay written by Ben Hecht. Capone returned to Florida after his release from Leavenworth Prison, but the ravages of time and an apparent syphilis infection left him grossly overweight and mentally disoriented. Stricken by a cerebral hemorrhage on January 19, 1947, Capone lived for six more days and then passed to his eternal reward at the age of forty-eight.

Like Herbert Hoover, Britain's Ramsay MacDonald was a self-made man, and so was MacDonald's chancellor of the Exchequer, the acerbic Philip Snowden. And like the American President, they refused to adopt unorthodox schemes of economic stimulation to pull their nation out of the deepening depression. "A well-balanced budget is not a luxury which is to be avoided," Snowden tartly informed Churchill in 1930. "It is a necessity which is to be provided for." And so Parliament dutifully raised taxes by £47 million in 1930 in a futile effort to balance the budget. By 1931, the economic situation had deteriorated to such a point that MacDonald felt compelled to invite the two opposition parties to form a coalition—the National government—which naturally intensified the drift to the right. Unemployment benefits were slashed (despite the fact that 1.5 million workers were jobless), public works were postponed, and military salaries were cut (provoking a strike by a company of sailors), but the devastating deflationary spiral continued until Britain finally, and most reluctantly, was forced to abandon the gold standard in late 1931.

In Germany, the government of Chancellor Heinrich Brüning adopted a similar policy of reducing expenditures and raising taxes. This classic and chilling remedy succeeded only in increasing unemployment to six million. Sparked by the failure of the Austrian *Kreditanstalt* in May 1931, the German banking system collapsed altogether, touching off a chain reaction of failures in financial institutions throughout Europe and the United States. Hindenburg appealed to Washington for help in postponing Germany's international obligations. Prompted by Hoover, who was primarily (and quite properly) concerned about the effects of the financial crisis on the United States, the Allies grudgingly consented to a moratorium on reparations and war debts payments. Although this "standstill agreement"—which the French deliberately sabotaged shortly after it was signed—was originally intended to form a temporary stopgap, international commercial arrangements had been thrown so completely out of whack by the depression and the ensuing tariff war (aggravated by the United States' infamous Smoot-Hawley Tariff of 1930) that payments on both reparations and war debts were never resumed, thus writing an effective end to the Young Plan.

By 1932, nearly 40 percent of the German work force was unemployed. Brüning responded by tightening the screws further, relentlessly cutting prices, wages, and benefits. In May, Hindenburg requested Chancellor Brüning's resignation. He replaced him with the aristocratic Franz von Papen, who immediately ordered new elections. Again the Nazis employed the economic crisis to expand their representation in the Reichstag. After several successive cabinet failures, Hindenburg (who had been overwhelmingly reelected to the presidency of the republic) finally—and very reluctantly—asked Hitler to take the reins of government in January 1933. Within months, Hitler had effectively deprived Hindenburg of all powers and assumed dictatorial control of Germany himself.

He took a desperate, confused nation and remade it in his own perverted image. Power was centralized in the hands of the Fuehrer and his inner circle of lieutenants; in the name of the National Socialist revolution, storm troopers seized the offices of the state governments and arrested anyone who protested; all vestiges of an independent labor movement vanished as trade union leaders were thrown into concentration camps along with dissident politicians, religious leaders, and intellectuals; fulfilling his cherished dream of supremacy as head of the Ministry of Enlightenment and Propaganda, Joseph Goebbels ruled the German press, radio, and movies as an unchallenged dictator. Hitler then embarked on a furious campaign of public works, rebuilding Berlin and revitalizing the nation's transportation system, adding over a thousand miles of new roads and doubling the capacity of the railways. Most important, he found ways to circumvent the Versailles Treaty restrictions on the size and power of the German armed forces, and when he could no longer hide his intentions he openly broke the restrictions and dared the Allies to challenge him.

Under the impetus of this massive spending program and a vast expansion in social services, the German economy—freed of the burden of reparations payments—revived and reasserted its natural primacy in Europe. And then the German military machine carried the national resurgence into new territories, assuaging the painful memories of 1919. Between 1933 and 1941, the Third Reich nearly doubled in size, from 180,976 to 323,360 square miles; by the end of 1941, the Reich governed 106 million people, a vast increase from the 65 million of 1933. By the time he was fifty-two years old, Hitler was the most powerful man in the world.

On the evening of March 1, 1932, the twenty-month-old child of Charles and Anne Lindbergh was kidnapped from their home near Hopewell, New Jersey. Ten weeks later, the child's lifeless body—the offspring of America's most beloved hero—was found partially buried in a woods about a mile away. An itinerant carpenter named Bruno Hauptmann was convicted of the crime and executed. The tragedy deepened Lindbergh's already paranoid suspicions of the press, which had turned both the hunt for the child and the trial into a cruel circus, full of sensational and mean publicity stunts, and so he and his wife soon abandoned America for Europe, where they withdrew further into seclusion.

Witnesses claimed that Calvin Coolidge seemed to have aged ten years between 1929 and 1932. His face and neck grew gaunt; the former President had a haggard, haunted look about him in the last twelve months of his life. No longer was Silent Cal a popular folk hero. His fading health permitted him to make only a few speeches on behalf of Hoover during the presidential campaign in the autumn of 1932. "I have been out of touch so long with political activities that I feel I no longer fit in with these times," Coolidge sadly admitted to a friend after the election. "We are in a new era to which I do not belong, and it would not be possible for me to adjust myself to it." He died shortly after noon on January 5, 1933, alone at his home in Northampton.

On July 1, 1932, on the fourth ballot at the Democratic National Convention in Chicago, Governor Franklin Delano Roosevelt received his party's presidential nomination, defeating rivals Al Smith, Owen Young,

Congressman John Nance Garner, and Newton Baker, an internationalist attorney who had served as secretary of war in Woodrow Wilson's cabinet. Embittered by his defeat at the hands of his former protégé, Smith (who had earlier denounced Roosevelt's innovative state unemployment relief program with the sarcastic comment "This is no time for demagogues") stormed out of the convention hall and petulantly refused to release his delegates, thereby preventing a nomination by unanimous consent.

Four months later, after a strenuous if not particularly edifying campaign in which prohibition, and not the depression, was the most controversial issue, Franklin D. Roosevelt (supported by substantial financial contributions from Bernard Baruch and Joseph P. Kennedy) captured the White House in a stunning but hardly unanticipated landslide that matched Hoover's defeat of Smith four years earlier. Roosevelt swept all but six states, winning 22,800,000 votes to Hoover's 15,750,000.

Although the new President succeeded in restoring the invaluable blessings of hope to the anxious American public, and though he did launch desperately needed programs of direct federal unemployment relief that mitigated the most damaging human effects of the economic catastrophe, Roosevelt's inauguration in March 1933 did not immediately dispel the black clouds of depression that stubbornly hung over the nation. Nor did the New Deal, with its contradictory impulses and frequently chaotic administrative style, ever succeed in restoring the United States to full economic health. Not until 1939–40, when the Roosevelt administration—facing fascist aggression on the continent of Europe and in the Far East—launched a substantial rearmament program that pumped vast sums of federal funds into the economy, did the last enduring effects of the Great Crash disappear.

Broken in health and beset by political difficulties, not the least of which was an official, independent investigation headed by puritanical judge Samuel Seabury, which had uncovered vast evidences of corruption in his administration of New York City, Jimmy Walker abruptly resigned as mayor on September 1, 1932. Five years later, Walker's successor, Fiorello La Guardia (whom Walker graciously described as "the greatest mayor New York ever had"), invited Jimmy to serve as "czar" of industrial and labor relations in the city's $250 million garment industry, a post Walker held until 1945. Walker lived the last years of his life quietly in New York City, and died in November 1946 at the age of sixty-five.

Between December 1929 and December 1932, the resources of National City Bank declined from $2.2 billion to $1.6 billion. The bank was forced to write off loans worth $86 million; deposits fell by 21 percent. In

1929, National City had turned a profit of $22.8 million; in 1932, it suffered a loss of $12.6 million. The shares of its stock tumbled from $520 all the way down to $23.

In January 1933, Charlie Mitchell was called to testify before a Senate subcommittee investigating "practices of stock exchanges with respect to the buying and selling and the borrowing and lending of listed securities, the values of such securities, and the effects of such practices." In response to a question from Senator Brookhart of Indiana, Mitchell candidly admitted that he had sold those 18,300 shares of National City stock "for tax purposes" in late 1929. Five days after his Senate testimony, Mitchell resigned as chairman of National City Bank and its affiliated companies. In March, he was arrested and charged with defrauding the government of $850,000 in income taxes; after a trial that lasted for six weeks, a federal jury acquitted him of the criminal charges, whereupon the federal government initiated civil proceedings to collect the back taxes. Mitchell appealed the case all the way to the Supreme Court, which finally ruled in favor of the government and ordered the banker to pay taxes, interest, and penalties totaling $1.1 million.

Despite his mounting personal financial difficulties, Mitchell resolutely refused to declare bankruptcy—he said he didn't think that would be the "square" thing to do—and eventually repaid all his debts and settled his tax dispute with the Treasury. He was elected chairman of the investment banking firm of Blyth and Company and transformed it into one of the leading brokerage houses on Wall Street. Genial and gregarious to the end, Charlie Mitchell died on December 14, 1955, at the age of seventy-eight.

Between 1929 and 1932, the reported net worth of J.P. Morgan and Company tumbled from $118 million to $53 million. Like Charlie Mitchell, Jack Morgan was called to testify before the Senate Banking Subcommittee investigating Wall Street. He admitted that he had paid no income taxes at all for the years 1930, 1931, and 1932, claiming that his losses in the stock market had more than offset his income. Indeed they may have done, at least on paper, and yet Morgan's vast personal fortune remained almost undiminished by the crash. Within months after his appearance before Congress, Morgan retired from the active management of the firm that bore his father's name, nominating Thomas Lamont as his successor. He suffered a fatal stroke at his Florida estate in March 1943.

For the first few months of the New Deal, President Roosevelt neglected to provide Joseph P. Kennedy with any tangible reward for his monetary contributions to the triumph of the national Democratic ticket.

In a fit of pique, Kennedy petulantly threatened to call in all his loans to the Democratic party, whereupon Roosevelt unexpectedly offered the unscrupulous financier the chairmanship of the newly established Securities and Exchange Commission, the organization responsible for preventing the sort of stock market abuses that had contributed to the crash (and, in no small measure, to Kennedy's personal fortune). It was a controversial appointment, to say the least, but Roosevelt apparently was acting on the time-honored premise that required one to set a thief to catch a thief. Kennedy fulfilled his SEC responsibilities with laudable vigor for a year; then, after contributing further substantial sums to Roosevelt's 1936 reelection campaign, he was named ambassador to Great Britain in December 1937. Again it seemed a most ironic appointment for the feisty Irishman. Nevertheless, Kennedy served at the Court of St. James for three years, earning the enduring enmity of the British political establishment for his profoundly defeatist attitude in the face of the Nazi military threat to the empire. (The ambassador also earned the derisive nickname "Jittery Joe" for his unseemly habit of fleeing London nearly every night during the blitz.) Roosevelt relieved him of his responsibilities at the end of 1940, whereupon Kennedy retired from active public service, made fitfully isolationist noises for a short time, and then contented himself with the management of his sons' political careers. He died in November 1969 after a long, wasting illness.

Civil war raged in Nicaragua for three more years after 1929. On January 1, 1933, the last remnants of the United States Marine garrison departed after six years of warfare against the Sandinista guerrillas. One month later, General Sandino arrived in Managua to attend a peace conference called by recently elected President Juan Bautista Sacasa. The warring parties quickly negotiated and signed a settlement terminating all hostilities, and the rebels laid down their arms. In February 1934, several officers of the National Guard, commanded by Anastasio Somoza, kidnapped and executed General Sandino at the Managua airfield. Two years later, Somoza overthrew the duly elected civilian government and ruled Nicaragua as dictator until his assassination in 1956, whereupon he was succeeded by his two sons.

Admiral Richard Byrd led a second expedition to Antarctica in 1933. Following a six-month vigil at an isolated base near the South Pole, during which time he saw no other living thing, Byrd became a convert to pacifism, and accepted a post as honorary chairman of the No Foreign-War Crusade soon after his return to the United States in 1935. Over the next fifteen years, he commanded two more polar expeditions, including the navy's Antarctic Developments Project in 1947, the most ambitious undertaking of its kind in history. On March 11, 1957, Admiral Byrd died in his sleep at his home in Boston, a victim of heart failure brought on by overexertion at the age of sixty-eight.

King George V died at Sandringham on January 20, 1936. As his life ebbed away on that last evening, the British Broadcasting Company maintained a respectful radio silence, save for the ticking of a clock in the background; every quarter hour, an announcer told the nation in hushed tones that "the King's life is moving peacefully towards its close." Upon the death of his father, the Prince of Wales was crowned King Edward VIII and ruled for fewer than eleven months. In December, he abdicated in order to marry an American divorcée named Wallis Warfield Simpson. "You must believe me when I tell you that I have found it impossible to carry the heavy burden of responsibility and to discharge my duties as King as *I* would wish to do without the help and support of the woman I love," he said as he renounced the throne. "I now quit altogether public affairs, and I lay down my burden." He seldom set foot in England again. His brother, Albert, succeeded him as George VI.

F. Scott Fitzgerald completed one final novel, *Tender Is the Night*, published in 1934, and then moved to Hollywood to write screenplays. He suffered a fatal heart attack on December 23, 1940. He was forty-four years old, haunted by ghosts of years of glory past, and when he died many Americans did not remember who he was.

Pursued by the demons that swept through her mind, Zelda Fitzgerald lived in and out of sanitariums for the rest of her life. In March 1948, she was a patient in a hospital just outside Asheville, North Carolina, when one night a fire raged swiftly through the top floors of the building. Zelda perished in the flames.

Desite the withdrawal of his financially hard-pressed business partners, John D. Rockefeller, Jr., pushed ahead with his plans for the vast building complex in downtown Manhattan that later became known as Rockefeller Center. Although the nation was obviously heading into a severe economic downturn, Rockefeller bravely decided to fund the project alone, suffering losses of more than $3 million a year on lease payments and taxes. "I don't know whether it is courage or not," he admitted years later. "Often a man gets into a situation where there is just one thing to do. There is no alternative. He wants to run, but there is no place to run to. So he goes ahead on the only course that's open, and people call it courage." It had been estimated that the mammoth construction effort provided jobs for 225,000 workers during the worst years of the depression. On November 1, 1939, two years after the death of his beloved father, Rockefeller himself drove in the last rivet of the project.

Al Smith severed his political ties with Franklin D. Roosevelt shortly after Roosevelt's inauguration and became a vociferous opponent of the New Deal, which he savagely denounced as nothing short of radical socialism. Smith eventually became so obsessed with his hatred for Roosevelt that he actively campaigned for Republican presidential nominee Alf Landon in the election of 1936. Following Landon's landslide defeat, Smith retreated from the public spotlight. He died in October 1944.

John J. Raskob did not lose a fortune in the stock market crash of 1929. He emerged from the depression a very wealthy man. And he, too, became a violent opponent of Roosevelt's New Deal program, particularly after the President's supporters ousted him as head of the Democratic National Committee. Along with Al Smith, Raskob subsequently served as a leader of the American Liberty League, a reactionary organization of "disgruntled corporate tycoons" dedicated to thwarting Roosevelt's bid for renomination in 1936. Failing in that endeavor, Raskob withdrew from political life and concentrated on his duties as a director of General Motors and Du Pont. In 1946, he resigned from both corporations' boards and retired to his three-thousand-acre estate on the Eastern Shore of Maryland, where he passed away on October 15, 1950, at the age of seventy-one.

During the last years of the Hoover presidency, Owen Young served as chairman of various unemployment relief fund-raising committees and commissions to stimulate business activity. In 1933, he resigned as chairman of RCA. Unlike many Democratic business leaders, the iconoclastic Young fully supported most of Roosevelt's New Deal programs, and on several occasions actually urged the President to move even faster in the pursuit of social and economic justice. He relinquished the chairmanship of General Electric at the end of 1939 and retired to his farm in Van Hornsville, New York, where he became, in his words, a "rocking chair consultant" to government and industry.

Although he suffered greater losses in the crash and ensuing deflation that he cared to admit (possibly on the order of $5 million), Bernard Baruch still possessed a fortune of approximately $16 million in 1931. Like Young, Baruch welcomed the New Deal's activist philosophy, though he did object strongly to some of its more liberal social measures and tax proposals. As one of the most influential—albeit unofficial—economic advisers to the Roosevelt and Truman administrations, Baruch (who was a genius at self-promotion) became known as the "park bench statesman" owing to his penchant for holding informal conferences with government officials and businessmen on a bench in Lafayette Park, just outside the White House gates.

In 1946, President Truman selected Baruch to head the U.S. delegation to the United Nations Atomic Energy Commission, where he presented a plan for the control of atomic energy production that the Soviet Union brusquely and quite understandably rejected, primarily because it would have maintained a virtual American monopoly on nuclear weapons. For the last decade of his life, Baruch became a sort of folk hero to Americans, an elder statesman of industry and finance, and occasionally a self-acknowledged public bore. He died of a heart attack on June 20, 1965, at the age of ninety-four.

By 1940, the Soviet Union had completed the horrifying ordeal of forced collectivization and industrialization. After a decade of unmitigated terror, Stalin had forged an industrial machine that trailed only Germany and the United States as a producer of steel, aluminum, and electrical energy, holding second place in oil production and machine building, and leading the world in the production of synthetic rubber. Yet the human costs of the brutal Stalinist program had been almost incalculable. "The number of victims here—the number, that is, of those who actually lost their lives, runs into the millions," wrote veteran American diplomat and historian George F. Kennan. "But this is not to mention the broken homes, the twisted childhoods, and the millions of people who were half-killed: who survived these ordeals only to linger on in misery, with broken health and broken hearts."

And one must add to this appalling record the twenty million or more human beings Stalin locked away in prisons, concentration camps, and forced-labor camps during the Terror and the purges of the 1930s.

After eliminating his only serious rivals in 1929, Stalin ruled the Soviet Union unchallenged until his death on March 5, 1953.

In May 1940, Winston Churchill became Prime Minister and High Constable of England, replacing the discredited Neville Chamberlain. As a reward for guiding the British Empire safely through the war, Churchill was turned out of office by the voters and replaced by a Labour government in the spring of 1945. He returned as leader of a Conservative cabinet in 1951, and served as Prime Minister until his resignation in 1955. He lived in retirement for ten more years, filling his days with his paintings, his memoirs, and his account of the history of his nation.

Franklin Delano Roosevelt won reelection to the White House in 1936, 1940, and 1944. By the time the Second World War advanced to a bloody conclusion in the spring of 1945, Roosevelt was a very, very tired man. Early on the afternoon of April 12, 1945, while vacationing in Warm Springs, Georgia, the President suffered a massive cerebral hemorrhage. Several hours later—at 3:35 P.M.—he died. When the news reached Washington, a crowd gathered in front of the White House and stared helplessly at the entrance to the President's home.

Shortly after noon on April 30, 1945, as Allied troops closed in on Berlin, Adolf Hitler shot himself in a closed room in a bunker deep underneath the city. Joseph Goebbels gave fatal doses of potassium cyanide to his wife and children and then swallowed the poison himself.

India received its independence from Great Britain in 1947. On January 30, 1948, while on his way to the prayer grounds outside his home, Mohandas K. Gandhi was shot and killed by a Hindu fanatic.

Ernest Hemingway won the Pulitzer Price for fiction in 1953 for his novel *The Old Man and the Sea.* The following year, he was also awarded the Nobel Prize. Hemingway subsequently suffered severe bouts of depression, and turned in desperation to shock treatment for relief. Perhaps he was still obsessed by his father's suicide when he shot himself with a shotgun at his home in Ketchum, Idaho, on July 2, 1961. He was wearing a robe and pajamas when he died.

No one was ever convicted for the murder of Arnold Rothstein, the king of easy money.

More than any other individual, Herbert Clark Hoover bore the burdens of the Crash of 1929. Blamed, quite unfairly of course, for the collapse of the stock market, vilified for his seemingly heartless policies during the depression (shanty towns of homeless men were known as "Hoovervilles" in mock tribute to the Great Engineer), and shattered by his crushing electoral defeat at the hands of Franklin Delano Roosevelt in November 1932, Hoover never again sought public office. After he left the White House, he retired briefly to his home in Palo Alto, California, and then took up residence at the Waldorf-Astoria Hotel in New York City in 1934. Soon he began denouncing various New Deal programs as "fascistic" and militaristic imitations of the totalitarian platforms of Hitler and Mussolini in Europe. Yet Hoover adamantly refused to join the Liberty League, or any other reactionary anti-Roosevelt organizations. He did, however, actively aid the isolationist forces that opposed the administration's lend-lease policies in the spring and summer of 1940.

When peace at last returned to the world in 1945, Hoover returned to the work he performed best. At the request of President Truman, the Great Engineer supervised and coordinated the United States' postwar emergency relief effort, and led a series of bipartisan study commissions to reduce government expenditures and increase the efficiency of the executive branch.

Deaf and practically blind, Hoover died of cancer on October 21, 1964, at the age of ninety. He had lived longer than any American president except John Adams. Although history has rehabilitated his reputation (perhaps more than he deserves), and time has assuaged the worst memories of the economic cataclysm that struck the United States during his time in the White House, to the end of his days and long afterward the name of Herbert Hoover has been inextricably linked with the Crash of 1929 and the Great Depression.

Groucho Marx deserves the last word.

After moving to Hollywood in the summer of 1930, the Marx Brothers made a series of wildly successful film comedies that included the marvelous *Horse Feathers* (1932), *Duck Soup* (1933), and *A Night at the Opera* (1935). Subsequent efforts were second-rate, however, and the act disbanded in 1949.

Years later, Groucho visited a stockbroker friend on Wall Street. The broker suggested they visit the New York Stock Exchange, a notion that pleased Groucho immeasurably. As they sat in the visitors' gallery observing the frantic activities of the traders on the floor, Groucho suddenly stood on his chair and started to sing "When Irish Eyes Are Smiling."

Everything came to a dead stop on the floor. Since Groucho was not wearing a mustache at the time, no one recognized the lunatic baritone in the gallery. The sergeant-at-arms told Groucho's broker friend, who by this time was visibly embarrassed, to quiet him down. "Groucho," the poor broker whispered, "I'm afraid they don't appreciate clowning in the Stock Exchange."

But Groucho continued to sing at the top of his voice until the sergeant-at-arms finally shouted at him to hush up or else he'd have to call the cops.

"Listen, you crooks," Groucho retorted, "you wiped me out of two hundred and fifty thousand dollars in 1929. For that kind of dough, I think I'm entitled to sing if I want to."

# Source Notes

Throughout these source notes of quoted material, newspapers and periodicals are identified by the following abbreviations:

BW:     Business Week
LD:     Literary Digest
LT:     Times (London)
MG:     Manchester Guardian
NAT:    Nation (U.S.)
NR:     New Republic
NY:     The New Yorker
NYT:    New York Times
Sun:    Baltimore Sun
WP:     Washington Post
WSJ:    Wall Street Journal

All dates of newspapers or journals refer to the year 1929 unless specifically noted otherwise.

The first citation of a published source always includes an abbreviated title; subsequent citations employ only the author's last name, unless I have used more than one book by that author.

### PART ONE: VANITY

PAGE:

4.  "His fortune was of the sort . . . ": *LD,* Oct. 19.
5.  "Tell them they can go . . . ": *WP,* Nov. 6, 1928.
6.  "If the Rothstein papers . . . ": *LD,* Oct. 19.
6.  "Not exactly . . . ": Fowler, *Beau James,* p. 232.
7.  "Mr. President . . . ": Stokes, *Chip Off My Shoulder,* p. 141.
9.  "Dwight, I am not . . . ": *NYT,* March 2.
9.  "Do not work too hard . . . ": *NYT,* Jan. 6.
9.  "The man who builds . . . ": Leuchtenberg, *Perils of Prosperity,* p. 188.
10. "makes new thoughts . . . ": Cochran and Miller, *Age of Enterprise,* p. 311.
11. "The business structure . . . ": *LD,* Oct. 6, 1928.
11. "In the intensive . . . ": quoted ibid.
12. "It was a great game . . . ": Rogers, *Autobiography,* p. 214.
12. "This is still a . . . ": *LD,* August 18, 1928.

13. "a flood of credit . . . ": White, *Puritan in Babylon,* p. 360.
14. "There will be nothing more . . . ": ibid.
14. "However much . . . ": ibid., p. 362.
14. "You know, Cal . . . ": Rogers, p. 180.
16. "We offer one . . . ": *NAT,* July 18, 1928.
16. "He was not the . . . ": Stokes, p. 236.
17. "a foolish attempt . . . ": *Time,* Nov. 17, 1928.
17. "so happy and so poor . . . ": Burner, *Hoover,* p. 14.
19. "That man . . . ": Schriftgiesser, *Normalcy,* p. 248.
20. "One of the oldest . . . ": ibid., p. 263.
20. "while both were . . . " *Time,* August 8, 1928.
20. "Hoover will be a little better . . . ": *LD,* Aug. 18, 1928.
20. "What is happening . . . ": ibid.
21. "This was the battle . . . ": Stokes, pp. 234–35.
21. "The two men . . . ": Mencken, *Carnival,* p. 186.
21. "Cocky, vulgar . . . ": ibid., pp. 185–86.
21. "a circus with bands . . . ": Stokes, p. 235.
21. "the almost physical . . . ": ibid., p. 245.
21. "an America healthy in body . . . ": *Time,* Oct. 29, 1928.
22. "the dirtiest political fight . . . ": *NAT,* Oct. 3, 1928.
22. "It will take two . . . ": Rogers, p. 191.
22. "this diabolical . . . ": *LD,* Sept. 22, 1928.
22. "degraded pimps . . . ": Mencken, p. 185.
23. "Naturally Mr. Hoover . . . ": *NAT,* Oct. 3, 1928.
23. "Most politicians . . . ": *Time,* Oct. 29, 1928.
23. "the soundest business proposition . . . ": *WSJ,* Nov. 1, 1928.
23. "No prosperity is possible . . . ": *WSJ,* Nov. 2, 1928.
24. "The country needs a leader . . . ": *NAT,* Sept. 26, 1928.
25. "Tell him I'll be glad . . . ": Creamer, *Babe,* p. 318.
25. "If he has any . . . ": *NR,* Nov. 7, 1928.
25. "It is in the air . . . ": *NYT,* Nov. 2, 1928.
25. "The fact of the matter . . . ": *NYT,* Nov. 4, 1928.
27. "This is going to be the greatest lesson . . . ": Rogers, p. 192.
27. "It was the only time . . . ": Harpo Marx, *Harpo Speaks!,* p. 254.
28. "Smith is not only . . . ": *WSJ,* Nov. 8, 1928.
28. "the wet sidewalks of our cities . . . ": Leuchtenberg, p. 236.
28. "vigor, his frankness . . . ": *NYT,* Nov. 7, 1928.
28. "won the battle for the allegiance . . . ": Leuchtenberg, p. 236.
29. "One cannot challenge his integrity . . . ": *NAT,* Oct. 17, 1928.
29. "The election has been . . . ": *NYT,* Nov. 7, 1928.
29. "He will bring to the White House . . . ": *NYT,* Nov. 8, 1928.
29. "His brain power . . . ": ibid.
30. "a man of action . . . ": ibid.
30. "Wall Street now feels . . . ": *WSJ,* Nov. 8, 1928.
31. "a mob, a little maddened . . . ": Seldes, *Years of the Locust,* p. 41.
31. "had the party incorporated . . . ": Patterson, *Boom and Panic,* p. 59.
31. "Good feeling was contagious . . . ": ibid.
31. "Off in a corner . . . ": ibid., p. 60.

34. "Few meals ever tasted . . . ": Byrd, *Little America*, p. 91.
35. "Roth by then was . . . ": ibid., pp. 131–32.
35. "Never had the Antarctic . . . ": Lt. Harry Adams, *Beyond the Barrier*, p. 165.
37. "I wanted to show . . . ": Kracauer, *From Caligari to Hitler*, p. 183.
38. "I cannot understand . . . ": *NYT*, Jan. 20.
38. "Professor Einstein is not eccentric . . . ": *Time*, Feb. 18.
38. "a satisfactory way of bringing . . . ": *LT*, Jan. 2.
38. "This Einstein has proven . . . ": *NYT*, Feb. 1.
39. "If A is success . . . ": *NYT*, Aug. 18.
40. "No question can fairly rise . . . ": *Time*, Jan. 14.
40. "Germany's capacity . . . ": Stresemann, *Diaries*, pp. 405–6.
41. "We in Germany . . . ": ibid., p. 413.
41. "The burned-out villages . . . ": Kessler, *In the Twenties*, pp. 348–49.
42. "We have given . . . ": Martin Gilbert, *Churchill, Part One*, p. 1339.
44. "The bourgeois state . . . ": Reimann, *Goebbels*, p. 73.
45. "God bless and keep you . . . ": *NYT*, Jan. 1.
46. "chief U.S. Democrat . . . ": *Time*, Jan. 7.
47. "Most people who are . . . ": ibid., p. 31.
47. "feeling much fitter . . . ": *NYT*, Nov. 5, 1928.
47. "If I could keep on . . . ": *NYT*, Nov. 2, 1928.
49. "Whole sections of the city . . . ": Fitzgerald, *Crack-Up*, p. 31.
49. "I think 90% of all the . . . ": Hemingway, *Letters*, pp. 289–90.
50. "I'm Scott Fitzgerald . . . ": Turnbull, *Fitzgerald*, p. 188.
50. "By this time . . . ": Mizener, *Far Side of Paradise*, p. 232.
50. "Many people who were not . . . ": Fitzgerald, *Crack-Up*, p. 30.
51. "luxurious bars . . . ": ibid., p. 31.
51. "dusky dream . . . ": quoted in Shaw, *Jazz Age*, p. 58.
51. "At first I was happy . . . ": James Collier, *Ellington*, p. 97.
52. "Jimmy was the extrovert . . . ": Walsh, *Walker*, p. x.
52. "Here was a politician . . . ": Cantor, *Take My Life*, p. 190.
53. "When the lives of innocent . . . ": *LD*, July 21, 1928.
53. "a snobbish, self-centered . . . ": *LD*, Jan. 12.
53. "whatever may be necessary . . . ": *NYT*, Jan. 3.
53. "there is no such thing . . . ": *Baltimore Evening Sun*, Jan. 1.
54. "You could talk about . . . ": Brooks, *Once in Golconda*, p. 82.
54. "Nothing matters . . . ": *Baltimore Evening Sun*, Jan. 1.
55. "a very well set-up . . . ": Cleveland and Huertas, *Citibank*, p. 87.
55. "He saw himself . . . ": Anonymous, *Mirrors of Wall Street*, pp. 158–59.
55. "What General Motors was . . . ": Cleveland, p. 114.
56. " 'Look down there' . . . ": F. L. Allen, *Lords of Creation*, p. 304.
56. "As I see it . . . ": ibid., p. 313.
57. "Business is entering . . . ": *NYT*, Jan. 1.
57. "In the industrial world . . . ": White, p. 412.
57. "the end of the general . . . ": *WSJ*, Dec. 31, 1928.
57. "the business outlook . . . ": *LD*, Jan. 19.
57. "The business world . . . ": *Baltimore Evening Sun*, Jan. 1.
57. "The public is in a happy . . . ": *WSJ*, Dec. 28, 1928.
57. "should be viewed not as . . . ": *WSJ*, Dec. 31, 1928.

57. "We have reached . . . ": ibid.
57. "The factors which make for . . . ": ibid.
58. "There is no doubt . . . ": *NYT,* Jan. 3.
58. "We are in the greatest . . . ": *LD,* Dec. 8, 1928.
58. "the gambling spirit . . . ": *LD,* Nov. 24, 1928.
58. "The great majority of . . . ": *LD,* March 16.
58. "Taxi drivers told you . . . ": Baruch, *Public Years,* p. 220.
59. "became a recognized . . . ": *North American Review,* April 1929.
59. "hard losers and naggers . . . ": Patterson, p. 18.
59. "Brokers say that not one woman . . . ": *LD,* Nov. 17, 1928.
60. "And if, after the . . . ": *North American Review,* April 1929.
60. "We're gambling on continued . . . ": *LD,* Dec. 8, 1928.
61. "In the early stages . . . ": *LD,* Nov. 17, 1928.
61. "He hates to take . . . ": *NR,* Jan. 2.
62. "thousands of buyers . . . ": *LD,* Dec. 8, 1928.
62. "conditions are in a . . . ": ibid.
62. "persistent and premature . . . ": *NYT,* Jan. 4.
62. "Don't kid yourself . . . ": Kahn, *Swope,* p. 315.
62. "Nineteen twenty-nine . . . ": Harpo Marx, p. 255.
63. "the very concoction . . . ": *NY,* Nov. 3, 1928.
63. "We didn't bathe . . . ": Arce, *Groucho,* p. 34.
63. "there was generally . . . ": Arthur Marx, *Life with Groucho,* p. 15.
64. "The only ambitions . . . ": Harpo Marx, pp. 100–1.
65. "I hate it . . . ": Arce, p. 83.
66. "I see we have the . . . ": Arthur Marx, p. 96.
66. "Aren't you up past . . . ": ibid.
67. "Until I came along . . . ": Harpo Marx, p. 172.
67. "Groucho may have given . . . ": Maxine Marx, *Chico,* p. 52.
67. "Knowing how wary . . . ": Arthur Marx, pp. 120–22.
68. "Julius, get yourself . . . ": ibid., p. 121.
69. "played by some three or four . . . ": Brooks, p. 68.
70. "There *was* an element . . . ": ibid., pp. 71–72.
71. "a born optimist . . . ": Pound, *They Told Barron,* p. 106.
71. "Assume that the . . . ": ibid., p. 35.
72. "I was for getting . . . ": Weisberger, *Dream Maker,* p. 139.
74. "a money collecting machine . . . ": Gustin, *Durant,* p. 227.
74. "success in the stock market . . . ": Weisberger, p. 306.
74. "Acting as a sort of . . . ": Gustin, p. 238.
74. "in Wall Street . . . ": Thomas and Morgan-Witts, *Day the Bubble Burst,* p. 45.
75. "Instead of using their wealth . . . ": *LD,* Sept. 15, 1928.
77. "There are no older . . . ": *Time,* Dec. 31, 1928.
78. "Rather, it was about . . . ": Christian, *Nicaragua,* p. 5.
79. "I will not abandon . . . ": Macaulay, *Sandino Affair,* p. 159.
80. "His prematurely lined . . . ": Selser, *Sandino,* p. 118.
80. "the entire country is in the most . . . ": *NYT,* Jan. 1.
80. "Patriotism compels me . . . ": *Baltimore Evening Sun,* Jan. 16.
81. "by the beginning . . . ": Macaulay, p. 134.

81. "further progress . . . ": ibid., pp. 85–86.
82. "I did everything . . . ": Case and Case, *Young,* p. 432.
82. "The bloom is off the rose . . . ": ibid.
83. "an American-owned . . . ": ibid., p. 177.
84. "The bank rate affects . . . ": *LD,* Feb. 9.
85. "Here is the ace . . . ": *LD,* Feb. 2.
85. "He greeted us . . . ": Lindbergh, *Bring Me a Unicorn,* pp. 75–76.
86. "For that brief . . . ": Strauss, *Men and Decisions,* p. 81.
86. "I cannot too emphatically . . . ": Forbes, *Morgan,* pp. 67–68.
87. "It would be difficult . . . ": Anonymous, *Mirrors of Wall Street,* p. 51.
87. "dirty little wop . . . ": Forbes, p. 116.
88. "Those debts should be . . . ": ibid., p. 125.
88. "Of all American business men . . . ": *NYT,* Jan. 13.
89. "Many thanks for your . . . ": Pecora, *Wall Street,* pp. 32–33.
90. "was told that he . . . ": Donaldson, *Edward VIII,* p. 148.
91. "There is a feeling . . . ": ibid., p. 139.
91. "Unemployment is not yet . . . ": *MG,* Nov. 9, 1928.
92. "While Wall Street . . . ": *MG,* Nov. 14, 1928.
92. "strongly of the opinion . . . ": *LT,* Jan. 22.
92. "Why should we . . . ": *MG,* Nov. 9, 1928.
93. "Most of these people . . . " *Time,* Jan. 28.
94. "There's many a time now . . . ": *LT,* Jan. 29.
94. "For each man . . . ": *Time,* Feb. 11.
94. "I have been deeply touched . . . ": *NYT,* Feb. 1.
95. "A ruling class . . . ": James, *British Revolution,* p. 492.
95. "He was full of promise . . . ": *LT,* Jan. 10.
95. "We have to march . . . ": James, *British Revolution,* p. 495.
95. "There is no . . . ": *NYT,* Feb. 24.
96. "frankly inconceivable . . . ": James, *British Revolution,* p. 500.
96. "I have got full faith . . . ": *LT,* Jan. 1.
96. "An Englishman never respects . . . ": James, *British Revolution,* p. 500.
96. "Either grant to India . . . ": *Time,* Jan. 7.
97. "We have paused . . . ": *Time,* March 11.
97. "In the first place . . . ": *LT,* Jan. 14.
98. "Had you succeeded . . . ": ibid.
98. "You have also prevented me . . . ": Lacey, *Kingdom,* p. 211.
99. "You Jews wanted . . . ": Meir, *My Life,* p. 134.
100. "The late 1920s were . . . ": ibid., pp. 105–6, 108–9.
100. "sour cereals, unrefined oil . . . ": ibid., p. 88.
100. "Because the soil . . . ": Harari, *Memoirs,* pp. 64–65, 67.
103. "From the time I entered . . . ": Fosdick, *Rockefeller,* p. 195.
103. "I have tried to do . . . ": ibid., pp. 200–1.
104. "You are altogether . . . ": ibid., p. 89.
105. "Nine aging lawyers . . . ": White, p. 412.
105. "It is easier . . . ": *Times,* Feb. 25.
105. "These people are trying . . . ": White, pp. 415–16.
106. "The closing months . . . ": *NYT,* Jan. 29.
107. "The Gulf Stream is alive . . . ": Hemingway, p. 292.

109. "hanging over their tickers . . . ": *NYT,* Jan. 17.
109. "Today, I do not feel . . . ": *NYT,* March 6.
110. "It is the phenomenal growth . . . ": *NYT,* Jan. 15.
111. "doomed the worker . . . ": *LD,* Feb. 16.
111. "the most ominous problems . . . ": *NR,* Feb. 6.
112. "1929 just brings on . . . ": Rogers, p. 194.
112. "The cycle will turn . . . ": *NYT,* Feb. 13.
114. "A village of whose members . . . ": *NR,* Feb. 20.
114. "The Federal Reserve Act . . . ": *NYT,* Feb. 7.
115. "The United States . . . ": ibid.
116. "I do not think that the . . . ": *NYT,* Feb. 8.
116. "Called off on account of . . . ": Rogers, p. 199.
116. "Any sudden drop . . . ": *NYT,* Feb. 9.
117. "has simply resulted . . . ": *NYT,* Feb. 10.
117. "The credit situation . . . ": *NYT,* Feb. 9.
117. "the most notorious . . . ": *Time,* Feb. 25.
117. "It is preposterous . . . ": *NYT,* Feb. 13.
118. "There is not a thing . . . ": *NYT,* Feb. 12.
118. "The real trouble . . . ": *NR,* Feb. 20.
119. "Any group of eight men . . . ": *NYT,* Feb. 28.
120. "useless parasites . . . ": Barron, *More They Told Barron,* p. 120.
120. "I doubt if he knows . . . ": Brown, *Imagemaker,* p. 194.
120. "It was the miracle . . . ": Lacey, *Ford,* p. 297.
121. "We are from . . . ": *NR,* March 6.
121. "It seems that the . . . ": *Time,* March 4.
122. "in dots and . . . ": *NAT,* Feb. 13.
122. "Political boundaries . . . ": ibid.
122. "Machinery is accomplishing . . . ": *NYT,* Jan. 1.
122. "I am sure they had the . . . ": *Times,* Dec. 31, 1928.
122. "I own a golf course . . . ": *NYT,* Feb. 21.
122. "No successful boy . . . ": *LD,* Dec. 29, 1928.
123. "Ultimate panic . . . ": *NYT,* Feb. 12.
124. "I fear Chicago . . . ": *NR,* Feb. 27.
127. "Nobody shot me . . . ": Kobler, *Capone,* p. 246.
127. "Only Capone . . . ": ibid.
127. "Chicago is on a . . . ": *NYT,* Feb. 16.
128. "vote early and vote . . . ": Kobler, p. 198.
128. "Thompson is a buffoon . . . ": ibid., p. 197.
129. "His face looked . . . ": ibid., p. 14.
130. "are marshalled in opposing armies . . . ": *NR,* March 13.
130. "It is this matter . . . ": ibid.
131. "the spider in the center . . . ": *LD,* Aug. 25, 1928.
131. "Ever since Prohibition . . . ": *LD,* March 2.
131. "Remove Prohibition . . . ": ibid.
131. "From Big Business . . . ": *NR,* March 13.
131. "The so-called 'insolence' . . . ": ibid.
132. "I give the public . . . ": Kobler, pp. 209–10.
132. "I thought you people . . . ": ibid., p. 210.

133. "Capone hires nothing but . . . ": *NYT*, July 10.
133. "Capone is living the life . . . ": *NYT*, Feb. 25.
133. "It's a racket . . . ": Patterson, p. 21.
133. "We got a 'cold bang' . . . ": *NYT*, Feb. 27.
134. "The police probably . . . ": *NYT*, March 1.
134. "It's a war to the finish . . . ": *Time*, Feb. 25.
134. "I invited Capone . . . ": *NYT*, Feb. 25.


PART TWO: GREED

139. "What's the weather . . . ": *NYT*, March 5.
140. "You've been tagged . . . ": *NYT*, March 5.
142. "I wish to get accustomed . . . ": ibid.
142. "I remember listening . . . ": Krock, *Memoirs*, pp. 123–25.
143. "When I first went down . . . ": Anonymous, *Mirrors of Wall Street*, p. 268.
143. "would make an ordinary married . . . ": Grant, *Baruch*, p. 9.
144. "If the Continent could . . . ": Baruch, p. 157.
145. "A nation's economy cannot . . . ": ibid., p. 167.
145. "I could see where a new surge . . . ": ibid., pp. 217–18.
145. "As we strolled along . . . ": ibid., p. 222.
145. "What you want to do is gamble . . . ": ibid., p. 223.
146. "an industrial boom . . . ": Grant, p. 230.
146. "For the first time . . . ": ibid., p. 231.
147. "the fact that so many . . . ": *NR*, Feb. 27.
148. "My attention was called . . . ": *Hearings Before a Subcommittee . . . to Thoroughly Investigate Practices of Stock Exchanges . . .* (hereinafter cited as *Hearings,*) p. 2172.
149. "Well, that is your . . . ": ibid., p. 2176.
149. "I told him that I was . . . ": ibid.
149. "sit still on that . . . ": ibid., p. 2177.
150. "History, which has a . . . ": *NAT*, March 20.
150. "are too high in price . . . ": *NYT*, March 15.
151. "Investors in stocks . . . ": *LD*, March 30.
152. "There are two things . . . ": *NYT*, April 3.
152. "The morning smash was . . . ": *NYT*, March 27.
153. "whatever might be the attitude . . . ": Cleveland and Huertas, p. 132.
153. "So far as this institution . . . ": Patterson, p. 72.
154. "Paying 15 per cent . . . ": *NYT*, March 30.
155. "financial disaster of . . . ": Weisberger, p. 328.
155. "Let the Federal Reserve Board . . . ": *NYT*, April 15.
155. "But at the point when . . . ": *NYT*, April 19.
156. "money needed at home is being drawn . . . ": *NYT*, April 12.
157. "hampering the flow of . . . ": *NYT*, March 15.
157. "if the speculators continue . . . ": *NR*, April 10.
157. "creating an abnormal . . . ": *NYT*, April 30.
158. "rather forgo . . . ": Strauss, pp. 78–79.
158. "Wall Street, at the moment . . . ": *NYT*, April 17.
159. "We are subject to no orders . . . ": *LD*, July 6.

161. "The new bank does not change . . . ": *NR*, June 19.
162. "Neither the figures . . . ": *NYT*, April 13.
162. "If our committee is not . . . ": *Time*, May 6.
162. "The kind of proposals . . . ": *Time*, May 20.
163. "throughout the German republic . . . ": *Time*, April 29.
163. "recognize the signs of the times . . . ": *NYT*, March 3.
163. "through unreasonable policies . . . ": *NYT*, March 5.
163. "Would the future history . . . ": *NYT*, Jan. 22.
163. "If Hell is anything like Paris . . . ": Forbes, p. 164.
164. "Sunshine and prerogatives . . . ": *NYT*, May 6.
164. "You have established yourself . . . ": Case and Case, p. 458.
164. "It did not augur well for the . . . ": Schacht, *Confessions*, p. 228.
164. "The report is not entirely . . . ": *Time*, June 17.
166. "from an economic point of view . . . ": Schacht, p. 228.
166. "I became convinced . . . ": Thyssen, *I Paid Hitler*, pp. 88–89.
167. "death penalty on the . . . ": Fest, *Hitler*, p. 260.
167. "a slave people . . . ": Davison, *Making of Hitler*, p. 278.
168. "A maniac . . . ": *LD*, July 13.
168. "the greatest of all . . . ": *Time*, June 17.
170. "That man in that book . . . ": Williams, *Huey Long*, p. 34.
171. "Where are the schools . . . ": ibid., p. 274.
172. "No sooner had this bill . . . ": ibid., and *NYT*, March 29.
173. "What the impeachment did . . . ": Williams, p. 411.
175. "You might be glad to invite . . . ": *NYT*, March 10.
175. "No period in history . . . ": *NYT*, July 5.
176. "the greatest superpower system . . . ": *NYT*, July 31.
176. "Now there is a fine man . . . ": *NYT*, July 8.
176. "I am not a candidate . . . ": *NYT*, July 22.
176. "the most completely one-man . . . ": *NR*, April 17.
177. "When you're serving . . . ": *NYT*, April 14.
178. "Hoover does not run away . . . ": *NR*, June 12.
179. "as possible hard times . . . ": Burner, p. 247.
179. "gilt-edged . . . ": ibid.
180. "I don't know anything . . . ": *NYT*, March 21.
180. "I told them there was . . . ": Kobler, p. 258.
181. "A mere $250 contribution . . . ": *Time*, June 17.
182. "Sometimes, I'd get so punchy . . . ": Arthur Marx, p. 108.
182. "He had the four cells . . . ": Harpo Marx, p. 256.
183. "insisted on painting . . . ": Chandler, *Hello*, p. 166.
183. "The director never made up . . . ": *NR*, June 12.
184. "This colored cafe band . . . ": *Variety*, April 24.
184. "People will walk out . . . ": *Los Angeles Times*, Nov. 4, 1928.
184. "When she goes home that evening . . . ": *NR*, May 22.
186. "made Al Capone look like . . . ": Goodwin, *Fitzgeralds and Kennedys*, p. 338.
186. "Here I am, a boy . . . ": Beschloss, *Kennedy and Roosevelt*, p. 65.
187. "There is no star in Hollywood . . . ": Goodwin, pp. 383–84.
187. "It looks to me . . . ": ibid., p. 420.

188. "The laughter was not her own . . . ": Milford, *Zelda,* p. 191.
188. "My latest tendency . . . ": ibid., pp. 192–93.
189. "If you decide that . . . ": Hemingway, p. 298.
189. "He was a big rough tough . . . ": Callaghan, *That Summer in Paris,* p. 124
189. "He was about the size . . . ": ibid., p. 166.
189. "He is thin to the point of . . . ": Secrest, *Dali,* p. 110.
189. "He couldn't even cross . . . ": ibid., p. 104.
189. "He was the absolute victim . . . ": ibid.
190. "There were Americans at night . . . ": Milford, p. 193.
190. "That year, Paris was . . . ": Callaghan, p. 194.
191. "all that was reckless . . . ": ibid.
193. "sipping whisky and soda . . . ": Manchester, *Last Lion,* p. 822.
194. "I want to see the country . . . ": Martin Gilbert, *Churchill, Part Two,* p. 10.
195. "certainly was *not* . . . ": Lindbergh, *Bring Me a Unicorn,* p. 89.
195. "a tall, slim boy . . . ": ibid.
195. "Who has moved men . . . ": ibid., p. 95.
196. "The world's mind is on . . . ": *NYT,* Feb. 14.
197. "Uh, glad to see you . . . ": *Time,* June 17.
198. "one of the most dramatic . . . ": *NYT,* May 21.
199. "the pessimistic feeling . . . ": *NYT,* May 23.
199. "the long bull market . . . ": *Variety,* May 29.
199. "The call-money market . . . ": *NYT,* May 23.
199. "frightful orgy of speculation . . . ": *NYT,* June 5.
199. "lured more innocent amateur . . . ": ibid.
199. "sarcastic and inaccurate . . . ": *NYT,* June 6.
199. "The proposition is so ridiculous . . . ": ibid.
200. "I asked the super . . . ": *NAT,* Oct. 9.
200. "The boss man wants our labor . . . ": ibid.
201. "Once I mashed . . . ": *NAT,* May 15.
201. "I ain't a-feared . . . ": *Time,* May 13.
201. "we find the whole trouble . . . ": *NR,* May 1.
202. "RED RUSSIANISM . . . ": *NAT,* April 24.
203. "The blood of these men . . . ": *NAT,* June 19.
203. "Come all of you . . . ": *NAT,* Oct. 9.
204. "No matter where industry prospers . . . ": *NYT,* June 1.
205. "The purpose of the Five Year Plan . . . ": *LD,* July 20.
205. "The figures make one . . . ": *NAT,* June 5.
205. "The Soviet Congress . . . ": *LD,* July 20.
206. "to strengthen his position . . . ": *NAT,* May 29.
206. "There is actually no difference . . . ": *NYT,* March 2.
207. "he will slaughter . . . ": Ulam, *Stalin,* p. 307.
209. "This country is enjoying . . . ": *LD,* July 20.
209. "as the year progresses . . . ": ibid.
210. "On the whole, he kept himself . . . ": White, p. 426.
210. "Our insurance companies . . . ": *NYT,* May 9.
211. "I have all the money . . . ": *NYT,* May 7.
211. "I have heard some . . . ": ibid.
212. "probably no man in New York . . . ": ibid., pp. 244–45.

213. "With his genius for organization . . . ": *NYT,* July 9.
214. "Say what you will . . . ": Weisberger, p. 329.
214. "lining up with the destructive forces . . . ": ibid., p. 330.
215. "while being seated . . . ": Davis, *FDR,* p. 125.
215. "a fifty per cent increase . . . ": ibid., p. 133.
215. "most of the working class . . . ": quoted in *NAT,* Oct. 30.
216. "The United States ought to be . . . ": *NAT,* July 24.
217. "put stockholders of the country . . . ": *NYT,* Aug. 10.
217. "Any business that can't survive . . . ": *NYT,* Aug. 13.
217. "only another blunder . . . ": *NYT,* Aug. 10.
218. "This will mean not only here . . . ": ibid.
218. "The end of the story . . . ": *NR,* Aug. 21.
218. "By Stock Exchange opening time . . . ": Brooks, p. 106.
219. "We were crowded . . . ": *LD,* Aug. 31.
219. "Scores of thousands . . . ": *LD,* Aug. 24.
219. "The Big Bull Market . . . ": F. L. Allen, *Only Yesterday,* p. 315.
219. "as little an intrest . . . ": *NYT,* Sept. 1.
220. "Money is king . . . ": Brooks, p. 108.
220. "People sang louder . . . ": Hecht, *Child of the Century,* p. 383.
220. "the great wealth of . . . ": Friedrich, *Before the Deluge,* pp. 284–85.
221. "If the republic wants to go native . . . ": *NAT,* June 26.
221. "Americans are crazy people . . . ": *LD,* Sept. 7.
221. "It matters not how long . . . ": *Variety,* July 24.
222. "no one now playing . . . ": *NR,* July 10.
222. "Their entertainment is verbal . . . ": *NR,* Jan. 16.
223. "George Gershwin is a leader . . . ": *LD,* Jan. 5.
223. "financial whoopee": Baruch, p. 224.
223. "GENERAL SITUATION . . . ": Grant, p. 235.
224. "After I got . . . ": Baruch, pp. 224–25.
224. "a wonderful . . . ": Manchester, *Last Lion,* p. 824.
225. "We have had really . . . ": Lindbergh, *Hour of Gold,* p. 68.
225. "He spoke slowly . . . ": *NYT,* Aug. 18.
225. "I have discovered . . . ": ibid.

### PART THREE: DESTRUCTION

230. "determined to speculate . . . ": *Hearings,* part 3, p. 1010.
230. "I call it panic . . . ": Seldes, p. 40.
230. "being pushed up as if . . . ": Thomas and Morgan-Witts, p. 277.
231. "As the fall begins . . . ": *BW,* Sept. 7.
231. "stock prices are generally . . . ": ibid.
231. "This has been a highly . . . ": *NYT,* Oct. 16.
232. "I repeat what I said . . . ": *NYT,* Sept. 6.
233. "with terrible news . . . ": Thomas and Morgan-Witts, p. 282.
233. "annihilate the Arab nation . . . ": *LD,* Sept. 14.
234. "When the attack first started . . . ": *NYT,* Sept. 1.
234. "I have returned from the . . . ": *NYT,* Sept. 2.
235. "Lead on! . . . ": *Time,* Sept. 9.

235. "Practically all the indicators . . . ": *NYT*, Sept. 10.
235. "Business optimism . . . ": *BW*, Sept. 14.
236. "You fellers are going to get . . . ": *NYT*, Sept. 16.
236. "ELLA MAY, SLAUGHTERED . . . ": ibid.
237. "Irrespective of its source . . . ": *NYT*, Sept. 15.
237. "You cannot drive out . . . ": *LD*, Sept. 21.
237. "no Communist is worse than a . . . ": ibid.
238. "How it grieves the heart . . . ": *NAT*, Oct. 9.
238. "Things have never . . . ": Thomas and Morgan-Witts, p. 290.
238. "Money is all right . . . ": *NYT*, Sept. 21.
239. "must be prepared to face . . . ": *LT*, Sept. 27.
239. "There are plenty of clouds . . . ": *MG*, Sept. 28.
239. "There is a premature . . . ": *BW*, Sept. 21.
239. "By the middle of the . . . ": *NYT*, Sept. 25.
240. "melting away, like a . . . ": *NYT*, Sept. 26.
240. "about the most nervewracking . . . ": ibid.
240. "I'm sorry you can't see it . . . ": Gustin, p. 244.
240. "Immediately after arriving . . . ": Baruch, p. 225.
241. "It seems probable . . . ": *BW*, Oct. 19.
242. "The question which now . . . ": *NYT*, Sept. 28.
242. "Mr. Hemingway is a writer . . . ": Meyers, *Hemingway*, p. 220.
242. "You just have to . . . ": Hemingway, p. 306.
242. "No Real Progress . . . ": Bruccoli, *Some Sort of Epic Grandeur*, p. 287.
242. "It was going into . . . ": Milford, p. 193.
243. "We have reached the limit . . . ": *Time*, Aug. 26.
243. "The thin ice of . . . ": *BW*, Sept. 28.
243. "Tightness of money . . . ": *NYT*, Oct. 1.
244. "It may be fairly said . . . ": *NYT*, Oct. 2.
244. "This historic building . . . ": ibid.
244. "Fear is in the saddle . . . ": *NYT*, Oct. 4.
244. "The midnight blackness of the year's . . . ": *BW*, Oct. 5.
244. "We are broke . . . ": *NYT*, Oct. 4.
244. "A new form of wolf . . . ": *Time*, Oct. 14.
245. "While the Nationalist . . . ": *NAT*, Oct. 16.
245. "He was a man of . . . ": Case and Case, p. 468.
245. "an irreparable loss . . . ": Kessler, p. 368.
246. "clean out . . . ": *Hearings*, p. 2177.
246. "There is a more or less . . . ": *NYT*, Oct. 7.
246. "a carnival in . . . ": Pilpel, *Churchill in America*, p. 88.
246. "a grave simple . . . ": Manchester, *Last Lion*, p. 825.
247. "He is a marvelous . . . ": Martin Gilbert, *Churchill, Part Two*, p. 97.
247. "There is money enough . . . ": ibid., p. 87.
247. "We do not want to be . . . ": *NYT*, Oct. 5.
248. "forget its troubles . . . ": *NYT*, Oct. 8.
248. "We would go through . . . ": *NYT*, Oct. 10.
249. "Business has really passed . . . ": *LD*, Oct. 19.
249. "the present level of business . . . ": ibid.
250. "with little provision . . . ": *NYT*, Oct. 12.

250. "The market is going to be here . . . ": *NYT,* Oct. 16.
250. "has one good day . . . ": *Time,* Oct. 21.
251. "Run a legal poolroom . . . ": *NYT,* Sept. 23.
252. "I have learned not to . . . ": *NYT,* Oct. 12.
253. "what looks like a . . . ": *NYT,* Oct. 16.
253. "Although in some cases . . . ": ibid.
254. "The rule was to attempt . . . ": *NYT,* Oct. 20.
255. "Why, Henry's even got . . . ": *LD,* Nov. 2.
256. "Not since March . . . ": Galbraith, *Great Crash,* p. 96.
256. "There's been a slight . . . ": Arthur Marx, p. 124.
257. "Taken as a whole . . . ": *NYT,* Oct. 22.
257. "in my opinion, current . . . ": ibid.
257. "Do you believe in the flag . . . ": *LD,* Nov. 2.
258. *"great* people who ought . . . ": Turnbull, *Wolfe,* p. 145.
258. "the bee bores . . . ": Daniels, *Time Between the Wars,* p. 177.
259. "CONFIDENTIAL . . . ": Grant, p. 237.
259. "The present market decline . . . ": *WSJ,* Oct. 23.
260. "I realize that this . . . ": *Hearings,* pp. 2177–78.
260. "In brokerage offices in Wall Street . . . ": ibid.
261. "It will send back to work . . . ": ibid.
261. "I need to know . . . ": Thomas and Morgan-Witts, p. 353.
262. "It was a minute or two . . . ": Josephson, *Money Lords,* pp. 89–90.
262. "like a bolt out of . . . ": Thomas and Morgan-Witts, p. 355.
262. "In the crowd there's a . . . ": ibid., p. 356.
263. "a sort of silent army . . . ": Brooks, p. 117.
263. "Photographs taken around . . . ": ibid.
264. "probably the most demoralized . . . ": *WSJ,* Oct. 25.
264. "By eleven-thirty . . . ": Galbraith, p. 99.
264. "a fat, perspiring man . . . ": Thomas and Morgan-Witts, p. 358.
264. "Fear, running through . . . ": *NY,* Nov. 2.
264. "It will not be safe . . . ": *NAT,* Nov. 6.
265. "The spectacle that met . . . ": Pilpel, pp. 93–94.
265. "one saw men looking . . . ": F. L. Allen, *Only Yesterday,* p. 329.
266. "There seems to be . . . ": *WSJ,* Oct. 25.
267. "Very glad indeed . . . ": Forbes, p. 167.
268. "Now that the long . . . ": *NYT,* Oct. 26.
268. "The crash of the . . . ": ibid.
269. "A year ago I said . . . ": *WSJ,* Oct. 25.
269. "it was a gambler's market . . . ": ibid.
269. "I am not surprised at what . . . ": ibid., and *NYT,* Oct. 25.
269. "with available funds . . . ": *NYT,* Oct. 25.
269. "We believe that present . . . ": ibid.
269. "I had a perfectly stunning time . . . ": Thomas and Morgan-Witts, p. 372.
270. "He was a pathetic . . . ": Arthur Marx, p. 125.
270. "a handful of . . . ": Shaw, *Jazz Age,* pp. 227–28.
271. "The fundamental business of the country . . . ": *WP,* Oct. 26.
272. "The number of citizens . . . ": *LD,* Nov. 9.
272. "We have by no means . . . ": *WSJ,* Oct. 26.

272. "In my long association . . . ": ibid.
272. "The business outlook . . . ": ibid.
272. "At this time it is especially . . . ": *BW*, Oct. 26.
272. "No Iowa farmer . . . ": *LD*, Nov. 9.
273. "Just as the stock-market profits . . . ": ibid.
273. "a collapse of the stock market . . . ": *WP*, Oct. 25.
273. "it is not good to go . . . ": Davis, p. 146.
274. "all German commercial transactions . . . ": *NYT*, Oct. 21.
276. "But I shall not be sorry . . . ": *NYT*, Oct. 28.
276. "Whatever may be the sequel . . . ": ibid.
276. "Since Jan. 1 . . . ": *NYT*, Oct. 27.
277. "If the stock market goes . . . ": *Variety*, Oct. 30.
278. "So many shares . . . ": *NYT*, Oct. 29.
279. "FORCED TO SELL . . . ": Harpo Marx, p. 262.
280. "down on his back . . . ": *Sun*, Oct. 30.
280. "Brown, things are . . . ": *Hearings*, p. 2178.
281. "Now, if this thing . . . ": ibid., p. 2179.
282. "screaming like a . . . ": Thomas and Morgan-Witts, p. 391.
282. "hunted . . . ": ibid.
282. "It ruined me . . . ": *NYT*, Nov. 1.
282. "Everybody was groaning . . . ": *Hearings*, p. 2180.
283. "The next morning . . . ": ibid.
283. "trying to stem . . . ": *NYT*, Oct. 30.
283. "The day was past . . . ": Baruch, p. 226.
283. "It was such a . . . ": *NYT*, Oct. 30.
283. "Show pictures . . . ": ibid.
284. "The office they met in . . . ": Thomas and Morgan-Witts, p. 278.
284. "a street of tarnished hopes . . . ": *NYT*, Oct. 30.
285. "Tell the boys I can't . . . ": ibid.
285. "I have been in Washington . . . ": Rogers, p. 211.
285. "We are not watching . . . ": *NYT*, Oct. 30.
285. "The Wall Street slump . . . ": ibid.
286. "They're liquidating now . . . ": Hemingway, p. 311.
286. "Anyone who buys a stock . . . ": Meredith, *Kaufmann*, p. 424.
286. "dwarfs in extent any reaction . . . ": *WSJ*, Oct. 30.
287. "Sixty bucks . . . ": Cantor, p. 214.
287. "I was scared . . . ": Freedland, *Berlin*, p. 102.
287. "SEND $10,000 IN 24 HOURS . . . ": Harpo Marx, p. 262.
287. "In raising the dough . . . ": ibid., p. 266.
289. "under my very window . . . ": Pilpel, p. 94.
289. "The [vital] factors . . . ": *NYT*, Oct. 30.
290. "What can be said . . . ": ibid.
290. "The stock market crash . . . ": ibid.
290. "LET'S GO! . . . ": *BW*, Nov. 2.
290. "Our October sales are . . . ": *WP*, Oct. 30.
290. "the pendulum has swung . . . ": *NYT*, Oct. 30.
291. "never before in the history . . . ": *NYT*, Nov. 3.
291. "Believing that fundamental . . . ": *WP*, Oct. 30.

291. "It is our belief . . . ": *NYT,* Nov. 1.
291. "No one who has gazed . . . ": Manchester, *Last Lion,* p. 827.
292. "We have gotten our minds . . . ": Grant, p. 241.
294. "It surely looks as though . . . ": *NYT,* Nov. 7.
294. "LOOKS LIKE ALL . . . ": Grant, p. 241.
294. "Let Mitchell . . . ": *NYT,* Nov. 13.
295. "unduly and repeated optimistic . . . ": *WP,* Oct. 31.
295. "has encouraged speculation . . . ": *WP,* Nov. 2.
295. "false, vicious, wholly unwarranted . . . ": *NYT,* Nov. 5.
295. "was whacking his thigh . . . ": Swanson, *Swanson,* p. 404.
296. "urged me to withhold . . . ": *NYT,* Nov. 10.
296. "the Country Trust Company . . . ": ibid.
296. "You can go to . . . ": O'Connor, *First Hurrah,* p. 246.
297. "I need your money . . . ": *NYT,* Nov. 5.
297. "so strong that otherwise . . . ": *NYT,* Nov. 13.
298. "banks all over the . . . ": *Baltimore Evening Sun,* Oct. 29.
298. "The purpose is obvious . . . ": *NYT,* Nov. 14.
298. "It is practically inconceivable . . . ": *NYT,* Nov. 6.
298. "unrestrained and unintelligent . . . ": *BW,* Nov. 9.
298. "a rather decided feeling . . . ": *NYT,* Nov. 9.
298. "retrenchments will have to be made . . . ": *BW,* Nov. 9.
299. "New business has been light . . . ": *NYT,* Nov. 7.
299. "The remainder of this year . . . ": *BW,* Nov. 9.
299. "People were in no mood . . . ": *Variety,* Oct. 30.
299. "The investing public . . . ": *Baltimore Evening Sun,* Nov. 2.
300. "some reassuring utterances . . . ": *NYT,* Nov. 15.
300. "Any lack of confidence . . . ": *NYT,* Nov. 16.

**PART FOUR: DESPAIR**

305. "those who voluntarily . . . ": Case and Case, p. 470.
306. "I am going to work . . . ": *NYT,* Nov. 20.
306. "Liquidate labor . . . ": Davis, p. 150.
307. "The people will take care . . . ": *Time,* Jan. 20, 1930.
307. "Prosperity cannot be commanded . . . ": *NAT,* Dec. 25.
307. "Confidence hasent left . . . ": Donald Day, *Rogers,* p. 250.
307. "You can no more stop . . . ": Baruch, p. 231.
307. "The golden bull has been . . . ": *BW,* Jan. 25, 1930.
307. "Every section of the United States . . . ": *BW,* Dec. 7.
307. "No one knew . . . ": Mumford, *Sketches,* p. 473.
308. "I dident have anything . . . ": Donald Day, pp. 249–50.
308. "too absurd to be . . . ": *NYT,* Nov. 13.
308. "Mitchell had his back . . . ": Cleveland and Huertas, p. 164.
308. "I am 40 years . . . ": *Hearings,* p. 2180.
308. "There's no justice . . . ": Arthur Marx, pp. 126–27.
308. "Father was worrying himself . . . ": ibid., p. 127.
309. "Martial law had been . . . ": Harpo Marx, p. 266.
309. "For him, committed . . . ": Callaghan, pp. 225–26.

309. "Ernest would never . . . ": ibid., p. 229.
309. "to forget bad times . . . ": Milford, p. 194.
309. "Somebody had blundered . . . ": Fitzgerald, *Crack-Up*, p. 21.
310. "The American crisis . . . ": *NYT*, Nov. 23.
310. "We are attacking capitalism . . . ": *NAT*, Nov. 27.
311. "Villages do not follow . . . ": *Time*, Jan. 13, 1930.
311. "a veritable earthquake . . . ": *NAT*, Nov. 27.
311. "The kulak must be . . . ": *NAT*, Feb. 3, 1930.
311. "the chances are on the side . . . ": *NAT*, Nov. 27.
312. "Everywhere we looked . . . ": Carter, *Little America*, p. 125.
312. "Now, with the full panorama . . . ": Byrd, p. 337.
313. "There was nothing . . . ": ibid., pp. 341–42.
313. "The recession at the end of . . . ": *BW*, Jan. 11, 1930.
314. "If you are interested . . . ": *Time*, Dec. 23.
314. "a young broker who had . . . ": Baruch, p. 226.
314. "By December a mood of . . . ": Brooks, p. 119.
314. "The sound went on . . . ": ibid.
316. "it was obvious that nobody was . . . ": Fest, p. 268.
316. "A sense of total discouragement . . . ": ibid., p. 269.
317. "The jury's verdict is . . . ": *NR*, Jan. 1, 1930.
317. "We had a very good Christmas . . . ": Forbes, p. 168.
317. "We have again arrived . . . ": *NR*, Jan. 29, 1930.
318. "Passed the Potter's Field . . . ": Rogers, p. 218.
318. "the usual New Years prosperity . . . ": ibid.
318. "A general feeling of confidence . . . ": Cleveland and Huertas, p. 165.
318. "Everybody's busted . . . ": Fowler, *Schnozzola*, p. 146.
319. "Business conditions . . . ": *BW*, Jan. 11, 1930.
319. "an orgy of . . . ": *BW*, March 12, 1930.
320. "There are clear signs . . . ": *BW*, Feb. 22, 1930.
320. "the U.S. is headed . . . ": *Time*, Jan. 20, 1930.
320. "With keen regret . . . ": *Time*, May 5, 1930.
320. "We're just a couple of . . . ": *Time*, March 3, 1930.
320. "I have been in the movies . . . ": ibid.
321. "In other periods of depression . . . ": White, p. 427.
322. "America is too rich . . . ": *Time*, April 7, 1930.
323. "After the second . . . ": *Time*, March 17, 1930.
323. "As the chief of state . . . ": *Time*, March 24, 1930.
324. "Throw the scum . . . ": Fest, p. 276.
324. "Strike down the political . . . ": Davison, p. 287.
324. "Never in my life . . . ": ibid., p. 270.
324. "What we felt . . . ": Toland, *Hitler*, p. 242.
325. "There are times . . . ": Mumford, p. 469.
325. "The situation is serious . . . ": Davis, p. 159.
326. "We shall face either . . . ": *Time*, April 14, 1930.
326. "You won't accomplish . . . ": Walsh, p. 212.
326. "From all parts of the scene . . . ": *LD*, March 22, 1930.
326. "A few lawless policemen . . . ": ibid.
327. "verily, trade and business . . . ": *Time*, May 5, 1930.

327.   "We are out of training . . . ": *BW,* April 30, 1930.
327.   "America needs leadership . . . ": *Time,* April 14, 1930.
328.   "a public nuisance . . . ": *Time,* May 5, 1930.
328.   "It's no crime to let a . . . ": ibid.
328.   "We endorse, commend, and urge . . . ": ibid.
329.   "I'm here for the rest . . . ": *Time,* April 28, 1930.
329.   "We are going to put you . . . ": Goodwin, p. 423.
329.   "It's dreadful, it's horrible . . . ": Milford, pp. 195–96.
329.   "Our ride to Switzerland . . . ": ibid., p. 198.
330.   "traitor to the cause . . . ": Macaulay, *Sandino Affair,* p. 160.
332.   "one vast soup . . . ": Manchester, *Last Lion,* p. 828.
332.   "retreated into a cloud . . . ": James, *British Revolution,* p. 513.
333.   "to diagnose and suggest . . . ": *BW,* May 14, 1930.
335.   "Today fear . . . ": Baruch, p. 231.

EPILOGUE

338.   "They are just ready . . . ": Leuchtenberg, p. 262.
338.   "wholesome thing in . . . ": Gelderman, *Ford,* p. 293.
338.   "To bring on the revolution . . . ": Leuchtenberg, p. 261.
339.   "He made what was probably . . . ": Stokes, p. 275.
339.   "This is not an issue . . . ": ibid., p. 277.
339.   "I do not sympathize with those . . . ": Leuchtenberg, p. 250.
340.   "By gum, they missed . . . ": Burner, p. 332.
340.   "I haven't a dollar . . . ": Weisberger, pp. 352–53.
340.   "I am still a little . . . ": *NYT,* May 2, 1931.
341.   "A well-balanced budget . . . ": Garraty, *Depression,* p. 15.
343.   "I have been out of touch . . . ": White, p. 439.
344.   "This is no time for . . . ": Leuchtenberg, p. 265.
347.   "I don't know whether it is . . . ": Fosdick, p. 266.
351.   "Groucho, I'm afraid . . . ": Arthur Marx, pp. 206–7.

# Select Bibliography

A great deal of the material for this study was drawn from contemporary newspapers and journals, the most helpful of which were the *New York Times, Wall Street Journal,* Washington *Post,* Baltimore *Sun, Time, Business Week, New Republic, Nation, Literary Digest, Times* (London), Manchester *Guardian,* and *Variety.*

Besides the invaluable *Congressional Record,* the most useful collection of government documents on the Great Crash was the eighteen-volume transcript of hearings held by a Senate investigating committee (known informally as the Pecora Committee, after the belligerent government prosecutor Ferdinand Pecora) in the winter and spring of 1933, cited as *Hearings Before a Subcommittee of the Committee on Banking and Currency,* U.S. Senate, Seventy-Second Congress, Second Session, re Senate Resolution 84 and Senate Resolution 239: *Resolutions to Thoroughly Investigate Practices of Stock Exchanges with Respect to the Buying and Selling and the Borrowing and Lending of Listed Securities, the Values of Such Securities and the Effects of Such Practices.*

For general readers, the best study of the Great Crash (excluding the volume you are holding in your hands, of course) remains John Kenneth Galbraith's *The Great Crash,* although Robert T. Patterson's *The Great Boom and Panic* is much underrated, and *The Day the Bubble Burst,* by Gordon Thomas and Max Morgan-Witts contains a great deal of fascinating human interest material. Frederick Lewis Allen's *Only Yesterday* and *The Lords of Creation* are unquestionably the most witty and pungent commentaries on the period. John Brooks' *Once in Golconda* is elegantly written, as usual, and contains valuable insights into the inside (and often unsavory) trading practices of Wall Street.

David Burner's biography of Herbert Hoover provides an excellent interpretation of the Great Engineer's personality and career up to the time Hoover left the White House; after that, it is deliberately very sketchy. Hoover's memoirs, however, are unreliable on many details and represent an extreme example of the sort of sour self-justification that mars many political testaments of our times. Actually, the autobiographies of Harpo Marx, Ben Hecht, and Lewis Mumford are far more interesting and instructive guides to the spirit of the period. Kenneth Davis' *FDR: The New York Years* is a wonderful piece of research and a joy to read, as is James McGregor Burns' *Roosevelt: The Lion and the Fox.* The best sources of information on some of the other major characters in this book may be found in the relevant biographical studies by Gene Fowler (on Jimmy Walker), James Grant (Bernard Baruch), Robert Rhodes James and William Manchester (Winston Churchill), Robert Lacey (Ford), Josephine Young Case and Everett Needham

Case (Owen Young), William Allen White (Calvin Coolidge), and Bernard Weisberger (William Durant).

On developments in Germany, readers should consult John Toland's *Hitler* and Eugene Davison's excellent *The Making of Adolf Hitler.* My understanding of Soviet affairs was aided immeasurably by Adam Ulam's monumental biography of Stalin and George Kennan's classic study of *Russia and the West Under Lenin and Stalin.* For a judicious and gracefully written analysis of events in Britain, see Robert Rhodes James' *The British Revolution,* along with the encyclopedic *Britain Between the Wars* by Charles Loch Mowat.

The following is a more complete list of the published sources used in writing this study:

Adams, Lt. Harry. *Beyond the Barrier with Byrd.* Chicago: Goldsmith, 1932.

Adams, Samuel Hopkins. *A. Woollcott: His Life and His World.* New York: Reynal & Hitchcock, 1945.

Adamson, Joe. *Groucho, Harpo, Chico, and Sometimes Zeppo.* New York: Simon & Schuster, 1973.

Allen, Frederick Lewis. *Only Yesterday.* New York: Harper & Row, 1957.

———. *The Lords of Creation.* New York: Harper & Brothers, 1935.

Allen, William Sheridan. *The Nazi Seizure of Power.* New York: Franklin Watts, 1984.

Anonymous. *The Mirrors of Wall Street.* New York: Putnam's, 1933.

Arce, Hector. *Groucho.* New York: Putnam's, 1979.

Ashworth, William. *An Economic History of England, 1870–1939.* London: Methuen, 1960.

Barron, Clarence W. *More They Told Barron.* New York: Arno, 1973.

Baruch, Bernard. *The Public Years.* New York: Holt, Rinehart & Winston, 1960.

Beaton, Cecil. *Self Portrait with Friends: The Selected Diaries.* London: Weidenfeld & Nicolson, 1979.

Beschloss, Michael R. *Kennedy and Roosevelt: The Uneasy Alliance.* New York: Harper & Row, 1980.

Bilby, Kenneth. *The General: David Sarnoff.* New York: Harper & Row, 1986.

Blotner, Joseph. *Faulkner: A Biography.* Vol. 1. New York: Random House, 1974.

Blum, John Morton, ed. *Public Philosopher: Selected Letters of Walter Lippmann.* New York: Ticknor & Fields, 1985.

Blythe, Ronald. *The Age of Illusion: 1919–1940.* Boston: Houghton Mifflin, 1940.

Brooks, John. *Once in Golconda.* New York: Harper & Row, 1969.

Brown, William R. *Imagemaker: Will Rogers and the American Dream.* St. Louis: University of Missouri Press, 1970.

Bruccoli, Matthew J. *Some Sort of Epic Grandeur: The Life of F. Scott Fitzgerald.* New York: Harcourt Brace Jovanovich, 1981.

Buckle, Richard. *Diaghilev.* New York: Atheneum, 1979.

Burner, David. *Herbert Hoover: A Public Life.* New York: Knopf, 1979.

Burns, James MacGregor. *Roosevelt: The Lion and the Fox.* New York: Harcourt, Brace, 1956.

Byrd, Richard Evelyn. *Little America.* New York: Putnam's, 1930.

Callaghan, Morley. *That Summer in Paris.* New York: Coward-McCann, 1963.

Cantor, Eddie. *Take My Life.* Garden City, N.Y.: Doubleday, 1957.

Caro, Robert A. *The Years of Lyndon Johnson: The Path to Power.* New York: Knopf, 1982.

Carter, Paul A. *Little America.* New York: Columbia University Press, 1979.

Case, Josephine Young, and Everett Needham Case. *Owen D. Young and American Enterprise: A Biography.* Boston: Godine, 1982.

Chandler, Charlotte. *Hello, I Must Be Going.* Garden City, N.Y.: Doubleday, 1978.

Chaplin, Charles Spencer. *My Autobiography.* New York: Simon & Schuster, 1964.

Charles-Roux, Edmonde. *Chanel.* New York: Knopf, 1975.

Childers, Thomas, ed. *The Formation of the Nazi Constituency, 1919–1933.* London: Croom Helm, 1986.

Christian, Shirley. *Nicaragua: Revolution in the Family.* New York: Random House, 1985.

Cleveland, Harold van B., and Thomas F. Huertas. *Citibank, 1812–1970.* Cambridge: Harvard University Press, 1985.

Cochran, Thomas C., and William Miller. *The Age of Enterprise.* New York: Harper & Row, 1961.

Coit, Margaret. *Mr. Baruch.* Boston: Houghton Mifflin, 1957.

Collier, James Lincoln. *Duke Ellington.* New York: Oxford University Press, 1987.

Collier, Peter, and David Horowitz. *The Fords: An American Epic.* New York: Summit, 1987.

———. *The Kennedys: An American Dream.* New York: Summit, 1984.

———. *The Rockefellers: An American Dynasty.* New York: Holt, Rinehart & Winston, 1976.

Corey, Lewis. *The House of Morgan.* New York: Grosset & Dunlap, 1930.

Cowley, Malcolm. *Exile's Return.* New York: Viking, 1951.

Creamer, Robert W. *Babe: The Legend Comes to Life.* New York: Simon & Schuster, 1974.

Daniels, Jonathan. *The Time Between the Wars.* Garden City, N.Y.: Doubleday, 1966.

Darrow, Clarence. *The Story of My Life.* New York: Scribner's, 1932.

Davis, Kenneth S. *FDR: The New York Years, 1928–1933.* New York: Random House, 1985.

Davison, Eugene. *The Making of Adolf Hitler.* New York: Macmillan, 1977.

Day, Donald. *Will Rogers.* New York: David McKay, 1962.

Day, Richard B. *The "Crisis" and the "Crash."* London: NLB, 1981.

Donaldson, Frances. *Edward VIII.* Philadelphia: Lippincott, 1975.

Durocher, Leo. *Nice Guys Finish Last.* New York: Simon & Schuster, 1975.

Eccles, Marriner S. *Beckoning Frontiers.* New York: Knopf, 1951.

Elliott, Lawrence. *Little Flower: The Life and Times of Fiorello La Guardia.* New York: Morrow, 1983.

Ewen, David. *George Gershwin.* Westport, Conn.: Greenwood Press, 1977.

Fausold, Martin L. *The Presidency of Herbert C. Hoover.* Lawrence: University Press of Kansas, 1985.

Fest, Joachim C. *Hitler.* New York: Harcourt Brace Jovanovich, 1974.

Fitzgerald, F. Scott. *The Crack-Up.* Edmund Wilson, ed. New York: New Directions, 1945.

———. *The Letters of F. Scott Fitzgerald.* Andrew Turnbull, ed. New York: Scribner's, 1963.

———. *The Stories of F. Scott Fitzgerald.* Malcolm Cowley, ed. New York: Scribner's, 1951.

Forbes, John Douglas. *J. P. Morgan, Jr.* Charlottesville: University of Virginia Press.

Fosdick, Raymond B. *John D. Rockefeller, Jr.: A Portrait.* New York, Harper, 1956.

Fowler, Gene. *Beau James: The Life and Times of Jimmy Walker.* New York:Viking, 1949.

———. *Schnozzola: The Story of Jimmy Durante.* New York: Viking, 1961.

Freedland, Michael. *Irving Berlin.* New York: Stein & Day, 1974.

Friedrich, Otto. *Before the Deluge.* New York: Harper & Row, 1972.

Gaines, James R. *Wit's End.* New York: Harcourt Brace Jovanovich, 1977.

Galbraith, John Kenneth. *The Great Crash: 1929.* Boston: Houghton Mifflin, 1979.

Garraty, John A. *The Great Depression.* San Diego: Harcourt Brace Jovanovich, 1986.

Gelderman, Carol. *Henry Ford: The Wayward Capitalist.* New York: Dial, 1981.

Gilbert, Julie Goldsmith. *Ferber.* Garden City, N.Y.: Doubleday, 1978.

Gilbert, Martin. *Winston S. Churchill. Vol. 5, Companion Parts One and Two, Documents: 1929–1935.* Boston: Houghton Mifflin, 1981.

Goldberg, Isaac. *George Gershwin.* New York: Ungar, 1958.

Goodwin, Doris Kearns. *The Fitzgeralds and the Kennedys.* New York: Simon & Schuster, 1987.

Grant, James. *Bernard M. Baruch: The Adventures of a Wall Street Legend.* New York: Simon & Schuster, 1983.

Greider, William. *Secrets of the Temple.* New York: Simon & Schuster, 1987.

Gustin, Lawrence R. *Billy Durant: Creator of General Motors.* Grand Rapids: Eerdmans, 1973.

Harari, Manya. *Memoirs: 1906–1969.* London: Harvill Press, 1972.

Hayes, Will H. *Memoirs.* Garden City, N.Y.: Doubleday, 1955.

Hecht, Ben. *A Child of the Century.* New York: Simon & Schuster, 1954.

Hemingway, Ernest. *Selected Letters, 1917–1961.* Carlos Baker, ed. New York: Scribner's, 1981.

Hersh, Burton. *The Mellon Family.* New York: Morrow, 1978.

Hirst, Francis W. *Wall Street and Lombard Street.* New York: Macmillan, 1931.

Hodson, H. V. *Slump and Recovery, 1929–1937.* New York: Garland, 1983.

Hoover, Herbert. *Memoirs: The Cabinet and the Presidency, 1920–1933.* New York: Macmillan, 1952.

———. *Memoirs: The Great Depression, 1929–1941.* New York: Macmillan, 1952.

James, Robert Rhodes. *Churchill: A Study in Failure, 1900–1939.* New York: World, 1970.

———. *The British Revolution: 1880–1939.* New York: Knopf, 1977.

Jones, Thomas. *Whitehall Diary. Vol. 2: 1926–1930.* Keith Middlemas, ed. London: Oxford University Press, 1969.

Josephson, Matthew. *Life Among the Surrealists.* New York: Holt, Rinehart & Winston, 1962.

——. *The Money Lords.* New York: Weybright & Talley, 1972.

Kahn, E. J. *The World of Swope.* New York: Simon & Schuster, 1965.

Kempner, S. Marshall. *Inside Wall Street.* New York: Hastings House, 1973.

Kennan, George. *Russia and the West Under Lenin and Stalin.* New York: New American Library, 1960.

Kessler, Harry. *In the Twenties.* New York: Holt, Rinehart & Winston, 1971.

Kobler, John. *Capone: The Life and World of Al Capone.* New York: Putnam's, 1971.

Koskoff, David E. *Joseph P. Kennedy: A Life and Times.* Englewood Cliffs, N.J.: Prentice-Hall, 1974.

Kracauer, Siegfried. *From Caligari to Hitler.* Princeton: Princeton University Press, 1947.

Krock, Arthur. *Memoirs: Sixty Years on the Firing Line.* New York: Funk & Wagnalls, 1968.

Lacey, Robert. *Ford: The Men and the Machine.* Boston: Little, Brown, 1986.

——. *The Kingdom: Arabia and the House of Saud.* New York: Harcourt Brace Jovanovich, 1981.

Lacouture, Jean. *Ho Chi Minh.* New York: Random House, 1968.

Laqueur, Walter. *Weimar: A Cultural History.* New York: Putnam's, 1974.

Lees-Milne, James. *Harold Nicolson: A Biography, 1886–1929.* London: Chatto & Windus, 1980.

Leuchtenberg, William E. *The Perils of Prosperity, 1914–1932.* Chicago: University of Chicago Press, 1958.

Lindbergh, Anne Morrow. *Bring Me a Unicorn: Diaries and Letters, 1922–1928.* New York: Harcourt Brace Jovanovich, 1971.

——. *Hour of Gold, Hour of Lead.* New York: Harcourt Brace Jovanovich, 1973.

Lippmann, Walter. *Interpretations, 1931–1932.* New York: Macmillan, 1932.

Long, Huey. *Every Man a King.* New Orleans: National, 1933.

Lundberg, Ferdinand. *Imperial Hearst: A Social Biography.* New York: Equinox Cooperative Press, 1936.

Lyons, Eugene. *David Sarnoff.* New York: Harper & Row, 1966.

Macaulay, Neill. *The Sandino Affair.* Chicago: Quadrangle, 1967.

Manchester, William. *The Arms of Krupp, 1587–1968.* Boston: Little, Brown, 1968.

——. *The Last Lion: Winston Spencer Churchill, Visions of Glory, 1874–1932.* Boston: Little, Brown, 1983.

Marx, Arthur. *Life with Groucho.* New York: Simon & Schuster, 1954.

Marx, Harpo. *Harpo Speaks!* New York: Robson, 1976.

Marx, Maxine. *Growing Up with Chico.* Englewood Cliffs, N.J.: Prentice-Hall, 1980.

Matz, Mary Jane. *The Many Lives of Otto Kahn.* New York: Macmillan, 1963.

McCormick, Anne O'Hare. *The World at Home.* Marion Turner Sheehan, ed. New York: Knopf, 1956.

McDonald, Forrest. *Insull.* Chicago: University of Chicago Press, 1962.

Meir, Golda. *My Life.* New York: Putnam's, 1975.

Mencken, H. L. *A Carnival of Buncombe.* Malcolm Moos, ed. Baltimore: Johns Hopkins University Press, 1956.

Meredith, Scott. *George S. Kaufman and His Friends.* Garden City, N.Y.: Doubleday, 1974.

Meyers, Jeffrey. *Hemingway: A Biography.* New York: Harper & Row, 1985.

Middlemas, Keith, and John Barnes. *Baldwin: A Biography.* New York: Macmillan, 1969.

Milford, Nancy. *Zelda.* New York: Avon, 1970.

Minton, Bruce, and John Stuart. *The Fat Years and the Lean.* New York: International, 1940.

Mizener, Arthur. *The Far Side of Paradise: A Biography of F. Scott Fitzgerald.* New York: Avon, 1974.

Moorhouse, Geoffrey. *India Britannica.* New York: Harper & Row, 1983.

Mosley, Leonard. *Lindbergh: A Biography.* Garden City, N.Y.: Doubleday, 1976.

Mowat, Charles Loch. *Britain Between the Wars.* Boston: Beacon Press, 1971.

Mowry, George. *The Twenties: Ford, Flappers and Fanatics.* Englewood Cliffs, N.J.: Prentice-Hall, 1963.

Muggeridge, Malcolm. *The Thirties.* London: Hamish Hamilton, 1940.

Mumford, Lewis. *Sketches from Life.* New York: Dial, 1982.

Myers, William Starr, and Walter H. Newton. *The Hoover Administration: A Documented Narrative.* New York: Scribner's, 1936.

Nicholls, A. J. *Weimar and the Rise of Hitler.* London: Macmillan, 1968.

Nichols, Beverly. *The Sweet and Twenties.* London: Weidenfeld & Nicolson, 1958.

Nicolson, Harold. *Diaries and Letters, 1930–1939.* Nigel Nicolson, ed. New York: Atheneum, 1966.

———. *Dwight Morrow.* New York: Arno, 1975.

Oates, Stephen B. *William Faulkner.* New York: Harper & Row, 1987.

O'Connor, Harvey. *Mellon's Millions.* New York: Day, 1933.

O'Connor, Richard. *The First Hurrah: A Biography of Alfred E. Smith.* New York: Putnam's, 1970.

Patterson, Robert T. *The Great Boom and Panic: 1921–1929.* Chicago: Regnery, 1965.

Pecora, Ferdinand. *Wall Street Under Oath.* New York: Kelley, 1968.

Perrett, Geoffrey. *America in the Twenties.* New York: Simon & Schuster, 1982.

Pilpel, Robert. *Churchill in America.* New York: Harcourt Brace Jovanovich, 1976.

Pool, James, and Suzanne Pool. *Who Financed Hitler?* New York: Dial, 1978.

Pound, Arthur, and Samuel Taylor. *They Told Barron.* New York: Harper, 1930.

Pruessen, Ronald W. *John Foster Dulles: The Road to Power.* New York: Norton, 1982.

Rees, Goronwy. *The Great Slump.* London: Weidenfeld & Nicolson, 1970.

Reimann, Viktor. *Goebbels.* Garden City, N.Y.: Doubleday, 1976.

Roberts, Randy. *Jack Dempsey: The Manassa Mauler.* Baton Rouge: Louisiana State University Press, 1979.

Robinson, Harlow. *Sergei Prokofiev.* New York: Viking, 1987.

Rogers, Will. *The Autobiography of Will Rogers.* Donald Day, ed. Boston: Houghton Mifflin, 1949.

Roosevelt, Franklin D. *F.D.R.: His Personal Letters, 1928–1945.* Vol. 1. Elliott Roosevelt, ed. New York: Duell, Sloan, 1970.

Ross, Walter S. *The Last Hero: Charles A. Lindbergh.* New York: Harper & Row, 1976.

Schacht, Hjalmar Horace Greeley. *Confessions of "The Old Wizard."* Westport, Conn.: Greenwood Press, 1974.

Schedvin, C. B. *Australia and the Great Depression.* Sydney: Sydney University Press, 1970.

Schriftgiesser, Karl. *This Was Normalcy.* Boston: Little, Brown, 1948.

Schwartz, Charles. *Cole Porter: A Biography.* New York: Da Capo, 1979.

Schwarz, Jordan A. *The Speculator: Bernard A. Baruch in Washington.* Chapel Hill: University of North Carolina Press, 1981.

Secrest, Meryle. *Salvador Dali.* New York: Dutton, 1986.

Seldes, Gilbert. *The Years of the Locust: America, 1929–1932.* Boston: Little, Brown, 1933.

Selser, Gregorio. *Sandino.* New York: Monthly Review Press, 1981.

Shachtman, Tom. *The Day America Crashed.* New York: Putnam's, 1979.

Shaw, Arnold. *The Jazz Age.* New York: Oxford University Press, 1987.

Shirer, William. *The Collapse of the Third Republic.* New York: Simon & Schuster, 1969.

———. *The Rise and Fall of the Third Reich.* New York: Simon & Schuster, 1960.

Smith, Denis Mack. *Mussolini.* New York: Knopf, 1982.

Smith, Gene. *The Shattered Dream: Herbert Hoover and the Great Depression.* New York: Morrow, 1970.

Smith, Rixey. *Carter Glass.* New York: Longmans, Green, 1939.

Sobel, Robert. *Inside Wall Street.* Norton, 1977.

———. *RCA.* New York: Stein & Day, 1986.

———. *The Big Board: A History of the New York Stock Market.* New York: Free Press, 1965.

———. *The Great Bull Market.* New York: Norton, 1968.

Stannard, Martin. *Evelyn Waugh: The Early Years.* New York: Norton, 1987.

Stokes, Thomas L. *Chip off My Shoulder.* Princeton: Princeton University Press, 1940.

Strauss, Lewis L. *Men and Decisions.* Garden City, N.Y.: Doubleday, 1962.

Stresemann, Gustav. *His Diaries, Letters, and Papers.* 3 vols. Eric Sutton, ed. New York: Macmillan, 1940.

Swanberg, W. A. *Citizen Hearst.* New York: Scribner's, 1961.

Swanson, Gloria. *Swanson on Swanson.* New York: Pocket Books, 1980.

Teichmann, Howard. *George S. Kaufman.* New York: Atheneum, 1972.

———. *Smart Aleck: The Wit, World, and Life of Alexander Woollcott.* New York: Morrow, 1976.

Thomas, Dana. *The Money Crowd.* New York: Putnam's, 1972.

Thomas, Gordon, and Max Morgan-Witts. *The Day the Bubble Burst.* Garden City, N.Y.: Doubleday, 1979.

Thompson, Craig, and Allen Raymond. *Gang Rule in New York.* New York: Dial Press, 1940.

Thyssen, Fritz. *I Paid Hitler.* New York: Farrar & Rinehart, 1941.

Tint, Herbert. *France Since 1918.* New York: Harper & Row, 1970.

Toland, John. *Adolf Hitler.* New York: Ballantine, 1976.

Turnbull, Andrew. *Scott Fitzgerald.* New York: Ballantine, 1971.

———. *Thomas Wolfe.* New York: Scribner's, 1967.

Ulam, Adam. *Stalin: The Man and His Era.* New York: Viking, 1973.

Von Papen, Franz. *Memoirs.* New York: Dutton, 1953.

Walsh, George. *Gentleman Jimmy Walker.* New York: Praeger, 1974.

Weisberger, Bernard A. *The Dream Maker: William C. Durant, Founder of General Motors.* Boston: Little, Brown, 1979.

White, William Allen. *A Puritan in Babylon: The Story of Calvin Coolidge.* New York: Capricorn Books.

Williams, T. Harry. *Huey Long.* New York: Knopf, 1969.

Woolf, Virginia. *The Diary of Virginia Woolf.* Vol. 3. Anne Olivier Bell, ed. New York: Harcourt Brace Jovanovich, 1980.

Wykoff, Richard D. *Wall Street Ventures and Adventures.* New York: Greenwood Press, 1968.

# Index